Reclaiming Pluralism in Economics

T0293493

Until the end of the early 1970s, from a history of economic thought (HET) perspective, the mainstream in economics was pluralist, but once neoclassical economics became totally dominant it claimed the mainstream as its own. Since then, alternative views and schools of economics increasingly became minorities in the discipline and were considered 'heterodox'.

This book is in honour of John Edward King who has an impressive publication record in the area of economic theory with specific interest in how economic thought in the past shapes current economic theory and enforces certain paths of economic policy and economic development. This book is divided into five themes based on King's interests. The first theme looks at the challenge in trying to reclaim pluralism in economics. The second faces head-on the direct collision of mainstream economics with HET and heterodox economics. The third addresses classical economic ideas, their central influence in the past and how they can still primarily guide modern pluralist economics. The fourth spans a variety of heterodox theories with a view to providing a diverse yet coherent pluralist approach to the modern capitalist economy. The final theme critiques neoliberal policy that has entrenched itself in capitalist economies which have led to financial, industrial, labour, and behavioural/consumerist crises. A concluding chapter synthesizes the previous 18 chapters into a pathway out of the niche heterodoxy edge to a new pluralist centre of economics learning, research and policy-making.

This text aims to provide a clear path for pluralism to serve the economics discipline as its standard bearer, and to no longer be merely a heterodox challenge to the mainstream. This book is of interest to those who study economic theory, history of economic thought, political economy and heterodox economics.

Jerry Courvisanos is Associate Professor of Innovation and Entrepreneurship at Federation University Australia, Ballarat, Australia.

James Doughney is Professorial Fellow at the Victoria Institute of Strategic Economic Studies, Victoria University, Australia.

Alex Millmow is Associate Professor of Economics at Federation University Australia, Ballarat, Australia.

Routledge advances in heterodox economics

Edited by Wolfram Elsner
University of Bremen
and
Peter Kriesler
University of New South Wales

Over the past two decades, the intellectual agendas of heterodox economists have taken a decidedly pluralist turn. Leading thinkers have begun to move beyond the established paradigms of Austrian, feminist, Institutional-evolutionary, Marxian, Post Keynesian, radical, social, and Sraffian economics—opening up new lines of analysis, criticism, and dialogue among dissenting schools of thought. This cross-fertilization of ideas is creating a new generation of scholarship in which novel combinations of heterodox ideas are being brought to bear on important contemporary and historical problems.

Routledge advances in heterodox economics aims to promote this new scholarship by publishing innovative books in heterodox economic theory, policy, philosophy, intellectual history, institutional history, and pedagogy. Syntheses or critical engagement of two or more heterodox traditions are especially encouraged.

Reclaiming Pluralism in Economics

Essays in honour of John E. King

Edited by Jerry Courvisanos, James Doughney and Alex Millmow

Routledge
Taylor & Francis Group

LONDON AND NEW YORK

First published 2016
by Routledge
2 Park Square, Milton Park, Abingdon, Oxon OX14 4RN

and by Routledge
711 Third Avenue, New York, NY 10017

First issued in paperback 2017

Routledge is an imprint of the Taylor & Francis Group, an informa business

British Library Cataloguing in Publication Data
A catalogue record for this book is available from the British Library

Library of Congress Cataloging in Publication Data
Names: Courvisanos, Jerry, 1949- editor. | Doughney, Jamie, editor. | Millmow, Alex, editor.
Title: Reclaiming pluralism in economics / edited by Jerry Courvisanos, Jamie Doughney and Alex Millmow.
Description: 1 Edition. | New York : Routledge, 2016. | Includes index.
Identifiers: LCCN 2015037771| ISBN 9781138951761 (hardback) | ISBN 9781315668024 (ebook)
Subjects: LCSH: Economics--Philosophy. | Pluralism.
Classification: LCC HB72 .R43 2016 | DDC 330.01--dc23
LC record available at http://lccn.loc.gov/2015037771

ISBN 13: 978-1-138-49872-3 (pbk)
ISBN 13: 978-1-138-95176-1 (hbk)

Typeset in Times New Roman
by Taylor & Francis Books

Contents

Preface

In July 2013, the three editors of this book attended John King's farewell function from his Australian university after 25 years of service. This marked a significant juncture in John's distinguished academic career in economics, including admission as Fellow of the Academy of the Social Sciences in Australia. Given his massive contribution to various strands of economic theory and the history of economic thought (HET) – all that lie outside neoclassical economics – the three of us were inspired to honour this career by more than a few nice drinks and cocktails. The idea of a festschrift had already been mooted by our very close colleague, Peter Kriesler. As Melbourne was John's home 'town' for the last quarter of a century, the editors resolved to organize some unique events here and in nearby Ballarat.

The issue of pluralism in economics is not incidental to John's retirement. In today's university environment, research assessment metrics determine the ranking of universities and fields of research of their departments. In the field of economics, the dominant mainstream is neoclassical theory, a study of economics that espouses a set of approaches focused on resource allocation at the margin in a hypothesized process of maximizing profit and utility by both individual firms and customers, respectively, in accordance with rational choice theory. The vast majority of economists subscribe to some version of neoclassical economics and, in epistemological terms, the mainstream restricts investigation of economic phenomena to this single theoretical construct. Thus, the mainstream rates neoclassical economics as the only 'good' economics, and all the university research assessment metrics reflect this view. In that light, John's immense publication record in non-neoclassical economics did not register as valid economics research in the ranking structure.

Pluralism is the formal term in the philosophy of science for phenomena requiring multiple methods to account for their nature. The monism of neoclassical economics has led to the need to reclaim pluralism in economics. Why reclaim? To answer this question, the editors have taken the unique decision to feature an original recently written essay by John as the first chapter of this book. It recounts his initiation in the discipline by a pluralist academy at the time. It describes how this pluralism was subverted and eventually disappeared from the mainstream. The remainder of the book addresses the issue of how to reclaim pluralism.

Reclaiming Pluralism in Economics: Essays in Honour of John E. King is the result of activities held over the period 14–16 April 2014, generously sponsored by Federation University Australia and Victoria University, Melbourne. It consisted of a public lecture on neoliberalism and launch of a major HET literature collection in Ballarat, Victoria, followed by a conference in Melbourne that concluded with a panel discussion on reclaiming pluralism. It was attended by academics, PhD and undergraduate students and political activists. A special call for papers was extended to two groups of economists. One was the group who worked with John over his academic life. John expressed a desire for them to gather on this momentous occasion. The other group were those supervised by John through to successful PhDs. A few overseas colleagues could not attend but were moved to submit papers nevertheless. The conference papers were peer-reviewed and evaluated for book publication. All papers accepted for the book were then reviewed and copy edited into the final chapters of this volume. The final chapter was written exclusively for the book to reflect and synthesize all the book contributions, as well as the final discussion by all participants at the panel. A structure was developed to arrange the chapters into five themes on which John contributed significantly over his career. A short introduction to each theme by the editors explains the significance of the themed chapters in reclaiming pluralism. All the chapters in the book are underpinned by HET, for it is only an examination of the role that economics has played throughout history that can provide an action-oriented perspective for the future. Pluralism dominated economics in the past; it can dominate in the future, too.

Thanks must go first to three colleagues who helped the editors set up the festschrift conference activities in the first place, namely Gillian Hewitson, Therese Jefferson and Peter Kriesler. Thanks also to all the reviewers who contributed to the quality of this book by their thorough and thoughtful feedback. A set of John's colleagues who were unable to contribute chapters to the book must be thanked for their support and valuable contributions in different ways that only they will know. They are Miriam Bankovsky, Riccardo Bellofiore, Donatella Cavagnoli, Marc Lavoie, Greg Moore, Mario Seccareccia and Tony Thirlwall. Appreciation is extended to Andy Humphries and Laura Johnson at Routledge for their encouragement, support and understanding of time-poor academic editors who are doing this out of their respect and admiration of John E. King. Diane Carlyle (again) did a great job of providing an excellent index. Finally, thanks to our families for giving us the time to edit the book and to John's partner, Mary Nicholls, for her profound support for this project, even while recovering from a major accident at the time of the conference.

Jerry Courvisanos, James Doughney
and Alex Millmow
Melbourne, August 2015

Contributors

Arnaldo Barone, Victoria University, Melbourne, Australia

Harry Bloch, Curtin University, Perth, Australia

Jerry Courvisanos, Federation University Australia, Ballarat, Australia

James Doughney, Victoria University, Melbourne, Australia

Sheila Dow, University of Stirling, Stirling, UK and University of Victoria, Victoria, Canada

G.C. Harcourt, University of New South Wales, Sydney, Australia

Neil Hart, University of New South Wales, Sydney, Australia

M.C. Howard, University of Waterloo, Waterloo, Canada and Balsillie School of International Affairs, Waterloo, Canada

Therese Jefferson, Curtin University, Perth, Australia

Steven Kates, RMIT University, Melbourne, Australia

J.E. King, Federation University Australia, Ballarat, Australia and La Trobe University, Melbourne, Australia

Peter Kriesler, University of New South Wales, Sydney, Australia

Heinz D. Kurz, University of Graz, Graz, Austria

John Lodewijks, University of New South Wales, Sydney, Australia

Alex Millmow, Federation University Australia, Ballarat, Australia

Patrick O'Leary, Federation University Australia, Ballarat, Australia

Michael Schneider, Federation University Australia, Ballarat, Australia

Frank Stilwell, University of Sydney, Sydney, Australia

Tim Thornton, La Trobe University, Melbourne, Australia

Jan Toporowski, University of London, London, UK and University of Bergamo, Bergamo, Italy

Theme I

The challenge to reclaim pluralism in economics

What is the 'pluralism in economics' that needs to be 'reclaimed'? John King in Chapter 1 provides the answer by reflecting on his career. He notes in his chapter that, when starting out in 1962, the economics that 'I learned ... was not monolithic or intolerant of diversity, in the way that it has become today'. King revelled in the 'vigorous intellectual debate' exhibited at that time in his native United Kingdom (UK). This was the 'mainstream' as King perceived it back then. As we travel with King through his career, he expresses his abhorrence to the 'transformation' that began in the United States of America (USA) in the 1940s into a discipline of 'aggressive economics imperialism'.

Epistemological (or methodological) pluralism is the formal term used in the philosophy of science to describe the view that phenomena observed require multiple methods to account for their nature. This contrasts with the epistemological monism of neoclassical economics which restricts investigation of phenomena to a single approach, the 'mainstream' in economics today. Such monism asserts a research process that aims to find relations in some few basic accepted and unquestioned precepts. King ends with some reflections on what can be done to reclaim the pluralism in economics that attracted him to this discipline. These reflections are tinged with deep sadness on what has been lost and how difficult the challenge is to reclaim it.

What is the economics to reclaim from a pluralist perspective? Should it be the pluralism of the UK in 1962? The challenge that Frank Stilwell addresses in Chapter 2 is the nature of what should be reclaimed. The concept of pluralism in economics should be reclaimed by rejecting epistemological neoclassical monism. The challenge is, however, to develop a new approach to economic pluralism, one for the twenty-first century with its complexity, uncertainty and crises. Stilwell identifies a form of diversity in current mainstream economics that embraces a vast variety of theoretical innovations from game theory to complexity. However, the underlying assumptions of 'methodological individualism and systemic stability through market forces' remain pervasive. For this reason, Stilwell sees pluralism coming out of the variety of heterodox traditions. What Stilwell makes clear is that where heterodoxy is a political economy position in opposition to neoclassical orthodoxy, pluralism is a commitment to an epistemological position. Heterodox economists must 'keep on talking' amongst themselves, to any mainstream economist who is willing to listen and to the wider community, many of whose members regard economics as a monolithic capitalist ideology.

So what should pluralist economics in the twenty-first century look like? For Stilwell, it needs to be a diversity that is compatible with both teaching and public policy discourse. This is a demanding challenge that requires unity across a diversity of traditions. Sheila Dow focuses on unity in diversity in Chapter 3. The conclusion a reader can take from her cogent analysis is that pluralism in economics needs to be structured. Consistency is needed to 'rule' in order that a coherent pluralist economics can be researched, learned, communicated and acted upon.

At the top is philosophical consistency, based on open-system ontology, with many possibilities depending on the problem at hand. Essentially, pluralism must reject a formal consistency on the basis of a theoretically perfect 'economic behaviour driven by rational choice' – a theoretically pure neoclassical system. Such mainstream consistency demands closed-system microfoundations across its research and teaching, a consistency that breaks down in the communication and policy domains (e.g. the aftermath of the global financial crisis). Consistency is important within any specific analytical construct adopted, but pluralism entails communication between different approaches and their appropriate use in policy.

1   Pluralist economics in my lifetime

J.E. King

At the end of a teaching career that spanned almost half a century, I reflect on the nature of the subject that I taught and on the ways in which it has changed, not often for the better. I begin with some recollections of the people who taught me economics in the 1960s and the characteristics of the discipline that they professed, which was pluralist in the sense that a variety of theoretical and methodological approaches to the subject was not just accepted but (at least implicitly) welcomed. Then I show how economics has come to be dominated by a monolithic and intolerant mainstream, in the process losing its earlier pluralism and commitment to interdisciplinary cooperation. I stress that economics is alone among the social sciences in turning out this way. This leads to the next stage in the argument, where I ask what it is about economics that has made it like this and attempt to explain why it has come about. I stress the role of two factors unique to the discipline of economics: physics envy, and the insidious influence of politics and profits. Finally I ask what, if anything, can be done about it all.

If you can remember the 1960s, you probably weren't there

My formal education in economics began in 1962 in the sixth form at Bromley Grammar School for Boys in south London, and ended just five years later when I graduated from Oxford University with a degree in Philosophy, Politics and Economics. Thus I have one thing in common with Trevor Swan (1918–1989), probably the greatest economist Australia has ever produced: our highest academic qualification, a first-class honours degree. I was part of the last generation of British academic economists who could make a career for themselves without undergoing any formal postgraduate training. Before 1970 this was common practice in the UK (Fourcade 2009); today, of course, it would be inconceivable.

I was lucky enough to have some very good teachers, beginning with my school economics teacher, Alan Huntington Charnley (1929–2011), who treated his sixth-form classes like university tutorials, expecting his students to read, prepare and argue with him. I still have the school's copy of Keynes's *General Theory* that he gave me, presumably in the belief that I was the only one of his pupils likely to read it before taking the A-Level examination. This I duly did, though I cannot be confident how much of it I understood (and doubts remain on this score to the present day).

At Charnley's prompting I applied to read PPE at St. Peter's College, Oxford, a rather undistinguished institution that did have a quite remarkable economics fellow. John Corina (1931–2001) taught me economic theory and applied economics, two of the eight units in the degree, often in demanding one-on-one tutorials that required careful preparation and rewarded the vigorous expression of personal, preferably well-informed, opinions, much as Charnley's classes had done. In this way I learned how to become argumentative.

Corina himself was a labour economist, an eccentric man who was extremely well read but published very little. Our plans to write a full-length textbook together ran into the sand; see his brief but incisive book (Corina 1972), where one J. King is thanked in the preface along with several much more eminent authorities. In terms of his analytical affinities Corina was an institutionalist who took a rather dim view of human capital theory and similar neoclassical inventions and refused to accept that the economic analysis of the labour market could be separated from the study of industrial relations. He made me read Kurt Rothschild's *Theory of Wages*, which combines elements of neoclassical theory, institutionalism and Marxism and has a final chapter entitled 'The limitations of a purely economic theory of wages' (Rothschild 1954). Corina also introduced me to the work of Henry Phelps Brown, another profound and eclectic thinker whose work straddled labour history, industrial relations and both neoclassical and institutional labour economics and is the subject of a special issue of the *Review of Political Economy* that I edited (see King 1996 and the papers that follow).

There were two compulsory units in philosophy, which I found uninspiring, and two in politics, which were only a little better. In the third year students had to choose two optional units to make up the eight for the PPE degree. Possibly at Corina's prompting I opted for 'British Economic History 1870–1939', which involved two terms of individual tutorials with the Australian economic historian Max Hartwell (1921–2009), and 'Development Economics', where I joined what seems to have been a graduate seminar run by the young Bob Sutcliffe (b. 1939). These two teachers could not have been more dissimilar. Hartwell was a free-market liberal whose 'optimist' defence of capitalism had embroiled him in a famous controversy with the 'pessimist' Marxist historian Eric Hobsbawm over what happened to the standard of living of the English working-class during the industrial revolution; see Voth (2004) for a recent assessment, which inclines towards Hobsbawm's position. Hartwell was a member of the Mont Pèlerin Society, though he kept quiet about that when talking to smelly socialist students in 1966–67, and was later its official historian. But he took me through the mainstream economic history literature without intruding his own political views in any obvious way, and I learned a great deal from him.

By contrast Sutcliffe was – and remains – an open-minded and non-sectarian Marxist, who would soon achieve fame (or notoriety) as the co-author of the influential book on *British Capitalism, Workers and the Profits Squeeze* (Glyn and Sutcliffe 1972). He introduced his class to all the contemporary debates in development economics, paying due attention to structuralist and other non-neoclassical authorities. Sutcliffe made me read Paul Baran's *Political Economy of Growth*, which left a big impression on me (Baran 1957). It was the only book by a Marxist that was recommended reading for any of the eight units in the PPE degree. I took my revenge by insisting on the three volumes of *Capital*, and Trotsky's *History of the Russian Revolution*, as part of the College book prize that I received as a reward for my first-class examination results.

Which of the three disciplines in the mid-1960s most closely resembled the intolerant, authoritarian, single-mainstream subject that economics has since become? Not economics, obviously. Not politics, where the only shared position of the people who taught me was an apparent aversion to theoretical generalizations of any sort. No, it was philosophy, where the dogmatic analytical school was at the peak of its influence and nothing else was tolerated. We students knew that there were alternatives to linguistic philosophy, and a samizdat copy of Ernest Gellner's *Words and Things* was in circulation (Gellner 1959), but we used to joke that if Gellner himself were to visit Oxford he would be apprehended at the station and put on the next train back to London. Marx and – God forbid! – Hegel were not names that we were expected to recognize.

As the absence of Marx suggests, the Oxford PPE degree did have serious problems (and the absence of any compulsory teaching in econometrics was probably just as difficult to justify). But it did have very real strengths, as can be seen from the characteristics of my three teachers in economics. They were quite different in the approach that they took to the subject and made no secret of their criticisms of the alternatives, but they also respected each other and were happy to engage in vigorous intellectual debate with economists of differing viewpoints. They were all pluralist by conviction if not by name, and also implicitly or explicitly multidisciplinary in their perspectives on the subject. The economics that I learned from them was not monolithic or intolerant of diversity, in the way that it has become today. In the almost fifty years since I graduated, something has gone very badly wrong with academic economics.

When economics changed

In the United States, where the process had originated, it was already almost complete. The great transformation 'from interwar pluralism to postwar neoclassicism', to quote the title of one important book on the question (Morgan and Rutherford 1998), began in the 1940s and was pretty well complete by 1970, despite a brief and unsuccessful attempt by 1960s radicals to challenge the dominance of mainstream orthodoxy. In Britain the change was already under way when I began my studies in the early 1960s, and

Oxford was probably lagging well behind other, less parochial, institutions that were beginning to adopt the American model (there were already mutterings about Essex and York). The assault on pluralism in economics in the United Kingdom after 1970 has been documented by Fred Lee (2009, chapters 7–9), with due emphasis on the role of the government's successive Research Assessment Exercises in strengthening the monopoly of the mainstream. Something very similar has occurred in Australia, as Tim Thornton has shown (Thornton 2013, forthcoming). And the same story can be told, with only minor variations, in many European countries.

It has been accompanied by an aggressive 'economics imperialism', based on the belief that the theoretical framework and research methods of neo-classical economics are greatly superior to those employed by the other social sciences and should thus be adopted by the practitioners of those disciplines if they wish to become truly scientific. This is sometimes referred to as a reflection of 'physics envy', the belief that the social sciences should adopt the methods and underlying philosophy of the natural sciences (above all, physics) and the claim that economics, alone among the social sciences, has made substantial progress in this direction.

Like other forms of colonial expansion, economics imperialism is often underpinned by ill-disguised contempt for the primitive practices of the backward natives. 'A political scientist', in words attributed (entirely plausibly) to the Chicago economist George Stigler, 'is someone who thinks that the plural of anecdote is data' and has therefore failed to appreciate the explanatory power that is wielded by formal models of constrained maximization.

Some critics of economics imperialism claim that it has succeeded, if not in the original form in which it was promoted by competitive market theorists like Gary Becker. Thus Ben Fine and Dimitri Milonakis are particularly critical of the 'new style' of economics imperialism that, they maintain, originated with George Akerlof, in which 'the non-economic, and previously neglected aspects of the economic, are addressed as the response to market imperfection'. This has proved to be 'a more successful economics imperialism by breadth of subject matter and influence, and encroachment on other disciplines' (Fine and Milonakis 2009, p. 12; see also pp. 119–20). They describe the new economics imperialism as 'devilish' (2009, p. 110), and its practitioners as 'parasitic, arrogant, ignorant and contemptuous' of their colleagues in other disciplines (2009, p. 123). They also accuse mainstream economics of 'plunder' (2009, pp. 84, 166) and of 'asset-stripping' (2009, p. 153) the intellectual resources of the other social sciences.

But plunder is very different from systematic colonization, and it is the latter that is usually intended when economics imperialism is being promoted (or, for that matter, opposed). It is clear, however, that while mainstream economics probably has indeed overrun marketing, management and some of the related business disciplines it has failed to colonize the other social sciences. Instead they continue to display a very high degree of independence and also considerable theoretical and methodological diversity.

I offer four pieces of evidence to support this claim. One comes from Oxford. Writing in the inaugural issue of the alumni magazine, the head of the Department of Politics and International Relations described his department in the following terms: 'We are self-avowedly pluralist in our teaching and research with enough of us to operate on the zoo principle – two of everything' (Whitefield 2011, p. 4). I doubt whether there is a single university economics department in the world today that would claim to operate on this principle. Peter Riach made a valiant attempt to apply it at De Montfort University in the 1990s, but he could only afford one of everything, and the brave experiment soon failed.

My second piece of evidence is the recently web-published autobiography of the eminent sociologist Neil Smelser (2014). If anyone in the social sciences might be expected to reveal the impact of intellectual colonization it would be Smelser, an economic sociologist whose research has always had economic themes at the centre of its subject matter. And yet there is not the slightest sign of such subjugation anywhere in the book, and very few references to economists in the index.

Third, there is the case of another cognate discipline, international political economy, which proves to be a many-splendoured thing. In existence for less than half a century, Benjamin Cohen tells us, it has 'proceeded to develop along sharply divergent paths followed by different clusters of scholars', thereby displaying 'a lively competition of ideas'. And this is a good thing. 'A research community without factions', Cohen writes, 'is like a monoculture in farming, dominated by a single biological species' (Cohen 2014, p. 6). Fortunately there are 'multiple versions of IPE, each with its own distinct personality' (2014, p. 7). In fact, Cohen suggests, there is a danger of excessive diversity, leading to unproductive fragmentation and the isolation of the different intellectual communities from each other. This is not a problem that economics confronts today.

Finally, there is the authoritative *History of the Social Sciences since 1945* edited by Roger Backhouse and Philippe Fontaine, which demonstrates that economics is indeed unique in having a single dominant mainstream. There has never been such a thing as 'orthodox psychology' or 'orthodox political science', and in those disciplines where functionalism might once have aspired to such hegemony (sociology and social anthropology), its supremacy proved to be temporary. Economic geography, too, 'at least since the early 1960s, has been multi-paradigmatic, at every scale of that concept' (Backhouse and Fontaine 2010, p. 175). 'In contrast, after 1945, economists increasingly adopted the view that scientific rigour required that theories be formulated as mathematical models, so that their implications could be derived rigorously, which implied a higher level of abstraction' – and a single-minded commitment to neoclassical theory (2010, p. 41).

Why economics changed

I have been asking myself for many years why economics has turned out this way, and I am still not sure that I have the full answer. Two important factors,

I am sure, are physics envy and the toxic combination of politics and money. The first has already been touched upon. In Edward Lazear's proud words:

> The power of economics lies in its rigor. Economics is scientific; it follows the scientific method of stating a formal refutable theory, testing the theory, and revising the theory based on the evidence. Economics succeeds where other social sciences fail because economists are willing to abstract. (Lazear 2000, p. 102)

'Real science' demands equations, and mainstream economists have provided them. In macroeconomics these equations must set out a Dynamic Stochastic General Equilibrium model, and any rival macroeconomic paradigm that fails to provide rigorous RARE microfoundations – the acronym denotes representative agents with rational expectations – must be rejected for this reason alone (King 2012). Post Keynesian 'theory', in particular, is simply not scientific economics.

This is a powerful factor internal to the discipline of economics that militates against any possibility of theoretical pluralism, but external influences are also important. Much more than is the case in any of the other social sciences, huge sums of money are at stake in economic controversies, and this renders the co-existence of alternative theoretical approaches much more difficult to sustain. As Marx noted in 1867:

> In the domain of Political Economy, free scientific inquiry meets not merely the same enemies as in all other domains. The peculiar nature of the material it deals with, summons as foes into the field of battle the most violent, mean and malignant passions of the human breast, the Furies of private interest. (Marx 1867, p. 10)

As early as 1830, he believed, these 'Furies' had been able to destroy the scientific achievements of classical political economy:

> It was thenceforth no longer a question, whether this theorem or that was true, but whether it was useful to capital or harmful, expedient or inexpedient, politically dangerous or not. In place of disinterested inquirers, there were hired prize-fighters; in place of genuine scientific research, the bad conscience and the evil intent of apologetic. (Marx 1873, p. 15)

This was an extreme position, from which Marx himself sometimes retreated (King 1979), but it does seem uncannily to foreshadow some of the most significant developments in financial economics in recent decades. The thoroughgoing deregulation of finance that began with the collapse of Bretton Woods and culminated in the Global Financial Crisis of 2007–08 would not have occurred without the ideological contribution of what Philip Mirowski (2013) describes as 'the neoliberal thought collective'. This contribution began with the case for floating exchange rates made by the monetarists and the revival in New Classical macroeconomics of Say's Law and the doctrine of the neutrality of money, repudiating the Keynesian principle of effective demand. Crucially, there was the Capital Asset Pricing Model, which applied the New Classical principle of rational expectations to financial transactions, with the implication that financial markets invariably produce the 'right price' and therefore require only the lightest of government regulation. This reinforced the deeply held neoliberal belief that market failure is almost always less serious than state failure, undermining the case for any form of regulation, micro or macro.

The connections between economic theory and financial deregulation are traced by several of the contributors to Wolfson and Epstein (2013), including Thomas Palley, who notes that 'regulatory capture' applies to macroeconomic policy institutions no less than to their microeconomic counterparts: to central banks as well as to industry regulators. Palley emphasizes the need for central banks to be more intellectually open-minded and to recognize the dangers of 'cognitive capture' by the financial markets. He is especially critical of the way in which in the United States the Federal Reserve is 'protected by its patronage of academia, which includes its own revolving door with university economics departments' and so 'buys the Federal Reserve intellectual cover and legitimacy' (Palley 2013, p. 640).

It needs to be emphasized that trillions of dollars were at stake here, since the process of financialization and the resulting massive increase in the profits of the FIRE sector of the global economy (finance, insurance and real estate) would not have occurred without the intellectual cover provided by theoretical economics. Nothing remotely comparable has ever been at stake in controversies in anthropology or human geography. This is not to deny that these subjects, and the related academic disciplines of political science, social psychology and sociology, do have an important ideological dimension. But 'the Furies of private interest' are so much stronger in the case of economics.

What is to be done?

I have also pondered this question for many years, and am even less sure of the answer (if indeed there is one). However, I do believe that heterodox economists would do well to consider three distinct but mutually reinforcing strategies as potential contributors to their intellectual and institutional survival: closer co-operation with each other, more interdisciplinary collaboration with the other social sciences, and pressure for political economy to be taught as a discipline in its own right, separate from departments of (mainstream) economics.

The first strategy has been in evidence for several decades, though whether this was due to dire necessity ('huddling together for warmth in an increasingly cold climate') or the result of a genuine desire for greater cross-paradigm integration is open to question. A characteristically extreme position was taken by the late Fred Lee, who claimed to have identified 'a group of broadly commensurable economic theories – specifically Post Keynesian-Sraffian, Marxist-radical, Institutional-evolutionary, social, feminist, Austrian, and ecological economics' (Lee 2010, p. 19). This led him to conclude that 'heterodox economists in the United States [had] coalesced into a professional community by 2000' (2010, p. 25).

Lee himself was a member of the Association for Evolutionary Economics (AFEE), the Association for Institutional Thought (AFIT), the Association for Social Economics (ASE), the European Association for Evolutionary Political Economy (EAEPE), the International Confederation of Associations for Pluralism in Economics (ICAPE, of which he was Executive Director from 2006 to 2010) and the Union for Radical Political Economics (URPE). He was also a member of the Business History Conference, the (UK) Conference of Socialist Economists, the Progressive Economics Forum, and history of economic thought associations on three continents. At the time of his death in late 2014 he was president-elect of AFEE (see King 2015a).

I myself was never convinced by Lee's argument. The differences within the various schools of heterodox economics – let alone between them – seem to me to be so substantial that any such intellectual Popular Front would prove to be a very unstable affair (see King 2013 and Lee 2013 for an extended discussion of this question). This does not mean that greater cooperation would not be a very good thing indeed. As a preliminary, it would be helpful if we all started to think seriously about the ideas that unite us with other non-mainstream schools and those that will continue to divide us. I have made a start on this in a recent book, comparing Post Keynesian economics with nine other heterodox paradigms, adding behavioural economics to Fred Lee's list but subtracting social economics (King 2015b, chapter 9).

I am attracted to the position – less extreme than Lee's – that is advanced by Edward Fullbrook, the founding editor of what used to be known as *Post-Autistic Economics Review* and is now *Real-World Economics Review*, one of the e-journals published by the World Economics Association that was established by Fullbrook and colleagues in 2011. Fullbrook maintains that non-neoclassical economists are at last beginning to come together for their own protection, on the basis of ten shared principles of a 'New Political Economy' that distinguish it from the 'Old Political Economy' that they all reject (Rosenberg 2014). I think this deserves serious consideration.

The second proposal is even more obvious, though perhaps even more difficult to implement: greater multidisciplinary cooperation. One characteristic that is shared by most, if not all, heterodox schools is an acknowledgement that institutions and history matter, so that economics cannot be carried out successfully without the incorporation of ideas and information from the other social sciences, in particular from politics, psychology and sociology. Almost certainly dissenting economists have something to offer them in return. In Australia we have always been very happy to welcome political scientists, sociologists and even the occasional anthropologist to the annual conferences of our Society of Heterodox Economists, and they presumably feel themselves to benefit from the experience, as they keep coming back for more.

This recognition of mutually beneficial exchange makes a strong case for trade with other disciplines, but not for plunder or (still less) the territorial annexation proclaimed by Lazear, for whom mainstream economics should 'expand the boundaries of economics and simply replace outsiders as analysts of "noneconomic" issues, forcing non-economists out of business, as it were, or at least providing them with competition on an issue in which they formerly possessed a monopoly' (2000, p. 104). Even without such naked intellectual aggression, however, problems will inevitably arise in the course of inter-disciplinary collaboration. To some extent the practitioners of different academic disciplines do speak, write and think in different languages, and there will always be subtle difficulties in the process of translation. But we need to try harder to overcome them.

Finally there is the project that Tim Thornton advocates, inspired by the forty-year success story of the political economy programme at the University of Sydney that is described by the contributors to Butler, Jones and Stilwell (2009). Thornton argues that the 'social science wing' of economics should constitute itself as a separate, independent discipline of 'political economy' within faculties of social science (Thornton 2013, forthcoming). The potentially very strong student support for such an approach has been demonstrated not just by the experience of Sydney but also by the global interest that was aroused when, in late 2013, the Post-Crash Economics Society at the University of Manchester began to campaign for reform of their own unduly narrow economics syllabus. By mid-2014 there was a thriving International Student Initiative for Pluralism in Economics, bringing together forty-two university economics associations in nineteen countries, from Australia to Uruguay, and calling for the introduction of theoretical, methodological and interdisciplinary pluralism into the core of the economics curriculum. They are demanding the same broad, pluralistic education in economics that I was fortunate enough to have received in Oxford all those years ago, and they deserve to get it.

Postscript

As I was finishing the final draft of this chapter, in March 2015, I was heartened to learn of the formation of a group of British academics calling itself Reteaching Economics UK,[1] devoted to the promotion of pluralism in tertiary economics courses in the UK and actively promoting a new film on the subject by the Monty Python celebrity Terry Jones, entitled *Boom Bust Boom*. Readers sympathetic to the drift of this chapter might like to make contact with this group, and also with the other organizations mentioned above: the International Confederation of Associations for Pluralism in Economics, the World Economics Association and the International Student Initiative for Pluralism in Economics (www.isipe.net).[2] It is good to know that we are not alone.

Notes

1 See http://reteachingeconomics.org.
2 See www.icape.org, www.worldeconomicsassociation.org and www.isipe.net.

References

Backhouse, R.E. and Fontaine, P. (eds.) (2010), *The History of the Social Sciences since 1945*. Cambridge: Cambridge University Press.

Baran, P.A. (1957), *The Political Economy of Growth*. New York: Monthly Review Press.

Butler, G., Jones, E. and Stilwell, F. (compilers) (2009), *Political Economy Now! The Struggle for Alternative Economics at the University of Sydney*. Sydney: Darlington Press.

Cohen, B.J. (2014), *Advanced Introduction to International Political Economy*. Cheltenham, UK and Northampton, MA, USA: Edward Elgar.

Corina, J. (1972), *Labour Market Economics: A Short Survey of Recent Theory*. London: Heinemann.

Fine, B. and Milonakis, D. (2009), *From Economics Imperialism to Freakonomics: the Shifting Boundaries between Economics and Other Social Sciences*. London and New York: Routledge.

Fourcade, M. (2009), *Economists and Societies: Discipline and Profession in the United States, Britain and France, 1890s to 1990s*. Princeton, NJ: Princeton University Press.

Gellner, E. (1959), *Words and Things: A Critical Account of Linguistic Philosophy and a Study in Ideology*. London: Gollancz.

Glyn, A. and Sutcliffe, B. (1972), *British Capitalism, Workers and the Profits Squeeze*. Harmondsworth: Penguin.

King, J.E. (1979), Marx as an Historian of Economic Thought, *History of Political Economy* 11(3), pp. 382–394.

King, J.E. (1996), Introduction to special issue on E.H. Phelps Brown, *Review of Political Economy* 8(2), pp. 125–127.

King, J.E. (2012), *The Microfoundations Delusion: Metaphor and Dogma in the History of Macroeconomics*. Cheltenham, UK and Northampton, MA, USA: Edward Elgar.

King, J.E. (2013), Post Keynesians and Others, in F.S. Lee and M. Lavoie (eds.) (2013), *In Defense of Post-Keynesian and Heterodox Economics: Response to Their Critics*. London and New York: Routledge, pp. 1–17.

King, J.E. (2015a), In Memoriam: Frederic Sterling Lee (1949–2014), *Review of Keynesian Economics* 3(2), pp. 226–232.

King, J.E. (2015b), *Advanced Introduction to Post Keynesian Economics*. Cheltenham, UK and Northampton, MA, USA: Edward Elgar.

Lazear, E. (2000), Economic Imperialism, *Quarterly Journal of Economics* 115(1), pp. 99–146.

Lee, F.S. (2009), *A History of Heterodox Economics: Challenging the Mainstream in the Twentieth Century*. London and New York: Routledge.

Lee, F.S. (2010), Pluralism in *Heterodox Economics*, in R. Garnett, E.K. Olsen and M. Starr (eds.), *Economic Pluralism*. London and New York: Routledge, pp. 19–35.

Lee, F.S. (2013), Heterodox Economics and its Critics, in F.S. Lee and M. Lavoie (eds.) (2013), *In Defense of Post-Keynesian and Heterodox Economics: Response to Their Critics*. London and New York: Routledge, pp. 104–132.

Pluralist economics in my lifetime 13

Lee, F.S. and Lavoie, M. (eds.) (2013), *In Defense of Post-Keynesian and Heterodox Economics: Responses to Their Critics*. London and New York: Routledge.

Marx, K. (1867), Preface to the first German edition of *Capital*, volume I. Moscow: Foreign Languages Publishing House (1961), pp. 7–11.

Marx, K. (1873), Afterword to the second German edition of *Capital* volume I. Moscow: Foreign Languages Publishing House (1961), pp. 12–20.

Mirowski, P. (2013), *Never Let A Serious Crisis Go to Waste: How Neoliberalism Survived the Financial Meltdown*. London and New York: Verso.

Morgan, M.S. and Rutherford, M. (eds.) (1998), *From Interwar Pluralism to Postwar Neoclassicism*. Durham, NC: Duke University Press.

Palley, T. (2013), Monetary Policy and Central Banking after the Crisis: the Implications of Rethinking Macroeconomic Theory, in M.H. Wolfson and G.A. Epstein (eds.) (2013), *The Handbook of the Political Economy of Financial Crises*. Oxford and New York: Oxford University Press, pp. 624–643.

Rosenberg, P. (2014), New Paradigm Economics versus Old Paradigm Economics: Interview with Edward Fullbrook, *Real-World Economics Review* 66, pp. 131–143. At http://www.paecon.net/PAEReview/issue66/whole66.pdf, accessed 15 June 2015.

Rothschild, K.W. (1954), *The Theory of Wages*. Oxford: Blackwell.

Rothschild, K.W. and King, J.E. (2009), A Conversation with Kurt Rothschild, *Review of Political Economy* 21(1), pp. 145–155.

Smelser, N.J. (2014), *Wanderlust in Academia*. At http://escholarship.org/uc/item/9j2082pm, accessed 9 March 2015.

Thornton, T.B. (2013), The Narrowing of the Australian University Economics Curriculum: an Analysis of the Problem and a Proposed Solution, *Economic Record* 89 (S1), pp. 106–114.

Thornton, T.B. (forthcoming), *From Economics to Political Economy: The Promise, Problems and Solutions of Pluralist Economics*. London and New York: Routledge.

Voth, H.-J. (2004), Living Standards and the Urban Environment, in R. Floud and P. Johnson (eds.), *The Cambridge Economic History of Modern Britain: Industrialisation, 1700–1860, Volume 1*. Cambridge: Cambridge University Press, pp. 268–294.

Whitefield, S. (2011), Welcome, *Inspires*, Trinity Term, 4.

Wolfson, M.H. and Epstein, G.A. (eds.) (2013), *The Handbook of the Political Economy of Financial Crises*. Oxford and New York: Oxford University Press.

2 Pluralism in economics

Challenges by and for heterodoxy

Frank Stilwell[1]

In May 2014, the organizers of the newly-formed International Student Initiative for Pluralism in Economics[2] issued a statement calling for reconstruction of economics and its teaching. Among other things, their statement said:

> we have no doubt that economics students will profit from exposure to different perspectives and ideas. Pluralism could not only help to fertilize teaching and research and reinvigorate the discipline. Rather, pluralism carries the promise to bring economics back into the service of society.

These words echo the view expressed in a petition circulated by economics students in Paris in 2000, lamenting that:

> Out of the approaches to economic questions that exist, generally only one is presented to us. This approach is supposed to explain everything by means of a purely axiomatic process, as if it were THE economic truth.
> (Fullbrook 2003: 14)

The characterization of mainstream economics as monist – focusing on only one approach to the subject rather than a plurality of approaches – has been a shared feature of almost all criticisms of economic method, teaching and political influence. Indeed, long before the dissident French students launched their Autisme-Economie movement (Movement for Post-Autistic Economics), there had been many similar written critiques (Australian examples including Wheelwright and Waters 1973; Stilwell 1988; Jones 1994). The formation of the Union for Radical Political Economics in the USA in 1968, the Australian Political Economy Movement in 1976 and the Association for Heterodox Economics in the UK in 1999 provided some organizational basis for collective activities and cohesion among those dissatisfied with the mainstream. In the last decade, the chorus of oppositional voices has swelled with the development of other international organizations such as the World Economics Association (WEA) and the International Initiative for the Promotion of Political Economy (IIPPE).[3] The global financial crisis beginning in 2007–08 triggered further calls for change, bringing the issues out from the academic realm into the broader public domain. Even the British Queen became publicly involved in asking what had gone wrong (Dow et al. 2009).

To the extent that the monist character of mainstream economics is the problem, then the general remedy is clear – to replace it with pluralism. However, seeking to confront monism with a pluralist alternative raises some interesting questions about what form the latter should take in a discipline like economics. What competing currents of thought should be considered? Is pluralism a desirable destination or a way-station on the road to a more coherent synthesis? Does pluralism enhance or detract from the capacity of heterodox economics to challenge the orthodoxy? And through which avenues can the challenge be mounted? This chapter considers how we can deal with these concerns. It looks at teaching, exploring what it means to adopt a pluralist approach and the potential consequences for students' learning. It also looks at how pluralism affects the acceptability and influence of heterodox economics in the wider realms of public economic discussion and economic policy formulation.

It is to John King's credit that he has opened up consideration of many of these important concerns through his own academic contributions, including his critiques of mainstream economics and the advocacy of a pluralist alternative. Exploring pluralism in the context of a book honouring John King should, therefore, occasion little surprise. King has been persistently pluralist in his research, writing and teaching. Among his research and publications are important contributions to Marxian political economy, Keynesian and Post Keynesian economics and industrial relations scholarship. There is recurrent attention also to diverse issues of public policy, ranging from wages and incomes policies to macroeconomic problems and policies to reduce unemployment. His teaching has also ranged widely over the history of economic thought, labour economics, monetary economics, macroeconomics and applied microeconomics, industrial relations, Post Keynesian and Marxian economics, globalization, modern world economy, and economics and ethics. This versatility is impressive, but it is the underlying pluralist commitment that gives coherence in method and educational intent. On this reading, pluralism is not 'anything goes'. On the contrary, it is a necessary means to an end – working at the interface between diverse currents of thought in pursuit of truths, or at least 'interim truths', that enrich our understanding of the world in which we live and enhance the possibility of changing it for the better.

This chapter develops these themes in further exploring pluralism in theory and practice. It refers to two articles in which King has explicitly addressed the case for pluralism in economics, using them as a springboard for considering the nature of pluralism, its prominence in the past and its scientific and strategic significance in the continuing challenge to mainstream economics. Subsequent sections consider: (1) the nature of the heterodox economics challenge to orthodoxy; (2) the relationship between heterodoxy and pluralism; (3) the question of 'how much' pluralism is appropriate; (4) how the 'classroom test' may help to indicate what works most effectively; (5) the reproduction of economic beliefs in economic discourse; and (6) the potential for mounting effective challenges to orthodoxy in economic policy. This is an interconnected set of issues, involving considerations of theory and ideology, methodology, pedagogy and practical impact. In the spirit of King's work, and that of other political economists seeking to blend theory with action, the ultimate purpose of reclaiming pluralism is to contribute to strategic judgements about 'what is to be done?'

Heterodoxy challenging orthodoxy

The development of a heterodox economics movement in recent decades is an interesting phenomenon. Regular heterodox economics conferences have been held in many countries, including those held annually by the Society of Hetero-dox Economists (SHE) in Australia. Books and journals using the heterodox economics identifier have proliferated. Worldwide associations like WEA and IIPPE have developed with an explicit commitment to the promotion of hetero-dox alternatives to the mainstream. Driving all these ventures are two central beliefs: first, that the economics profession is dominated by a particular orthodoxy that is frequently, indeed usually, unhelpful for understanding 'what is going on out there'; and second, that an effective challenge to that orthodoxy should embrace an array of alternative approaches to economic inquiry.

King has taken a particularly strong stance on the first of these two pro-positions, arguing that 'economics is unique among the social sciences in having a single monolithic mainstream, which is either unaware of or actively hostile to alternative approaches' (King 2013, p. 17). This monist character of economics is strikingly at odds with most social science disciplines. Interna-tional political economy, a major growth area for research and teaching in recent decades, is a case in point. Surveying the field, a recent book by Cohen (2014) celebrates its continuing pluralist character, notwithstanding the push for dominance by an American-based political science school.

In economics, core knowledge is defined in terms of neoclassical theory, based on assumptions of individuals maximizing utility in markets that create mutually-advantageous outcomes for buyers and sellers. It is a theory that leads to a recurrently favourable view of markets, competition and trade and corre-sponding aversion to government 'intervention' and institutional developments that may 'impede' the proper functioning of the market. Mainstream economists generally view economic phenomena through this lens. There are many different theoretical variations and developments within the mainstream, many of which are technically sophisticated and elegant, even intriguing (Milonakis and Fine 2009; Davis and Hands 2011; Wolff and Resnick 2012, pp. 251–310). However, they are mainly variations around a central theme – that a market economy, subject to a limited set of conditions, is a want-satisfying mechanism, creating the informational signals necessary for productive economic efficiency and the incentives necessary for increasing material wealth.

This brief restatement of the essential character of the orthodoxy is only needed here because some economists have claimed that the mainstream has itself become heterodox in recent times. Diane Coyle (2007) and David Colander (2009) are among those who have propounded this view. They posit that the embrace of game theory, new growth theory, behavioural and experimental economics, complexity economics and other theoretical innovations have reduced the dominance of neoclassicism. The argument is not convincing, for at least three reasons. First, while these developments do indeed give the appearance of some diversity in the forms of economic analysis, the underlying assumptions of methodological individualism and systemic stability through market forces remain pervasive. Second, the developments have not displaced neoclassical economics from the core curriculum that is taught to students, although they sometimes form the basis for electives in later years of study. Because what is taught in the foundation years determines the basis on which the discipline and profession is defined and reproduced, the changes are neither fundamental nor transformative. Third, if an academic profession is to be judged ultimately by its external influences and effects, it is evident that it is still largely 'business as usual' for an orthodox economics that functions as an entrenched feature of modern capitalist ideology. The close association between neoclassicism in the academy and neoliberalism in the realm of public policy remains much in evidence. Even Diane Coyle, notable for her previous emphasis on the flexibility of the economics discipline, has conceded that the catastrophic impact of the global financial crisis of 2007–08 has had little impact on how the academic orthodoxy in economics is constructed and reproduced (Coyle 2013).

The implication is clear: pluralism must be sought outside the mainstream, in the heterodoxy. The fundamental challenges to the orthodoxy come from political economists developing Marxian, institutional, Post Keynesian, feminist and ecological alternatives, not from those economists creating minor product differentiation within the mainstream. This is the common ground on which most of the critics of the mainstream stand. It is territory on which King has firmly stood for decades. It is territory needing to be defended, developed and extended, and King has played an important part in these processes too. In this respect he has worked resolutely in tandem with others in challenging the orthodoxy – to quote the title of my own (complementary, not competing!) festschrift (Schroeder and Chester 2014). But the challenge is not a simple or straightforward clash, like that between two sporting teams in an arena seeking to score more runs or goals to determine the winner. The rules of the contest are not agreed beforehand and there is no impartial umpire. Even the criteria by which interim success, let along eventual victory, are judged, are contestable. It is in this context that understanding the relationship between heterodoxy and pluralism is important.

Heterodoxy embracing pluralism

Does the case for pluralism arise primarily because of the dominant character of the orthodoxy in economics? In my own previous writing I have tended to take this view, emphasizing the strategic significance of the array of competing currents of economic thought from which we can usefully draw. On this reasoning, the commitment to pluralism is essential because it ensures that critics of orthodoxy do not fall into the same trap by espousing a single alternative to replace the orthodoxy.

Yet heterodoxy and pluralism are not synonymous. Heterodoxy is defined in relation to orthodoxy: it entails the embrace of, or at least the provision of a fair hearing for, unorthodox views. Pluralism, on the other hand, is a methodological position that embraces diversity as a matter of principle. In this latter case, the existence or otherwise of orthodoxy is not formally a central concern: pluralism is desirable per se, variously justified as the required method for 'real science' or as the hallmark of an 'open society'. In struggles for progress in economics, heterodoxy and pluralism often seem to be such close relatives that they are indistinguishable, but it is pertinent to recall the conceptual difference. Pluralism is an 'in principle' position, based on ontological, epistemological and ethical propositions (as discussed by Mariyani-Squire and Moussa 2013), whereas the espousal of heterodoxy is a tactic for creating space in which alternatives to the orthodoxy can get a hearing.

The case for, and nature of, pluralism in economics has been extensively explored in the literature of the last two decades (see, for example, Salanti and Screpanti 1997; Dow 2002; Fullbrook 2008). Good personal stocktakings are provided by two of King's own papers in which he explicitly addresses these issues (King 2002, 2013). The earlier, shorter paper is a rather tentative contribution, being mainly a review of arguments for pluralism put forward by other scholars from within heterodox economics (Kurz and Salvadori 2000; Hodgson 2001; Chick and Dow 2001). As King notes, Kurz and Salvadori, who are generally associated with the 'classical' tradition within political economy, emphasize the inherent difficulty of the questions that economists address and, hence, the unlikelihood of finding simple answers. They advocate pluralism because, in conditions of inherent complexity and uncertainty, different theories may have complementary contributions to scientific advancement. Hodgson has a somewhat different slant: as might be expected of an institutional political economist, he emphasizes historical specificity and contingency. From this perspective, the quest for a single general theory, particularly one that abstracts from historical processes, is misconceived. Chick and Dow, well-known contributors to Post Keynesian economics, make a case for pluralism that rests on the somewhat similar view that 'economic statements may therefore be true in some historical and institutional circumstances, but false in others' (King 2002, p. 84). They argue that the costs of the formalism that mainstream economists are so keen to adopt have to be set against its benefits. A more blended method, including the use of common-sense or ordinary logic in generating knowledge that is 'imperfect, partial or vague', is implied.

King's short review of these three perspectives seeks to find points of agreement and concludes that 'no single case for pluralism in economics emerges' (King 2002, p. 87). Is this a healthy and desirable situation? Well, yes, if only because it accommodates the diversity of views among heterodox economists. In King's words, 'Sraffians, institutionalists and Post Keynesians do quite different things, often in radically different ways – as do Marxists, social economists, feminists, greenies and other schools of political economy' (King 2002, p. 87). By inference, the case for pluralism is that they all deserve to get a hearing. King ends his article by referring to a remark attributed to radical US activist Abbie Hoffman in 1968 when he and his comrades were on trial for conspiracy against the state: 'Conspire? We couldn't agree on lunch!' In conclusion, it is the willingness to just 'keep on talking' which 'in the last resort is what pluralism is all about' (King 2002, p. 88).

It would be hard to disagree with such an affable case for pluralism. King makes the case significantly more strongly, however, in his 2012 Keith Hancock Lecture, subsequently published in the *Economics and Labour Relations Review* (King 2013). This devastating critique of mainstream economics also goes on to explain the deeply unfortunate educational and social consequences arising from retention of the orthodoxy. The monist character of the mainstream imposes a template that impedes an understanding of contemporary political economic processes and events. It simultaneously has structurally adverse consequences because it results in the marginalization of economic history and the history of economic thought, producing an ahistorical approach that creates a widespread 'amnesia'. Worse, 'self-harm' arises from the view that there is only one acceptable way to do economics, as is evident in the dysfunctional policies enacted in the name of 'sound economics' since the onset of the global financial crisis. As King also notes, the recent processes of official research evaluation, such as the 2011 Excellence in Research for Australia (ERA), do much damage to the standing of non-mainstream approaches, thereby operating to compound all the above problems. In effect, this is a story of circular and cumulative causation, with monism in the mainstream excluding the very elements that could enable economics to better explain real-world concerns in historical context. It is a thoroughly unhealthy vicious circle. Only the widespread embrace of pluralism could correct it. But, ah, there's the rub …

Establishing the case for pluralism may be regarded as the easy bit. Since its monist character makes economics an aberrant discipline within the social sciences, the onus of self-justification should lie with its mainstream practitioners rather than its critics. But they evidently aren't listening (being conspicuous by their absence from King's otherwise well-attended public presentation of the 2012 Hancock lecture in Sydney, for example), still less acting to change their ways. For the critics, however, many related concerns still need to be addressed – most obviously what form of pluralist alternative might most effectively counter the intransigence from within the mainstream. It is to this issue that we now turn.

How much pluralism?

It may seem odd to pose a 'how much?' question. The key concern of pluralism is not quantitative – a lot or a little? Rather, it relates to how broadly to cast the net in considering alternative approaches to economic inquiry. In principle, whatever range of analytical positions is demonstrably useful should be included. Does that mean 'anything goes'? Well, yes, if one subscribes to the anarchist approach to the theory of knowledge propounded by Feyerabend (1975); and indeed there is good reason not to apply exclusionary processes like those that mainstream practitioners use to define and defend their territory. However, most contributors to the literature on pluralism in economics are evidently wary of this position. They point to the need for a common concern with the 'reality' of the modern world economy largely organized on capitalist principles, albeit looking at it from different perspectives. The acid test becomes the capacity to illuminate that real world, drawing on and contributing knowledge of its character, contradictions, evolution and political economic possibilities.

In practice, at least eight schools of political economic thought have legitimate grounds for inclusion, including: (1) Marxian political economy (including various modern applications of this long-standing tradition); (2) institutional economics (certainly the 'old' institutionalism of Veblen, Commons, Myrdal and Galbraith, and sometimes the 'new' institutionalism of Coase, Williamson and their followers); (3) Post Keynesian economics (in its various forms, including the 'classical' tradition shaped by the influence of Sraffa, and other works deriving from the contributions of pioneers such as Robinson, Kalecki and Kaldor, as well as Keynes himself); (4) the Austrian school (including Hayek's work which is methodologically non-neoclassical but politically incompatible with all the other heterodox schools of thought); (5) analysis of the political economy of land in the tradition of Henry George (which is usually included in principle but ignored in practice); (6) evolutionary economics (building on the themes within the work of Schumpeter, Nelson and Winter); (7) feminist political economy; and (8) environmental political economy.

The last two are prominent influences in modern heterodox economics, but they are different in character from the other schools of thought because they are defined to a considerable extent by their subject matter rather than by their method. Since some orthodox economists apply neoclassical tools to gender and environmental issues, heterodox economists have to differentiate the nature of their contributions (e.g. by distinguishing the ontology of 'ecological economics' from environmental economics that draws on neoclassical modelling). These points signal some of the complex boundary problems.

So, we need to be clearer about the grounds on which pluralism is justified. Only then can we determine what are the most appropriate characteristics and limits of heterodox economics in practice.

In my own previous publications (especially Stilwell 2006), I have put four arguments for pluralism. Mariyani-Squire and Moussa (2013) characterize these as the 'way station' argument, the 'political openness' argument, the 'epistemic progress' argument and the 'critical creativity' argument, emphasizing that they are not altogether consistent. The first two arguments focus on the role of pluralism in coping with the existing problems in economics.

Argument one posits open-mindedness to alternative approaches as the most sensible approach to an economic discipline that is inherently flawed, if not in perpetual disarray. Argument two contends that a pluralist approach is the best antidote to political bias: because the competing schools of thought are ideology-laden, we should select them to cover the full range of political positions from left to right, particularly in teaching. Beyond these concerns about coping with an inherently problematic discipline, however, pluralism can be advocated as being conducive to future progress. This is where arguments three and four come into play. Argument three regards juxtaposition and/or attempted synthesis of the competing schools of thought as the method most conducive to effective scientific progress. Argument four also sees this form of pluralism as conducive to critical creativity rather than the perpetuation of 'tunnel vision'.

Wherein lies the inconsistency between these arguments? Most fundamentally, it relates to the question of whether economics is in a 'pre-scientific' state or is inherently incapable of scientific progress. The 'way station' and 'epistemic progress' arguments imply the former, whereas the 'political openness' and 'critical creativity' arguments imply the latter. Mariyani-Squire and Moussa (2013) develop this critique more fully, also pointing out that the marginalization of discussions of methodology (alongside its 'partner in invisibility', the history of economic thought) makes the economics discipline largely impervious to these arguments for pluralism in practice. This last point is particularly important because, ultimately, the restructuring of the economic discipline along pluralist lines requires the mainstream practitioners to come on board. Well, to the extent that mainstream economists already regard themselves as heterodox, as posited by Coyle (2007) and Colander (2009), the advocacy of pluralism is 'water off a duck's back'. Take your pick: either mainstream economics does not need to be pluralist (because it is head and shoulders above anything else in terms of its 'scientific' pretensions and achievements) *or* it is already pluralist. This dual defence against criticisms from heterodox economists may be slippery, but few economists seem to care. And it is not difficult to see why. Implementing pluralism in teaching and research is never easy, usually requiring big investments of lecturers' time. Moreover, there is seldom any personal career progression advantage from changing track. Indeed, for academics below the rank of full professor, there are almost invariably more career risks in being seen to align with dissident heterodox economists.

These latter considerations take us to the practical heart of the matter – in the sociology of a conservative profession for which a particular orthodoxy is a defining feature. They also have important strategic implications. Ultimately, it would be nice to 'win over' mainstream practitioners, of course, but the immediate task is for radical critics to define the terrain on which progress can be made. We need to identify 'what works' and the real-world arenas in which that pragmatic test applies. Three arenas spring immediately to mind: the classroom, public discourse (including the media) and public policy processes. Beyond the territory of academic writing and publishing in which heterodox economists are usually more comfortable, these are the principal arenas in which mainstream economics has to be challenged. An effective heterodox economics, embracing pluralism, needs to make substantial inroads into each. The next three sections of this chapter consider each in turn.

Pluralism in the classroom

Economics is a notably 'taught' discipline, in that what is taught, especially to undergraduates, effectively defines what constitutes the orthodoxy and provides for its reproduction. If heterodox economics is effectively to challenge the orthodoxy it must do so, first and foremost, by establishing its place 'in the classroom'. This is the reason for giving primacy to pedagogy in putting the case for a 'classroom test' of what constitutes a useful practical definition and range of heterodox economics.

'Teaching a subject is the best way to understand it' is a familiar academic truism. It is certainly a good test of 'what works'. Hence it is pertinent to review experiences with pluralist approaches to teaching economics. On this there is a quite considerable literature in journals such as the *Journal of Pluralism and Economics Education* and the *Australasian Journal of Economics Education* (see also Dawson 2007 for further consideration of how the difference between monist and pluralist approaches is reflected in textbooks). There is no single model for structuring heterodox economics courses (as emphasized by Mearman 2014) but pluralist approaches always contrast with the more typical micro-macro course structures in mainstream economics education. Exploring 'what works' in teaching economics from a pluralist perspective is a field in which I may assert some small claim to personal experience, even comparative advantage, having helped to design the pluralist introductory course in political economy at the University of Sydney when it was introduced in 1975 and taught in it every year from 1977 to 2011. It is the first unit of study in a course that the author of an international survey has described as 'the world's most distinctive undergraduate program in heterodox economics' (Nesiba 2012).

Undoubtedly, as Earl (2008) emphasizes, a pluralist pedagogy makes substantial demands on both students and teachers. For students, it requires moving beyond the passive view of their role as recipients of received wisdom, requiring them to be active participants in processes of debate that involve personal judgement. For teachers, it requires a willingness to self-educate in bodies of thought which they were not themselves taught when they were students. It also requires teachers to be able to cope with resistance from some students who perceive a pluralist approach to be making excessive demands on them or challenging their passive approach to learning 'accepted truths'. Yet experience suggests that, if the pluralist pedagogy is pursued with careful explanation and sustained commitment, it can be highly effective. Certainly that is the experience of the Political Economy programme at the University of Sydney (as further described in Stilwell 2011, 2012b). The pluralist approach to the introductory unit of study in political economy has been remarkably effective by a range of criteria, ranging from student evaluations to impact on students' personal values and perceptions of the nature of economic inquiry.

The latter aspect, involving understanding of the nature and purpose of political economy, is particularly significant. Mainstream economics has sometimes been criticized for its tendency to turn students into trainee versions of *homo economicus* because it inculcates values of narrow self-interest, encouraging competitiveness rather than co-operation and interpreting success in narrowly material terms (see, for example, Frank, Gilovich and Regan 1993). A pluralist approach to teaching can create markedly different outcomes. A student survey in ECOP 1001 at the University of Sydney in 2010 found that 65 per cent of students agreed with the statement that, as a result of their study, 'I have become more concerned about social justice'; while 76 per cent agreed with the proposition, adapted from Joan Robinson, that 'the answers to economic problems are usually political questions' (Stilwell 2012a, p. 156).

The processes of students' course selection and attitudinal change are subject to complex influences. For example, orthodox economics courses may tend to attract students already predisposed to self-interested competitive behaviours, while heterodox courses may attract students who are already more interested in matters of social justice or political controversy (Rubinstein 2006). Indeed, it is likely that the 'attraction' and 'creation' effects are interactive and synergistic: heterodox courses attract more questioning students and the pluralist pedagogy then develops their critically inquiring attributes. Meanwhile, some students with more closed attitudes and expectations will be 'lost' to mainstream economics. But you can't win them all! Indeed, it is hard to see how that could be otherwise, short of the utopian prospect of all economics teachers adopting a pluralist pedagogy. Notwithstanding all the arguments and evidence about the benefits of pluralist pedagogy, that just is not going to happen, given the strength of the socialization processes encouraging, and sometimes enforcing, conformity to the mainstream (Thornton 2013).

Staying in the realm of reality, we can concentrate our efforts on making pluralism effective in the teaching spaces we can establish. O'Donnell (2014) provides powerful evidence on discipline-specific knowledge, generic skills and students' attitudes to show what can be done – and with evidently striking success. My own experience at the University of Sydney is that successful learning outcomes depend significantly on: (1) the repeated explanation of the reasons for considering competing schools of economic thought; (2) the introduction of competing schools of thought in historical context, showing the economic issues they were designed to address; (3) considering the principal tools and insights provided by these schools, as described in my textbook (Stilwell 2012a), comparing and contrasting them in a clearly structured manner; (4) putting recurrent emphasis on the ongoing influence of the rival political economic ideas in current economic policy discussions; and (5) encouraging the students to be active participants in political economic debates right from the outset. This is education rather than cloning. It needs to be done well because only then is a groundswell of student enthusiasm likely to be fostered. In other words, effective pluralist teaching can create students' 'demonstration effects' as well as being a socially responsible approach to education.

Pluralism in public discourse

The bigger arena in which a pluralist approach to heterodox economics has to prove its capacity to challenge mainstream economics is beyond the universities and in the broader realm of public discourse. How do intelligent citizens interpret political economic events? Through what lens do they see? Can heterodox economics contribute to changing the nature of economic discourse in the media and popular understandings of how the economy might better serve social needs? Can it break the stranglehold of mainstream economics on what is considered legitimate and useful in analysing economic issues in the broader society?

Therein are enormous challenges. The reproduction of beliefs about how the economic system operates involves a contest of economic interests as well as economic ideas. It is shaped by an array of institutions, most notably the media – through which economic information and commentary is disseminated. The proposition that 'we are what we eat' has its clear parallel in the proposition that 'we are what we read' – where 'read' can be taken here as signifying the various channels of information and 'infotainment' through which people currently get their peculiar diet of value-laden knowledge of political economic issues.

Although a comprehensive analysis of the media is beyond the scope of this chapter, it is pertinent to note some aspects of the institutional landscape that influence the possibilities for 'unorthodox' economic ideas to get a hearing. The media effectively defines the legitimate and accepted range of discourse, particularly on economic and political issues. It is helpful to understand this process in terms of three journalistic zones: a 'sphere of consensus', a 'sphere of legitimate controversy' and a 'sphere of deviance' (Hallin 1986). 'Conventional wisdoms' are perpetuated in the first sphere, subject only to the modest modifications permitted within the second sphere, while views that are effectively beyond the pale are consigned to the third sphere and duly ignored. What came to be known in Australia in the 1980s as 'economic rationalism' (the local forerunner of more fully-fledged neoliberalism) provides an example. It became effectively unnecessary for the media to elaborate the case for 'microeconomic reform', 'contestable markets' or reductions in the 'barriers to international trade'. Simply to mention this agenda was enough: anyone who did not subscribe to it was presumed suspect of 'economic illiteracy'. Hence the virtually across-the-board support in the mainstream media for competition policy, tariff-reductions, and deregulation of financial and labour markets. This is not to posit that alternative voices could never get a hearing.

Alternative media – including newspapers run by left parties rather than capitalist corporations, journals run by genuinely independent groups, local community radio stations and contributions by academics and other individuals to Internet blogs, for example – have recurrently challenged the 'conventional wisdom' in economic matters. It is important that heterodox economists contribute to these alternative channels, thereby seeking to broaden the zone of legitimate debate to some extent. Keeping critical perspectives and radical alternatives alive during otherwise barren periods of conservative hegemony is a rock-bottom position.

More positively, there are at least three reasons for some optimism about heterodox views being able to get a hearing. One is that the 'official ideology' of the media includes recognition of the role that the 'freedom of speech' plays in fostering a 'free society'. Setting aside the undoubtedly complex aspects of these terms, both in theory and practice, the simple point is that a pluralist approach must be seen as fundamentally legitimate in this context. The 'fourth estate' feature of the media is its saving grace, notwithstanding the recurrent 'third sphere' tendencies to suppression and marginalization of dissident views. There are always some journalists looking for views that challenge the status quo; and there is always some avenue through which those dissident views will out.

Second, the media has a persistent concern with describing the changing conditions in the real world. Indeed, without changes there are no news stories. Analyses that focus on illuminating the political economic forces driving those changes have an intrinsic advantage over mainstream economic views that emphasize 'equilibrium' conditions. 'New ideas for new times' could indeed be a pertinent masthead for modern political economy. Many of the currents of thought within heterodox economics have long and distinguished pedigrees, of course, but it is their relevance to current economic and social changes that gives them potential popular appeal.

Third, the intense political economic stresses that exist in the current era create numerous opportunities for radical analyses to get a hearing. The political economic order is recurrently threatened by the intensity and recurrence of financial crises, the intensification of ecological stresses (climate change most obviously) and the redistribution of income towards a wealthy elite (the top 1 per cent and, even more strikingly, the top 0.1 per cent of households). Continuation of these trends would threaten stability, sustainability and social cohesion. The big test for heterodox economists is to provide explanations and guidance that are intelligible to journalists and their audiences. That is easier said than done, of course. There is no obvious mass political demand for analyses that would challenge the bases of corporate power, the legitimacy of private property in environmental assets or the culture of consumerism and the drivers of capital accumulation.

That heterodox economists face an uphill battle in the public area is not a reason for passivity. Indeed significant victories can be periodically achieved when they join forces with political activists to challenge policies with damaging social effects. The battle to derail the 'WorkChoices' industrial relations agenda of the Howard Government in Australia in 2005 was a case in point. King was prominent among those showing what could be done. It was his initiative in penning a strongly-worded article warning that 'Australian unions are facing their most serious threat for over a century' (King 2005, p. 277) that prompted the editors of the *Journal of Australian Political Economy* to devote a special issue to the topic, for which King was invited to co-author the introduction. This journal's special issue was the first of many substantial academic contributions that strengthened the evidence base of opponents of the Howard Government's assault on the interests of labour, contributing eventually to its demise. The 2014 Budget of the Coalition government led by Tony Abbott is a more recent example where widespread public disquiet created abundant opportunities for critical political economic views to be heard.

The public policy challenge

Can heterodox economics also have direct influence on public policy for-mulation? This question takes us into a third realm, beyond the classroom, beyond public discourse and into the very heartlands of public policy for-mulation. Achieving influence there would certainly be a signal of success in shifting from margin to mainstream. Perhaps it is asking too much. For some heterodox economists, particularly those coming from within the Marxian tradition, policy prescription is a reformist activity that runs counter to their analyses of the capitalist state and sources of real economic power (Bramble 1994, Bryan 2002). That is not the dominant view, however. Criticism of the status quo and advocacy of a preferred alternative, no matter how unlikely it is to be embraced by incumbent governments, is the more typical political economic inclination. The recent book by Higgins and Dow (2013), drawing lessons from the history of social democratic politics and economic reform in Sweden, makes an explicit case for embracing that positive view of the possi-bilities and scope for economic reform. For heterodox economists who embrace the notion of 'radical reformism' (Gorz 1999), policy prescription is central to making a difference.

This is where heterodox economics gets explicitly political. In the current era, this necessarily means an engagement with neoliberalism, because that otherwise screens out any such progressive alternatives. This was explicit in former UK Prime Minister Margaret Thatcher's famous assertion that 'there is no alternative' to the harsh policies she implemented to address economic problems. The ascendancy of neoliberalism, to which she contributed, has developed into a deeply embedded set of political ideologies and practices. The combination of 'free market, strong state' is one way of characterizing its distinctive political economic character. Its familiar policy elements are privatization of public enterprises, liberalization of trade, deregulation of business behaviours and limitation of union power. Over the last three decades it has become the default position for economic policy in many countries across the OECD. It has continuing traction even (or perhaps especially) in the aftermath of the global financial crisis.

Can heterodox economics contribute to undermining this neoliberal dominance? This surely is a major test of the effectiveness of the challenges mounted against orthodox economics by heterodox economists who advocate pluralism in relation to public policy formulation, as well as for academic inquiry and teaching. To their credit, heterodox economists are often vigorously engaged in this process, e.g. reasserting Keynesian macroeconomic principles against those pursuing the currently dominant neoliberal 'politics of austerity'. But to turn the tables is a tall order. The proponents of neoliberalism – and the interest groups that benefit from its dominance in the public arena – are not inclined to roll over because academic economists of heterodox inclination claim more explanatory and predictive capacity for their analyses. A high R^2 is not enough! Issues of political economic power are involved. It is to King's credit that this has been yet another of the fields to which he has contributed, analysing neoliberalism in the context of recent and likely future trajectories of the capitalist system (Howard and King 2008; King 2012).

However, when it comes to policies that could help drive economic change in a different direction, the proponents of pluralism face an obvious disadvantage. This is because advocacy of specific policy proposals is the normal expectation in the policy arena. Governments and bureaucrats seeking policies that will 'solve' current economic problems are unlikely to be impressed by being told that: (1) there are many ways of seeing; (2) that the implementation of one short-term policy solution is likely to give rise to a different range of problems at a later time as the underlying economic contradictions reassert themselves in new forms; or (3) that the choice between alternative policy responses ultimately depends on the relative weight placed on an array of social goals that necessarily shape the policy process. The response is predictable: 'look, do you guys have a "fix" for the current economic problem or not?!'

Having a 'fix' for the problems of modern capitalism is an ultimately impossible demand. Heterodox economists emphasize the contradictory character of the system and its evolving nature, contrasting with the neoclassical economists' focus on the 'equilibrium' tendencies within the system. The contradictions are manifest in class conflict, ongoing crisis tendencies, environmental degradation and a host of related problems. Moreover, as Erik Olin Wright memorably demonstrated in one of his early books, policies that overcome particular constraints on capital accumulation in any one historical period tend to give rise to different types of constraints developing in the next period, thence to new economic problems requiring different strategic responses (Wright 1978). The point is also implicit in the reasoning presented in the more recent book by Higgins and Dow (2013). Indeed, the policy formulation process is necessarily complex because the implementation of any one set of policies creates structural economic changes that precipitate new problems and new policy needs.

Policies to deal with climate change are a case in point. Mainstream economists have an apparently neat 'solution' on offer. They advocate fixing the problem by 'putting a price on carbon', thereby internalizing the externalities that otherwise result because the private cost of burning of fossil fuels does not reflect the full social costs of that environmentally-damaging activity. This is the neoclassical logic that has led to the establishment of emissions trading systems as the preferred policy response across most OECD nations (with the glaring exception of Australia, where the current government has been more strongly influenced by climate change sceptics and short-sighted corporate interests). Taking that step creates other predictable hazards, however: the environment becomes more 'privatized' as use of resources like clean air becomes a matter of ability to pay, while secondary markets in emissions permits develop as new avenues for speculative profit-seeking. 'Selling the environment in order to save it' is indeed a somewhat bizarre process. Only a neoclassical economist could really believe that it creates a stable, sustainable equilibrium outcome. The task for heterodox economists is clear: to join forces with environmental scientists and activists in providing deeper analyses and remedies that address the underlying political economic causes of the problem (as signalled by Diesendorf 2014; Bryant 2014).

Conclusion

This chapter has taken John King's outstanding contributions to pluralism in economics as a springboard for discussing an array of concerns relating to economics as a discipline and how dissidents may seek to change it in progressive and effective ways. It has argued that heterodox economics is a necessary challenge to orthodox economics, that pluralism is a centrepiece for that challenge both in method and pedagogy, but that progress depends on getting more traction beyond 'the groves of academe' in the broader territories of public discourse and public policy.

King has made important contributions in all these respects: seeking to address the big issues of the era while maintaining emphasis on academic rigour. He has firm grounds for his renowned pessimism of the intellect. Yet optimism of the will evidently remains a driving force, as it does for so many other dissident and heterodox economists, particularly those actively engaged in organizations such as the WEA and SHE. Quite a lot has already been achieved. Many journals and books advancing heterodox political economic analysis provide both publication credits for authors and intellectual fuel for readers seeking to understand 'what is going on out there'. Attempts to make incursions into the media are also notable, as are linkages with other organizations challenging neoliberal capitalist hegemony. But much remains to be done.

These considerations illustrate the strengths of pluralism, but also signal some of the associated tensions. As a counter to monism, pluralism is intellectually admirable, just as freedom of speech is preferable to dogma and intellectual suppression. As a basis for seeking to topple the dominance of mainstream economics, however, it is necessary but not sufficient. More unity, analytically and organizationally, is helpful in a conflict situation like this. Working together to extend and broaden the critique of mainstream economics and its pernicious influences, both on students and in the wider world of public policy, remains the main challenge. Concurrently, seeking syntheses of the principal progressive, non-neoclassical currents of analysis is important in developing effective and influential alternatives. Let a hundred flowers bloom, but let's make this garden more impressive than the superficially tidy but unsustainable one that currently occupies the central place.

Notes

1 Thanks are due to David Primrose for his help with developing this chapter, including valuable suggestions and comments on an earlier draft.
2 See www.isipe.net.
3 See www.worldeconomicsassociation.org and http://iippe.org/wp/.

References

Bramble, T. (1994), Interventionist Industry Policy: a Marxist Critique, *Journal of Australian Political Economy* 33, pp. 65–89.
Bryan, D. (2002), Alternative Economic Strategies: an Evaluation, *Journal of Australian Political Economy* 50, pp. 153–162.
Bryant, G. (2014), When the 'Green Economy' Undermines Sustainability: Political, Economic and Ecological Dimensions of the Crisis, in S.K. Schroeder and L. Chester (eds.), (2014), *Challenging the Orthodoxy: The Contributions of Frank Stilwell to Political Economy*. Heidelberg: Springer-Verlag, pp. 243–255.
Chick, V. and Dow, S. (2001), Formalism, Logic and Reality: a Keynesian Analysis, *Cambridge Journal of Economics* 25(6), pp. 705–721.
Cohen, B.J. (2014), *Advanced Introduction to International Political Economy*. Cheltenham, UK and Northampton, MA, USA: Edward Elgar.
Colander, D. (2009), Moving Beyond the Rhetoric of Pluralism: Suggestions for an 'Inside the Mainstream' Heterodoxy, in R. Garnett, E.K. Olsen and M. Starr (eds.), *Economic Pluralism*. London and New York: Routledge, pp. 36–47.
Coyle, D. (2007), *The Soulful Science: What Economists Really Do and Why it Matters*. Princeton, NJ: Princeton University Press.
Coyle, D. (2013), The State of Economics and the Education of Economists, World Economics Association Curriculum Conference, *The Economics Curriculum: Towards a Radical Reformulation*. At http://curriculumconference2013.worldeco nomicsassociation.org/wp-content/uploads/WEA-CurriculumCon ference2013-COYLE.pdf, accessed 22 May 2013.
Davis, J.B. and Hands, D.W. (eds.) (2011), *The Elgar Companion to Recent Economic Methodology*. Cheltenham, UK and Northampton, MA, USA: Edward Elgar.
Dawson, R. (2007), Judging Economics Teaching and Textbooks, *Journal of Australian Political Economy* 60, pp. 73–97.
Diesendorf, M. (2014), A Genuinely Green Economy Must Be Ecologically Sustainable and Socially Just, in Schroeder, S. and Chester, L. (eds.), (2014), *Challenging the*

Orthodoxy: The Contributions of Frank Stilwell to Political Economy. Heidelberg: Springer-Verlag, pp. 223–242.

Dow, S. (2002), *Economic Methodology: an Inquiry.* Oxford University Press: Oxford.

Dow, S., Earl, P., Foster, J., Harcourt, G.C., Hodgson, G.M., Metcalfe, J.S., Ormerod, P., Rosewell, P., Sawyer, M.C. and Tylcote, A. (2009), An Open Letter to the Queen, reprinted in *Journal of Australian Political Economy* 64, pp. 233–235.

Earl, P. (2008), In the Economics Classroom, in Fullbrook, E. (ed.), (2008), *Pluralist Economics.* London: Zed Books, pp. 193–214.

Feyerabend, P.K. (1975), *Against Method: Outline of an Anarchistic Theory of Knowledge.* London: New Left Books.

Frank, R.H., Gilovich, T.D. and Regan, D.T. (1993), Does Studying Economics Prohibit Cooperation? *Journal of Economic Perspectives* 7(2), pp. 159–171.

Fullbrook, E. (2003), *The Crisis in Economics: The Post-Autistic Economics Movement: The First 600 Days.* London and New York: Routledge.

Fullbrook, E. (ed.) (2008), *Pluralist Economics.* London: Zed Books.

Gorz, A. (1999), *Reclaiming Work: Beyond the Wage-based Society.* London: Pluto Press.

Hallin, D.C. (1986), *The 'Uncensored War': the Media and Vietnam.* Los Angeles: University of California Press.

Higgins, W. and Dow, G. (2013), *Politics against Pessimism.* Berne: Peter Lang.

Hodgson, G.M. (2001), *How Economics Forgot History.* London and New York: Routledge.

Howard, M.C. and King, J.E. (2008), *The Rise of Neoliberalism in Advanced Capitalist Economies: a Materialist Analysis.* Basingstoke, UK: Palgrave Macmillan.

Jones, E. (1994), The Tyranny of A Priorism in Economic Thought, *History of Economics Review* 22, pp. 24–69.

King, J.E. (2002), Three Arguments for Pluralism in Economics, *Journal of Australian Political Economy* 50, pp. 82–88.

King, J.E. (2005), Industrial Relations: a Minimum Program for the States, *Journal of Australian Political Economy* 56, pp. 277–283.

King, J.E. (2012), The Future of Neoliberalism, in D. Cahill, L. Edwards and F. Stilwell (eds.) *Neoliberalism: Beyond the Free Market.* Cheltenham, UK and Northampton, MA, USA: Edward Elgar, pp. 251–266.

King, J.E. (2013), A Case for Pluralism in Economics, *Economics and Labour Relations Review* 24, pp. 17–31.

Kurz, H.D. and Salvadori, N. (2000), On Critics and Protective Belts, in H.D. Kurz, and N. Salvadori (eds.), *Understanding Classical Economics: Studies in Long-Period Theory.* London and New York: Routledge, pp. 232–255.

Mariyani-Squire, E. and Moussa, M. (2013), Stilwell's Pluralism and Beyond, paper presented to conference on The State of Political Economy: Past, Present and Future, University of Sydney, April 2013.

Mearman, A. (2014), Teaching Political Economy, in S.K. Schroeder and L. Chester (eds.), (2014), *Challenging the Orthodoxy: The Contributions of Frank Stilwell to Political Economy.* Heidelberg: Springer-Verlag, pp. 39–55.

Milonakis, D. and Fine, B. (2009), *From Economics Imperialism to Freakonomics: The Shifting Boundaries between Economics and other Social Sciences.* London and New York: Routledge.

Nesiba, R. F. (2012), What Do Undergraduates Study in Heterodox Economics Programs? An Examination of the Curricula Structure at 36 Self-identified Programs, *On the Horizon* 20(3), pp. 182–193.

O'Donnell, R. (2014), What do Graduate Attributes Have to do with Political Economy? in S.K. Schroeder and L. Chester (eds.), (2014), *Challenging the Orthodoxy: The Contributions of Frank Stilwell to Political Economy.* Heidelberg: Springer-Verlag, pp. 57–77.

Rosenberg, P. (2014), New Paradigm Economics versus Old Paradigm Economics: Interview with Edward Fullbrook, *Real-World Economics Review* 66, pp. 131–143. At http://www.paecon.net/PAEReview/issue66/whole66.pdf, accessed 15 June 2015.

Rubinstein, A. (2006), A Sceptic's Comment on the Study of Economics, *The Economic Journal* 116(510), pp. C1–C9.

Salanti, A. and Screpanti, E. (eds.) (1997), *Pluralism in Economics: New Perspectives in History and Methodology.* Cheltenham, UK and Northampton, MA, USA: Edward Elgar.

Schroeder, S. and Chester, L. (eds.), (2014), *Challenging the Orthodoxy: The Contributions of Frank Stilwell to Political Economy.* Heidelberg: Springer-Verlag.

Stilwell, F. (1988), Contemporary Political Economy: Common and Contested Terrain, *The Economic Record* 64(1), pp. 14–25.

Stilwell, F. (2006), Four Reasons for Pluralism in the Teaching of Economics, *Australasian Journal of Economics Education* 2(1–2), pp. 42–55.

Stilwell, F. (2011), Teaching a Pluralist Course in Economics: the University of Sydney Experience, *International Journal of Pluralism and Economics Education* 2(1), pp. 39–53.

Stilwell, F. (2012a), *Political Economy: the Contest of Economic Ideas.* Melbourne: Oxford University Press.

Stilwell, F. (2012b), Teaching Political Economy: Making a Difference? *Studies in Political Economy* 89, pp. 147–163.

Thornton, T.B. (2013), The Narrowing of the Australian University Economics Curriculum: an Analysis of the Problem and a Proposed Solution, *The Economic Record* 89(S1), pp. 106–114.

Wheelwright, E.L. and Waters, W. (1973), University Economics: A Radical Critique, *The Australian Quarterly* 45(3), pp. 51–65.

Wolff, R.D. and Resnick, S.A. (2012), *Contending Economic Theories: Neoclassical, Keynesian, and Marxian.* Massachusetts and London: MIT Press.

Wright, E.O. (1978), *Class, Crisis and the State.* London: New Left Books.

3 Consistency in pluralism and the role of microfoundations

Sheila Dow[1]

Introduction

As a highly-respected chronicler of the state of modern economics and its history, and in particular in his promotion of pluralism in economics, John King provides ample material on which to base a further consideration of pluralism. It is challenging to single out any particular publications by John King, given the breadth and depth of his knowledge, and the careful analysis and bold argument he consistently displays in his work. Nevertheless, for the purposes of this chapter, I focus on two papers which I have found particularly striking. A central piece of work for the focus of this volume is his discussion of the case for pluralism (King 2002). My purpose here is to relate that paper to another striking paper arguing against the significant drive within modern economics to specify microfoundations. I first heard this argument as a paper presentation at the IMK/FMM[2] annual conference in Berlin in 2008 and then at a symposium on microfoundations at SOAS[3] in 2009; since then he has published a more full account of his analysis of microfoundations in his 2012 monograph. Both papers were thought provoking, in terms of reflection on the two conceptual areas and on the different stances on them which were revealed. The discussion here is a set of reflections provoked by these papers.

The first paper considers three different arguments for pluralism within heterodox economics. It is important to establish at the start what is being meant by pluralism, since it can refer to any of the levels of philosophy, methodology and theory (see further Dow 1997). The three arguments refer primarily to the philosophical level, i.e. *methodological pluralism* – the acceptance of, and respect for, a range of methodological approaches on the grounds that no one approach can be demonstrated to be best given the nature of the subject matter. The meaning at the level of methodology is *pluralist methodologies*, i.e. particular approaches which advocate use of a range of methods. Methodological pluralism could in principle allow for a methodological approach which advocates only one method. But the prime case of such a methodology is the mainstream insistence on mathematical formalism, which takes a methodological monist approach. There is further *theoretical pluralism*, i.e. a range of theories. Since the methodological approach is regarded in mainstream discourse as settled, this is usually the meaning of pluralism employed there. While there is a variety of theories within mainstream economics, nevertheless they are all conditioned by the shared ontology, epistemology and methodology by which mainstream economics is defined (Dow 2007).

While methodological pluralism involves acceptance that there will be a range of approaches to economics, it does not mean that any economist should use several approaches simultaneously, since to do so would in effect mean developing a new, synthetic approach. Rather it means that any economist should be sufficiently methodologically aware to be able to make the case for her own approach relative to others. No approach can be definitively demonstrated to be superior, but that does not mean that argument for one's own approach cannot be forceful. Heterodox economists are inevitably methodologically aware in that the case has to be made relative to the mainstream approach. Nevertheless there are some apparent expressions of monism in heterodoxy as a challenge to pluralism (see Dow 2008 for a flavour of the debate). At the very start of the pluralism paper, John King nails his colours firmly to the mast: 'Is there a single correct alternative to neoclassical economics? The purpose of this short paper is to suggest that there is not'.

King (2002) focuses on the Sraffian, Post Keynesian and institutionalist arguments for pluralism, all of which are based on an ontology which defies any prospect of one general overarching theory or theoretical approach. But all have exclusions from this openness to different approaches. These exclusions are different but overlapping: Sraffians exclude neoclassical economic theory, Post Keynesians exclude exclusive use of mathematical formalism, while institutionalists exclude any theory which purports to be general. All the arguments about exclusion involve some application of the principle of consistency, although at different levels. Sraffians point to theoretical inconsistency in neoclassical economics with respect to capital, while Post Keynesians and institutionalists focus more on inconsistencies between ontology and epistemology in criticizing methodological and theoretical exclusiveness, respectively. But is it inconsistent for a pluralist to exclude methodologies or theories in this way, or is this just one implication of structured pluralism? John King's paper concludes that differences between pluralists can be overcome by communication, but how far is communication between different approaches itself open to inconsistencies of meaning?

The second paper similarly pulls no punches, demonstrating further differences among heterodox economists, given that many, like orthodox economists, employ the concept of microfoundations which he so effectively critiques, drawing on the philosophy literature. Again consistency is a continuing theme. The case for microfoundations has been based on the view that macroeconomics and microeconomics should be consistent, although John King goes on to explain that neither need be foundational to the other. He argues however that, while some inconsistency between the two levels is to be expected, nevertheless one aim should be to reduce inconsistency. Further, John King argues not only for theory to be consistent with the economist's social and philosophical approach, but that this approach should be foundational. Here we see an echo of the arguments for pluralism in the earlier paper, based on consistency between theory on one hand and ontology and epistemology on the other.

While the concept of consistency arises in both papers, it is worth reflecting further on what exactly is being meant by this term too. The purpose of this chapter is to try to unpack the different ways in which the consistency concept applies to both papers. We consider consistency at three levels, but in the reverse order to the outline of pluralism above: the theoretical, methodological and philosophical levels. We therefore start with theoretical consistency, which then raises the issue at the methodological level of the system of logic within which consistency is being applied, in particular whether it is classical logic or human logic. Next we consider philosophical consistency, between ontology, epistemology, methodology and theory. In the process we consider further John King's argument for social and philosophical foundations. We then consider the issue of consistency with respect to communication. This involves consideration of the concept of vagueness. Finally we review the implications of this discussion of consistency for the future direction of heterodox economics, and in particular for Post Keynesian economics.

King (2008) highlights the powerful role of metaphor in the history of ideas right at the start of the microfoundations paper. In the process of the exploration here of consistency in relation to pluralism and microfoundations, we will bear in mind the powerful metaphor which King develops from Geoff Harcourt's account of Post Keynesian methodology: 'horses for courses' (see further Harcourt 1987, 1996). This metaphor captures the idea that methodology should reflect the problem at hand and the real context in which it arises. There is disagreement between the three heterodox groups represented in the pluralism paper in terms of their respective views on formalism, with openness to different methods for specific problems being greatest for institutionalists and least for Sraffians; this can be understood as a different choice as to the appropriate type of horse for a particular course.

King (2002) points out that the need for some consistency puts some limits on the horses. With respect to theoretical consistency, he points to inconsistencies in mainstream economics, concluding that each horse must 'have four legs and a jockey and proceed anti-clockwise around the course' and further that 'all four legs must be pointing in the same direction'. But his argument that more theoretical consistency is desirable requires further reflection on what exactly is meant by that. At risk of torturing the metaphor, we will see how we might develop it further as the discussion proceeds. We return to an early statement of the 'horses for courses' position in the final section on Post Keynesian economics.

Theoretical consistency

The argument for theoretical consistency arises in both papers. It is central to the microfoundations paper, where mainstream economics is shown to have been driven by a commitment to increase consistency between the micro and macro levels of analysis – indeed to make the two levels of theory perfectly consistent. John King's main argument is against requiring the micro level to be established prior to the macro level (or indeed vice versa), such that one level provides the foundation for the other. 'Foundations, to repeat, *must come first*. The constitutive nature of the foundational metaphor is most evident, and most damaging, here' (King 2008, p. 36, emphasis in original).

A secondary argument is against giving priority in economics practice to the exercise of promoting consistency. Nevertheless, other things being equal, increased consistency is to be pursued:

> The position that I shall be defending is this: consistency between microeconomics and macroeconomics is desirable, but it does not entail that the former is the *foundation* of the latter. In more general terms, the fact that there is (or may be, or appears to be) some inconsistency between two related bodies of knowledge, A and B, does not entail that A must become the foundation for B, or for that matter that B must become the foundation for A.
>
> (King 2008, pp. 3–4)

Keynesian economics has been criticized by the mainstream on the grounds of lack of consistency between the macro and micro levels. It has therefore been particularly appealing to heterodox economists to point out that the mainstream itself involves serious theoretical inconsistencies. The one to which most attention has been paid is the mainstream treatment of capital, where inconsistency completely undermines the whole theoretical edifice built on the principle of substitution, which, it is shown, does not apply to capital (Kurz and Salvadori 2000). John King highlights this critique of mainstream economics in relation to the Sraffian case for pluralism – but a pluralism without mainstream economics. For Sraffians therefore theoretical consistency is so crucial that its violation justifies rejection, even by pluralists.

If it is to be taken for granted that theoretical consistency is desirable, where does that leave heterodox economics, where inconsistencies persist, notably between the micro and macro levels within any one approach? Inconsistencies persist also between theories within heterodox schools of thought, such as Post Keynesian economics, as seen in the debates between the different Post Keynesian approaches to monetary theory (see for example Arestis and Sawyer 2006). There are even more inconsistencies between heterodox schools of thought.

Clearly there are inconsistencies and inconsistencies, and some are more important than others; indeed when is an inconsistency a sign of incoherence and when is it just a difference (see further Dow 1990)? A clue to how to deal with this is given in King's account of Chick's (2002) justification for not pursuing completely consistent Post Keynesian microfoundations, whose title refers to 'necessary compromise': 'Chick therefore rejected the possibility of impeccably logical microfoundations, which could be provided only at the expense of "the logic of the whole'" (King 2008, p. 11). The stumbling block in any effort to develop consistent microfoundations is the fictional nature of the auctioneer. The nature of the theoretical relationship between microeconomics and macroeconomics then is something open to reasoned argument and persuasion rather than definitive logical demonstration.

Consistency takes its meaning from logic, but there is more than one logic on which methodology can be based, and there is more than one sphere of logic. First we consider two main types of logic: classical logic and human logic, as applied to theory. But we cannot go far with this without considering the sphere of application – what is the 'whole' to which Chick refers? In particular, we need to think about the justification for using one or other type of logic at the philosophical level – this will be the subject of the following section.

Logical consistency: classical and human logic

It is common to equate logic with classical logic, which has indeed dominated Western thought. This system of logic is deductivist, deriving conclusions by means of deductive logic from premises which are taken to be true. If the logic is correct the conclusions are then also true. If the logic is incorrect this can be proved by identifying a logical contradiction – an inconsistency. Within this type of logic, inconsistency can be identified definitively and is something to be eradicated since it undermines the entire argument. Where a body of theory follows classical logic, it takes the form of a deductivist system, all of which is founded on premises which refer to the lowest level, i.e. it is reductionist.

This is the type of logic employed by mainstream economics and which underpinned the drive for microfoundations of macroeconomics: that macro-economic propositions should be derivable from the axioms of rational opti-mizing behaviour which are taken to be true, or at least 'as if' true. The theoretical system which is built on such principles is a closed system and lends itself to formal mathematical expression. (In terms of the racehorse metaphor, whatever the racecourse and its current condition, there is only one type of horse which is acceptable.) Further, within such a system the notion of consistency is unambiguous and is closely aligned with the notion of rigour. No wonder there is such unquestioning support for consistency as a principle.

The presumed truth of the premises is critical to classical logic. In the case of economics, the axioms of rational choice have been the object of sustained questioning. Within mainstream economics, such questioning (as in the new behavioural economics) is aimed at establishing more robust axioms. But in heterodox economics, the prospect of *any* axioms being established as true is questioned and an alternative logic preferred in order to deal with the absence of certainty about any assumptions. This is the type of logic employed by Keynes, variously termed 'ordinary logic' or 'human logic' (Gerrard 1992). For Keynes (as for Hume), reason (and thus deductivism) was insufficient for justifying belief as the basis for action. Because of the complex, evolving nature of the economic system, we can never expect to uncover true causal mechanisms, far less predict on their basis. Rather than relying on one reasoned argument, he argued that beliefs are more soundly based if they draw on a range of types of argument and/or of language (Harcourt 1984, 1987). Further, since contexts of analysis differ, choice of types of argument and evidence should reflect the problem at hand: 'horses for courses'.

This logic can be characterized, in contrast to the Cartesian/Euclidean character of a system of thought based on classical logic, as Babylonian thought, based on the Babylonian style of mathematics (Dow 2012). This approach builds up knowledge by means of a range of arguments which are incommensurate (otherwise they could collapse into one argument). Thus one line of argument might use the *ceteris paribus* argument to focus on one sector, treating the rest of the economy as exogenous. Another line of argument might focus on the interrelations between that sector and another with which it interacts, treating all the rest as exogenous. This would seem unexceptional to a mainstream economist, but their expectation would be that the two analyses could then be combined in an overarching formal analysis, derivable from the rationality axioms. Within human logic, rather, the expectation is that different types of argument will help to build up the strands of an argument, but there is no basis for treating any of the provisional assumptions as axioms. In terms of the 'horses for courses' metaphor, we can consider each horse as encompassing a particular combination of characteristics, each characteristic representing one method or line of argument. Schools of thought may emerge around a particular range (a stable) of combinations of types of argument within human logic (different horses), providing some structure to what in principle would be endless possibilities (the category 'horse' is bounded).

From a classical logic point of view, the human logic approach is riddled with inconsistencies. But within human logic it is inevitable that different (inconsistent?) assumptions will be used for different purposes. The issue is the domain of application of an assumption, which is universal in the case of classical logic and local in the case of human logic. This follows from the closed nature of a system of classical logic, such that any contradiction undermines the whole system. Herein lies the force of the heterodox critiques of orthodoxy which identify inconsistencies in terms of classical logic, as in the capital controversies. In an open system there will be differences between lines of reasoning and the assumptions on which they are built, but these need not involve inconsistency. Inconsistency is only definitive within any one partial analysis, for example if perfect foresight were assumed for some agents and uncertainty for others within one model. Within human logic it is therefore not legitimate necessarily to regard different assumptions as entailing inconsistency since the domains are different. There is no overarching closed deductive edifice to be challenged by apparent contradiction.

Whitehead (1938, p. 76) concludes his discussion of consistency as follows: 'Thus inconsistency is relative to the abstraction involved'. A microeconomic theory may involve different assumptions from a macroeconomic theory, but if they are each treated as partial systems rather than part of a formal overarching system, no inconsistency *need* be involved. There is an important distinction between models (which require provisional closure) and theoretical systems:

> The key is how far the theoretical system is identified with its models. Within an open theoretical system, there is scope for changing the assumptions, boundaries or *ceteris paribus* conditions to suit the theorist's immediate purpose, as for example assuming that long-term expectations are fixed in one model but not in another. Discussion surrounding these models extends beyond the models in order to take account of what has been 'kept at the back of one's head'. A closed theoretical system on the other hand tends to be identified with its models.
>
> (Chick and Dow 2005, pp. 369–70)

Whitehead (1938, p. 75) had seemed to imply that inconsistency was not an issue within what we now refer to as an open-system mode of thought: '[b]y means of process the universe escapes from the limitations of the finite. Process is the immanence of the infinite in the finite; whereby all bounds are burst, and all inconsistencies dissolved.' This has echoes of postmodernism, which celebrates paradox as one of its features, something which is anathema to classical logic (and different from the reasoned compromise over consistency in the Post Keynesian approach, for example). But to see the prevalence of process is not to give up on theoretical argument. I have argued elsewhere (Dow 2001a) that postmodernism runs the risk of presenting itself in terms of classical logic, and thus as employing the dual of modernist classical logic, which is absence of logic. In terms of the 'horses for courses' metaphor, there would be no horserace.

Of course postmodernists do in fact employ logic, for example to justify general arguments, but this is inconsistent with the dual of classical logic. Similarly, McCloskey (1986) has shown that mainstream economists aren't consistent either in their use of logic – an example of methodological inconsistency. While classical logic is central to the official discourse in publications, informal, unofficial discourse in fact employs a range of types of argument more in line with human logic. It should not be surprising that deductive logic is insufficient to demonstrate the superiority of one line of argument over another. The failure of the Bourbaki project to represent mathematics as a completely closed system provides ample illustration of the problems. Indeed the continuing inconsistency between pure and applied work in mainstream economics can be understood in terms of the primacy of the consistency principle in pure mathematics, when compared to applied mathematics (Weintraub 2002). But even in empirical work, the drive for internal consistency has overridden concerns with realism (Wren-Lewis 2011).

But the implication is that a completely internally consistent closed formal system representing the economy is unattainable, however persistently it is pursued. But in practice the charge of theoretical inconsistency in terms of classical logic has proved to be insufficient for theory rejection, as we have seen by the waving aside by the orthodoxy of heterodox arguments about inconsistencies with respect to capital, even though such methodological inconsistency is straightforward since the stated primacy of consistency within mainstream economics takes its meaning from classical logic.

It clearly matters whether inconsistency is understood in terms of classical logic or human logic. It is appropriate to critique mainstream economics for theoretical and methodological inconsistency on its own, classical logic, terms. For heterodox economics, a critique on grounds of theoretical inconsistency within the body of theory as a whole (rather than any partial analysis) needs to be expressed in terms of human logic. Similarly methodological inconsistency is only relevant if it is identified in terms of human logic. But to understand what that entails we need to return to Chick's 'logic of the whole'. The discussion above has been straying from issues of methodological consistency into issues of philosophical consistency. We have seen the importance of ontology, or how we understand the subject matter. We turn now to consider philosophical consistency: the logic of the whole.

Philosophical consistency

While King (2008) argues against the notion of theoretical foundations, he does advocate social and philosophical foundations. I understand his discussion of social foundations as referring to ontology and the philosophical foundations as referring to epistemology. What he is arguing therefore is that theorizing should not only be consistent with a particular ontology, and also a particular epistemology, but that these are both prior to theorizing. When heterodox economists argue that the nature of the social world is such that it does not yield law-like behaviour and thus any prospect of demonstrating which is the best theory to represent it, they are making a consistency argument – not consistency within a closed theoretical system, but consistency between the theoretical system and the nature of the subject matter. (In terms of the 'horses for courses' metaphor, it is the understanding of the nature of the racecourse and its current conditions which determines the choice of horse to run.) Thus Lawson (1997) argues for open-system theorizing (which employs human logic) to address an open-system reality. Since there is no demonstrably best form of theorizing about an open system, as King (2002) explains, there will be a range of open theoretical systems each employing its own range of methods, i.e. pluralism. (Different owners will have a range of horses in their stables, based on their understandings of the nature of the course.)

That each of these systems adopts different ranges of assumptions and methods implies inconsistency in the sense of differences at the methodological and theoretical levels between different approaches. But for heterodox economics there is consistency with the particular open-system ontology of each system. In contrast, Lawson (1997) points out that the closed-system theorizing of mainstream economics is only consistent with a closed-system reality. To the extent that many mainstream economists in fact believe the real social world to be open, they are being philosophically inconsistent. (There is only one type of horse to be run, even if the owner knows it to be unsuited to any course on which the race will be run.)

This argument implies that philosophical consistency trumps theoretical consistency (which in any case depends on epistemology including the type of logic employed). The case for pluralism rests on philosophical consistency. Further it would appear that philosophy (ontology and epistemology) should indeed be foundational. I am associated with this view, not least because of the title of my recent book, *Foundations for New Economic Thinking*, but also because I have long argued for increased awareness of the philosophical assumptions implicit in economic theory and the need to ensure philosophical consistency. So it might seem perverse to raise issues with it. Nevertheless I would like to raise again some issues with a uni-directional version of foundations (see further Dow 2001b).

Everything follows from ontology. Yet our understanding of reality is a complex product of socially-mediated experience. Indeed the philosophy of economics is performative to the extent that our understanding of reality and the corresponding appropriate epistemology can be the result of our assimilation into a mainstream approach to economics. For society at large, the reality may be performative too, to the extent that the media, government and business organizations accept the mainstream account of the real social world and the appropriate way to build knowledge about it. In particular, if mainstream economics succeeds in representing formal mathematical systems as the most rigorous and inconsistency within these systems as a sign of defective science, economists and economic agents alike are encouraged to understand economic behaviour as driven by rational choice and mathematical modelling as the best way to proceed in building up knowledge. We have had ample evidence in the financial crisis of this performativity, when financial deregulation, confidence in the capacity for risk assessment and even reregulation took this view, with real consequences. Ontology is then affected by epistemology and methodology.

This reverse causation can also occur in a more constructive way. Where philosophy is foundational, economists may be expected to follow instruction from philosophers, something which mainstream economists in particular have been notably reluctant to do. Even where lip service is paid to philosophy of science, such as the work of Popper or Lakatos, the practice has not been consistent with it (Blaug 1980). Where the argument for focusing on philosophical foundations stands the best chance is where there is significant input from practising economists, not least because practice informs philosophy. This is not just a matter of rhetoric, but a matter of developing methodological principles through practice.

These two arguments may seem like quibbles relative to the important argument for social and philosophical foundations, but they are in fact symptomatic of the particular philosophical foundations of heterodox economics, that the different levels interact and in both directions. Ontology and epistemology are foundational in that they need to be addressed consciously when developing and justifying one's approach. This is not incompatible with acknowledging that, from a systemic perspective, ontology and epistemology are themselves ultimately endogenous.

Communication and consistency

King (2002) notes the inconsistencies between the three arguments for pluralism he sets out. But I agree with his conclusion that pluralism does not mean methodological or theoretical uniformity, even when making the case for pluralism – in fact the point of pluralism is that it does not. Rather pluralism entails communication between different approaches. There is sufficient philosophical commonality – essentially each approach is identified with an open-system ontology out of the many possibilities and an open-system epistemology out of the many possibilities.

Communication itself requires some level of consistency, which different ontologies and epistemologies might be thought to belie. But the philosophical foundations provide the solution. For a closed-system ontology and epistemology, meanings are fixed and precise such that there should be no scope for communication difficulties. Indeed it is one of the arguments for mathematical formalism that it ensures just such a commensurability. Mathematics is regarded as a particularly precise language, but its precision is internal and does not extend to application. Incommensurability arises for mainstream theory outside the system in terms of the subject matter which is excluded because of the mathematical method, but more generally in terms of the translation of formal terms into real experience, i.e. in application to the real world (see Harcourt 1984 for an account of the history of this line of argument). Since mainstream methodology is exclusively mathematical there is no solution other than to treat application as an art requiring a different methodology which is inconsistent with the methodology which produced the pure theory which is to be applied (Colander 2002). In order to avoid methodological contradiction, the solution has been to separate off the area of application where meanings lose their precision and inconsistencies may arise.

For open-system epistemologies, identification and definition of categories is provisional within an evolving environment. Context is of critical importance, requiring adaptation of theories and concepts. Not only may different strands of argument employ different 'languages' (Harcourt 1984), but verbal language has a particular advantage in being vague, allowing overlapping meanings which allow conversation. The issue of the precision (or otherwise) of language arose within the debates between rationalism and common sense philosophy early in the twentieth century in Cambridge (see Coates 1996 and Davis's 1999 review article). While rationalist argument aimed for precision, this precision was less clearly appealing when arguments were applied to the real world. Harcourt (1992, p. 276) suggests that Marshall made the choice in favour of real-world application at the cost of precision: 'it is better to be vaguely right than precisely wrong' (an expression acquired from Wildon Carr, via Gerald Shove). The vagueness of ordinary language, corresponding to ordinary logic, has the virtue of allowing greater scope for correspondence between reasoned argument and the real world. The scope for ambiguity allows for change in the subject matter, because the meaning of verbal language is more flexible than the meaning of mathematical terms or data series. The meaning of verbal terms further tends to be complex rather than singular, incorporating a range of connotations.

But even in mathematics and the physical sciences terms are vague in the sense that their meaning has changed over the years. The metaphors we use in economics benefit from their vagueness. Game theory for example draws on the metaphor of the game and the cluster of meanings attached to it (Coates 1996, chapter 2). Similarly, the metaphor of the market benefits from its vagueness. That is what allows Becker to extend market analysis into the family context. It may be that the market is precisely defined for the purposes of deductive theory, in terms of preferences defined in a precise way with respect to the abstract concept of rational economic man. But what the rhetoric literature has taught us is that how we actually understand and discuss this theory and these concepts draws on our wider understanding of the world. This is made possible by the vagueness of our use of what are intended to be precise terms.

But vagueness is only helpful where there is significant overlap of meaning. Where meanings are very different the use of a common language can impede communication. The confusion caused by the different meanings of rationality is a case in point, just as here we are focusing on distinctions between different meanings of 'consistency'.

Conclusion: Post Keynesian economics and consistency

King (2008) makes clear the quite different (methodological and theoretical) positions taken on microfoundations within heterodox economics. If heterodox economics is to progress within the hoped-for pluralist economics, then it is important to address differences which imply incoherence. But shared philosophical foundations and the vagueness of language should facilitate communication and therefore debate. We have also argued that theoretical 'inconsistencies' are inevitable within heterodox economics given the open-system approach and the human logic by which it is pursued. It is consistency with ontology which is the most important.

This issue of consistency within heterodox economics, and particularly within Post Keynesian economics has come up before, implicitly in comparison with mainstream economics, which emphasizes internal consistency. In 1988, Hamouda and Harcourt published an account of three strands within

Post Keynesian economics and posed the question of how far this school of thought is coherent. This paper elicited a response from Backhouse (1988) which in effect focused on the coherence of mainstream economics in comparison to Post Keynesian economics. Because Post Keynesian economics does not prioritize theoretical consistency – indeed argues against doing so – then it inevitably qualifies as a degenerating Lakatosian research programme (because of what Backhouse perceives as ad hocery). Alternatively, he suggests that a Kuhnian interpretation would classify Post Keynesian as immature relative to mainstream economics. It is clear that the conclusion that Post Keynesianism is deficient was based on the charge of theoretical and methodological inconsistency in its classical logic sense.

There was a further round of debate when Walters and Young (1997) published a set of arguments that Post Keynesianism lacked coherence, but this time referring also to different accounts of philosophical foundations. This paper drew a strong response from Arestis, Dunn and Sawyer (1999) who explained the prevalence of commonalities in what Walters and Young had identified as differences. The possibility of differences at the philosophical level requires serious attention. The pluralist methodology of Post Keynesian economics requires that there be multiple strands of reasoning, involving different methods and generating different partial theories. But a school of thought is defined by its shared methodology, which requires a shared ontology and epistemology.

In considering the future of Post Keynesian economics, or indeed heterodox economics more generally, it is therefore important that we distinguish between inconsistencies within partial analyses, within methodologies and between these and the underlying philosophical foundations. The philosophical position does not allow for 'anything goes'. John King has drawn our attention to the one important example of apparent inconsistency: the stance on microfoundations. For him it is consistency between the philosophical foundation on one hand and methodology and theory on the other which is of primary importance. He has argued for a movement in the direction of more consistency between theory at the micro level and the macro level. But the guiding principle is consistency of each of micro and macro theory with the nature of the subject matter, rather than necessarily with each other.

At the same time as pursuing consistency in this sense, it is important not to be distracted by other charges of inconsistency which do not in fact make sense within a pluralist methodology or open-systems epistemology. But the challenge is greater for such an approach relative to the simplicity and clarity of the consistency criterion in classical logic. The argument has to be made on a case-by-case basis for particular segmentations of analysis into the multiple pluralist strands, based on consistency with understanding of the real context at hand, and then judgement needs to be applied in forming a conclusion based on this pluralist analysis. Consistency is important *within* partial analyses, but inconsistency in the sense of differences between analyses is to be expected, as long as it does not involve inconsistency with philosophical foundations.

In seeking to summarize the case for this analysis of consistency, it is hard to put it better than the concluding statement in Hamouda and Harcourt (1988, pp. 24–25, emphasis in original):

> What we have tried to show is that, within the various strands which we have discerned and described, there *are* coherent frameworks and approaches to be found, though obviously there remain within each unfinished business and unresolved puzzles. The real difficulty arises when attempts are made to synthesize the strands in order to see whether a coherent whole emerges. Our own view is that this is a misplaced exercise, that to attempt to do so is mainly to search for what Joan Robinson called 'only another box of tricks' to replace the 'complete theory' of mainstream economics which all strands reject. The important perspective to take away is, we believe, that there is no uniform way of tackling all issues in economics and that the various strands in post Keynesian economics differ from one another, not least because they are concerned with different issues and often different levels of abstraction and analysis.
>
> An important implication of the above conclusion is that the policies which may be rationalized by post Keynesian analysis are very much geared to concrete situations, the historical experiences and the sociological characteristics of the economies concerned. More generally, this approach which was that, for example, of Keynes, Kalecki, Joan Robinson and Arthur Okun, sometimes and most appropriately, has been dubbed the 'horses for courses' approach.

As John King puts it, within any partial analysis, each horse must 'have four legs and a jockey and proceed anti-clockwise around the course' and further that 'all four legs must be pointing in the same direction'. There needs to be consistency in terms of the choice of methods to use (the horse) and ontology (the understanding of the nature of the racecourse and its current conditions) if there is to be a good chance of generating useful analysis (winning the race). Different open-system ontologies justify different choices of method (different types of horse). Relying exclusively as does mainstream economics on one method regardless of ontology (one type of horse chosen, e.g. for its aesthetic appeal) cannot reasonably be expected to succeed. But here the metaphor breaks down. Were it the case that all agreed on epistemology and thus on the criteria for success (the rules of the race), we would end up with a monist choice of approach (a clear winner). Rather the metaphor applies to the stage of planning for the race and placing bets – even under uncertainty, practising economists must adopt one approach or another within the plurality on offer. We support the stable we judge to have the best range of horses to address the course as we understand it, and the ability to make the best choice of horse for particular conditions.

Notes

1 This chapter has benefited from helpful comments and suggestions from Geoff Harcourt and from an anonymous referee.
2 Macroeconomic Policy Institute (IMK) at the Hans-Boeckler-Foundation, Research Network Macroeconomics and Macroeconomic Policies (FMM). See http://www. boeckler.de/index_netzwerk-makrooekonomie.htm.
3 University of London. See https://www.soas.ac.uk/.

References

Arestis, P., Dunn, S.P. and Sawyer, M. (1999), On the Coherence of Post-Keynesian Economics: a Comment on Walters and Young, *Scottish Journal of Political Economy* 46(3), pp. 339–345.

Arestis, P. and Sawyer, M. (eds.) (2006), *Handbook of Alternative Monetary Economics*. Cheltenham, UK and Northampton, MA, USA: Edward Elgar.

Backhouse, R. (1988), Comment on Hamouda and Harcourt, *Bulletin of Economic Research* 40(1), pp. 35–41.

Blaug, M. (1980), *The Methodology of Economics*, second edition. Cambridge, UK: Cambridge University Press (reissued in expanded form in 1992).

Chick, V. (2002), Keynes's Theory of Investment and Necessary Compromise, in S.C. Dow and J. Hillard (eds.), *Keynes, Uncertainty and the Global Economy: Beyond Keynes*, volume 2. Cheltenham: Edward Elgar, pp. 55–67.

Chick, V. and Dow, S.C. (2005), The Meaning of Open Systems, *Journal of Economic Methodology* 12(3), pp. 363–381.

Coates, J. (1996), *The Claims of Common Sense*. Cambridge, UK: Cambridge University Press.

Colander, D. (2002), The Lost Art of Economics, *Journal of Economic Perspectives* 6(3), pp. 191–198.

Davis, J.B. (1999), Common Sense: A Middle Way between Formalism and Post-structuralism? *Cambridge Journal of Economics* 23(4), pp. 503–515.

Dow, S.C. (1990), Beyond Dualism, *Cambridge Journal of Economics* 14(2), pp. 143–158, reproduced in J.B. Davis (ed.), *Recent Developments in Economic Methodology*, volume 2. Cheltenham, UK and Northampton, MA, USA: Edward Elgar (2006), pp. 261–275. Also reproduced in S.C. Dow, *Foundations for New Economic Thinking: a Selection of Essays*. Basingstoke, UK: Palgrave Macmillan (2012).

Dow, S.C. (1997), Methodological Pluralism and Pluralism of Method, in A. Salanti and E. Screpanti (eds.), *Pluralism in Economics: Theory, History and Methodology*. Cheltenham, UK and Northampton, MA, USA: Edward Elgar, pp. 89–99.

Dow, S.C. (2001a), Modernism and Postmodernism: a Dialectical Process, in S. Cullenberg, J. Amariglio and D.F. Ruccio (eds.), *Postmodernism, Economics and Knowledge*. London and New York: Routledge, pp. 61–76.

Dow, S.C. (2001b), Methodology in a Pluralist Environment, *Journal of Economic Methodology* 8(1), pp. 33–40.

Dow, S.C. (2007), Variety of Methodological Approach in Economics, *Journal of Economic Surveys* 21(3), pp. 447–465.

Dow, S.C. (2008), Plurality in Orthodox and Heterodox Economics, *Journal of Philosophical Economics* 1(2), pp. 73–96.

Dow, S.C. (2012), The Babylonian Mode of Thought, in J. King (ed.), *The Elgar Companion to Post Keynesian Economics*, second edition. Cheltenham, UK and Northampton, MA, USA: Edward Elgar, pp. 15–19.

Gerrard, B. (1992), Human Logic in Keynes's Thought, in P. Arestis and V. Chick (eds.), *Recent Developments in Post-Keynesian Economics*. Aldershot: Edward Elgar, pp. 1–16.

Hamouda, O.F. and Harcourt, G.C. (1988), Post Keynesianism: From Criticism to Coherence? *Bulletin of Economic Research* 40(1), pp. 1–34.

Harcourt, G.C. (1984), Reflections on the Development of Economics as a Discipline, *History of Political Economy* 16(4), pp. 489–517.

Harcourt, G.C. (1987), Theoretical Methods and Unfinished Business, in D.A. Reece (ed.), *The Legacy of Keynes*. San Francisco: Harper and Row, pp. 1–22, reprinted in C. Sardoni (ed.), *On Political Economists and Modern Political Economy: Selected Essays of G.C. Harcourt*. London and New York: Routledge (1992), pp. 235–249.

Harcourt, G.C. (1996), How I do Economics, in S.G. Medema and W.J. Samuels (eds.), *Foundations of Research in Economics: How do Economists do Economics?* Cheltenham, UK and Northampton, MA, USA: Edward Elgar, pp. 93–102.

Harcourt, G.C. (1992), Marshall's Principles as Seen through the Eyes of Gerald Shove, Dennis Robertson and Joan Robinson, in C. Sardoni (ed.), *On Political Economists and Modern Political Economy: Selected Essays of G.C. Harcourt*. London and New York: Routledge, pp. 265–280.

King, J.E. (2002), Three Arguments for Pluralism in Economics, *Journal of Australian Political Economy* 50, pp. 82–88, reprinted in *Post-Autistic Economics Review* 23, article 2 (2004).

King, J.E. (2008), Microfoundations? Paper presented to the Macroeconomic Policies on Shaky Foundations – Whither Mainstream Economics? Conference, Research Network Macroeconomics and Macroeconomic Policies (FMM) 12th annual conference, Berlin.

King, J.E. (2012), *The Microfoundations Delusion: Metaphor and Dogma in the History of Macroeconomics*. Cheltenham, UK and Northampton, MA, USA: Edward Elgar.

Kurz, H.D. and Salvadori, N. (2000), On Critics and Protective Belts, in H.D. Kurz and N. Salvadori (eds.), *Understanding 'Classical' Economics: Studies in Long-Period Theory*. London and New York: Routledge, pp. 235–258.

Lawson, T. (1997), *Economics and Reality*. London and New York: Routledge.

McCloskey, D.N. (1986), *The Rhetoric of Economics*. Brighton, UK: Wheatsheaf.

Walters, B. and Young, D. (1997), On the Coherence of Post-Keynesian Economics, *Scottish Journal of Political Economy* 44 (3), pp. 329–349.

Weintraub, E.R. (2002), *How Economics Became a Mathematical Science*. Durham, NC: Duke University Press.

Whitehead, A.N. (1938), *Modes of Thought*. Cambridge, UK: Cambridge University Press.

Wren-Lewis, S. (2011), Internal Consistency, Price Rigidity and the Microfoundations of Macroeconomics, *Journal of Economic Methodology* 18(2), pp. 129–146.

Theme II

The role of history of economic thought in the path to pluralism

How can the history of economic thought (HET) assist in drawing up a path to pluralism? Chapters 4 to 6 set out battles and influences that HET has had on economics as a discipline. These interactions with the discipline, respectively adversarial and abetting, add a dimension to economics that transcends the monism of the neoclassical mainstream. Steve Kates explains in Chapter 4 how HET is an integral part of the study of economics and not merely part of a broader sociology of knowledge. The 'enemies' of HET, as Kates describes them, exist in the mainstream and correlate HET with extinct 'old' economic theories or critiques of neoclassical views. These 'enemies' are adamant that HET should leave the economics discipline. Kates explains this obdurate behaviour as aiming to preserve the theory without questioning where it came from or what options exist to advance it (not only techniques to elucidate existing precepts). Revisiting economic theory in historical context is needed for the early twenty-first century. Kates concludes by setting out six reasons HET can make economics and economists better. HET therefore provides the path for pluralism that will provide an appreciation of different approaches and their appropriate use.

The path to pluralism faces many roadblocks and detours. In Chapter 5, John Lodewijks provides two Australian case studies, some six years apart, of barriers raised by Kates's 'enemies'. In both cases, the 'barbarians' were 'repulsed' at the gate. The first was an attempted official re-classification of 'Economic History and the History of Economic Thought' from its own research code into the generalist non-economics group of 'History, Archaeology, Religion and Philosophy'. The second was the proposed downgrading in the Australian rankings of the major international HET journal. The History of Economic Thought Society of Australia conducted vigorous campaigns that created scholarly, bureaucratic and political pressure to prevent these two attacks on pluralism. Hope and guidance on how pluralism in economics might be regained can be attained from these two almost military campaigns.

An enlightening example of pluralism is provided by Alex Millmow in Chapter 6. This is set out as a case study of 14 young Australian scholars who went to Cambridge University during the period 1945–60, 'intent upon furthering their economics education'. In the inter-war period, Cambridge had led economics in espousing the new Keynesian theory, as well as being home to economists such as Piero Sraffa and others with diverse views. This attracted Australian scholars raised in the British tradition. Two lessons for advancing pluralism can be perceived. One is how a leading pluralist UK department exerted considerable impact when these scholars came back to Australia. This provided a long-lasting impetus to alternative visions to those dominated by the mainly US-based neoclassical school. The other is that pluralism should not be seen through rose-coloured glasses. Cambridge, the young scholars discovered, was fractured over ideas, and its disputes were often rancorous.

4 The history of economic thought and its mainstream enemies

Steven Kates

The study of the history of economic thought has been on a downwards trajectory since the end of World War II. It is now observable that for the mainstream of the economics profession, there is no history of their own subject that is worth so much as a semester of a student's time, nor are such courses on offer to students who might themselves wish to study the history of economic thought (HET) if such an option were made available. There are a number of reasons for this trend but the one that will be discussed below is the active hostility of the mainstream to the study of the history of thought, not in spite of the fact that students will come upon other theories that conflict with mainstream views but because of it. HET is now seen as a preserve for the heterodox tradition and therefore filled with older ideas that have been, in their view, rightly discarded.

But in studying the history of thought, much of what is studied consists of the very beliefs and ideas held by the mainstream of the economics profession at an earlier time. They are thus potentially plausible alternatives to contemporary approaches to economic thought. Where once one could teach HET as a kind of Whig history, as a story of progress from more primitive levels of understanding towards greater scope and depth, this is no longer the case. The heterodox tradition now contains theoretical structures as deep and plausible as anything found in the mainstream. The war on the history of economic thought is in many respects an attempt by the mainstream to protect its monopoly position on the study of how economies operate in the modern world.

The central issue of this chapter is whether the history of economic thought is an integral part of the study of economics and thus part of the social sciences, or whether it is an element of the history and philosophy of science and therefore a part of the humanities. This is no minor issue to historians of economics. The confluence of the attempt by the OECD to tidy up its classifications codes with the desire by some historians of economics, aided by many in the economics mainstream, to see HET removed from the economics classification and become part of the history and philosophy of science, has created serious dangers for the future of the study of HET, and indeed to the future of economic theory itself.

The argument presented in this chapter is that the history of economic thought is part of the social sciences. An economist studying the history of economic thought is doing the work of an economist and is contributing to the study of economics. Economic theory is improved and deepened because of the work that historians of economic thought undertake.

Fighting the classification wars of 2007 and 2011

The first explicit challenge to the presence of the history of economic thought as an integral part of economic theory occurred in Australia in 2007. The Australian Bureau of Statistics (ABS) took it upon itself to remove the history of economic thought from within the economic theory classification. This decision came out of the blue as far as the HET community was concerned, even though the proposal had been previously vetted by a series of committees that had included many economists. In an important sense, the entire episode can be traced back to the decision by the OECD to separate out the study of social sciences, which it placed in one section of its recommended academic classification scheme, and the history of sciences, which it placed in another.

This is probably a reasonably sensible approach to take with most subject areas. The study of physics and the study of the history of physics are almost entirely separate areas of research with little overlap in who undertakes such work and almost no overlap at all in relation to what the actual issues are. A historian of physics does not attempt to advance the study of physics but has an interest that is more in keeping with the sociology of knowledge. And while this division might be appropriate for most subject areas, it is completely inappropriate for economics.

Importantly, in understanding these events the formal mechanism for the classification system in each national system is not determined nationally but is based on an international standard. The classification systems used in every country are designed around what is called the 'Frascati Manual' which has been issued by the OECD (see OECD 2013). The Manual is not intended to influence the structure of research but merely reflect the underlying reality. Nevertheless, to have placed the history of economic thought outside of economics, as it did in 2007, caused national statistical agencies to view the history of economic thought as part of the humanities.

In Australia, the ABS attempted to reclassify the history of economic thought into its new category, 'History, Archaeology, Religion and Philosophy', which, in its view, would have brought the Australian classification system into conformity with their interpretation of the Frascati Manual. We historians of economics in Australia believed that their interpretation was incorrect (see Kates and Millmow 2008a, 2008b, 2008c) which was confirmed by the success of what turned out to be an extraordinarily intense lobbying effort that involved economists at every facet of economic theory and practice in Australia – particularly economists in the public sector and tertiary schools of economics. In this, there was virtual unanimity that the history of economic thought was an integral element of economic theory. When confronted with the submissions that descended upon it, which argued that isolating the history of economic thought from the 'Economics' classification was wrong in both principle and practice, the ABS reversed its earlier decision and reinstated the history of economic thought within the economics classification.[1]

Four years later, in 2011, this issue came up again, this time through a similar initial decision by the European Research Council (ERC) to place the history of economic thought in a social sciences category which they proposed to call, 'The Study of the Human Past: Archaeology, History and Memory'. Again after a series of submissions in relation to this decision that explained how inappropriate this shift in classification would have been, the ERC reversed its original decision and retained the history of economic thought within the 'Economics' classification.

HET as a special case

Why then is the history of economic thought a special case that must be understood separately and differently from the history of natural sciences? This has been discussed in a book of mine that arose out of the two attempts at reclassification. The arguments presented below elaborate the perspective presented in the book, titled *Defending the History of Economic Thought* (Kates 2013).

1 The word 'history' in the 'history of economic thought' has a long history of its own. Because the word 'history' is found in the subject name is no reason for assuming HET can be subsumed into other forms of actual historical study, which HET is not.
2 Economists have been using historical doctrine as a focal point for new directions in economic theory since at least the time of Adam Smith who built the arguments of *The Wealth of Nations* around his criticisms of Thomas Mun and mercantilist doctrine which was, by then, more than a century old.
3 The first histories of economics were contained as part of actual economics texts. J.R. McCulloch's 1825 textbook on economic theory is titled *The Principles of Political Economy: With Sketch of the Rise and Progress of the Science* and does indeed begin with a thirty-page discussion of the history of economic theory to that point. Similarly, John McVickar, the author of the first economics text published in the United States, *Outlines of Political Economy* (also 1825), commences his text with an extended discussion of the history of economic theory to that point.
4 The history of economic theory provides essential guidance to the meaning of the theory. Without an appreciation of the way in which theory had developed, it is more difficult to understand what the theory means in practice.

5   Economic theory is frequently taught in an historical setting. Both the Marginal Revolution and the Keynesian Revolution are part of the education of every economist, along with other discussions of how theory became what it is. There is less emphasis than in the past as far as the mainstream goes, but for all non-mainstream traditions, from Austrian to Marxian, the historical development of the theory is an essential part of providing an understanding of the theory.

6   Virtually all studies of the history of economic thought are undertaken by economists. Unlike histories of the natural sciences, which are dominated by the philosophy of science and not written by natural scientists themselves, historians of economics are economists working within economic departments of their universities. Virtually every paper published in a history of economic thought journal has been written by an economist. Virtually the only readers of papers on the history of economic thought are other economists. This is a literature written by economists for other economists. There are, of course, exceptions to this but they are few. Studies in the history of economic thought are by and for economists.

7   The history of economic thought is a prerequisite for the development of economic theory. Unless economists are to continue to chase their tails, going over old ground and repeating old arguments as if they were fresh and new, there needs to be an appreciation within the profession of that old ground that had been gone over. This should not necessarily be a deterrent from going over this ground, which in many cases may even provide a valuable alert. The Keynesian Revolution was influenced by and possibly even inspired by John Maynard Keynes's 1932 reading of Malthus's *Principles*, which had been published in 1820.

8   Studying the history of economic thought deepens an economist's understanding of textbook theory. It helps to define terms and clarify arguments. There are many examples where discussions of what an economist might or might not have meant have been important means of thinking through the theoretical developments that had been initiated. Keynesian economics is notorious for its 'what did Keynes really mean?' discussions. But this is far from unique, as the debate over the proper interpretation of the Coase Theorem, first stated in 1960 or perhaps even in 1937 (with even the date controversial), has not yet subsided.

9   Having a pool of historians of economic thought within the profession provides a stimulus to others. Not everyone needs to be a scholar in these areas but it helps all economists if such specialists are around who enter into such debates. To reclassify the history of economic thought as a separate study beyond the area of economics will deter individual economists from taking up such studies and therefore the pool of historians of economic thought within economic theory will diminish. It will therefore weaken the actual study and development of economic theory since the pool of historically knowledgeable economists within schools of economics will be diminished both in number and in stature.

10 The issue of stature is important. While in some ways, the system of classification may be seen as nothing more than a minor issue, the authority of historians of economics in providing both guidance and critique on economic issues will be diminished and therefore their ability to influence the direction of the subject matter will be diminished. The classification system is intended to be a neutral element that does not influence the scope or standing of any forms of research, but to remove historians of economic thought from within the economics classification must with certainty do this.

11 Properly crafted classification systems are designed to promote productive study. The classification system should therefore follow the contours of these studies, not define them in an unnatural way relative to the nature of the subject. If classification schemes are not flexible enough in their design to permit the kind of exception that economic theory requires, amendments should be made that do not induce classification agencies, which typically do not have expertise in the subject areas, to introduce classification schemes that have a perverse effect on the nature of the study itself.

12 Historians of economic thought recognize the specific nature of their area of study that many economists without this expertise often fail to appreciate. The following was written by the editor of *History of Political Economy* during a 2013 controversy in Australia about how to rank economic journals in relation to their impact.

> The field of history of economics, although the specialty of a relatively small number of scholars, is nearly as old as economics itself. It is a serious, vibrant, and international field with national and international professional associations, frequent conferences, and international scholarly exchanges. Through its history, its luminaries have included not only specialists known primarily to other specialists, but also such distinguished economists as Lionel Robbins, who first penned the standard definition of what economics is ('Economics is the science which studies human behaviour as a relationship between ends and scarce means which have alternative uses'), Joseph Schumpeter, Jacob Viner, Don Patinkin, and the Nobel laureates Paul Samuelson, George Stigler, John Hicks, and Amartya Sen.

13 Some of the most illustrious names in economics, including Nobel Prize winners, have devoted many years of serious scholarship to the study of history of economic thought and in doing so thought of themselves as working entirely within the field of economics. They did not step out of their role as economists in undertaking this work but saw themselves as contributing to scholarship within economics as economists.

You would therefore think that the history of economic thought was on reasonably safe ground since it ought to be apparent that pretty well every economist would see its significance and defend its role as part of the study of economics.

Yet HET has its enemies

The history of economic thought, nevertheless, has its share of critics within economics itself. The problem was highlighted by Roy Weintraub in his article on what he called the 'Economic Science Wars':

> In economics departments in the U.S., doing the history and methodology of economics came to be seen as doing no economics at all. It was even worse, of course, for those doing history and methodology of economics were generally seen as critics, often hostile critics, of mainstream economics.
>   This last point is the crucial one.
>
> (Weintraub 2007, p. 277)

Historians of economics, not all but many, in their studies of the history of economic theory come upon alternative perspectives on economic issues that are quite different from the views and approaches of the mainstream. If historians of economics were a harmless lot who looked only at various philosophical and methodological matters that had no implications for the practice of economics, the kinds of hostility Weintraub points to would not exist. And while mainstream economists might consider such studies irrelevant to their own concerns, they would feel no hostility.

Among economists, approximately half of those who take an interest in the history of their subject are critics of the mainstream. Historians of economics are almost entirely already economists. They are economists with a heightened interest in their own field of study which has taken them into some area of historical research. Journals of the history of economic thought are populated by members of schools of economics, as are conferences on the history of economic thought. Indeed, the level of knowledge one must have to comment sensibly on just about any theoretical economic question can only be attained by someone who has studied the subject to a reasonable depth. Moreover, looking from the other side of the ledger, there are few beyond economics who would actually be interested in what an historian of economic thought might write. HET is a specialist area of economics in which economists write for other economists.

But many of those who study the history of economic thought are not part of the mainstream but are its critics. This is noted by Weintraub who sees this division as the central part of the problem now affecting the history of economics:

> There are a variety of impulses that lead professional economists to 'take up' the history (and methodology) of economics. It cannot be surprising that many historians who begin as critics of mainstream economics link their historical projects with critical appraisals of modern economics.... This association of heterodoxy with history of economies is real; a quick

examination of the program of any History of Economics Society meeting will locate two dominant poles: work on 'old' economics (Physiocracy, Adam Smith, etc.), historically engaged in contextualization, and the work on issues treated in mainstream economics today, in which there is a critical component, heterodox economics if you will.

(Weintraub 2007, pp. 277–78)

With such a large proportion of HET specialists critical of mainstream analysis, in the fight for scarce academic resources, all historians of economics, both the traditional and heterodox, were driven from the field. Nothing official. 'Economists simply appropriate[d] without public comment or notice the faculty positions and tenure lines of retiring historians and use[d] those resources for more "mainstream" work' (Weintraub 2007, p. 279). In Weintraub's view, the right approach would be for historians of economics to withdraw from within economics departments and go elsewhere.

If historians of economics can shed their professional identification with the community of economists and thus refuse to take sides in the mainstream-heterodox controversies, their return to history, to constructing narratives of context, might brighten their institutional future.… The history of economics needs to locate academic sites in North America that can provide more support than do research departments of economics. Since a number of historians of economics have intellectual affinities to the science studies community broadly understood, that realization can lead to their evolving connection with a potentially more welcoming scholarly community.

(Weintraub 2007, pp. 279–280)

And thus we have a convergence of the views of an influential segment from among historians of economic thought with parts of the mainstream who would therefore follow the recommendations of the Frascati Manual, not because it is good for the development of economic theory but because it would help preserve economic theory as it now is from criticisms by other economists who are not mainstream in their perspectives.

Conclusions

In the Frascati Manual at present economics is classified as a social science while the history of economics is classified as part of the humanities. That is, the two areas are distinct with no overlap of any significance. And while this may make sense in regard to other sciences, it is completely wrong when applied to the study of economics. But wrong as it may be, it led to two attempts by classification agencies, the first in Australia in 2007 and the second in Europe in 2011, to remove the history of economics from the economics classification. In Australia, the economics community was able to persuade the ABS not to make the change. In Europe, the change was actually made. The ERC removed HET from the economics classification. The effort was therefore devoted to asking the ERC to reverse a decision that had already been made, which was ultimately successful. This is from the original ERC decision. The concern referred to – your concern – is that HET would be removed from the economics classification: 'Addressing your concern, "history of economics" is divided between SH1 and SH6 ("The study of the human past: archaeology, history and memory").'

Anyone who believes because they are historians of economic thought that they are economists undertaking economics work, and who therefore believes that they would find it unproblematic to explain the importance of their work to their head of department in a school of economics, when the official classification has them listed as working in an area described as 'the study of the human past: archaeology, history and memory' (and in Australia the classification would have been, 'History, Archaeology, Religion and Philosophy'), can only be seen as an optimist. And to the extent that they could get funding for their work, these would have been the panels they would have needed to apply to.

These, moreover, are not battles won. These are battles historians of economics remain in the midst of. The history of economics has its enemies within the ranks of economists who will sideline the study of HET if they can. The history of economic thought makes economics a better subject and makes economists better economists. Below is a summary of the reasons why this is so:

1   economists looked at individually have a stronger grasp of economic theory and therefore make better economists if they have studied the history of economic thought,
2   economics as a discipline looked at as a collective enterprise is much improved by the existence and work of such historians of economics,
3   economic theory is improved by the work of historians of economics who are able to bring insights from the work of economists of the past into the current conversation,
4   economic theory is improved if economists generally actively look amongst the work of economists of the past for a theoretical understanding of contemporary issues,
5   it improves the skills and abilities of the community of economists as economists if they collectively and individually have a greater understanding of economic theory's past and the different perspectives it provides, and
6   the history of economics as a subject area must remain part of economic theory, recognized as such by both economists and the official classification agencies of government.

There remains work to do to defend the history of economic thought but there is even more work needed to promote its importance to economists. The importance is subtle and often imperceptible. Economists widen their perspectives and see other possibilities than the narrow range provided by whatever mainstream view may happen to exist at any moment in time. That is only one part of the value the history of economic thought provides to economists, but it is surely important enough to ensure such threats as those described above do not become a reality.

Note

1 See John Lodewijks's account of this episode in Chapter 5 of this volume.

References

Kates, S. (2013), *Defending the History of Economic Thought*. Cheltenham UK and Northampton MA, USA: Edward Elgar.

Kates, S. and Millmow, A. (2008a), A Canary in the Coalmine: the Near Death Experience of History of Economics in Australia, lead article in a symposium on the role of history of economics within economics, *History of Economic Ideas* XVI(3), pp. 79–94.

Kates, S. and Millmow, A. (2008b), A Canary in the Coalmine: a Rejoinder, final rejoinder in a symposium on the role of history of economics within economics, *History of Economic Ideas* XVI(3), pp. 112–118.

Kates, S. and Millmow, A. (2008c), The History Wars of Economics: the Classification Struggle in the History of Economic Thought, *History of Economics Review* 47, pp. 110–124.

Organisation of Economic Co-operation and Development (OECD) (2013), Revision of the Frascati Manual, at http://www.oecd.org/sti/inno/frascati-manual-revision.htm, accessed 17 June 2015.

Weintraub, E.R. (2007), Economic Science Wars, *Journal of the History of Economic Thought* 29(3), pp. 267–282.

5 The history of economics 'down under'

Repulsing the barbarians at the gate

John Lodewijks

Scholarship in the history of economics and heterodox economics has come under considerable attack both in Australia and overseas. In terms of heterodoxy one only needs to read the pessimistic account of the United Kingdom situation documented by Lee et al. (2013) and a disturbing local example (Lodewijks 2013/14). The history of economics has also long come under assault and this was the subject of a special issue of *History of Political Economy* (*HOPE*) that covered the disappointing experiences of a wide range of countries (Weintraub 2002). Locally the topic has been extensively treated in Kates (2013).[1] The connections between heterodoxy and the history of economics have been documented (Lodewijks 2003).

The reasons for the attacks on heterodox and historical approaches to the discipline are puzzling as in both areas Australian researchers have a well-established reputation internationally. The work of Geoffrey Harcourt, John King, Phil O'Hara, Steve Keen, Tony Aspromourgos, Jerry Courvisanos, Peter Kriesler and Peter Earl is justifiably lauded in heterodox circles. The excellence of Australian scholars in the history of economics has been noted in Lodewijks (2002, 2004). Indeed, it can be argued that Australian economists have a clear comparative advantage in these two areas. That cannot be said for most other economics sub-disciplines. The attacks then are hard to fathom on scholarly grounds. However, these are not our concerns here, for scholarly debate about the merits and value of these approaches has played an insignificant role in the developments to be examined here. Nor do we speculate about the future of these two areas, however gloomy the projections are. We focus very narrowly on two specific assaults on the history of economics in Australia where the end results were positive. An examination of these two episodes, the strategies employed and the phases of the battles are worth preserving for their own sake, as much of the communication occurred electronically and some of the files have since been deleted, and as a guide for future confrontations that will inevitably arise.[2]

A near-death experience

The first assault on Australian history of economics to be examined can be dated from Monday 27 August 2007. On that date an email was circulated stating that the Australian Bureau of Statistics (ABS) was replacing the term 'Research Fields, Courses and Disciplines' with a new simpler term 'Fields of Research'. It also proposed changes for each discipline area and was seeking feedback on the proposed changes by 13 September. This seemingly innocuous development could easily have been overlooked. Closer examination of the proposed changes generated disbelief and shock.

What was being proposed was that the research classification 'Economic History and the History of Economic Thought', which had been privileged with its own four digit research code, was to be deleted entirely from the 'Economics' research classification and relocated into a category of 'History, Archaeology, Religion and Philosophy'. The changes were to be effective from 2008 and it was further proposed that in any future revision separate 'History of Economic Thought' (HET) and 'Economic History' classifications might be eliminated entirely.

What a bombshell! With barely two weeks to object. This is certainly not the way that academic deliberations normally proceed within a single institution let alone for such a far-reaching change with dire implications for the study of the field as a whole and for its practitioners in terms of tenure, promotion, access to research funding and even redundancy. If research in the history of economics no longer counts as 'Economics', or even 'Business' research, then its days in the discipline are numbered. Broader debate in the literature about historians of economics 'breaking-away' and finding a better fit in the history and philosophy of science fields, which most had dismissed as an unviable alternative, was now a distinct prospect. So what could be done?

Given the gravity of the situation, and the very tight timeline, William Coleman on 2 September suggested that a 'War Cabinet' be formed to develop strategy and coordinate the response. This proved to be a very effective mechanism to channel dissent. The War Cabinet comprised William Coleman, Steven Kates, Alex Millmow, Tony Aspromourgos and John Lodewijks. Coleman suggested that universities had to be alerted, the Economic Society of Australia (ESA) had to get on board, Ministers and Shadow Ministers informed, the Academy of the Social Sciences in Australia (ASSA) contacted and the North American History of Economics Society involved. Prior to that Steven Kates had already developed a seven point strategic plan that included identifying who the decision-makers are and more importantly, who will make the final decision to accept or reject this proposal. These persons need to be personally approached in face-to-face meetings. Communication had to remain open so that we were aware of what individual submissions were saying and sympathetic international supporters needed to be sounded out.

The first priority was to alert the troops. Cobbling various email lists together, urgent emails were sent out far and wide indicating the potential harm that these ABS proposals could cause and requesting everyone to write to the ABS expressing their concerns and getting those higher up in their own institutions to voice concerns. The response from Michael Schneider at La Trobe University was exactly what was needed. Schneider immediately contacted his Head of

Department, who then contacted the Head of School, who contacted the Acting Dean who 'strongly urged [La Trobe's Deputy Vice-Chancellor] DVC (Research) to oppose the changes' to the research codes. The DVC (Research) formally did so. Tony Aspromourgos was also quick off the mark. On 29 August he wrote to the Director of the University of Sydney Research Office asking that they oppose the reclassification of the history of economics.

So far so good, but we were working in the dark. Why were these changes to research codes made? Who was responsible? Who were the key decision-makers that might be influenced? What pressures could be brought to bear? Answers to several of these questions uncovered a vast array of acronyms like DEST, ARC, CHASS, RQF, FASTS, ASSA and UA. Some of these are well known, such as the Australian Research Council (ARC), but the vast bulk does not enter the daily lives of the average university academic. They were all a bit of a mystery. We needed to find out what these various interest groups did, as their influence was extensive, while individual scholars or even scholarly societies, such as the History of Economic Thought Society of Australia (HETSA), were not even consulted. As Steven Kates quipped: 'Was there anyone there who actually knows anything about what we do?'

Steven Kates and Alex Millmow discovered that the Department of Education Science and Training (DEST) had commissioned a review of the use of the Australian Standard Research Classification (ASRC) and the ABS was conducting the review. DEST's role raised more alarms as this institution officially recognizes and collates all research publications and so has a pivotal role in certifying academic research performance. Seven 'peak bodies' were invited to send representatives to the Reference Group guiding the review, including the Council for the Humanities, Arts and Social Sciences (CHASS), the ARC, Universities Australia (UA) and the Federation of Australian Scientific and Technological Societies (FASTS).

Alex Millmow uncovered that a Dr David Brett at the ABS was the driving force behind the research code reclassifications. He contacted Brett directly to ask for a justification for the expulsion of the history of economics and economic history from the economics classification. Brett replied on 30 August that:

> One change was the relocation of codes relating to history or philosophy of specific subject areas to one location, in the then proposed History, Archaeology, Religion and Philosophy division. History of Economic Thought and Economic History were two codes that were included in this process. Expert consultation for the economics division was conducted through the Academy of the Social Sciences, however we did not receive any response regarding this change during this process. The Academy of the Humanities, who managed the expert consultation relating to the history and philosophy of specific fields, recommended the two economics codes be merged into one code entitled 'History and Philosophy of Economics'....
>
> Classification consistency with regards to the use of processes [was] the key driver of classification location. This assumes that the processes used

in history of economic thought are primarily historical and philosophical rather than economic. This is the critical issue from the perspective of a classification and a rule that has been widely applied throughout the classification....

Groups (formerly disciplines) which are not useful for describing either the breadth of R&D [research and development] or how spending is apportioned, were restructured. The discipline Economic History and History of Economic Thought only contained two codes, which is not sufficiently broad. It also represented only 1.2% of all public sector R&D in economics.... Less than $1M of R&D expenditure was recorded against each of the codes for Economic History and History of Economic Thought ... and the amounts have been declining ... unless there is an upswing in recoded activity in these fields both would most probably be deleted at the next revision....

If this change is undesirable to your research community, we can contemplate undoing these changes on the following grounds: Evidence that R&D activity is significantly underreported or anticipated to significantly increase.... Evidence that the assumption that History of Economic thought R&D primarily involves processes that are historical and philosophical is false.... Should you argue for returning this field to Economics we will also require a suggested location within this division. The Economic History and History of Economic Thought group will not be reinstated.

Now at least we had some grounds to raise objections. It did raise some awkward questions about the role of the ASSA in this process. Why were they silent? Why did they not contact HETSA for advice? Did they contact their economist members? On the last point at least two of their members indicated very quickly that they were not consulted and fired off emails objecting to the changes. Peter Groenewegen, a fellow of the ASSA, wrote on 2 September to Brett protesting about the 'rather peculiar reclassification' and as:

> one of the leading persons involved in the history of economic thought in the Academy, I was not consulted on this matter, nor, to my knowledge, were the other historians of economics (Geoff Harcourt and John King). ... [Moreover] research work on the history of economic thought is largely undertaken by people who see themselves primarily as economists [and] involves detailed knowledge of economic theory and economic ideas ... [and] is impossible without a deep understanding of economic theory.... Removing history of economic thought from economics would make Australian practice different from best international practice and in some ways a laughing stock.

On 17 September, Geoffrey Harcourt wrote to Brett that 'I do not recognise your descriptions of the processes used in the history of theory ... I hope ... both HET and Economic History may be classified under the rubric of economics. Australian economists have punched above their weight in both fields'. Alex Millmow had taken the initiative to contact the ASSA directly. On 31 August he wrote to John Beaton, Executive Director, ASSA. Beaton replied on the same day that he was aware of the situation and would take appropriate action.

Millmow, Kates and Coleman were vigorously using their contacts to put pressure on the ABS and make them aware of the serious impact this reclassification would have. Those Millmow contacted included Bruce Chapman, President of the ESA, Ken Henry from Treasury, Ian Macfarlane, former Governor of the Reserve Bank of Australia, Peter Shergold at Prime Minister and Cabinet and Ian Castles, a former Australian Statistician. Kates contacted Gary Banks, Productivity Commission, Ian Watt from the Department of Finance, Mark Paterson, Secretary of the Department of Industry, Geoff Allen, Chairman of the Australian Statistics Advisory Council, which is the board that advises the ABS, and more senior people at ABS. Coleman contacted Ian Castles and Glenn Withers, CEO of Universities Australia. We do not have the details of what action all these senior people took but a few have shared their communications. Glenn Withers was very quick to 'lend name and any words as desired to your feedback to ensure inclusion under economics' and suggested various other prominent people to contact. Ian Castles wrote to Brian Pink, the Australian Statistician, with 'surprise and concern' over the ABS proposal to delete HET and Economic History as distinct research fields in economics. He urged that the matter be reconsidered. He went on to say that 'I know that Australian scholars are at the forefront of research in substantial areas of the history of economic thought … as for economic history, this is a major field of research'.

Subsequently, Steve Crabb of the ABS invited Ian Castles to a meeting about this matter. Ian Macfarlane wrote to Brett on 8 September saying that:

> I regard both of these areas as being intrinsic to the study of Economics … and came increasingly to rely on them to help with practical policy decisions.… I felt this was of more use to understanding the current economic situation than any other approach. I urge you to reconsider your proposal.

Warren Hogan also directly contacted the 'most senior person I know at the ABS … and wrote at much greater length … to the Minister for Education, Science and Training'. We do not know the impact all this had but it is highly likely that it was far more significant than those communications received from individual academic historians of thought venting their spleen. Alex Millmow believes that Castles's intervention in particular would have carried immense weight.

The North American History of Economics Society SHOE email list also proved an excellent vehicle to solicit assistance. A plea for help was circulated on 31 August which elicited sixty-four individual postings in the month of September

2007. Many of these postings reprinted formal letters of complaint sent to the ABS by individual academics. We will not cover these in detail as they are all on the public record on the History of Economics Society (HES) website.[3] The posting of 7 September by Deirdre McCloskey of a letter she sent to Brett gives an indication of some of the response by these North American colleagues:

> I have heard of the astonishing proposal to take the history of economics (the study of past economics) and even economic history (the study of past economies) out of departments of economics. You will do permanent damage to the prestige of Australian economics by doing so.... To make Australia the only country in the world to adopt such an anti-intellectual line is to reinforce the incorrect but widespread impression that Australian is a land of ignoramuses and glad of it.

Some commentators even threatened legal action against the ABS. Later we heard that Brett had complained about receiving abusive emails on the reclassification issue – all of which came from overseas. By 8 September the ABS had received thirty emails from overseas, one in support of what they were proposing and twenty-nine against. As helpful as these individual contributions were, more important was that they served as catalysts for action by international scholarly societies. Sandra Peart, President of the North American History of Economics Society, was exceedingly quick off the mark. On 5 September she had already sent off a letter to Brett, co-signed by nine others (and later signed off by many more) including past presidents, vice-presidents and executive committee members. In part the letter read that the relocation:

> will be costly both for the economics profession as a whole and also for the students we teach. The history of economic thought has ... shown the richness of the roots of economic theory and provided a base for the debate and discussion of the competing schools of economic ideas.... A relocation of the History of Economic Thought and Economic History will privilege technical approaches over the literary approach. We suggest that economics needs both approaches.... The typical economics professor today has had little training in moral reasoning or civic engagement, and his or her interests are narrowly defined by formal modeling and statistical testing. This means that the economics major, absent the historical approach, is becoming less and less appropriate for students interested in business or public policy. An education in economics that includes room for historical approaches to economic thinking ... offers students opportunities for applied moral reasoning and policy analysis.... For all these reasons, we urge you to reconsider your decision.

Tony Brewer wrote on 6 September that he would make sure that the issue was discussed at the UK annual HET conference, which was scheduled the following week, and would personally contact the conference organizer and the editor of the HET newsletter. He had already mailed the President and the Vice-President of the European Society for the History of Economic Thought (ESHET). Mary Morgan was exceedingly helpful. She wrote on 8 September that:

> In the last 24 hours, the President of our Royal Economic Society, the Chair of the Economics section of the British Academy and the President of the (British) Economic History Society have all responded to my request to write about this matter to the ABS. These letters have been strongly supportive of HET.

The Greek Society for the History of Economic Thought sent a letter to Brett on 11 September signed by twenty-eight of its members. Among the points raised was that:

> Teachers of HET and economic history will cease to exist in economics departments... Economists whose research is primarily in other fields will be discouraged to contribute to HET and economic history in this competitive age of quantitatively assessed research output. This would be unfortunate, since there is a long line of illustrious economists who have contributed to HET while their major contribution is in other fields. This list includes Nobel Laureates such as George Stigler, Friedrich Hayek, Paul Samuelson, James Buchanan, Kenneth Arrow, Gerard Debreu, Lawrence Klein, Robert Solow, Herbert Simon and Vernon Smith. In truth, you cannot teach economics, or practice it, without a knowledge of history of thought and of economic history.... We think that you agree with the principle that a Statistics Bureau should not create reality but depict it.

Aldo Montesano, President of the Italian Association for the History of Political Economy, wrote to Brett urging him to reconsider the decision, as did Yasunori Fukagai, board member of the Society for the History of Economic Thought of Japan on 15 September.

Given the mounting volume of correspondence reaching the ABS about the harmful effects of the proposed reclassification, it is interesting to see how they reacted. It might also be mentioned that media interest was increasing. Millmow wrote a long letter to *The Australian* titled 'A Goodbye to History' while Kates had an article in the *Australian Financial Review* on 10 September titled 'An Historical Injustice'. Yet the ABS's initial reaction was one where adjectives like condescending, obstinate, digging their heels in and refusing to budge come to mind. Sam Bostaph wrote on the HES list on 6 September that the 'appropriate answer to uninformed bureaucratic petty tyranny ... is to move higher up the ladder and let corrective measures flow downhill'. Warren Young had written the same day that Brian Pink, head of the ABS, should be the person to have contact with.

The official attitude to our objections at this time was best summed up by Tim Sealey, Assistant Director, Statistics and Data Analysis, Universities Australia. He felt we were misreading the situation, the review's objectives and consequences, and our response was a storm in a teacup. Sealey formally wrote to Millmow to express these views on 7 September and mentioned that he had the concurrence of both Barney Glover (the nominated UA representative) and David Brett of the ABS. He noted our 'rather peculiar view' and that the 'issues raised have little to do with the integrity of the classification system but more to do with apparent benefits of visibility of various subject matter areas within the classification structure'. He went on to say that:

> the History of Economic Thought and Economic History have been classified appropriately by the ABS. A further important point that should be made is that the revision is made on the basis of needs in relation to the ABS. Therefore, talk of the revision impacting on RQF [Research Quality Framework] funding or an area's viability are not only premature but not likely to come to fruition.... I trust that this helps to ease the concerns expressed by your colleagues.

Far from easing concerns this was a red flag to increasingly agitated bulls. It was clearly apparent that the ABS would not easily be moved despite the increasing avalanche of protests. The ABS clearly did not comprehend the implications of what it was doing or thought such considerations were irrelevant. The ABS was interested in principles of classification based on consistency and research funding (an economic measure of research activity). However, the revised classification would be used by DEST and the ARC for quality-ranking exercises and the allocation of research funding. It is on the basis of these indicators that conference funding, hiring and promotion and all else depend. With the reclassification, HET publications would no longer count in the total for 'Economics' and the funding that is associated with it. However, it would count in 'History and Philosophy', which is located in Faculties of Arts and Social Sciences, where historians of economic thought are not primarily employed. As long as DEST, the ARC and research quality ranking exercises use these revised codes then Economic History and HET were effectively dead in economics departments or business faculties.

Pressure, however, was mounting on the ABS to change their position. Very high profile economists from Australia and overseas had been writing to voice their disapproval, including those who were chairs of our various economics societies. Steven Kates provided the first significant glimmer of hope in an email dated 11 September reporting on the outcome of a meeting he had with Brett and his manager at the ABS in Belconnen, Canberra. Kates said it was his view that both HET and Economic History would remain within the economics discipline. Surprisingly, he also noted that it was HET that they were more reluctant to keep as part of Economics compared with Economic History. In their response to individual submissions David Brett was increasingly conspicuous by his absence and those at higher levels such as Steve Crabb and Glyn Prichard now appeared to be more prominent. They were saying by 7 September that submissions were 'being carefully considered' and the arguments presented had 'substance'. By 10 September they were acknowledging that:

> the status of the initial draft proposal is very low. It was based largely on the relatively low amount of R&D expenditure reported for these fields in recent years. This is only one of the criteria being used for the review ... other measures of importance such as Ph.D completions and DEST publications ... will be also taken into account in finalizing the review's recommendations.

So the tide was turning, but not without another red herring. The ABS let it be known that we could stay in the economics classification if we remove the word 'history' from our title. For example, we might use the label 'Development of Economic Theory and Policy' or 'Review of Economic Analysis'. This was an unacceptable fig leaf. Steven Kates wrote that 'The ABS should not tell us what to call our subject area because it is convenient for their classification system. In my view we should not give an inch'. The protest letters kept pouring in. Not only was the quantity of submissions impressive but also the standing of the representation that was being made. Domestically, support came from the President, Economic Society of Australia; President, Economic History Society of Australia and New Zealand; President, History of Economic Thought Society of Australia; CEO, Universities Australia; senior staff, Productivity Commission; Australian Research Council Federation Fellows; a former Governor, Reserve Bank of Australia, and Executive Director, Academy of the Social Sciences in Australia. Internationally, there were letters of support from the President of the Royal Economic Society, UK, Chair of the Economics section of the British Academy, President of the (British) Economic History Society, President, North American History of Economics Society, President, Italian Association for the History of Political Economy, as well as the Society for the History of Economic Thought, Japan, and the Greek Society for the History of Economic Thought.

On 21 September we were informed that the battle was over and we had won. The original proposal was abandoned. The revised proposal was to keep both Economic History and HET within Economics. Economic History would appear under Applied Economics and HET under Economic Theory. It should be noted that this outcome was exactly what Steven Kates had proposed in his submission to the ABS dated 12 September. Jerry Courvisanos had also proposed exactly the same solution in his submission. In the space of three tumultuous weeks we had overturned the decision that effectively would have killed the history of economic thought and economic history in this country. But there was to be one more twist in the tale.

On 26 September in *The Australian* appeared an article titled 'Economic historians claim win on status' written by Bernard Lane. We were stunned to read that 'A small band of economic historians has kicked up enough fuss to make the Australian Bureau of Statistics rethink their place within a new system for classifying fields of research'. Apparently we had been saved by the economic historians! No mention whatsoever of our efforts in this process. They had taken all the credit. From the very start we had alerted the economic historians of the dire situation, particularly the president of the Economic History Society of Australia and New Zealand. We were aware that they were similarly rounding up the troops in a broadcast email on 3 September. Our understanding was that the ABS felt far more comfortable keeping economic history in economics than they did HET. Thus, HET staying in economics was a far harder case to win than that of economic history, a situation not recognized in the Lane article.

Final comments on the saga and its positive outcome are in order. First we must acknowledge the overwhelming support we received locally and overseas, not just from the history of thought community, but from economists generally, ranging from John Quiggin locally to Nobel Prize winners. On 14 September Edmund Phelps wrote saying that the move to dump HET from the economics research classification would be an 'unambiguous disaster'. The second point is that intellectual discourse played an insignificant role in the outcome. There were some spirited discussions on the HES list about the science wars and whether HET was a part of economics or better situated as intellectual history in the history and philosophy of science camp. The discussion had no impact whatsoever. Ivan Moscati, in an email dated 13 September, mentioned that in Europe, North America and other countries, historians of economics work primarily in economics departments, business schools or other institutions involved in economic research. A quick survey he conducted in 2006 revealed 87 per cent of participants at the ESHET conference, 80 per cent of HES participants and 79 per cent of younger historians of economics worked in economics departments. The vast majority of historians of economics are located in, and draw their sustenance from, the economics discipline. What did make an impact were sustained pressure and the sheer weight of numbers. As evidenced in Kates and Millmow (2008), Steven Kates and Alex Millmow, in particular, came out of this episode with considerably enhanced reputations. Whereas the average academic is content to fire off indignant emails, they worked the room, contacted the heavy hitters, attended the meetings and took the initiative to have the decision overturned.

A savage attack

The second assault on Australian history of economics to be examined can be dated from Monday 9 September 2013. However, some context is useful before we get to what happened on that day. For staff performance-appraisal purposes, academic managers and supervisors need to be able to evaluate the quality of a staff member's research outcomes. With respect to journal publications this is usually evaluated using journal ranking rubrics. This particularly gained prominence with the Excellence in Research for Australia (ERA) audit organized by the ARC. In the first round of this research quality audit – ERA1 (2003–08) – there was an explicit ranking of journals. It should be said that HET journals were fairly treated. *History of Political Economy* (*HOPE*) was ranked A* – the highest possible ranking. The two other major journals, the *Journal of the History of Economic Thought* (*JHET*) and the *European Journal of the History of Economic Thought* (*EJHET*), were both ranked A and the local journal, the *History of Economics Review* (*HER*), was ranked B. These rankings had been endorsed by the executive of HETSA, which spoke on behalf of the 150-plus members of that society in their submission to the ARC.

However, in the second round – ERA2 (2005–2010) – explicit journal rankings were dispensed with. The reasoning is outlined in an extract from the Higher Education Minister's statement dated Monday 30 May 2011 to the Senate Economics Legislation Committee titled 'Improvements to Excellence in Research for Australia (ERA)':

> I have been aware for some time of concerns within the sector about certain aspects of the exercise, particularly the ranked journal lists…. As the result of this process, I have approved … the refinement of the journal quality indicator to remove the prescriptive A*, A, B and C ranks…. There is clear and consistent evidence that the rankings were being deployed inappropriately within some quarters of the sector, in ways that could produce harmful outcomes, and based on a poor understanding of the actual role of the rankings. One common example was the setting of targets for publication in A and A* journals by institutional research managers. In light of these two factors – that ERA could work perfectly well without the rankings, and that their existence was focusing ill-informed, undesirable behaviour in the management of research – I have made the decision to remove the rankings, based on the ARC's expert advice.

The Australian Business Deans Council (ABDC), however, persisted with explicit journal rankings. Their 2010 rankings were not as generous as the ARC had been to the history of economics. They downgraded *HOPE* from A* to A, and both *JHET* and *EJHET* to B status. While a disappointing outcome, for a while we could ignore this slight and continue to use the earlier, more favourable, ARC rankings. Although the ARC increasingly discouraged the use of their rankings, over time the ABDC list, by default, became increasingly important in all Business faculties at the insistence of the Business Deans. The ABDC list increasingly guided the decisions of colleagues about where to publish the results of their research. In 2013 the ABDC began reviewing its journal rankings. Submissions were called for and Coleman, Aspromourgos and Millmow (on behalf of HETSA) provided reasoned argument as to why *HOPE* should be restored to A* status. The draft revised ABDC journal rankings were to be made available in September.

On 9 September we were again flabbergasted to read that instead of being upgraded, *HOPE* had been downgraded to a B; the same ranking as *JHET, EJHET* and *HER*. There were to be no A* or A HET journals. It was battle stations again and the War Cabinet sprang into action. The timeline, as usual, was ridiculously short. The ABDC website indicated that:

> Until 30 September, interested parties can provide feedback, on serious anomalies or errors in the revised list. Please note that this exposure period is not a forum for debating decisions. Disputing journal ratings on grounds already reviewed by the expert panels will not be considered.

So we had three weeks to overturn the decision. The process was far more restrictive this time as only Australians and New Zealanders, who met certain conditions, were allowed to comment. This meant that we could not use the international community of historians of economics to support us, as they had so enthusiastically done in the earlier episode.

We had to move quickly and find out why the decision had been made and how the decision could be reversed. Again, we immediately alerted the troops via broadcast emails and postings on the SHOE email listing. Very quickly it emerged that the 'culprit' was a health economist from the University of Technology Sydney, Elizabeth Savage, who appeared to be writing on behalf of the economics discipline as head. She recommended *HOPE* be downgraded from an A to a C. That submission was seriously considered, and although the ABDC thought a downgrade to a C was too severe it accepted a 'compromise' of a downgrade to a B. It was unclear as to why her views were accorded more weight than those of three well-known Australian historians of economics (all of whom had authored one or more books in the field). The plot thickened when we uncovered that not only had she recommended downgrading *HOPE*, she had also made the same recommendations for an economic history journal as well as heterodox journals such as the *Journal of Post Keynesian Economics* (*JPKE*) and the *Journal of Economic Issues* (*JEI*).

A further conundrum was the ABDC statement that:

> Another consideration was the stature of a journal within its field. Generally, the panel viewed the #1 journal in a field as deserving of A* status, even if the journal would not achieve this status by citation data alone. For example, the *Journal of Economic History* is regarded as the top journal in the important field of Economic History, and has significantly more citations than any other journal in that field, but would not make the top 50 based on citations alone. (Of course, a line must be drawn, somewhere, concerning which fields are considered 'important fields', and the panel used its judgment on that issue.)

Why did they regard Economic History as an important field, but not HET? Another wrinkle was that business history did appear important for the ABDC but not the history of economics. Specifically, the Combes citation index equally ranks *HOPE* with *Business History* and the *Business History Review* and actually ranks *HOPE* higher than *Labour History*. Yet those other three journals all get an A rating in the ABDC list. Why are business and labour history of more importance than the history of economics? This seemed a serious inconsistency across the discipline-specific rankings.

The Savage downgrade submission was clarified by Peter Docherty. Economics staff at UTS had not been consulted with respect to the submission. Docherty indicated on 24 September, after a meeting with the Dean and the Associate Dean for Research in the Business School, that:

> UTS as an institution does not have an official position on the journal list and does not endorse the downgrading of any particular journals. This implies that any submission made from UTS can only have had the status of an individual submission. I have urged them to make sure that this position is conveyed to those responsible for the ABDC List including the Economics Panel. In addition, the Dean has agreed to sign a further submission arguing that heterodox, HET and economic history journals not be downgraded from A to B. A number of others from UTS will also sign this submission. It will have the status of an individual submission since the institutional policy here has not changed, but hopefully Roy's [Roy Green's] individual stature as a Dean will carry some weight.

What determined Savage's conclusions is conjectural but the evidence she relied on related exclusively to citation counts. We had to get to the bottom of these citation-ranking studies. Paul Oslington on 13 September assembled the main published articles on citation studies and speculated that 'there is some ammunition there for a higher ranking for *HOPE*'. He noted that the recent addition of HET journals to the Social Sciences Citation Index (SSCI) reports means that as more of them are added the counts improve, but the historical citations are likely to be unreliable. A very valuable contribution to our understanding of these citation studies and the ABDC ranking exercise came from Jerry Courvisanos on 14 September with detailed 'Notes on the ABDC Ranking List 2013', along with more published studies on citation counts. Courvisanos's input was valuable because he was a member of BARDsNet (Business Associate Deans of Research [ADR] sub-committee of the ABDC). He surveyed the main citation indicators and concluded that 'There is no one "perfect" measure of citations for ranking. Even choosing the ranking algorithm is a subjective issue'. One can be quite selective in choosing which citation measures to highlight. Perhaps the most useful insight that Courvisanos provided was that the ABDC journal rankings are ultimately designed as management tools for evaluating staff research performance. They would be used as a proxy for research quality. Business Deans and their ADRs wanted a simple management tool for performance reviews and promotion applications to assess their staff members' research output. This management tool, Courvisanos explained, disadvantages those who publish in areas without many A or A* journals. Moreover:

> Good scholarship in [heterodox or HET] areas of inquiry does not require the same extent of citations referencing recent journal articles; instead they inevitably take a much longer-term view of the literature being cited. Both tend to quote many more books, book chapters and old 'seminal' articles than the mainstream. This reduces the citation impact factors for HET and heterodox economics (and economic history too) relative to the mainstream 'current' research. Mainstream researchers give faculties more 'bang for their buck' from every article published. Also there is the scale factor. Since HET, HE [heterodox economics] and EH [economic history] are niche areas with only a relatively few researchers ... there is even less ability to get strong global citation impacts. Many of the Deans and ADRs are not economists. Most of these 'managers' do not have an 'axe to grind' to get rid of HE, HET or EH. The downgrading of HE, HET and EH are merely 'collateral damage' in the managerialism of research output in business schools.

We were now better informed of what the key factors were, and now had some ammunition to raise doubts on the veracity of citation studies, but we needed a strategy to defeat the downgrading of *HOPE*. Positive media coverage is always helpful and Steve Keen published a supportive article titled 'Low-grade journal rankings are failing economics' in the *Business Spectator* on 18 September. Individual academics were strongly encouraged to put in submissions to the ABDC. In one 24-hour period ten academics indicated that they had or would give feedback to the ABDC supporting *HOPE*. They were Jeremy Sheamur, Toomas Truuvert, John Foster, Susan Schroeder, Evan Jones, Rob Leeson, Eric Sowey, Robert Dixon, Elias Khali and Bruce Littleboy. We were also approaching all seven branches of the Economic Society of Australia, and its Central Council, to see if we could get their support and for them to individually write to the ABDC. A number of HETSA members hold, or have held, management positions in these organizations. Despite our best efforts, the society was of little assistance. The ESA's Central Council met in Sydney on 19–20 September. They noted the controversial downgrades of both *HOPE* and the *Australian Economic History Review*, but the only action they agreed to proceed with was to recommend an upgrade of the *Economic Record* from A to A*. It was felt that, while many battles could have been fought, putting a single focus in the society's request would give it more impact. Unfortunately, the ESA's strategy would end in failure.

A submission by the former editors of the *HER*, Michael McLure and Gregory Moore, submitted on 13 September was particularly effective. They had got around the 250-word limit by emailing a letter directly to the ABDC. Here are some excerpts:

> If the 2013 panel decision is accepted, there will be no HET journal ranked as either A or A*. This contrasts with the Excellence in Research for Australia (ERA) exercise undertaken by the Australian Research Council in 2010 when there were three so bracketed.... We fail to see what has changed in the structure of the discipline of economics over the last three years to warrant this wholesale revision downwards of HET journals. If anything, these journals have continued to improve. Given that most university departments require junior academics to publish in A or A* journals before being eligible for promotion, the decision to downgrade *HOPE* from A to B (and thereby the associated decision to shunt all HET journals to B status or below) effectively eliminates HET as a career path for young academics. We cannot believe that this was the desired objective of the panel members and thereby attribute their decision to a failure to recognize this implication.... The submission calling for the revision downwards of the rank of *HOPE* was supported by one individual and, as far as we can tell, without wide consultation with others in the discipline of economics. By contrast, we notice that the other submissions for revisions, particularly from the University of Melbourne, were supported by thirty or more people from these institutions. The Melbourne approach of wide consultation reflects a mature and reasonable way to proceed on such matters. We do not, in short, believe that the revision of the *HOPE* ranking has really been the subject of wide consultation.

An identical strategy to get around the 250-word limit was employed to convey a letter to the ABDC dated 19 September from the editors and advisory board of *HOPE* itself. Of course this was a little tricky as all the contributors bar one were not from either Australia or New Zealand. Again, some excerpts are appropriate:

> We should make it clear that our main interest in this matter is not to assuage our wounded pride, but to support the community of scholars engaged in the study of history of economics in Australia against an action that will damage their professional prospects and undermine a serious field of academic research. Australian scholars in the history of economics are amongst the finest in the world and do not deserve to be undermined by an ill-conceived institutional judgment.... The community of scholars in the history of economics is relatively small, and consequently the number of citations is small relative to areas of economics with thousands of scholars.... [Yet it] is a serious, vibrant, and international field with national and international professional associations, frequent conferences, and international scholarly exchanges.... *History of Political*

Economy is the oldest journal devoted to the history of economics. It is widely recognized as the best journal in the field.... In downgrading *HOPE*, you fail to heed your own dictum that the ABDC 'exercise should be a conservative one'. It is not a conservative decision, but a radical one – one that tells Australian scholars, who make important and meaningful contributions to international research in the history of economics, that they have no journal in which to publish their work that will be counted as evidence of their having achieved the highest level of distinction in their field. To let this decision stand would be to commit an act of academic vandalism, which in effect tells Australian historians of economics that, because their field is specialized, it is not valued. It would set up incentives that would ultimately militate against the very existence of the field in Australia. Surely, that is not the intent of your council. So, we urge you to reconsider and to apply your own announced standards to the ranking of *HOPE* with the aim of giving wholly deserved support to the distinguished community of historians of economics in Australia.

While these letters were very helpful, the internal discussion among the Australian economic historians of thought was spirited and ongoing. Much of the anger was vented on the ABDC. One HETSA member complained that:

On a personal level it feels like theft. Someone has taken (stolen) my accumulated intellectual wealth. I have had my A* articles stolen from me and replaced with inferior B's. Another colleague has 'lost' 17 A's and had them replaced with 17 B's. Two staff were promoted on the basis of repeated publication in a journal that is to be removed from the ABDC list. Another colleague is crowing because the journal he publishes in (and is on the editorial board of) has just been upgraded to an A*. It is the arbitrariness of the process that offends. They are ransacking academics' intellectual capital like a bull in a china shop.

Several HETSA members were pessimistic about the outcome; even one of the members of the War Cabinet stated that 'I personally think we are unlikely to win this but should make the effort'. Another had anticipated a negative outcome in a proposed editorial on the issue. Harry Bloch wrote on 13 September that:

My understanding of the process is that the sort of campaign you are organising is not the most likely to have effect. The panel review process is limited and unlikely to respond to popular pressures. On the other hand, the panel recommendations are due for review by first the BARDsNET group and then ABDC. I suggest you would have more success with influencing these reviews.

Neil de Marchi on 3 November mused about a 'larger question: how ought minority styles of scholarship within a dominant and different academic culture, be evaluated?' He went on to say that:

> Histories of all sorts, including histories of economics, are part of a book culture as much as they are of one dominated by journals. Thus citations might be a less appropriate criterion than, say, in your average economics department or business school.... In any mixed bag of scholars and scholarship the easy alternative to asking those questions is to find some quantifiable scale. But that is necessarily too crude.

Needless to say we were thrilled, in this climate of negativity and dire foreboding of doom and gloom, to hear on 29 November that *HOPE* had been reinstated as an A-ranked journal. We had won the battle. The relevant passage from the ABDC document is:

> [Fifteen] different submissions came in to challenge the downgrading of the *History of Political Economy* (*HOPE*) from A to B. These included submissions from the editor of the journal and the President of the History of Economic Thought Society of Australia (HETSA). An argument was made that *HOPE* is the top journal in the field of 'History of Economic Thought' and, without *HOPE* as at least an A journal, this would significantly reduce the incentive for anyone in Australia to engage in this kind of research. Thus, despite *HOPE*'s citation record putting it squarely in the B category, the panel recommends that it be re-instated at the level A – one grade higher than its citation data implies.

Our representations had made the difference. We had fought a campaign singularly focused on maintaining *HOPE* as an A-ranked journal. We could have been distracted into aligning with other affected groups, but a tightly organized and strategic intervention proved effective.

Concluding thoughts

We learn from these episodes that pluralism – epitomized by both heterodox and historical approaches to economics – will always be under threat, be it from orthodox colleagues or bureaucrats with limited vision or performance algorithms that are far too crude to assess scholarly merit. So economists in the pluralist tradition need to be ever vigilant. Research codes will be up for review again and journal rankings will be revised. Nonetheless, historians of economics can take a small measure of self-satisfaction in having taken on far more powerful forces and winning at the end of the day. That cannot be said, in this latest episode, for the economic historians or the heterodox economists. Both those groups failed to reverse the downgrading of their journals. There was only one submission in favour of restoring *JEI* to an A and two for *JPKE*. The downgrading of those other journals is to be regretted. HETSA has now had two notable victories in battle, it behoves all economists in the pluralist tradition to gain hope and guidance from the success of HETSA, so that the challenge to the mainstream (interpreted as a 'war') to reclaim pluralism in economics can be won.

Notes

1 See also Chapter 4 of this volume.
2 The source material used comes primarily from material publicly accessible on 19 June 2015 at: the North American History of Economics Society (SHOE) email list, https://listserv.yorku.ca/archives/shoe.html; Adam Smith Lives! A History of Economic Thought Blog, http://adamsmithlives.blogs.com/thoughts/2007/09/index.html; the Australian Research Council's (ARC) website relating to the Excellence in Research for Australia (ERA) initiative, www.arc.gov.au/era/; the Australian Business Deans Council, http://www.abdc.edu.au/journalreview.html.
3 See http://historyofeconomics.org.

References

Kates, S. and Millmow, A. (2008), A Canary in the Coalmine: The Near Death Experience of History of Economics in Australia, *History of Economic Ideas* XVI (3), pp. 79–94.

Kates, S. (2013), *Defending the History of Economic Thought*. Cheltenham, UK and Northampton, MA, USA: Edward Elgar.

Lee, F.S., Pham, X. and Gu, G. (2013), The UK Research Assessment Exercise and the Narrowing of UK Economics, *Cambridge Journal of Economics* 37(4), pp. 693–717.

Lodewijks, J. (2002), The History of Economic Thought in Australia and New Zealand, *History of Political Economy* 34, pp.154–164.

Lodewijks, J. (2003), Research in the History of Economic Thought as a Vehicle for the Defense and Criticism of Orthodox Economics, in W. Samuels, J. Biddle and J. Davis (eds.), *A Companion to the History of Economic Thought*. Oxford: Blackwell, pp. 655–668.

Lodewijks, J. (2004), *HOPE* in the Antipodes, in T. Aspromourgos and J. Lodewijks (eds.), *History and Political Economy: Essays in Honour of P.D. Groenewegen*. London and New York: Routledge, pp. 245–255.

Lodewijks, J. (2013/14), Political Economy in Greater Western Sydney, *Journal of Australian Political Economy* 72, pp. 80–105.

Weintraub, E.R. (ed.) (2002), *The Future of the History of Economics, History of Political Economy* 34, annual supplement. Durham and London: Duke University Press.

6 The influence of the history of economic thought on pluralism

The Cambridge economic tradition and Australian economics

Alex Millmow[1]

This chapter assesses the influence Cambridge University has had upon the development of Australian economics including a commitment to pluralism in the post-war era. In particular, the chapter identifies some of the twenty-odd Australian economists who went to Cambridge during the period 1945–60 intent upon furthering their education. Some of their experiences are recounted in what was then one of the world's leading economics departments. It was, however, a time when the Cambridge Faculty of Economics and Politics was becoming fractured along doctrinal lines. It seems that nearly all of the Australian economists who went there found the experience profound. Some, like Geoff Harcourt, have written about how, initially at least, their supervision was plainly inadequate. More controversially, Murray Kemp has spoken about 'The dead hand of Cambridge economics', suggesting that the experience for most Australian economics students there had not been a happy one due to the lack of supervision and that, in short, 'they'd made a huge mistake in coming to England' (Coleman 2005, p. 7). Kemp was also implying that all the new and exciting developments in economics were being produced in the USA with Britain left behind.

The other side of Kemp's comments was that those who went to Cambridge came home and subsequently instructed their students about doctrinal disputes rather than cutting-edge economics. Kemp spent 1957 at Cambridge as a Nuffield Fellow but was not based at any of the colleges.[2]Harcourt (2006) has vigorously contested Kemp's contention. This chapter also challenges Kemp's view, listing some of the nine successful doctoral students and recording their experiences, negative and positive, there.

In tribute to John King, this chapter also takes the opportunity to touch upon some of the themes raised by him in his review article of Luigi Pasinetti's *Keynes and the Cambridge Keynesians* (2007). King pondered what impact the 'intellectual arrogance', 'exclusiveness' and 'the Cambridge *prima donna* syndrome' had on young postgraduates. In particular, King suggested (2011, p. 13) that it would make an interesting research project to explore whether the notoriously disputatious Cambridge faculty might have deterred those with Keynesian sympathies from studying there. In another place, King (2003) pondered just how many Australian economists had actually gone there up till the 1960s. In that regard, this chapter identifies some of the Australians who undertook a course of study there, focussing upon the brightest names in post-war Australian economics.

Some of the experiences of those who went to Cambridge are captured in correspondence with their lecturers back in Australia. As a caring head of department at the University of Melbourne, Wilfred Prest monitored the progress of all the Melbourne commerce graduates who traditionally went to Cambridge. After a brief discussion of postgraduate economics education in Australia in the second section of this chapter, biographical details of some of those who went to Cambridge are listed in the third. The fourth section of the chapter will undertake a simple audit of those who attended Cambridge during this period and highlight those who made a contribution to pluralist economics.

Underpinnings

Only a handful of Australian universities taught economics during the immediate post-war era (Williams 1965). None of them offered doctoral training in economics until the Australian National University (ANU) was established in 1948. Even then, it made a slow start in attracting young minds partly because it encountered difficulties establishing a putative research school. There was also a 'colonial tradition' that the finest social sciences postgraduates, including economists, headed overseas to complete their education (Williams 1965, p. 310). In the inter-war period there had been a trickle of Australian economists going abroad to further their studies, most of them funded by Rockefeller scholarships.

Imitation is the finest form of flattery and Copland, the inaugural Dean at the Faculty of Commerce at Melbourne, modelled the teaching of economics on Cambridge. In the post-war years, Melbourne remained Cambridge-dominated with most of its best and brightest gravitating there to complete their studies. Harcourt recalls that Marshall, Keynes, Pigou, the Robinsons, Richard Kahn, Nicholas Kaldor, Maurice Dobb, Michał Kalecki, Gerald Shove, Dennis Robertson and Piero Sraffa were almost 'household names' to Melbourne staff (Mongiovi 2001, p. 503). It meant that many Australian economists who went overseas during this period 'acquired the pure milk of the *General Theory*, first hand, from Robinson, Kahn and Kaldor' (King 2003, p. 143). Prest, who became the Truby Williams professor in 1946, told Stuart Wilson from the University of Sydney that 'We take the view that it is more important for students to read Keynes' own book rather than read articles about Keynes'.[3] Prest also informed the University Registrar at Cambridge that 'We try to keep the standard of the final exam comparable with that of the Cambridge Tripos'.[4] Melbourne could also call upon the graces of L.F. Giblin who, as a Supernumerary Fellow of King's College, was happy to sponsor students applying there. Also facilitating the Cambridge connection was that

Prest had his brother, Alan, as a fellow of Christ's College from 1948 until 1964. Another support in Cambridge was Brian Reddaway, who had spent two years in Melbourne in the 1930s. Reddaway was a sought after supervisor (Harcourt 2006, p. 147).

In 1935, Austin Robinson had told Copland that the Cambridge faculty had not catered well for the then influx of students and that it would have to better prepare for the future. As a response, Piero Sraffa was made Secretary of the Degree Committee and Assistant Director of Research, charged with overseeing the admission of research students and deciding upon which degree they would be undertaking and choice of supervisor (Marcuzzo 2012, p. 54). Within that ambit was the personal supervision of postgraduate students but the only successful case of a doctoral student Sraffa supervised through to completion was an Australian, Graham Tucker. However, as Marcuzzo (2012, pp. 54–55) points out, Sraffa's modest score on that count overlooks his influence over the direction taken by many graduate students who had also come to Cambridge partly because of his presence there. We will see, however, that there were grumblings by some of the Australians who had gone there just after the war. Nevertheless, when Sam Soper, then a lecturer at the University of Tasmania, sought advice about where to study overseas, Prest was adamant that English universities were still superior to anything in North America: 'Those US doctorates are designed for people having done very little serious work at the undergraduate level and there is a real risk of you being seriously disappointed at the standard – not to mention being bored stiff by the repeat courses'. That aside, Prest felt Chicago was better than Harvard, adding, though, that 'the place would drive me crazy – they cannot think of anything beyond the virtues of a freely operating price system – but in the technique of mathematical economics and statistics they are unsurpassed (except perhaps by Cambridge, England)'.[5] However, Prest warned Soper that in England 'The postgraduate student is too often left to sink or swim on his own. At the best he has to make himself a bit of a nuisance in order to get anyone to take an interest in him. This might be less true of London than it is of other English universities'.[6] Apart from his own knowledge of British universities, Prest came to this conclusion after hearing of the experiences of Australian students who had gone there. As Harcourt recalled, Cambridge supervisors were hardly expected to advise upon research methods or the writing of theses (cited in Shelton and Jacobs 2015, p. 4).

When Prest visited Cambridge in 1953 he took a more considered view of the place and the London School of Economics (LSE). It would presage what Pasinetti (2007) was to lament in his Caffe Lectures on Keynes and the Cambridge Keynesians. This is what Prest wrote in a memorandum on his sabbatical whilst at St John's College, Cambridge:

> I was rather shocked to find the Faculty there deeply divided on doctrinal, political and, indeed, racial grounds. On the one hand there is the Robertson party comprising, in addition to Sir Dennis himself such

diverse characters as Guillebaud, Richard Stone, R.F. Henderson and S.R. Dennison. This group has never quite accepted Keynes without reservation and its members are inclined to be conservative, politically and socially. On the other hand, there is the Kahn party comprising, in addition to Professor Kahn, Sraffa, Kaldor, Dobb, Rostas, Joan Robinson, Ruth Cohen and Harry Johnson. This group is neo-keynesian in outlook and is well to the left politically.... The conflict between the two parties is deep and bitter. It comes into the open on the controversy over 'the new monetary policy' in the *Oxford Bulletin of Statistics* last year when Dennis Robertson called Harry Johnson 'silly-clever'. In Faculty meetings I am told that squabbles develop over such things as the appointment of examiners and the arrangement of timetables. Because Dennis Robertson gives a course in interest rates, Kahn must give one too; then the timetable is mangled so that the student hears Kahn's version first![7]

It was the next sentence, however, that really caught the eye: 'The really good student may, of course, benefit from hearing different points of view but the ordinary student is more likely to be confused, and in any case far too much of the dons' energy seems to be absorbed in academic intrigue'. He went on to discuss the LSE, noting that the atmosphere there seems 'much healthier. Robbins has mellowed over the years and is more open-minded than he used to be. He has gathered around him an impressive group of colleagues (Meade, Paish, Phelps-Brown) and they seem to have been strengthened rather than weakened by Hayek's departure'.[8] Prest didn't know the half of it; he was unaware of the in-fighting within the Kahn group (Pasinetti 2007, p. 61).

The problem with the faculty, in a nutshell, was that Kahn, Robinson and Kaldor regarded themselves as the true inheritors of Keynes's mantle in both its analytic and political aspirations. And, to quote Pasinetti (2007, p. 38), 'they believed themselves to be masters of the place and of the theory, as if anybody else (in Cambridge and in the outside world) had accepted their ideas and authoritativeness'. Did this commotion, then, deter Australians from going there? Apparently not; apart from the glamour of going to Cambridge it was quite simply the place to be because 'an extraordinary flurry of ideas characterized Cambridge economics in that period' making it 'one of the major world sources of original economic thought' (Pasinetti 2007, p. 74). This is not to overlook the fact that some Australian scholars during this time went to 'the other place', Oxford. Equally, there were other Australian econo-mists studying in London. Bob Gregory was put off Cambridge not just by 'the snobbishness' but the fact that 'a number of really good tutors, good people ... had come back from ... Cambridge without finishing their doc-torate, so I was a little scared as well' (cited in Coleman 2009, 69). The first group of Australian economists who went to Cambridge after 1945, however, went there in high expectation.

Australian economists at Cambridge 1945–1960

Eric Russell 1947

Eric Russell was the first Australian economics scholar to arrive at Cambridge in the post-war era. He had been a student at Melbourne from 1939 till 1942 and was awarded a Kilmany Scholarship to study abroad. The class of 1942 at Melbourne was an extraordinary one with Peter Karmel and Donald Cochrane also given university travelling scholarships. The war, alas, would delay their use. Russell had been a temporary lecturer at Melbourne specializing in the history of economic thought and Keynesian economics. Giblin had arranged his entry into King's College where he would undertake Part II of the Tripos. Russell came under the influence of Shove who he felt set the tone of economics at King's. Russell hung on his every utterance: 'It is fascinating to hear his chance almost off hand and always modest remarks appearing in new dress – a feather here and a trick there – some nine months later'.[9] Austin Robinson and Richard Kahn were also excellent teachers. Robertson and Sraffa had spoken highly of a paper Russell presented to the Keynes Club on utility theory.[10] Russell would secure subsequent employment teaching at New England University College and afterwards the University of Adelaide. He would write a paper with James Meade for the *Economic Record* which analysed the causal dynamics behind the post-war Australian economy. His subsequent Statement of Evidence to the Arbitration Commission in the Basic Wage Case argued that average real wages be tied to 'effective Productivity', that is, national productivity adjusted for movement in the terms of trade. Harcourt considered him his teacher and mentor.

Don Cochrane 1947–48

Cochrane, 29, left Melbourne in December 1946 accompanied by Karmel, 24, and their respective wives. Both had been students at Melbourne. Cochrane had come to the study of economics through accounting and mathematics. He had been trained in pure mathematics, the theory of statistics, statistical method and mathematical economics. He had been Prest's research assistant for six months working on Melbourne's transport problems before volunteering for the Royal Australian Air Force in 1942. He resumed his appointment at Melbourne in March 1946 but this time as a temporary lecturer where he lectured on Keynesian economics. His first proposed research thesis was an econometric study on the English demand for foodstuffs. A Commonwealth Government post-war Rehabilitation Training Scholarship (CRTS) helped defray the cost of studying abroad with the only condition being that recipients had to return to Australia.

It was Russell who apprised Prest of how the two were faring. Their first conversation was mostly about English food and constrained budgets. Cochrane, who was at Clare College, was 'a little perturbed about the mathematical standard in the treatment of his subject'.[11] Cochrane's supervisor in Cambridge was Richard Stone who had just been appointed head of the Department of Applied Economics and was deeply engaged upon national income accounting. Prest had earlier informed him that Cochrane and Karmel were intent on coming to England to broaden their skills as economists.[12]

One of Cochrane's first letters to Prest contained disquieting news. Stone had left Cochrane to his own devices with the suggestion 'I call upon him whenever I desired help'. He added 'In general there is remarkably little advanced theory lectures at Cambridge'. He also sought from Prest a letter about his earlier research work that would allow Cochrane to qualify for the PhD in the shortest possible time.[13] It suggested that Cochrane had already undertaken work on his proposed doctorate whilst in Australia. Stone was helpful, however, in securing for Cochrane permission to attend Roy Allen's lectures in econometrics at the LSE and use of 'the statistical machine' there.[14] By this time, Cochrane had amended his doctoral research topic to 'A Study in Demand Analysis' looking at measurable economic relationships. His examiners were Allen and Charles Carter of Cambridge.

In his second year there, Cochrane took the opportunity to attend lectures that took his interest. Cochrane attended Kahn's lectures on 'The Economics of Government Intervention' and Dobb's lectures on 'Problems of a Collectivist Economy', which he found 'engrossing'. Both sets of lectures were, he admitted, 'divorced' from his main area of research but he had always been a little interested in the theory of socialism.[15] When he had first arrived he attended Dennis Robertson's lectures on Keynes reporting that they were very 'entertaining and that he did not attack or criticize Keynes himself but his followers and Mrs Robinson in particular'. Cochrane also listened to John Hicks from Oxford University give a lecture to the Marshall Society on the workings of the Keynesian system in an economy marked by shortages. He concluded that Hicks was 'the perfect model of an academic theorist' because 'he was not concerned what happened to his theories provided he satisfied himself of their validity'.[16]

Cochrane already had been enjoying academic fare. He attended the 1947 Marshall Lectures, which featured Lionel Robbins. His topic was 'The Economic Problem in Peace and War: Some Reflections on Objectives and Mechanisms'. Robertson introduced him 'delightfully', pointing out how he thought Robbins's rise to become one of the chief planners in the civil service during the war reminded him of Molière's play *Le medicin malgré lui*. [17] Like most of the Australians who went to Cambridge, Cochrane supervised undergraduates undertaking the Tripos. Overall Cochrane's sojourn at Cambridge was more notable, of course, for the work he did with Guy Orcutt which resulted in two path-breaking works on econometric technique published in the *Journal of the American Statistical Association*. These contributions became forever known in econometric practice as the Cochrane-Orcutt transformation. The influence of Cambridge lingered. When Cochrane became the Dean of the Faculty of Economics and Politics at Monash University in Melbourne in 1960, he not only adopted the light blue colours of the Cambridge faculty but also a commitment to pluralism in the economics Monash offered.

Peter Karmel 1947–48

For his part, Karmel had secured first class honours in economics and had been awarded the Wyselaskie scholarship in political economy. During the war he had been working at the Commonwealth Bureau of Census and Statistics in Canberra. As a public servant he lamented the 'distressing sameness in one's life' and wanting to get back to 'The Shop' (i.e. the University of Melbourne) as 'academic work is my line'.[18] His wishes were granted. He returned to Melbourne as a lecturer in economic history and the travelling scholarship facilitated his odyssey to Cambridge. Colin Clark and Giblin rated Karmel's quantitative skills highly. Karmel won a studentship to study at Trinity College and would be looking at population growth by focussing upon male fertility. First reports were that Karmel was a little disappointed at the statistical material available at Cambridge. Shove, his initial supervisor, 'admits that he knows little of my subject'.[19] Karmel's thesis supervisor at Cambridge was Stone and he was, like Cochrane, a little unimpressed about it:

> I hardly ever see Stone and, if so, I talk he nods his head sagely and finally says 'What are your conclusions?' It is really a bit of a farce and he doesn't do much for my five guineas a term. There is practically no one to talk about my stuff up here although Carter, the statistics man, is vaguely interested and Joan Robinson has shown some interest but not on the technical stuff.[20]

Carter was the lecturer in statistics who had replaced Colin Clark when he went off to Australia. In another letter, Karmel reported how Carter had taken some interest in his work but he had not seen Stone 'for ages'. He complained, too, how he gave him a paper that remained unread three months later. He reported that research student fees had gone up by two-and-a-half guineas 'which is rather maddening when one does not get anything in return'.[21] Like Cochrane, Karmel resolved to submit his doctorate in the earliest possible time, which meant residing in Cambridge for two academic years. Karmel seemed to mellow later and would later tell Prest that the research seminar for graduate students which Sraffa oversaw 'had improved with Reddaway attending and Joan Robinson is forever keen even aggressively critical'.[22] For his part, Cochrane, in the same seminar found her criticisms 'very clear and precise'.[23] Karmel marvelled at the international mix of graduate students attending Sraffa's seminar. Meanwhile he had all but finished his magnum opus by July 1948 with his wife, Lena, typing up the manuscript for him to submit in October. Karmel would eventually become the head of the Department of Economics at Adelaide in the 1960s and go on to an illustrious career in university administration.

Burgess Cameron 1950–52

Burgess Cameron was a student from the University of Sydney who secured a Masters from there and was employed at Canberra University College (CUC), where Heinz Arndt was head of department. Arndt had earlier supervised his Masters thesis at Sydney on 'Public Finance and the National Income of Australia 1925–38'. In 1950 he was awarded a Trinity College scholarship and would duly obtain his doctorate in 1952. He undertook the work at the Department of Applied Economics (DAE) supervised by Stone. The work, on general equilibrium theory and input-output analysis using Australian data, was titled 'The Determinants of Production – An Essay in General Equilibrium Analysis'. The theoretical part of his thesis was subsequently published as a textbook on general equilibrium theory by Cambridge University Press. In a subsequent job application, Arndt, acting as a referee, reported that both Kahn and Joan Robinson regarded Cameron 'as one of the best graduate students that they had had in the post-war years'.[24] Cameron's first letter from Cambridge spoke excitedly of being at Cambridge:

> Naturally, I'm enormously interested in everything that is happening here. I have been listening to Robertson, Kaldor – and have been meaning to attend other lectures – but one gets swamped with engagements and of course the seminars are getting underway – Sraffa's Research Seminar, the departmental seminar and another at King's.[25]

In another letter Cameron told Prest:

> Your brother has been most kind and suffered a long monologue from me last week on what I am planning to do. Reddaway has also offered a number of helpful criticisms and Dennis Robertson has been taking a rather paternal interest. I had a number of long talks with Leontief before he returned to the states. His presence was particularly good for my morale as none else (sic) in Cambridge is working in this field![26]

Cameron's progress caught the eyes of one of his compatriots: 'Burgess Cameron has all but finished his after only 4 terms here but I understand a good deal of work has been done on it whilst he was in Canberra.'[27]

Despite his swift progress, Cameron was unimpressed about Sraffa as Research Director and the level of supervision afforded him: 'I must say I'm extremely disappointed in Sraffa and his research seminar. On the whole the standard this past year has been rather poor – not a little of the blame for which rests with Sraffa himself for the conduct of the group is pretty inefficient. D.H. Robertson still comes pretty regularly but this is not an unmixed blessing when Joan comes too.'[28] Cameron later told Arndt that Robinson 'is certainly acute but somehow it seems to be argument for argument's sake – not very productive'.[29] Let us return to Cameron's earlier complaint:

Indeed I must confess myself disappointed with Cambridge in many ways. For one thing there is no good course in econometrics here – it is all or nothing, or, in other words, you train yourself. Moreover the people in DAE work in a very narrow field and Stone himself is almost impossible to see. I have yet to persuade him to read my work – which I think is rather shocking. Since Leontief is gone I find very few people with whom to discuss my work.[30]

In a later, more upbeat letter, Cameron spoke of lunching with Stone 'over 3 hours of solid drinking' that led the latter to whip up some interest in his student's project. Stone promised some material assistance in the form of Richard Goodwin who had just joined the faculty staff. Cameron also reported that Laszlo Rostas was appointed assistant to Sraffa and hoping he might be interested 'in my side of things for Sraffa gives little or no direction (or any other assistance) to Research Students'. He also reported that at the research seminars students 'give papers in turn on any subject they please ... the general standard has been far below my expectations and at least two were of below graduate standard, really extremely poor'.[31]

Cameron's ability was certainly recognized since Stone offered him a job of planning and directing a research project on inter-industry relations in the United Kingdom, 'but I'm not interested in staying in England, not enough Sun for one thing!'[32] Like Cochrane and Karmel, Cameron submitted his thesis whilst at Cambridge and, after a viva by Carter and Richard Goodwin, declared that his doctorate 'was in the bag'.[33] Plainly, Cameron was not enamoured with Cambridge; he spent the rest of his career in Canberra occupying a chair at the ANU and, apart from theoretical output, produced a number of textbooks.

Graham Tucker 1952–53

Another Melbourne-trained student, Graham Tucker was inspired by John La Nauze to pursue further studies in the history of economic thought (La Nauze 1982). After war service with the RAAF and with the assistance of the CRTS Tucker entered Melbourne in 1946 and scored first class honours. Tucker was to arrive at Cambridge at a time when Sraffa was engaged on his mammoth work of editing the works of Ricardo. Tucker's doctoral work, undertaken over two academic years, examined the theories of pre-classical and classical economists. It was subsequently published as *Progress and Profits in British Economic Thought 1650–1850* (Tucker 1950). It won the prestigious Ellen McArthur prize. Another Melbourne colleague, Jim Cairns, who was at Oxford, visited Tucker and informed Prest that 'Graham is getting on fine with Sraffa' and that 'he was the best possible man for him to work with'.[34] It was indeed a suitable pairing, but as Butlin (1980, p. 278) recalled Tucker was a committed scholar with a powerful intellect. Certainly, Tucker knew he was blessed: 'I am very lucky to be working under Mr Sraffa's supervision. He is always very interested and not nearly so inaccessible as popularly supposed.... I saw him 4 or 5 times last term and have already had a longish talk with him this term'. [35] Tucker conveyed the same sentiments to La Nauze reporting how 'Sraffa has been seriously injured in a climbing accident in Norway.... I shall be supervisor-less for a while' before adding 'I hope that Sraffa does not decide to pass me on to someone else. It seems that I am about the only research student in Cambridge who likes his supervisor' (cited in La Nauze 1982, p. 3).

Tucker gave an alternative account to Cameron's of what it was actually like to be in the research seminars:

> There are no holds barred at Mr. Sraffa's seminar, and one wonders beforehand just what is going to happen. Mr. Sraffa, as you know, delights in battle, and always has an array of inconvenient arguments to wage with great vigour against the propositions of the paper-reader. They are almost invariably unanswerable. I find his ability to argue not only with his voice, but his whole body – head, eyes, eyebrows, hands and even feet – most intriguing![36]

Harcourt (2012, 20) would encounter similar treatment a few years later. Tucker once made a rough note of the numbers hewing away at doctorates: 'If one compares the number of PhD candidates normally at work here with the number of PhDs awarded, it is evident that the wastage is very high. A sobering reflection!'[37] Harcourt believes the wastage rate was as high as 90 per cent.[38] Tucker was not one of them. He had loved being at Cambridge and revered Sraffa. They kept in touch. Sraffa acted as his referee when Tucker applied for the chair in economic history at the ANU in 1960.[39] Weighed down by an unrelenting flow of work and administration Tucker told Sraffa that 'Cambridge seems very long ago and very far away now. Soon it will be twenty years since I left.... I have been hoping to return on leave but each time something happens to prevent it'.[40] Tucker would never get back there.

Jim Wilson 1953–54

A graduate from the University of Sydney, Jim Wilson had unsuccessfully applied for an ANU scholarship at the Research School of Social Sciences. He had undertaken a Masters at Sydney on capital theory in 1952 which had been supervised by Arndt. Wilson was awarded a Rockefeller scholarship and a Cambridge postgraduate studentship in economics. The studentship was only awarded after Sraffa had contacted Arndt enquiring whether Wilson truly was 'an exceptionally strong candidate' to undertake a doctorate. Arndt replied that Wilson was well equipped to handle theoretical work in economics.[41] Arndt candidly added, however, that Wilson's chief failing was in marshalling his ideas in orderly fashion and expressing them lucidly and that he held some conceit about his own abilities. A period of disciplined study at

Cambridge, Arndt felt, would remedy this. From Trinity College Wilson wrote just one erudite letter confirming a 'fundamental cleavage' between 'the old brigade' and 'the new keynesians' but making the interesting observation that 'Almost without exception Marshall seems the unifying symbol.... Marshall's work really is a living thing giving rise to the use of a highly specialised private language and method of analysis which differs quite rudely from the Oxford-LSE amalgam'.[42]

Kaldor was Wilson's supervisor and he welcomed it because 'If I don't produce something worthwhile under his slave-driving I never shall'. He added that he had the 'greatest admiration' for Kaldor: 'He is ... exceedingly painstaking in his efforts to steer you on what he considers the right track'.[43] It seems, however, that Kaldor's 'slave-driving' did not work; Wilson's proposed thesis on the post-war trading system and why discriminatory measures like multiple exchange rates and quantitative restrictions would become prevalent came to nothing. Wilson's staff records at the University of Sydney reveal no Cambridge credential. Wilson returned to Sydney and became an associate professor there in 1970.

Geelum Simpson-Lee 1954–55

Another Sydney-sider, Simpson-Lee graduated from the University of Sydney in 1942 with second-class honours and joined the faculty the year after. Simpson-Lee attended Trinity College, Cambridge but his proposed dissertation and doctoral supervisor are unknown. Despite spending two years at Cambridge Simpson-Lee did not complete his dissertation. Simpson-Lee was elected Dean of the Department of Economics and appointed an official committee of inquiry, which ultimately recommended the establishment of a sequence of political economy courses for students seeking an alternative to mainstream economics (Stilwell 2002). He invited Joan Robinson to visit the faculty in 1975. He visited Cambridge for six months in 1979 to conduct research into Post Keynesian economics.

Wilfred Salter 1953–55

After an astonishing first degree at the University of Western Australia (UWA) with first class honours there was no doubt that Salter was ready made for academe. His honours thesis drew up an index of industrial production for Australia. Another recipient of a Hackett travelling scholarship, Salter went to Clare College where he was supervised by Reddaway. He found the research culture conducive and was helped by Rostas who had some background in taxation and measuring productivity. Salter won the 1954 Stevenson Prize for the best graduate essay. His thesis 'A Consideration of Technological Change with Special Reference to Labour Productivity' was, after revision, subsequently published as *Productivity and Technical Change* (Salter 1960). Apart from its views on investment and industrial policy, it would have a considered and profound bearing upon Australian wages policy. After a post-doctoral scholarship at Johns Hopkins University, Salter returned to Australia to take up an appointment as a research economist at the ANU. In 1960 he left the ANU to become an Assistant Secretary in the Economic Section of the Prime Minister's Department (Swan 1963, p. 486). He then went to work in Pakistan as part of the Harvard program. A year before his death from heart disease, he shared with Arndt how he was 'coming to the view that economists are living in a dream world when they talk about economic development in Asia. There is not really much economics in it. The basic things are political will, energy of the people, administrative structures and the distribution of wealth and power in society'.[44]

Keith Frearson 1954–56

Another Western Australian, Keith Frearson was the next to go to Cambridge but via Melbourne. Frearson, for all his gifts, never completed his doctorate. Not completing one's doctorate then was not as terminal to a fulfilling academic career as it would be today. A graduate of UWA where he had won first class honours, Frearson had worked on a theoretical and statistical analysis of the accelerator principle in the light of recent developments of trade cycle theory. He then worked as a trainee actuary for an insurance company in Melbourne before successfully applying for a lecturer position there. He was appointed because of excellent reports on his teaching but also because he would be the only member of the Melbourne staff with a mathematical qualification.

As a student at Clare College, Frearson was first supervised by Kaldor and then R.C.O. Mathews. He attended Joan Robinson's lectures on material that would later become her book *The Accumulation of Capital* (Robinson 1956). He became so entranced that one observer likened it 'to a religious experience' (cited in Harcourt 2000, p. 297). By mid-1956 he could only tell Prest that he was 'making only slow progress' on his doctorate on the formulation of models of economic growth, including a critique and synthesis of current growth models. Frearson was 'ashamed' about his lack of progress: 'I have been feeling very badly about my lack of tangible evidence of my time in Cambridge but still it has been wonderful to have been there, and to have seen and heard all these people, and I feel at least that I have learned an awful lot!'[45] A sympathetic Prest responded that perhaps he could give a seminar or contribute a chapter of this thesis to the *Economic Record* so that 'It could at least be something to show for your time in Cambridge'.[46] Prest was moved by Frearson's plight after hearing from Isaac who had run into him in London. Frearson had told him that he did not want to return to Australia as 'a failure' even though Isaac dismissed this as silly talk.[47] Frearson duly returned home and continued to work upon his doctorate.

It was to drag on and on. Three years later, Austin Robinson, on behalf of the Faculty Degree Committee at Cambridge, wrote to Prest:

> When a man has done a period of research at Cambridge we are natu-
> rally very anxious that he shall finish his work and submit. We have the
> impression ... that he is a very conscientious teacher who has been giving
> all his attention for the last year or so to his new job of teaching and that
> may be inevitably conflicting with his research.[48]

Robinson asked Prest to lighten his teaching load. This Prest did, responding that he had seen drafts of Frearson's work and was hopeful it would be submitted. He added, however, that 'part of Frearson's difficulty is his reluctance to commit things to paper'.[49] With Prest's support, Frearson won a further extension from Cambridge to March 1961. Robinson told Prest that he was happy to give a further extension provided Frearson was making steady progress but added 'When things come to a dead stop it seems better on both sides to face the fact and allow the thesis quietly to die'.[50]

Robinson was ultimately proved right. When Cochrane took up his appointment at Monash, he was keen to have Frearson join him. Cochrane's testimonial to the Registrar at Monash summed up why Frearson did not complete his Cambridge doctorate: 'Frearson sets an extremely high standard for himself and, as a result, he has refrained from completing his PhD, and also from publishing a number of papers he has written in the hope of perfecting them in the process of time'. Cochrane expressed confidence that, with encouragement, Frearson would come good with output. While a substantial piece of work on a survey of growth theory was published in *Australian Economic Papers* Frearson refused to publish papers 'unless he can make a grand contribution'.[51] Cochrane did emphasize that of even 'greater importance was that Frearson was a first class teacher'.[52] Frearson would spend all his sabbaticals at Cambridge where he was, as at Monash, immensely popular with staff and students alike. He was insistent upon introducing students to non-mainstream economics. In that regard, he was instrumental in inviting Joan Robinson to Australia on two occasions.

Geoff Harcourt 1955–58

Perhaps the most famous Australian economist to attend Cambridge in the post-war era, Harcourt also had a Melbourne pedigree. After an honours degree and then a Masters at Melbourne, Harcourt attended King's College. He was initially supervised by Kaldor before Ronald Henderson took over when the former went on leave. The supervision by Kaldor proved unfortunate but Harcourt could equally say the same of his experience as a Masters student at Melbourne where his supervisor gave him such a torrid time that it knocked his confidence (Isaac 2009, pp. 93–94). Harcourt has written several autobiographical pieces of his time at Cambridge. Like Frearson, he was in awe of Joan Robinson and locked himself away in his room for a term in 1956 to unravel *The Accumulation of Capital* (Mongiovi 2001, p. 504) which the young Harcourt felt would be something similar in impact to *The General*

Theory. Harcourt subsequently gave two seminars on the meaning of the work. Meanwhile he laboured away on his doctorate titled 'The Finance of Investment, Taxation and Retained Profits in Selected United Kingdom Industries, 1949–53' which was completed in Australia. While it sounded suburban it was pregnant with ideas for subsequent work on distribution, accumulation and growth within a Keynesian-Kaleckian setting (Mongiovi 2001, p. 505).

Harcourt found employment at Adelaide and took leave from there to be a university lecturer at Cambridge in the mid-1960s. In 1982 he left Adelaide to take up a permanent position at Cambridge. He was made a Fellow of Trinity Hall. He would become the great spokesman for the Cambridge tradition in economics, writing over 100 essays on Cambridge economics, Keynes and Kalecki and Joan Robinson and her circle (Harcourt 2012). He was asked by Mark Perlman, the then editor of the *Journal of Economic Literature*, to tell the economics profession about the importance of the capital debates that raged in the 1960s (Harcourt 1969). It was later expanded into a book (Harcourt 1972). Harcourt was, and continues to be, a great proponent of pluralism in the Australian economics curriculum.

Hugh Hudson 1957–58

A graduate from the University of Sydney, Hudson was a confident young man who rose to meet the expectations he set. He completed a Masters thesis at Sydney looking at the effects of inflation on the allocation of resources. He then lectured at CUC and then at Melbourne University as a temporary lecturer. He was accepted into King's College on a British Council scholarship with his supervisors being Kaldor and Reddaway. At Cambridge he gave seven seminars: three at King's College, three at the research students' seminar and one for the Cambridge–Oxford–London joint seminar. His thesis topic was 'Cyclical Fluctuations and Economic Growth'. In his second year there he won the 1958 Stevenson Prize for his essay on 'The Equilibrium Rate of Growth'. So successful was Hudson's research that he was awarded a King's College Studentship. Kaldor asked him to be his editorial assistant for one of his forthcoming books of essays. While Joan Robinson and Kahn rated Hudson the brightest of all the Australians they had seen (Harcourt 2006), he seemed to be talking his way out of completing his doctorate. Hudson reported how Reddaway had 'demanded' he present 'a proposed chapter-by-chapter outline' of his thesis and insisted on a definite date for the first draft, 'however, I'm not very hopeful about finishing before the end of the year'.[53] Around the same time, Hudson told Arndt that his work was proceeding 'with painful progress' and that the chances of him securing the doctorate were much poorer 'as the examining of a theoretical thesis seems to be pretty savage'.[54]

Like Frearson, Hudson, for all his promise, did not complete his thesis but it did not stop him from having a fulfilling academic career. Nor did he ever seem to regret it. He returned to Australia to take up a position at the NSW

Institute of Technology and then subsequently as a senior lecturer at the University of Adelaide. In 1965 he was elected to the South Australian parliament where he became the Minister of Education in the Dunstan Government. In 1979 he became Deputy-Premier of South Australia.

Allan Barton 1955–58

Allan Barton was one of the last Australians in the 1950s to derive a doctorate from Cambridge. Initially Sraffa wanted Barton to do two papers from the Tripos as part of the qualification to undertake a research degree because he felt that Barton was more an accountant than an economist. Prest assured him that Barton was an economic tutor at Melbourne and that 'I have therefore no doubt that Barton has considerable ability with a wide grasp of economics. I think he can do a very worthwhile piece of research in a borderland field and that means can be found to avoid his being diverted from this purpose by having to sit for the Tripos paper'.[55] Barton undertook his doctorate at the same time as Harcourt. Titled 'A Contribution to the Theory of the Multi-Product Firm' Barton's dissertation, supervised by Austin Robinson, was strictly in the economics domain and anticipated later work on the boundaries and internal organization of multi-product firms. Cornish, Harcourt and Holden (2013) describe the work as 'remarkable for its creativity and breadth' and say that Barton was too self-effacing about getting it published. Barton recalled that his supervision sessions with Robinson involved usually ten minutes on his thesis and fifty minutes on Keynes (cited in Shelton and Jacobs 2015, p. 5). Barton became one of the first accounting professors in Australia to hold a PhD, albeit in economics, and over a thirty-year career at the ANU, sought to bring the two disciplines together.

Michael Schneider 1956–57

Michael Schneider is an interesting case in that as an undergraduate he was an honours student in politics and history, not economics. He was awarded a twelve-month Shell overseas scholarship and went to Christ's College, Cambridge, arriving at the same time as Barton, who went to the same college. At Cambridge Schneider was initially enrolled in the Diploma of Economics, which requires at least a II.I in three of the Part II Tripos subjects and a minor thesis. Having achieved the former under the supervision of Alan Prest, he was invited to enrol in a higher degree with the support of his supervisor. This allowed Schneider to pursue an interest in the works of John A. Hobson, for which he was awarded a Masters in economics; the supervision of this thesis was by Kenneth (later Sir Kenneth) Berrill whose supervision Schneider recalls, untypically for Cambridge, as exemplary. Alan Prest was a referee for Schneider's first academic appointment as a Research Fellow at his Alma Mater, the University of Adelaide. Schneider recalled that while he was at Cambridge there was a colony of nine Australians undertaking studies within the faculty. In his later career Schneider became an eminent HET scholar focussing upon the works of J.A. Hobson and also the distribution of wealth.

Duncan Ironmonger 1957–59

A graduate from CUC and Melbourne, Ironmonger took leave from his work at Commonwealth Bureau of Census and Statistics and went to St Catharine's College, Cambridge. It appears he may have been accommodated by a public service postgraduate scholarship. His thesis, titled 'New Commodities, Quality Changes and Consumers' Behaviour', was supervised by Alan Brown from the DAE. His work on the characteristics approach to demand theory preceded the work of another Australian, Kelvin Lancaster (Williams 2009, p. 22). It was subsequently published as *New Commodities and Consumer Behaviour* (Ironmonger 1972). Ironmonger would become the deputy director of the Melbourne Institute of Applied Economic and Social Research, which was headed by Ronald Henderson who had come out from Cambridge.

An audit

This chapter has identified nine Australian economists out of a possible fourteen who successfully completed doctoral studies at Cambridge during the period under review. Interestingly, five of them submitted the doctorates whilst at Cambridge (Cochrane, Karmel, Cameron, Tucker and Salter) while the other four submitted their doctorates back in Australia (Harcourt, Barton, Ironmonger and the economic historian John McCarty). This is simply because they were funded for a maximum stay of two years when the PhD was normally a three-year programme. Despite some complaints about Stone as a supervisor, he is reputed to be the only economist in Cambridge all of whose doctoral supervisees were successful in getting their PhD.[56] Seven Australians failed to complete their economics doctorate, including Simpson-Lee, Frearson and Hudson. Overall, the doctoral success rate is commendable given how difficult it was to get a doctorate from Cambridge at the time. One factor to bear in mind was that Cambridge was not 'a PhD shop' in the way LSE was. Cambridge tended to regard the Tripos as the basis for a professional career in economics.[57] On that note, three Australians completed it (Russell, Max Newton and Austin Holmes), another completed the Diploma in Economics and three others the M.Sc. in Economics, including Schneider. Overall, a fair degree of human capital was imported back into the Australian economics profession. Even those who had failed to meet their degree requirements came home energized, ready to resume their academic careers. Indeed all who returned home were soon promoted, not necessarily because of their Cambridge qualification but their natural ability.

Some, however, like Russell, Salter, Karmel, Harcourt, Hudson, Simpson-Lee and Frearson, brought to Australia the torch of neo-Keynesian economics as represented by the works of Kahn, Kaldor, Robinson and Sraffa. Others like Barton, Cameron, Cochrane, Holmes, Karmel, Newton and Schneider adopted a mild-mannered brand of Keynesianism, nothing more. The transmission of neo-Keynesian ideas was furthered by Harcourt and Karmel, who, along with Wallace, produced a first-year textbook, *Economic Activity* (Harcourt et al. 1967), that bridged the divide between price theory and macroeconomics. Besides giving a careful exposition of Keynesian economics, it was the only Australian-produced textbook to win markets abroad. Simpson-Lee, in collaboration with his Sydney colleague, Cyril Renwick, published the secondary school economics textbook *The Economic Pattern* in 1950 (Renwick and Simpson-Lee 1950), which was essentially Keynesian in orientation.[58] Hudson, in conjunction with Harcourt, went further and established a new journal, *Australian Economic Papers*, which had a cosmopolitan feel (Harcourt 2014). In its first twenty years, that journal entertained a pluralistic ambit and an alternative to the *Economic Record*. Both Frearson and Hudson published some of the fruit of their Cambridge research there.

In terms of personal careers, all of the Australian economists who went to Cambridge during the period under study succeeded in academe. Eight of them became professors, four becoming Deans (Cochrane, Karmel, Cameron and Simpson-Lee), with Karmel being elevated to Vice-Chancellor status. Cambridge was an irresistible choice, with the place lit up in the afterglow of the Keynesian revolution and Kahn, Kaldor and Robinson, still in their prime, trying to thresh out a new economics but meeting resistance within the faculty itself. Just to eavesdrop on what was going on, or to attend perhaps any of the three sets of seminars, even perhaps the secret seminar, would have been exhilarating for most.

Conclusion

This chapter found that Cambridge exerted considerable impact upon the professionalization of Australian economics not just by the training of brilliant young minds but also in the sense that some carried the torch of a new Keynesian paradigm in economics back to their homeland. There was some rancour about graduate supervision, pastoral care and the standard of econometrics even right up till the 1960s. That said, others could not wait to get back to the place. Australian economics profited from sending some of its best and brightest to an economics faculty then in its heyday.

Notes

1 I am indebted to the late Alan Boxer, Peter Drake, John King, Marjorie Harper, Geoff Harcourt, Sue Howson, Joe Isaac, John Lodewijks, John Nieuwenhuysen, Jonathan Pincus, Michael Schneider, Frank Stilwell and Bob Wallace for their generous comments, advice and corrections on earlier drafts of this chapter. All primary sources used are contained in the following endnotes.
2 Kemp did his doctorate at Johns Hopkins in international trade supervised by Evsey Domar. It was, however, 'almost by accident' since his earlier doctoral work

on welfare economics, supervised by Carl Christ and Arnold Harberger, was apparently 'resisted' by the chairman of the department. 'The Enigmatic Professor Kemp: The Early Years' by Daniel Leonard appeared in *RECONaissance* 1(2) which was, for a while, the in-house magazine of the economics and commerce students of UNSW.

3 Prest to J.S.G. Wilson 28 May 1946, Prest Papers, University of Melbourne Archive (UMA).
4 Prest to J.C. Taupin 22 August1951, Prest Papers, UMA.
5 Prest to Soper 29 March 1950, Prest Papers, UMA.
6 Ibid.
7 Report of visit to Britain, January–March 1953, Prest Papers, UMA. Prest's appreciation of the faculty feuding was accurate except for linking Johnson with the Kahn camp.
8 Ibid.
9 Russell to Prest 9 April 1947, Prest Papers, UMA.
10 Prest to J.P. Belshaw 30 January 1947, Prest Papers, UMA.
11 Russell to Prest 15 March 1947, Prest Papers, UMA.
12 Prest to R.L. Stone 5 June 1946, Prest Papers, UMA.
13 Cochrane to Prest 4 March 1947, Prest Papers, UMA.
14 Cochrane to Prest 3 July 1947, Prest Papers, UMA.
15 Cochrane to Prest 24 January 1948, Prest Papers, UMA.
16 Cochrane to Prest 3 July 1947, Prest Papers, UMA.
17 'The doctor in spite of himself' (ibid.).
18 Karmel to Prest 28 October 1944, Prest Papers, UMA.
19 Karmel to Prest 9 April 1947, Prest Papers, UMA.
20 Karmel to Prest 19 July 1947, Prest Papers, UMA.
21 Karmel to Prest 2 September 1947, Prest Papers, UMA.
22 Karmel to Prest 25 December 1947, Prest Papers, UMA.
23 Cochrane to Prest 3 July 1947, Prest Papers, UMA.
24 Arndt to Registrar, University of Western Australia, 1954, Arndt Papers, National Library of Australia (NLA).
25 B. Cameron to Arndt 6 November 1950, Arndt Papers, NLA.
26 Cameron to Prest 5 February 1951, Prest Papers, UMA.
27 G.S.L. Tucker to Prest 23 January 1952, Prest Papers, UMA.
28 Cameron to Arndt 14 May 1951, Arndt Papers, NLA.
29 Cameron to Arndt 31 October 1951, Arndt Papers, NLA.
30 Cameron to Arndt 14 May 1951, Arndt Papers, NLA.
31 Cameron to Arndt 15 June 1951, Arndt Papers, NLA.
32 Cameron to Arndt 31 October 1951, Arndt Papers, NLA.
33 Cameron to Arndt 17 May 1952, Arndt Papers, NLA.
34 J.F. Cairns to Prest 23 January 1952, Prest Papers, UMA.
35 Tucker to Prest 23 January 1952, Prest Papers, UMA.
36 Tucker to Prest 23 January 1952, Prest Papers, UMA.
37 Ibid.
38 Personal communication with author.
39 Tucker to Sraffa 15 October 1960, Sraffa Papers, Trinity College Cambridge, UK.
40 Tucker to Sraffa 27 March 1970, Sraffa Papers, Trinity College Cambridge, UK.
41 Arndt to Sraffa 29 May 1952, Arndt Papers, NLA.
42 Wilson to Arndt 6 January 1953, Arndt Papers, NLA.
43 Ibid.
44 Salter to Arndt 18 December 1962, Arndt Papers, NLA.
45 Frearson to Prest 14 June 1956, Prest Papers, UMA.
46 Prest to Frearson 29 May 1956, Prest Papers, UMA.
47 Isaac to Prest 20 February 1956, Prest Papers, UMA.

48 A. Robinson to Prest 20 January 59, Prest Papers, UMA.
49 Prest to A. Robinson 11 February 1959, Prest Papers, UMA.
50 A. Robinson to Prest 27 July 1960, Prest Papers, UMA.
51 Cochrane to R. Downing 14 August 1968, Downing Papers, UMA.
52 Cochrane to F.H. Johnson, Registrar 6 January 1961, Frearson staff file, Monash University, Melbourne.
53 H. Hudson to Prest 22 March 1958, Prest Papers, UMA.
54 Hudson to Arndt 23 March 1958, Arndt Papers, NLA.
55 Prest to Sraffa 2 July 1956, Prest Papers, UMA.
56 I am grateful to Sue Howson for this point.
57 I owe these two comments to John Nieuwenhuysen.
58 In 1966, Burgess Cameron wrote a first year macroeconomics textbook, *The Theory of National Income and Employment*, complete with an Australian institutional background and statistics (Cameron 1966).

References

Butlin, N.G. (1980), G.S.L. Tucker, *Economic Record* 56(154), pp, 278–280.

Cameron, B. (1966), *The Theory of National Income and Employment*. Melbourne: Cheshire.

Coleman, W. (2005), A Conversation with Murray Kemp, *History of Economics Review* 41, pp. 1–18.

Coleman, W. (2009), The Power of Simple Theory and Important Facts: A Conversation with Bob Gregory, *Agenda* 16(2), pp. 61–89.

Cornish, S., Harcourt, G.C. and Holden, R. (2013), Allan Barton 1933–2012: A Tribute, *Economic Record* 89(285), p. 283.

Harcourt, G.C. (1969), Some Cambridge Controversies in the Theory of Capital, *Journal of Economic Literature* 7, pp. 369–405.

Harcourt, G.C. (1972), *Some Cambridge Controversies in the Theory of Capital*. Cambridge, UK: Cambridge University Press.

Harcourt, G.C. (2000), Keith Septimus Frearson 18 September 1922–2 February 2000: A Memoir and a Tribute, *Economic Record* 76(234), pp. 297–300.

Harcourt, G.C. (2006), Australians in Cambridge in the 1950s: A Comment on William Coleman's Conversation with Murray Kemp, *History of Economics Review* 43, pp. 146–149.

Harcourt, G.C. (2012), *The Making of a Cambridge Economist*. Basingstoke, UK and New York: Palgrave Macmillan.

Harcourt, G.C. (2014), AEP and Me: A Short(ish) Memoir, *Australian Economic Papers* 53(3–4), pp. 255–259.

Harcourt, G.C., Karmel, P. and Wallace, R.H. (1967), *Economic Activity*. Cambridge, UK: Cambridge University Press.

Ironmonger, D.K. (1972), *New Commodities and Consumer Behaviour*. Cambridge, UK: Cambridge University Press.

Isaac, J.E. (2009), The 1950s: Adjustment and Consolidation, in R. Williams (ed.), *Balanced Growth: A History of the Department of Economics, University of Melbourne*. Melbourne: Australian Scholarly Publishing, pp. 87–102.

King, J.E. (2002), *A History of Post Keynesian Economics since 1938*. Cheltenham, UK and Northampton, MA, USA: Edward Elgar.

King, J.E. (2011), The 'Cambridge Keynesians': Some Unanswered Questions, mimeo.

La Nauze, J. (1982), Graham Shardalow Lee Tucker: Some memories of the 1950s, *HETSA Newsletter.*

Marcuzzo, M.C. (2012), Piero Sraffa at the University of Cambridge, in M.C. Marcuzzo, *Fighting Market Failure: Collected Essays in the Cambridge Tradition of Economics.* London and New York: Routledge, pp. 46–69.

Mongiovi, G. (2001), The Cambridge Tradition in Economics: An Interview with G.C. Harcourt, *Review of Political Economy* 13(4), pp. 503–521.

Pasinetti, L.L. (2007), *Keynes and the Cambridge Keynesians: A 'Revolution in Economics' to be Accomplished.* Cambridge, UK: Cambridge University Press.

Renwick, C. and Simpson-Lee, G.A.J. (1950), *The Economic Pattern.* Melbourne: Longmans.

Robinson, J. (1956), *The Accumulation of Capital.* London: Macmillan.

Salter, W.E.G. (1960), *Productivity and Technical Change.* Cambridge, UK: Cambridge University Press.

Shelton, W. and Jacobs, K. (2015), Allan Douglas Barton: A Scholar Who Spanned Theory and Practice, *Accounting History* 20(1), pp. 20–42.

Stilwell, F. (2002), Obituary: Geelum Simpson-Lee, *Journal of Australian Political Economy* 47, p. 121.

Swan, T. (1963), Wilfred Edward Graham Salter, 1929–1963, *Economic Record* 39(88), pp. 486–487.

Tucker, G. (1950), *Progress and Profits in British Economic Thought 1650–1850.* Cambridge, UK: Cambridge University Press.

Williams, B.R. (1965), Economics in Australian Universities, *The Australian University*, 1(3), pp. 308–318.

Williams, R. (ed.) (2009), *Balanced Growth: A History of the Department of Economics, University of Melbourne.* Melbourne: Australian Scholarly Publishing.

Theme III

Pluralism begins – classical ideas, yesterday and today

Pluralism was everywhere in the study of economics until the end of the eighteenth century. Despite Ricardo's *Principles of Political Economy* marking a classical 'orthodoxy' (the word used by Sismondi) in the discipline, there arose major works from Karl Marx and William Stanley Jevons in the mid-nineteenth century that identified two major divergent approaches. The authors in Chapters 7 to 10 revisit classical ideas as they were espoused at that time of great fluidity within the discipline.

In Chapter 7, Heinz Kurz invokes the work of Piero Sraffa to accomplish two tasks. The first is to acclaim and revive the 'submerged and forgotten' classical theory of value and distribution (particularly Ricardo's) compatible with modern pluralist thought by dealing separately with the real facts of the economy and expectations of the future that influence those facts. The second is a critique that exposes the fallacies of both Marshall's partial equilibrium analysis and the general equilibrium approach that succeeded it. Sraffa's critique, again compatible with modern pluralist thought, not only revived 'the rich outlook on economic and social matters entertained by the classical economists', but it also helps 'to rid the profession of the fetters of mechanical marginalist thinking'.

In Chapter 8, James Doughney offers an immanent critique of the theory of the falling rate of profit by Marx (and Engels) in *Capital* volume III. By identifying false abstraction in Marx's work, Doughney notes: 'The profit rate will not tend to fall in consequence of relentless productivity-enhancing change that raises the relative value of the stock of constant capital (dead labour) against that required for variable capital (living labour). Rather, periods of strong accumulation are more likely to cause an increase in the rate of profit. Conversely, it will more likely fall in consequence of slowing or weakening investment and growth.' This analysis points to the need to incorporate a short-run analysis of investment decisions, drawing on the work of Michał Kalecki and other Post Keynesian and institutionalist economic thinkers.

Multiple discoveries of economic concepts elicit images of pluralism. Different theoretical schools can come up with identical or very similar concepts but within different contexts. Michael Schneider shows how the case of decreasing returns to land came into economic thought from different perspectives. The story is in effect about two concepts, where one is appropriated as 'Ricardo's theory' into a classical mainstream and the other absorbed into the neoclassical mainstream. This provides an excellent illustration of pluralism disappearing when confronted by determined dominance of the mainstream perspective.

Ricardo, as noted by Keynes, was the first Cambridge economist (along with his disputant Malthus). The role of Ricardo's *Principles* in the development of economics is examined through the divergent interpretations of the 'Magnificent Seven' Cambridge economists, and one interloper, in Chapter 10 by Geoff Harcourt and Peter Kriesler. Only one of these interpretations became integrated into the neoclassical mainstream, while the others are what Kurz describes as 'submerged and forgotten'.

7 Reclaiming the 'standpoint of the old classical economists'[1]

Heinz D. Kurz

In the first half of the twentieth century there existed a fairly wide consensus as to the nature of the classical economists' contribution to political economy, especially to the theory of value and distribution (on which the present chapter focuses attention) and its relation to marginal economics, which had or was about to become the mainstream in large parts of the profession at around the turn of the century. This position was well expressed by Alfred Marshall in his *Principles of Economics* (1890). He portrayed Adam Smith, David Ricardo and other authors he counted as 'classical' as precursors of his own theory of demand and supply. The classicals, he argued, were possessed of a fairly well-developed theory of production and thus supply, but lacked an equally developed theory of demand. Classical theory, which had provided us with the concept of marginal productivity in the theory of intensive diminishing returns, could easily be reconciled with modern theory, based on the concept of marginal utility. A judicious combination of the two, as he, Marshall, had elaborated, was considered to do the job and bring to full fruition the seed the classical economists had sown. Marshall thus disagreed strongly with William Stanley Jevons, who in his *Theory of Political Economy* (1871) had contended that the classical analysis was entirely useless. Jevons deplored what he called 'the mazy and preposterous' assumptions underlying the doctrine of the 'Ricardian school' and advocated its abandonment rather than its extension and completion.

There were, of course, still scholars who thought neither that the legacy of the classicals was without any value nor that it could easily be absorbed into marginalist theory. They felt that the classicals had developed a theory of value and distribution that was fundamentally different from the marginalist theory and that the former's shortcomings did not reflect deficiencies beyond remedy, as Jevons and his followers had contended. Interestingly, amongst those keeping the classical flag flying in various countries there was almost unanimous agreement that a defining characteristic of the classical approach to the theory of value and distribution was the labour theory of value. Classical, especially Ricardo's, economics was almost identified with the labour theory of value.[2] It was then only natural to consider Marx's labour-value based reasoning as firmly belonging to the classical tradition, although Marx (1867) himself had given *Capital* the subtitle *A Critique of Political Economy*, meaning, of course, first and foremost the political economy of Smith, Ricardo, James Mill, Torrens, etc.

With the benefit of hindsight one might say that both supporters and critics of classical theory as well as those who saw a continuity between the 'innovators', that is the marginalists, and the classicals got it more or less wrong. In particular, the idea that the classical theory stood or fell with the labour theory of value, on the one hand, and the idea that in the marginalist theory there was no room for it whatsoever, on the other, cannot be sustained. Scrutiny shows that despite their insistence on the novelty of their approaches, authors such as Jevons, Eugen von Böhm-Bawerk and John Bates Clark were all convinced that relative prices in long-run equilibrium in conditions of free competition equal relative labour values. What they essentially disputed was the causality invoked by the classical authors, which leads from cost of production in terms of amounts of labour to normal prices. Instead they argued that the natural starting point is the needy individual and its estimation of goods. The choices of individuals are then said to bring about a situation in which relative marginal utilities with respect to the various goods are equal to relative prices, which in turn are equal to the relative quantities of labour needed directly and indirectly in their production.

When I referred to the benefit of hindsight, I had, of course, in mind the situation subsequent to the publication of volume I of *The Works and Correspondence of David Ricardo* (1951) and Piero Sraffa's 'Introduction' therein and even more so to his *Production of Commodities by Means of Commodities* (Sraffa 1960).[3] Sraffa's interpretation of the classical economists as advocates of a 'surplus' approach to the theory of value and distribution changed not only our perspective on authors such as Smith and Ricardo totally, it also attributed to this approach a genuine significance that is fundamentally different from the marginalist one. After Sraffa, the situation was completely different from what it was before. This does not mean that there were no other authors who had anticipated elements of Sraffa's interpretation of the classicals (see, for example, Ladislaus von Bortkiewicz) or who had insisted on striking differences between the marginalist and the classical approaches (see, for example, the young Joseph Schumpeter). It means that only Sraffa managed to revolutionize our perception of the genuine significance of the classical approach, of how it compares to the marginalist one and of how insights derived from the former imply a criticism of the latter.

In this chapter I seek to clarify what Sraffa meant by 'the standpoint of the old classical economists from Adam Smith to Ricardo', why it was abandoned prematurely – 'submerged and forgotten', as Sraffa (1960, p. vi) put it – and why Sraffa's reformulation of it allows one not only to bring back to economics the rich outlook on economic and social matters entertained by the classical economists but also to rid the profession of the fetters of mechanical marginalist thinking. First, the chapter summarizes Sraffa's interpretation of the classical theory of value and distribution, which revolves around the concept of 'social surplus'. Second, it turns to the marginalist criticism that the classical theory of value and distribution is under-determined. It is shown that the criticism cannot be sustained. Third, the chapter deals with Sraffa's characterization of the marginalist theory and the role counterfactuals play in it. Fourth, it continues the discussion and argues that the kind of counterfactuals the marginalist authors invoke leads them onto treacherous ground.

The classical theory of value and distribution

The upshot of Sraffa's view on the difference between the classical and the marginalist approaches to the theory of value and distribution is to be found in the preface of his 1960 book. There he emphasizes that the classical economists' investigation 'is concerned exclusively with such *properties of an economic system* as do not depend on changes in the scale of production or in the proportions of "factors"' (Sraffa 1960, p. v; emphasis added). Since Sraffa's contribution in the book is explicitly designed to reformulate and revive the classical approach, 'No changes in output and ... no changes in the proportions in which different means of production are used by an industry are considered so that no question arises as to the variation or constancy of returns' (1960, p. v). Hence what the classical economists were concerned with, according to Sraffa's interpretation, are the properties of a given *system of production*, characterized by: (i) given gross output levels of the various commodities and (ii) given methods of production to produce these outputs.

This does not mean that changes in the scale of production or in the pro-portions of 'factors' were never analysed by the classical economists or even that they were unable to analyse them, given the deficiencies and limited scope of the analytical method at their disposal. It only means that the classical economists first analysed a given system of production and only in a second step investigated changes of the system (in the theory of capital accumulation and economic growth, in the theory of rent and, more generally, in the treatment of the problem of the choice of technique). Investigating the properties of a given system of production characterized by a division of labour and inter-dependent markets in conditions of free competition involved, of course, the elaboration of a theory of value and income distribution, that is the sharing out of the product amongst the various social classes, workers, capitalists and landlords, as wages, profits and rent. The question was whether the givens (i) and (ii) are both necessary and sufficient to ascertain the range of numerical values that the wage rate(s), the rent(s) of land, the general rate of profits and relative prices can assume – i.e. the magnitudes in which the classical economists were interested.

Sraffa showed that the answer to this question is yes. More specifically (and setting aside the problem of scarce natural resources, such as land) he showed

that the givens (i) and (ii) suffice to determine the competitive rate of profits
and relative prices if real wages are given and form a part of the physical real
costs of production: they are thus reckoned as necessary inputs in production.
This case regards 'wages as consisting of the necessary subsistence of the
workers and thus entering the system on the same footing as the fuel for the
engine or the feed for the cattle' (1960, p. 9). In the simple case of single-
product industries and thus circulating capital only, and normalizing gross
output levels of the different industries as unity, it is well known that we can
write the price equations of classical derivation as:

$$p = (1+r)Ap \quad or \quad p = r(I - A) - 1Ap = rHp \tag{1}$$

where p is the m-dimensional price vector $(p_1, p_2, ..., p_m)^T$, r is the general
rate of profits, and A is the $m \times m$ matrix of material inputs per unit of
output. The vector of inputs needed by an industry to produce its gross
output of one unit is given by the respective row of the matrix, I is the identity
matrix and $H = (I - A)^{-1}A$ is the matrix of vertically integrated input coefficients.
Each coefficient of matrix A gives the amount of a particular commodity used
up as a means of production in the production of a particular commodity
plus the amount of that commodity needed in the support of the workers
producing it. We may split up matrix A into a matrix giving only the material
means of production, M, and a matrix giving the necessary subsistence of
workers, S. On the simplifying assumption of a uniform real wage per unit of
labour employed in production, given by vector $w = (w_1, w_2, ..., w_m)$, and
denoting the quantities of (direct) labour needed per unit of output in the
different industries by $l = (l_1, l_2, ..., l_m)^T$ we have:

$$A = M + S = M + lw^T$$

and therefore

$$p = (1+r)(M + lw^T)p \tag{2}$$

With M, l and w given, and taking the bundle of non-negative quantities of
the different commodities $d = (d_1, d_2, ..., d_m)$ as the standard of value or
numeraire, that is setting its value equal to unity

$$d^T p = 1 \tag{3}$$

the general rate of profits r and the prices in terms of the standard d can be
ascertained.[4] No other data or known variables and especially no demand
and supply functions are needed to determine the unknowns.

Being concerned with the mathematical properties of a given system of production implies, as Sraffa (1960, p. v) noted perceptively, 'that no question arises as to the variation or constancy of returns'. This implication of the classical approach has met with disbelief amongst several commentators, including, for example, Paul Samuelson (2000). Trained in the marginalist way of thinking, returns play an important role, and it was simply considered impossible to elaborate a theory of value and distribution without an explicit assumption about them. Hence they were on the lookout whether, in his book, Sraffa had not secretly smuggled in such a premise. These critics then felt they had discerned the assumption of constant returns in Sraffa's concepts of the Standard system and Standard commodity (Sraffa 1960, chapter IV). However, this is a misunderstanding. These concepts constitute only an *analytical Hilfskonstruktion*, a tool or auxiliary device that allows the economist to look at the actual system of production from a particular perspective: they do not imply any material imputation of properties to the system. Since no changes in the scale of production are considered, the question of returns simply does not arise. The only purpose of the Standard system and Standard commodity is to render the features of the system more easily understandable: 'Particular proportions, such as the Standard ones,' Sraffa emphasized, 'may give transparency to a system and render visible what was hidden, but they cannot alter its mathematical properties' (1960, p. 23).

Could Sraffa have assumed constant returns to scale and yet remained faithful to the classical authors? No. Constant returns cannot possibly be assumed in a world in which an increase in the scale of production typically entails a deepening division of labour and dynamically increasing returns, as Adam Smith had insisted. In such a world an increase in output would lead to a new system of production that would typically not obey constant returns if compared with the old one. Let me try to clarify the issue in the following way. Let $\mathbf{x}_0 = (x_{10}, x_{20}, \ldots, x_{m0})$ be the vector of m quantities of commodities produced in the initial situation 0, employing technique $(\mathbf{M}_0, \mathbf{l}_0)$. These quantities are those in 'effectual demand', to use Adam Smith's (1776, chapter 7) concept. With a uniform real wage $\mathbf{w}_0 = (w_{10}, w_{20}, \ldots, w_{m0})$, competitive conditions give rise to prices in terms of the standard of value $\mathbf{p}_0$ and r_0. Let $\mathbf{x}_1 = (x_{11}, x_{21}, \ldots, x_{n1})$ be the vector of n quantities of commodities produced and in effectual demand in the new situation 1, employing technique $(\mathbf{M}_1, \mathbf{l}_1)$. The new system of production will typically be dimensionally different from the old one ($m \neq n$): certain commodities produced in the original situation will no longer be produced in the new one, while other commodities will be produced in the new situation which were not yet known in the old one. According to Adam Smith, the dimension of the commodity space can be expected to increase as a consequence of the deeper division of labour, that is, more new types of commodities will typically enter the picture than old types will be eliminated ($n > m$). This may affect the commodity substance of the real wage. Renumbering commodities and assuming a uniform real wage $\mathbf{w}_1 = (w_{11}, w_{21}, \ldots, w_{n1})$ competitive conditions give rise to prices in terms of the standard of value $\mathbf{p}_1$ and r_1. This standard may be the old one, provided it has been defined in terms of commodities that are a part of both the old and the new system.

Now there is obviously no reason whatsoever to presume that the transition from situation 0 to situation 1 is subject to constant returns to scale throughout the economy. Each situation can, however, be analysed as regards its properties with respect to income distribution and relative prices in terms of the classical approach. When analysing capital accumulation and economic growth, which involve transition processes of the kind alluded to, the classical economists did, of course, have to specify precisely which technical changes they thought were accompanying changes in gross output levels.

The classical economists did not put forward a scarcity or marginal productivity theory of profits. While Ricardo (and others) had a relatively clear idea of intensive diminishing returns in agriculture, he did not generalize it from homogeneous land to other factors of production, including 'capital'. He was clear that capital, whether employed by a single firm, an entire industry or the economy as a whole, consists typically of a heterogeneous bundle of commodities and that two different capitals could only be said to be equal in size if their respective physical components were each aggregated by means of prices. In the context of a discussion of the dependence of relative prices on income distribution, given the system of production, Ricardo wrote to J.R. McCulloch on 21 August 1823:

> I would ask what means you have of ascertaining the equal value of capitals? ... These capitals are not the same in kind – what will employ one set of workmen, is not precisely the same as will employ another set, and if they themselves are produced in unequal times they are subject to the same fluctuations as other commodities. Till you have fixed the criterion by which we are to ascertain value, you can say nothing of equal capitals.
>
> (Works IX, pp. 359–60)

And in a critical assessment of Robert Torrens's contribution he argued:

> Col. Torrens Means that if two equal capitals be employed for the same time the commodities produced will be of equal value. No one can doubt the truth of this proposition, but I may ask Col. Torrens what he means by equal capitals? ... [I] ask him to compare the capital of the clothier consisting of buildings, steam engines, raw materials & c., with the capital of the sugar baker consisting of a very different set of commodities, and then to tell me what he means by equal capitals – he must answer that by equal capitals he means capitals of equal value....
>
> (Works IV: 393–94)

Hence it did not occur to Ricardo that the 'quantity of capital' (of a firm, an industry or the economy) could be ascertained 'independently of, and prior to, the determination of the prices of the products' and thus the rate of profits, to use Sraffa's formulation (1960, p. 9). How then could the relative scarcity of a factor called 'capital' determine the general rate of profits? Put differently, the quantity of capital in the economy could not be taken as a known magnitude. *It was an unknown to be determined simultaneously with, rather than independently of, the rate of profits and prices.* In the case of the system discussed in terms of equations (1)-(3), the capital, **C**, employed in the system as a whole would amount to:

$$\mathbf{C} = \mathbf{e}^T \mathbf{A} \mathbf{p} = \mathbf{e}^T \mathbf{A}(r \mathbf{H} \mathbf{p}) = r \mathbf{e}^T \mathbf{A} \mathbf{H} \mathbf{p} \tag{4}$$

where **e** is the unit vector, and depends on prices and thus income distribution.

With a choice of technique, which we have up until now left out of consideration, things become invariably more difficult (see Sraffa 1960, part III; Kurz and Salvadori 1995, chapter 5). Here it suffices to draw attention to the fact that at different real wages different methods of production will in all probability be chosen by cost-minimizing producers, involving not only different proportions of given types of means of production, but typically also some different types of such means. How then could the analysis ever start from a quantity of capital whose magnitude and material composition could be known independently of the distribution of income, that is, real wages (or, alternatively, the rate of profits)? The marginalist way of thinking (see 'Sraffa on marginalist thinking' below) was totally foreign to Ricardo.

In a mirror-inverted manner, the same can be said about the majority of economists after the classical approach to the theory of value and distribution had been 'submerged and forgotten since the advent of the "marginal method"' (Sraffa 1960, p. v): their attitude towards the classical economists was (and still is) characterized by an almost complete lack of comprehension.[5] This lack of comprehension is typically expressed in terms of two objections: (i) the classical theory takes as given what are unknowns, and (ii) it is 'underdetermined'. Before we have a closer look at these objections, the obvious fact ought to be stressed that any kind of theory is bound to start from certain data or givens – it cannot be otherwise. The questions therefore are: (a) Do the data or givens suffice to determine the unknowns? (b) Is the sought determination convincing or is it beset with grave difficulties? These questions ought to be answered with respect to both the classical theory of value and distribution and its marginalist alternative. This will be done in the following. It will then be seen that the two theories start from different data and determine partly different unknowns. It will also be seen that while the difficulties besetting the classical theory, as it was handed down by Ricardo, can be overcome, the difficulties besetting the long-period marginalist theory cannot.

One equation to determine two unknowns?

William Stanley Jevons objected in *The Theory of Political Economy* (1871) that the classical-Ricardian theory of value and distribution was unsatisfactory because it started from the premise of given output levels and a given real wage rate. However, he insisted, these magnitudes are to be treated as unknowns, not as data in the theory of value. Even if one was to admit that the wage rate can be taken as known (reflecting the outcome of some Malthusian population mechanism), 'the doctrine is radically fallacious; it involves the attempt *to determine two unknown quantities from one equation*' (Jevons 1871, p. 258; emphasis added): (the rate of) profits and the level of output. What was badly needed, Jevons opined, was a theory of 'demand' in order to close the system and render it determinate.

The same kind of incomprehension of the classical approach is encountered in §368 of Léon Walras's *Elements of Pure Economics* (1874). Echoing Jevons's objection, Walras writes:

> Let P be the aggregate price received for the products of an enterprise; let *S, I* and *F* be respectively the wages, interest charges and rent laid out by the entrepreneurs, in the course of production, to pay for the services of personal faculties, capital and land. Let us recall now that, according to the English School, the selling price of products is determined by their costs of production, that is to say, it is equal to the cost of the productive services employed. Thus we have the equation
>
> $$P = S + I + F,$$
>
> and *P* is determined for us. It remains only to determine *S, I* and *F.* Surely, if it is not the price of the products that determines the price of productive services, but the price of productive services that determines the price of the products, we must be told what determines the price of the services. That is precisely what the English economists try to do. To this end, they construct a theory of rent according to which rent is not included in the expenses of production, thus changing the above equation to
>
> $$P = S + I.$$
>
> Having done this, they determine *S* directly by the theory of wages. Then, finally, they tell us that 'the amount of interest or profit is the excess of the aggregate price received for the products over the wages expended on their production', in other words, that it is determined by the equation
>
> $$I = P - S.$$

It is clear now that the English economists are completely baffled by the problem of price determination; for it is impossible for I to determine P at the same time that P determines I. In the language of mathematics *one equation cannot be used to determine two unknowns.*

(Walras 1874, §368)

The same kind of criticism can be found also in more recent times (see e.g. Arrow 1972, 1991).

From what has been said in the section above, it follows that the Jevons-Walras-Arrow criticism misses the target. The kind of criticism was explicitly refuted as early as the end of the nineteenth century by Knut Wicksell and the Russian mathematical economist Vladimir K. Dmitriev (1974, p. 51). Wicksell insisted that 'the way in which Ricardo develops his argument ... is a model of strictly logical reasoning about a subject which seems, at first glance, to admit of so little precision'; and that 'Ricardo's theory of value is, one finds, developed with a high degree of consistency and strictness' (Wicksell 1893, pp. 34, 40). He added: 'Since, according to Ricardo, wages represent a magnitude fixed from the beginning, and since – as he later shows – the level of rent is also determined by independent causes, the cause of capital profit is already settled. *It is neither possible nor necessary to explain capital profit in other ways, if the other assumptions are sound*' (1893, pp. 36–37; emphasis added). The real issue is indeed, as Wicksell stressed, whether the assumptions of the classical approach to the theory of value and distribution are 'sound'.

This was denied by its critics who therefore felt the need to elaborate an alternative theory. Before we turn to this theory, the following observations are apposite. First, Wicksell is granting Ricardo perhaps too much, because in Ricardo's own judgement his theory of value was far from complete. In a letter to Malthus of 17 April 1815, Ricardo called his theory a 'simple doctrine', designed to 'account for all the phenomena in an easy, natural manner', sidestepping 'a labyrinth of difficulties' (Works VI, p. 214). However, he could not leave things at that and eventually had to take on the difficulties head on. As his two manuscript fragments on 'Absolute Value and Exchangeable Value' document (Works IV), he incessantly worked on the problems until his premature death in September 1823. He was clear that his theory of value exhibited a number of loose ends. In the *Principles* he had adopted the labour theory of value, because he lacked a more satisfactory theory. He comforted himself with the thought that the labour theory involved a reasonable approximation to the truth. The error involved in basing one's argument on it, he felt, would not distort the results by too much. However, he never entertained the substantivist-essentialist view of Marx, according to whom 'Labour is the substance, and the immanent measure of value' (Marx 1867, p. 503).

One might speculate how Ricardo would have received John Stuart Mill's exuberant opinion that 'Happily, there is nothing in the laws of value which remains for the present or any future writer to clear up; the theory of the subject is complete' (Mill 1848, p. 456). Alas, things were quite different. Here is not the place to enter into a discussion of the debates that took place after Ricardo's death about his theory of value.[6] It suffices to notice that a growing number of critics saw the labour theory of value as the Achilles heel of his entire construction. Marx's use of the labour theory of value as the basis for a theory of 'exploitation' amplified the opposition to Ricardo's theory in circles of economists.[7] A full-fledged theory, based on marginal utility, appeared only six years after Mill's premature claim: Hermann Heinrich Gossen's *Entwickelung* (Gossen 1854). While Gossen's work fell flatly on the ground, the contributions of Jevons, Carl Menger and Léon Walras at the beginning of the 1870s didn't and accelerated the speed at which the classical approach to the theory of value and distribution was 'submerged and forgotten'. But was the new theory superior to the old one it replaced? And was the old one, as its critics contended, wrong beyond remedy?

Sraffa on marginalist theory

Major differences between variants of the new kind of theory notwithstanding, all share the following characteristic features: the contemplation of what would happen if some magnitude of the system – the total amount of one of the 'factors of production' or the consumption of one of the goods by individuals – was to *change* is an integral part of the story told. Without such hypothetical changes the central concepts on which marginal theory rests – marginal productivity and marginal utility – simply would not be there. Hence taking up Sraffa's (1960, p. v) formulation quoted in the second section, we could say that marginalist theory, in opposition to classical theory, 'is concerned exclusively with such properties of an economic system as do depend on changes in the scale of production or in the proportions of "factors"'. This involves *counterfactual reasoning* right from the beginning of the marginalist approach to the theory of value and distribution. The question is, whether the counterfactuals invoked by the marginalist authors are harmless or not. The answer is that they are far from being harmless. The main problem is the marginalist concept of capital: as Ricardo noted, how can we say that two capitals are equal or unequal independently of knowing prices and thus income distribution? What is the meaning of a marginal increase in the quantity of capital *ceteris paribus* available to an economy?

As Sraffa's papers kept at Trinity College, Cambridge, show, he tackled these puzzles at an early time of his reconstructive work. In a document composed in the summer or autumn of 1929, he compared the sets of given quantities used in different theories in order to determine value. The quantities involved may be classed in three groups. The first group encompasses quantities, as Sraffa notes:

> which cannot possibly be measured, because they are not defined in terms of the method of measuring them, e.g. marg. utility and sacrifice. No

definition at all is given for measuring them in the case of several individuals: in the case of one individual, they are defined as being proportional to certain quantities, i.e. prices, but this is, as Cairnes says, 'merely giving a name to the unknown causes of price'. Such quantities must be *excluded altogether*. At the worst, they may be used as a fictitious device for solving problems, but must not appear either in the premises nor in the conclusions.

(D3/12/13: 2–5; Sraffa's emphasis)

About the second group, Sraffa wrote:

At the opposite extreme there are quantities which can be, and in fact are, statistically measured. These quantities have an objective, independent existence at every or some instants of the natural (i.e. not interfered with by the experimenter) process of production and distribution; they can therefore be measured physically, with the ordinary instruments for measuring number, weight, time, etc. Such are quantities of various materials used or produced, of lands, quantities of labour (?), lengths of periods (?), etc.[8] These are the *only* quantities which must enter as constants in economic theory, i.e. which can be assumed to be 'known' or 'given'.

(D3/12/13: 2–5; Sraffa's emphasis)

To this Sraffa added: 'The "extensive" theory of rent, and the labour theory of value only assume this kind of knowledge.' Notice also his reference to the 'experimenter' who, differently from the detached 'objective' observer, is said to interfere in the process, thereby changing its properties. This distinction plays a crucial role in his argument. Its meaning becomes clear when we turn to the third group:

Finally, there is the class of quantities, which form the basis of Marshall's theory (or, rather, of Pareto's), such as demand and supply curves, marginal productivities (i.e. rate of growth of total), indifference curves, etc. Here the constant quantities have no names – they are the parameters of curves. The several quantities represented by these curves do not exist at any one moment, nor during any period of the recurrent steady process of production or consumption. They are alternatives, only *one* of which can exist in any one position of equilibrium, all the others being thereby excluded (even the one does not really exist if there is no change, since it is the rate of growth of a quantity, i.e. marginal product: it can be inferred from price, but so can marginal utility, which … we have agreed does not exist). Therefore, they cannot be found by merely observing the process or state of things, and measuring the quantities seen. They can only be found out by means of *experiments* – and these quantities in effect are always defined in terms of such experiments (successive doses applied to land; alternatives offered to the consumer; etc.)

(D3/12/13: 2–5; Sraffa's emphasis)

He continued:

> These experiments cannot be carried out (and never have been, as a matter of fact) for various reasons: 1) the practical difficulties, 2) the lack of definition of the conditions to be required, which are always summed up in the absurd 'other things being equal['].
>
> But even apart from these difficulties, which might conceivably be overcome, there remains something about these experiment[s] which is very curious: they are generally regarded as acceptable, as if they were calculated to reproduce under controlled conditions, so as to be able to measure them, facts which actually happen 'in nature' all the time but cannot directly be pinned down by observation. But the experiments have an entirely different significance: they actually *produce* facts which would otherwise not happen at all; if the experimenter did not step in first to produce them, and then to ascertain them, they would remain in the state of 'unknown possibilities', which amounts to the deepest inexistence.
>
> (D3/12/13: 2–5; Sraffa's emphasis)

Marginalist theory, Sraffa concluded, does not simply analyse a given system as it is, it rather presupposes a hypothetical (infinitesimal) change of the system. It does not accept the facts as they are, but first produces new 'facts' without which it cannot proceed. Counterfactuals in marginalist theory are a *sine qua non* right from the beginning: without them the theory would be incomplete and could not determine the unknowns.

For reasons that will become clear in the following, Sraffa thought that marginalist theory had chosen a methodologically highly speculative and risky, if not unsound, starting point. Yet before we come to this, two closely interrelated observations are apposite. First, in analysing a *given* system of production, classical theory can do entirely without such hypothetical changes. This does not mean that it is unable to study such changes. It certainly can and does so in a second step of the analysis (see, especially, part III of Sraffa's book). As regards marginalist theory, things are different. The invocation of counterfactuals, the contemplation of change, is a constitutive element of the theory itself. As Sraffa (1960, p. v) stressed: 'The marginal approach requires attention to be focused on change, for without change either in the scale of an industry or in the "proportions of the factors of production" there can be neither marginal product nor marginal cost'.

This brings us directly to our second observation, which refers to Sraffa's insistence that, in assuming the 'standpoint ... of the old classical economists from Adam Smith to Ricardo' in determining competitive values, 'no question arises as to the variation or constancy of returns' (Sraffa 1960, p. v). Already at an early time, Sraffa was aware of the difficulty of communicating his unusual point of view to an audience raised in marginalist thinking. A document probably written in the second half of 1928 is significantly titled 'Why I Neglect Incr. and Dim. Returns in Equations' (D3/12/7: 85–87) and

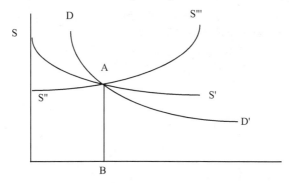

Figure 7.1 'Marshall's Curves'

provides a clear answer to the problem at hand. Sraffa's point of reference was, as so often, Marshall's analysis, as evident in Figure 7.1:

> The question is sure to be asked: what about variable returns?
> The reply is that these [i.e. Sraffa's] equations cannot possibly answer as to how or why prices change. They only explain why ... prices of different things bear to one another the proportions which they do. ...
> No system of equations, whether it considers variable returns or not, could tell this if time does not enter as a variable. Take a pair of Marshall's D. and S. curves. They tell that, given the conditions the price will be AB: to this effect it is quite indifferent whether the supply curve is SS′ or S″S‴. It may be thought that this is relevant to a case in which 'there is a change of demand'. ...
> The real point is that it is believed that Marshall's curves provide 'forces' which, in case the price falls below or above AB by 'chance', will restore it to AB.

This is in stark contrast with Sraffa's own theory:

> Now *I am not assuming any forces*: I simply say that, if the values will in reality be as given by the equations certain conditions will be satisfied: if not, they will not be satisfied. ...
> I am afraid it will be difficult to make it clear that *we are considering what has actually happened in the markets, and not what might have happened had things been different.* It will therefore be useful to explain that the reader may assume that constant returns prevail. Because, on the assumption of free competition, incr. and dim. costs are impossible.[9] Exclude internal economies and overhead costs. Then, through external economies, size of industry affects costs: but size of industry as a whole, not size of any one given industry. Therefore, transferring capital from one branch of industry to another does not affect external economies, and therefore not cost. Dim. ret.

in agriculture: land common to all agricultural products: if I transfer land and capital from wheat to potatoes there are no dim. ret. Finally if I transfer cap. from industry to agriculture, costs increase in industry because of less ext. econ., they increase in agriculture because of dim. ret.

The implication is close at hand:

> Therefore I cannot make a simple statement of the sort that is implied in a supply curve: 'if output increases 10%, cost falls 2%'. It cannot be unconditional: the result depends on *how* the demand increases, i.e. *whence* is the transference of cap. and lab. made. Entirely different results will take place if the increase in the demand for bicycles is due to a smaller demand of guns or of wine. And total demand, since it is simply the other name of total supply, is fixed.
>
> (D3/12/7: 85–87; Sraffa's emphasis)[10]

While this comment might be read as pertaining only to Marshallian partial equilibrium analysis, Sraffa's criticism was meant to go deeper and in fact aimed at the very foundation of long-period marginalist theory.[11] In this context, the role of counterfactuals in it was crucial. By construction, Sraffa maintained, the marginalist economist was bound to invoke counterfactuals, but, again by construction, the kind of counterfactuals were highly problematic.

Counterfactuals in marginalist theory

What was wrong with marginalism, as seen by Sraffa in the early phases of his work? The main criticism concerned its determination of value in terms of demand and supply functions or schedules. These functions, Sraffa insisted, have a 'fantastic character' and reflect 'inexistent possibilities'. He added: 'after all, the only explanation (cause) of a thing being what it is, is that, "if it were different, absurd consequences would follow". The mistake is to assume *direct* knowledge of these (inexistent) consequences' (D3/12/13: 4).

Inexistent consequences concern both the demand and the supply side. As regards the former, Sraffa in December 1927 counterposed the classical and the marginalist theory in terms of Francis Bacon's appeal to 'efficient causes' and 'final causes' (a distinction also used by Whitehead 1926, p. 11). Sraffa argued:

> 'Efficient causes' are facts of the past that act on the present: 'final causes' are facts of the future that act on the present. The existence of the latter is at best dubious and they are better called 'illusions'. The classical P.E. dealt only with the first sort of causes, i.e. of 'material things' that have existed in the past. Modern economics deals with the second class, i.e. hopes for the future, such as utility, abstinence, disutility, etc.; these things, it must be noticed, refer only to the foresight of *future acts*. The economists have noticed this point; and have tackled the question

whether it is the utility I *shall actually get in the future* through consumption that determines my demand price, or whether it is that very
different thing – the utility *I now imagine* that I shall get in the future.
(D3/12/10: 61(1–2))

Sraffa did not deny that expectations may and generally will have an influence
on the facts (as superstitions, for example, also do) and therefore 'have to be
taken into account as such by the economist. But the recognition of the fact
that the opinions of the actors have an influence must not lead the economist
to believe that they are the real facts themselves, or much less their objective
explanation, as Marshall does' (D3/12/9: 32).[12]

While Sraffa credited Vilfredo Pareto with having improved upon received
utility theory by introducing indifference curves and refining the general
equilibrium method, the main flaws of the theory had been left untouched.
The 'forces' the theory contemplated as bringing about a tendency toward
equilibrium, and which are reflected in the demand function, were essentially
the traditional ones. These have no objective contents: nothing corresponds to
them in the real world. It did not mean that needs and wants do not matter. It
rather meant that the *homo economicus* marginalist perspective on human
nature and society could not be sustained. In this regard, Sraffa agreed with
ethnologists and anthropologists like Bronislaw Malinowski and Raymond
William Firth. Some of the difficulties besetting the theory had recently also
surfaced in the writings of the more attentive marginalist authors themselves.
With reference to the works of Alfred Marshall, Henry Cunynghame, Francis
Y. Edgeworth and Arthur C. Pigou, Sraffa pointed out that the allowance for
external economies had undermined the strictly individualistic point of view.
Hence, general equilibrium theory was not only confronted with the phenomenon of great complexity, as Pareto had maintained; it was confronted with a
kind of complexity that could not, as a matter of principle, be captured in
terms of the individualistic approach. As to the problem of externalities and
demand, Sraffa stressed in a preparatory note for his lectures on 'Advanced
Value Theory' composed in the summer of 1927 'that it is not sufficient to
make utility of one commodity [a] function of all others consumed by [the]
"individual"'; it would have also to be made dependent on the consumption
of the 'community' as a whole. Sraffa drew the following parallel: 'It would be
as if in astronomy we said the movement of each star depends upon all the
others, *but we have not the faintest idea of the shape of the functions!*' (D3/12/3: 63;
emphasis added).

While in 1927 and 1928 Sraffa at first focused attention on the subjective
side of the marginalist doctrine, he almost in parallel began to scrutinize its
objective or production side and thus marginal productivity theory.[13] Sraffa
endorsed Bortkiewicz's principle that methods of production (and consumption) that are not actually used can have no effect on the rate of profits and
relative prices. Marginalist theory violates this principle. Sraffa was especially
keen to understand under what conditions the concept of 'marginal product of

capital' and that of a 'given quantity of capital' were well defined. The result was that only in the case of a one-commodity world – with 'corn' (wheat) as the only capital-alias-consumption good – do the two concepts have a clear and unambiguous meaning. As early as summer 1929 in a manuscript titled 'Normal Profits, Marginal Distribution, Self-identity' Sraffa insisted:

> In order to have a marginal theory of distribution (or, in fact, any such theory) *we must have a physical measure of the quantity of each factor, independent (i.e. that can be carried out without knowing ...) of its share in distribution.* – This physical measure implies that each factor is perfectly homogeneous with itself, i.e. all its composing particles are identical to one another ...
>
> (D3/12/13: 17(5); emphasis added)

However, in a world with heterogeneous capital goods, what does it mean to increase the quantity of capital in the system as a whole? A main difficulty of the theory, as seen by Sraffa, consisted in that it attempted to *measure* something that was not well defined. If the same methods of production are being used and if the proportions of outputs do not change and if there are constant returns to scale, then an increase in the amount of capital will be associated with a parallel increase in the amount of labour. But this does not lead to the concept of marginal productivity of capital. If, on the other hand, the amount of capital is supposed to be increased for a given employment of labour, what can possibly be meant by this? In a manuscript composed in summer 1929 and titled 'Puzzles on the Theory of Rent' Sraffa stressed: 'Great difficulties arise ... when there is, not only "corn", but a number of different products. *Most economists carefully keep clear of this problem, they simply ignore it.*' Marshall, Sraffa went on, while aware that both product and capital input ought to be measured in physical terms, decided to measure them in *value*. Yet what is the meaning of a sum of value, and of an infinitesimal change of such a sum? Values are the unknowns of the problem under consideration, but in this context they are taken to be known. The lack of self-identity of 'capital' is stressed by Sraffa in a document written in summer 1929. He expounded 'that "adding one dose to the 100 doses already employed" means "employing 101 doses where 100 were employed before".' This however does *not* mean, he insisted, '"employing *the same* 100 doses plus a new one". In other words, "after the increment the application is equal to the old one plus one dose", provided equality means *equal quantity* [in terms of value], *not identity* of objects or of ways in which the objects are used' (D3/12/13: 23(4–5); first emphasis added). So what do the 101 as opposed to the 100 doses in terms of value stand for physically? They may stand for entirely different types of commodities or different proportions of the same types of commodities.

Interestingly, even nowadays it can safely be said that 'most economists carefully keep clear of the problem mentioned, they simply ignore it'.

Sraffa's attempts to make sense of marginalist theory invariably led to the result that its concept of capital cannot be sustained. The kind of counterfactuals the marginalist theory invoked – how would an infinitesimal increase in the quantity of capital *ceteris paribus* affect the 'marginal product of capital' and thus the general rate of profits? – could not be rendered meaningful except in the uninteresting case of a one-commodity economy. Since the invocation of such counterfactuals was an integral part of the analytical core of the theory, the theory was difficult to sustain.

The marginalist theory under consideration was a long-period theory, revolving around the concept of a uniform rate of interest (or profits), just like the reformulated classical theory. Therefore it had to satisfy Sraffa's 1960 equations. It was thus natural for Sraffa to ask whether within the framework of his equations fundamental propositions of the marginalist theory could be shown to be valid by reversing 'cause' and 'effect' as contemplated by marginalist theory. Since it made no sense to invoke infinitesimal changes in the quantity of capital, what about invoking changes in the rate of interest and studying its logical implications? A change in the rate of interest was no doubt meaningful. Did a 'rise' ('fall') of the interest rate of necessity imply a fall (rise) of the amount (value) of capital per unit of labour employed, as the marginalist doctrine contended? Sraffa started to study this problem in the late 1920s, and he then took it up again in the early 1940s. In a working note dated 10 October 1943, Sraffa asked: did a given quantity of capital determine the rate of interest or did a given level of the rate of interest, by deciding the choice of technique by means of which given levels of output are produced, determine the wage rate, relative prices and the value of the capital employed in each industry and in the economy as a whole?

> Put it like this: We cannot say that r [the rate of interest] is 5 % ... because ... these methods are adopted, and so much capital is used. But we can say that these methods were adopted ... because ... r was 5 %.
>
> The fact is that however much we examine the method of production we cannot discover in it any circumstance that compels a rate of 5 % rather than any other. ... It is only when we consider the *alternative possible methods of production*, that we discover a connection between the particular method and the rate of 5 %. And the connection is, that at that rate that method is cheaper than any other. But does the reverse connection hold too? Is it true that, 'given the quantity of capital', a certain method will be adopted and a certain rate be verified?
>
> (D3/12/35: (1–2); emphasis added)

The answer to the last question was no. More generally, as early as in a short note written in November 1927 Sraffa had insisted that the 'fundamental fallacies in Marshall' were the 'principle of substitution' and the 'principle of continuity' (D3/12/11: 11). In the following years of the first period of his constructive work (1927–1930) and then with a much improved understanding of both the classical and the marginalist analytical structures in the second (1942–1946) and third periods (1955–1959) the meaning of this remark became ever more clear. Here a few observations must suffice.

Sraffa established that depending on the set of actually available methods of production from which cost-minimizing producers can choose, a lower (higher) rate of interest may correspond either to a lower (higher), or a higher (lower), or in the extreme even a constant capital-to-labour ratio of the economic system. Hence the marginalist doctrine which postulated an inverse relationship between the capital-to-labour ratio and the rate of interest could not generally be sustained. This destroyed what Sraffa called the 'monotonic prejudice' of the doctrine (see D1/91: 14, 27) according to which methods of production could generally be ordered with regard to their 'degrees of mechanisation' or capital-to-labour ratios. Sraffa had criticized this view as early as in the first period of his work, and then, in the early 1940s, had stressed that 'there is no assurance that, owing simply to a change in the rate of interest, the order is not reversed' (D3/12/15: 10). This undermined the received marginalist view as to the direction of *substitution* between the factors of production, capital and labour, as income distribution changed.

It also undermined the *continuity* assumption endorsed by Alfred Marshall, Eugen von Böhm-Bawerk, John Bates Clark and others. As Sraffa (1960, p. 76) stressed, output (or the rate of interest) 'may increase continuously, although the methods of production are changed spasmodically'. As a consequence, input proportions may change in an 'erratic' way. This has negative implications for the demand and supply functions postulated by marginalist theories of income distribution. These theories, Sraffa emphasized in a document dated 27 December 1942, 'assume knowledge of possibilities – i.e. of what would happen in certain hypothetical circumstances, knowledge not of points but of curves (Wicksteed Alphabet p. 55 they "*really exist*").[14] These italics are the strongest, most convincing evidence produced to date that the boxes are not empty' (D3/12/29: 25).[15]

Notes

1 I am grateful to an anonymous referee for useful comments on an earlier version of this chapter. Let me also add a personal remark about a good friend. I have known John King for many years, first from the literature and then personally. My wife and I are privileged by the fact that both John and his wife Mary love the Austrian mountains and the city of Graz. They have been recurrent visitors to our hometown and John has been a recurrent visiting professor to our department. He participated in the biannual Graz Schumpeter Summer School and gave papers in our research seminar. Conversations with him were always very fruitful to me. I have learned a great deal from him and admire his erudition, meticulousness and sober judgement. He has always been an independent thinker and resisted fads and fashions in the profession. I hope that he and Mary will visit us many more times. *Ad multos annos!*

2 For evidence with respect to the German-speaking world, see Kurz (1995).

3 On Maurice Dobb's role in the writing of Sraffa's introduction to volume I of the *Principles*, see Pollitt (1988).
4 For details, see Kurz and Salvadori (1995, chapter 4).
5 There are a few notable exceptions to the rule, especially Knut Wicksell. See the following section.
6 For a comprehensive discussion of these debates, see King (2013).
7 The irony is that many of the marginalist critics of Ricardo, including Jevons, Eugen von Böhm-Bawerk and John Bates Clark, maintained that in a long-run equilibrium relative prices are proportional to relative labour quantities needed in the production of the various commodities. Ricardo's 'law of cost', as Böhm-Bawerk called it, thus applied. However, these authors argued that Ricardo had (wrongly) started from cost of production, whereas the right starting point would have been (marginal) utility. Interestingly, while Ricardo acknowledged an impact of the rate of profits (or interest) on relative prices (through compound interest), the critics didn't. Böhm-Bawerk had famously developed his argument in terms of simple interest, which contradicts the assumption of free competition.
8 At the time, Sraffa still vacillated as to whether the magnitudes with a question mark in brackets could in fact be treated as constants. See on this Kurz and Salvadori (2005, section 3).
9 This was the conclusion at which Sraffa (1925) had arrived when scrutinizing Marshall's theory of particular equilibrium.
10 Elsewhere in his papers, Sraffa stressed that a given system of equations implies a given division of labour which in turn involves certain gains of specialization. See, for example, his reference to differential efficiencies a producer would have when working in different lines of production (D3/12/11: 89). Changes in output levels would lead to a new division of labour which in general would be incompatible with constant returns to scale.
11 Intertemporal general equilibrium theory had not yet seen the light of the day at the time under consideration. Marshall's analysis dominated the discipline, with Vilfredo Pareto's general equilibrium theory only slowly gaining ground. However, intertemporal general equilibrium theory would not have been exempt from Sraffa's criticism in that it also pretends to be possessed of a direct knowledge of all 'possible worlds'.
12 For Sraffa's discussion of expectations in the early period of his constructive work, see especially D3/12/9: 86(1–3).
13 This side had already been the object of Sraffa (1925, 1926), but there Sraffa, apart from a few remarks, set aside the problem of the circular flow of production.
14 The reference is to Wicksteed (1888, p. 55): 'Thus the curve *really exists*, whether he [the theorist] is able to trace it or not.'
15 Sraffa read Schrödinger's book *Science and Humanism* (1952) and annotated the latter's attack on the '*postulate of continuity of description*' (Schrödinger 1952, p. 26). In the margin of the following passage, Sraffa put a straight line: 'This habit of thought we must dismiss. *We must not admit the possibility of continuous observation.* Observations are to be regarded as discrete, discontinuous events. Between them there are gaps which we cannot fill in. There are cases where we should upset everything if we admitted the possibility of continuous observation' (1952, p. 29).

References

Arrow, K.J. (1972), Kosten und nachfragetheoretische Aspekte der Preis(bestimmungs) theorie, *Zeitschrift für Nationalökonomie* 32, pp. 47–57.
Arrow, K.J. (1991), Ricardo's Work as Viewed by Later Economists, *Journal of the History of Economic Thought* 13(1), pp. 70–77.

Dmitriev, V.K. (1974), *Economic Essays on Value, Competition and Utility*, edited by D.M. Nuti, Cambridge, UK: Cambridge University Press (translation by D. Fry of a collection of essays published 1904 in Russian).

Gossen, H.H. (1854), *Entwickelung der Gesetze des menschlichen Verkehrs, und der daraus fließenden Regeln für menschliches Handeln*. Berlin: Prager (1927).

Jevons, W.S. (1871), *The Theory of Political Economy*, London: Macmillan and Co.

King, J.E. (2013), David Ricardo, in *Great Thinkers in Economics*. Basingstoke, UK: Palgrave Macmillan.

Kurz, H.D. (1995), Marginalism, Classicism and Socialism in German-speaking Countries: 1871–1914, in I. Steedman (ed.), *Socialism and Marginalism in Economics: 1870–1930*. London and New York: Routledge, pp. 7–86.

Kurz, H.D. and Salvadori, N. (1995), *Theory of Production: A Long-period Analysis*. Cambridge, Melbourne and New York: Cambridge University Press.

Kurz, H.D. and Salvadori, N. (2005), Representing the Production and Circulation of Commodities in Material Terms: On Sraffa's Objectivism, *Review of Political Economy* 17(3), pp. 69–97, reprinted in Kurz, H.D., Pasinetti, L.L. and Salvadori, N. (eds.) (2008), *Piero Sraffa: The Man and the Scholar – Exploring his Unpublished Papers*. London and New York: Routledge, pp. 249–277.

Marshall, A. (1890), *Principles of Economics*, London: Macmillan.

Marx, K. (1867), *Capital*, volume I. London: Lawrence and Wishart (1954).

Mill, J.S. (1848), *The Principles of Political Economy with Some of Their Applications to Social Philosophy*, in *The Collected Works of John Stuart Mill*, J.M. Robson (ed.). Toronto: University of Toronto Press, London and New York: Routledge and Kegan Paul (1965).

Pollitt, B. (1988), The Collaboration of Maurice Dobb in Sraffa's Edition of Ricardo. *Cambridge Journal of Economics* 12(1), pp. 55–65.

Ricardo, D. (1951–73), *The Works and Correspondence of David Ricardo*, edited by Piero Sraffa with the collaboration of M.H. Dobb, 11 volumes. Cambridge, UK: Cambridge University Press. In the text referred to as: Works, volume number, page number.

Samuelson, P.A. (2000), Sraffa's Hits and Misses, in H.D. Kurz (ed.), *Critical Essays on Piero Sraffa's Legacy in Economics*. Cambridge, UK: Cambridge University Press, pp. 111–150.

Schrödinger, E. (1952), *Science and Humanism: Physics in Our Time*. Cambridge, UK: Cambridge University Press.

Smith, A. (1776), *An Inquiry into the Nature and Causes of the Wealth of Nations*, in *The Glasgow Edition of the Works and Correspondence of Adam Smith*, two volumes, edited by R.H. Campbell and A.S. Skinner,Oxford: Oxford University Press (1976).

Sraffa, P. (1925), Sulle Relazioni fra Costo e Quantità Prodotta, *Annali di Economia* 2, pp. 277–328.

Sraffa, P. (1926), The Laws of Returns under Competitive Conditions, *Economic Journal* 36(144), pp. 535–550, also in H.D. Kurz and Salvadori, N. (eds.) (2003), *The Elgar Companion to Piero Sraffa*, Cheltenham, UK and Northampton, MA, USA: Edward Elgar.

Sraffa, P. (1960), *Production of Commodities by Means of Commodities: Prelude to a Critique of Economic Theory*. Cambridge, UK: Cambridge University Press.

Walras, L. (1874), *Elements of Pure Economics*, English translation by W. Jaffé of the definitive edition of *Eléments d'economie politique pure*, Lausanne. London: Allen and Unwin (1954).

Whitehead, A.N. (1926), *Science and the Modern World*, Lowell Lectures 1925. Cambridge, UK: Cambridge University Press.

Wicksell, K. (1893), *Value, Capital and Rent*, English translation of *Über Wert, Kapital und Rente*. London: Allen and Unwin (1954).

Wicksteed, P.H. (1888), *The Alphabet of Economic Science* part I, *Elements of the Theory of Value or Worth*. London: Macmillan.

8 Problems in Marx's theory of the declining profit rate

James Doughney[1]

The 'Law of the Tendential Fall in the Rate of Profit' (Marx 1894, *Capital*, volume III, chapter 13) was pivotal for Karl Marx's political economy. He formulated it in the 1857–59 *Grundrisse* notebooks that preceded *A Contribution to the Critique of Political Economy* (Marx 1859), regarding it as 'in every respect the most important law of modern political economy' (Marx 1858–59, *Grundrisse*, pp. 747–78). The 23 notebooks of 1861–63 known as the *Theories of Surplus-Value* (Marx 1861–63*TSV*), volumes I–IV, rehearse formulations that reappear in the unfinished manuscript of *Capital*, volume III, written during 1864 and 1865, and in the final version of *Capital*, volume I (Marx 1867, completed between 1865 and 1867. Marx reiterated in chapter 13 (*Capital*, volume III, p. 319) that 'not one of the previous writers on economics succeeded in discovering [the law/tendency] … These economists perceived the phenomenon, but tortured themselves with their contradictory attempts to explain it.'

There is no evidence that he changed his opinion about the importance of the law/tendency or the significance of his own explanation. Indeed, it occupied an important position in his theory of the demise of capitalism (see e.g. *Capital*, volume III, chapter 15; Preface to the *Contribution; Grundrisse*, e.g. pp. 749–50, 763; cf. Dobb 1973, pp. 157–58). Moreover, a letter from Marx to Frederick Engels, written after he had rewritten and published the first volume of *Capital*, emphasized that '*The tendency of the rate of profit to fall as society progresses* … follows from what has been said in Book I [*Capital*, volume I] on the *changes in the composition of capital following the development of the social productive tendencies*. This is one of the greatest triumphs over the pons asinorum of all previous economics' (Marx and Engels 1844–95, p. 194, 11 July 1868; original emphasis).

This chapter reinvestigates the explanation that Marx offered. It does not consider the voluminous secondary literature but rather tests Marx's original concepts and formulations in their own terms. This involves careful scrutiny of Marx's use of abstraction. The chapter exposes flaws in Marx's explanation and demonstrates that the necessary corrections involve Kaleckian conclusions.

The profit rate and its constituent concepts

Marx's essential proposition was that the rate of profit would fall over time because productivity-enhancing change would increase the relative value of the stock of constant capital (dead labour) against that required for variable capital (living labour). The profit rate would fall because the growing value of this stock of machines, raw materials, buildings and the like would tend to outweigh the flow of profits that living labour could generate over a given interval of time.

To illustrate Marx's argument clearly, this preliminary section examines his formulation of the profit rate p'. Marx concentrated his concepts – surplus value s, constant capital c, variable capital v, rate of surplus value or exploitation $s' = s/v$, value composition of capital $c' = c/v$, technical composition and organic composition of capital[2] and so on – in the following familiar expressions:

$$p' = \frac{s}{c+v} = \frac{\left(\frac{s}{v}\right)}{\left(\frac{c}{v}\right)+1} = \frac{s'}{c'+1} \tag{8.1}$$

However, these are 'single-turnover' not annual expressions, as chapter 4 of *Capital*, volume III, 'The Effect of the Turnover on the Rate of Profit', explains. Turnover is a time variable. It represents the amount of time it takes to replenish through revenues the stock of money capital a firm holds to pay wages (i.e. variable capital *advanced* or the v in the denominator of Equation 8.1).

Two interesting things about chapter 4 are that Marx contributed only the title and that readers largely ignore it. Engels wrote both chapter 4 and similar corrective parenthetical paragraphs in chapter 13. He explained in his 1894 Preface to the third volume that, because 'the effect of the turnover on the profit rate' was of no less than 'decisive importance', he 'elaborated it' himself. His point was that it was 'apparent that the formula given for the profit rate in chapter 3 [and chapters 13–15] needed a certain modification if it was to have general validity' (*Capital*, volume III, p. 94). Engels's modifications of Equation 8.1 begin with the following definitions, which concern the role of productivity in determining the rate of exploitation:

> The mass of surplus-value appropriated in the course of a year is … equal to the mass of surplus-value appropriated in one turnover period of the *variable* capital, multiplied by the number of such turnovers in a year. If we call the surplus-value or profit annually appropriated S, the surplus value appropriated in one turnover period s, and the number of turnovers made by the variable capital volume in a year n, then $S = sn$ and the annual rate of surplus-value $S' = s'n$, as already set out in Volume 2, Chapter 16, 1.
>
> (*Capital*, volume III, p. 167; original emphasis)[3]

Before considering Engels's reformulation, an additional complication deserves attention. It is that Marx conjoined the single-turnover profit-rate formulation with the 'one-year assumption'. This simplifying contrivance holds that constant capital advanced turns over (i.e. fully depreciates or, in the case of raw materials, exhausts) in exactly one turnover of variable capital advanced, and variable capital turns over (i.e. exhausts itself as wages paid) exactly once a year. This confounded the necessary conceptual distinctions between stocks of constant and variable capital advanced and flows of value added. Therefore, it will help to make the necessary distinctions now.

For Marx, the 'Law of the Tendential Fall in the Rate of Profit' expressed the effects of productivity-enhancing, labour-saving technical change (*Capital*, volume III, p. 319). Productivity here means labour productivity only, output of commodities per unit of labour time. It is thus equivalent by definition to the inverse of average commodity value L/Y, in which, again by definition $L = S + V$, with all terms measured in flows of annual labour time. Now, an increase in productivity Y/L, being the capability to produce the same quantity of commodities in less time or more commodities in the same time, is likewise equivalent to a decrease in average commodity value (i.e. socially necessary labour time) or a devaluation of each of those commodities.

The value of labour power by definition is the labour time socially necessary to reproduce and sustain labour power. This is the labour time required to produce the annual wage-goods bundle V in those industries that *Capital* refers to as Department II. Marx also calls this necessary labour. To state the obvious, the time that workers spend producing capital goods in the industries comprising Department I[4] is time they do not spend producing the goods of their own subsistence (wage goods). The labour time devoted to Department I is thus social surplus labour.

Now, if productivity increases in the wage-goods industries less labour time will be required to produce a given output. The value of labour power V will fall along with the fall in the average value of the commodity use-values comprising workers' subsistence bundle.[5] Meanwhile, if productivity does not increase simultaneously in Department I, the value of capital goods will not fall because the same labour time will be required. In proportionate terms, surplus value will have increased against both total value and the value of labour power (an increase in relative surplus value), which is to say that surplus labour has increased in proportion to necessary labour or that the social rate of exploitation has increased. The annual ratio $S/V = ns/nv$ captures this dynamic. It is clearly equal by definition to the rate of exploitation or the rate of surplus value s' expressed in single-turnover form. However, there is a proviso: as the brief discussion above has demonstrated, the rate of surplus value $s' = s/v = S/V$ makes sense only as a ratio of two time-consistent flows.

Engels made an important additional point about variable capital advanced. Capitalists, he explained, would be unaware of the quantum of variable capital (i.e. of cash) they keep on hand, in the 'till'[6] or 'cash-box'[7], specifically to pay wages when they fall due (*Capital*, volume III, p. 167).

Rather, this quantity is part of working capital, 'cash-on-hand' for circulating capital expenses in general. Using an example from his business experience in Manchester, an example that Marx had also used in chapter 9 of *Capital*, volume I (pp. 327–29), Engels illustrated that variable capital advanced represented a mere 2.5 per cent of total capital advanced and that it turned over about 8.5 times per annum. That is, the business kept on hand about six weeks' wages as risk against uneven cash flows across a year (i.e. 52/8.5). Had this business had a greater appetite for risk against uneven revenue flows, the requirement for *v* advanced could well have been less. What Engels had demonstrated in effect was that turnover time is an artefact with little or no causal bearing on the rate of profit. In itself it is unimportant, a point that Marx seemed also to acknowledge (*Capital*, volume III, p. 251).

What was important, however, was the 'decisive' point that the 'rate of profit is calculated upon the total capital applied ... for a specific period of time, in practice a year. The proportion between the surplus value or profit made and realized in a year and the total capital [advanced], calculated as a percentage, is the rate of profit.' The single-turnover rate, therefore, 'is not necessarily identical with the rate of profit ... it is only if this capital turns over precisely once in the year that the two things coincide' (*Capital*, volume III, p. 334; see also p. 142). This then *is* the formula for the profit rate:

$$p' = \frac{sn}{c+v} = \frac{\left(\frac{s}{v}\right)n}{\left(\frac{c}{v}\right)+1} = \frac{s'n}{c'+1} = \frac{S'}{c'+1} \tag{8.2}$$

This formulation has 'general validity'. It helps to disentangle stocks from flows and, together with Engels's numerical examples, puts the constituent dimensions of the profit rate into better perspective (*Capital*, volume III, p. 168). The following example is similar but numerically simpler:

$$p' = \frac{100s \times 10n}{9,900c + 100v} = \frac{\left(\frac{100s}{100v}\right)10n}{\left(\frac{9,900c}{100v}\right)+1} = \frac{1s' \times 10n}{99c'+1} = \frac{10S'}{100(c'+1)} = 10\% \tag{8.3}$$

Note Marx's convention of presenting the symbol next to the number for clarity. It does not signify multiplication. Note also that the rate of surplus value $s' = 1.0$ is the same in annual flows $S/V = 1.000/1,000$, 'turnover period' flows $s/v = 100/100$, weekly flows = 19.2/19.2, daily flows 2.74/2.74 or flows over 10 years 10,000/10,000 = 1.0.

Abstraction and the formulations of chapter 13

Another preliminary section will be useful to clarify Marx's argument further. It examines the methodological question of abstraction and its application in chapter 13.[8] How do the abstractions and assumptions Marx employs affect the validity of his formulation of the law/tendency? One reason for asking is that Marx clearly knew that the only profit rate is one that takes a flow over a given interval against a given stock of capital advanced (e.g. *Capital*, volume III, pp. 243, 250, 478; *Grundrisse*, pp. 662, 718, 761; *Correspondence*, p. 192). His awkward imposition of the one-year assumption on the single-turnover formulation of the profit rate reflected this knowledge. So, is there something deeper in Marx's method that the preceding section (and Engels) missed?

Capital exhibits two kinds of abstraction. The first is generalizing, universalizing or defining (predicating) abstraction. Marx employs it when, for example, he says that rent, profit of enterprise and interest are surplus value by any other name. They are forms of the more abstract form surplus value, more concrete determinations or specifications of the determination surplus value. The essence of rent, interest and profit of enterprise is surplus value is another way of saying that the latter expresses, includes and takes in the former.

The second kind of abstraction is exclusive rather than inclusive. Its aim is to isolate more or less independent determinations and, possibly, the causal forces behind them, by way of isolation or closure. It is to take a one-sided approach or perspective in order to illuminate an aspect of a many-sided, more concrete problem. The experimental sciences achieve closure in the laboratory. In the open world of political economy, Marx sought to replace the power of experimentation with the power of abstraction, including that of the isolating, ceteris paribus kind (see *Capital*, volume I, Preface to the first edition). Then, having undertaken this exercise, the social scientist should bring the various one-sided determinations back together: reconstituting the diverse concrete by way of thought. The second kind of abstraction is at work in both investigation (examples being the *Grundrisse* and *TSV*) and, in reconstituting the concrete, presenting and explaining the results of the investigation (as in *Capital*, volume I).

Eventually, the first kind of abstraction should absorb the second. The conceptual results of the investigation, 'the intrinsic connection existing between economic categories' (*TSV*, volume II, p. 165), ideally should yield real essences by laying bare or revealing (*Capital*, volume I, Preface to the first edition, p. 92) 'the obscure structure ... the inner coherence, the actual physiology of bourgeois society' (*TSV*, volume II, pp. 165–66). As Engels put it in a letter to Karl Kautsky in 1884, 'Marx summarizes the actual content common to things and relations and reduces it to its general logical expression. His abstraction therefore only reflects, in rational form, the content already existing in the things' (*Correspondence*, p. 357).

The conceptual work achieved by both kinds of abstraction should expose the dominant real underlying causal powers that operate generally or universally. This is so even if counteracting forces confound the manner in which such causes operate, such that their effects manifest themselves in the way of tendencies. This indeed was how Marx conceived the 'Law of the Tendential Fall in the Rate of Profit'. Marx stressed two counteracting forces in chapter 14 of *Capital*, volume III. Both, like the increasing composition of capital itself, occur because of labour-saving or capital-intensive accumulation. The two counteracting forces are the more intense exploitation of labour (rise in the rate of surplus value) and the cheapening of the elements of constant capital.

What is the best way to describe the single-turnover one-year assumption in the light of this brief account?[9] Clearly, it does not fall under the first, generalizing, kind of abstraction. Engels made that point. Second, it is not a one-sided abstraction: a partly general or incomplete representation that might help later in reconstituting the concrete in thought. An example of the latter might be to consider productivity growth in Department II abstractly from change in Department I, as did the preceding section. Instead, the one-year assumption in single-turnover form manufactures then holds constant (i.e. imposes) a peculiar and unrealistic concrete possibility (all capital advanced turning over in exactly one year). This might be acceptable as an expositional device, perhaps, but it is unacceptable if it conceals what it is that one hopes to lay bare.

An altogether different and more subversive problem arises from Marx's moves in dealing with dominant and counteracting forces in chapter 13. His first move was to abstract from changes in the value of constant capital, explicitly setting aside the counteracting influence of cheapening of the elements of constant capital for chapter 14. To illustrate, Equation 8.4 abbreviates Equation 8.3 and includes only an increase in the magnitude constant capital by 11.22 per cent, from 9,900.0 to 11,011.1.[10] The technical composition rises and, therefore, so does the organic composition, which is equal in this case to the value composition $c' = c/v$.[11] *Ipso facto*, the profit rate falls. (Changes from preceding equations will be in bold.)

$$p' = \frac{1,000sn}{\mathbf{11,011.1}c + 100v} = \frac{1s' \times 10n}{\mathbf{110.1}c' + 1} = \frac{10S'}{\mathbf{111.1}(c' + 1)} = 9.0\% \quad (8.4)$$

If the rate of surplus value remains constant, the profit rate must fall. This is Marx's first formulation of the law/tendency (i.e. a rising organic composition of capital, reflecting a rising technical composition,[12] and a constant rate of surplus value). In principle, there is nothing wrong in presupposing a conclusion and presenting it one-sidedly ahead of a complete exposition. Marx is merely presenting his conclusion in a pure form, protected by a *ceteris paribus* device, emphasizing one-sidedly the presumed relationship between p' and c' to the exclusion of other causes of change.

However, to keep s' constant is to abstract from productivity growth, which must affect the relative values of s and v, as shown above. Marx's entire argument turned on productivity growth, especially in Department II. Productivity growth in Department II necessarily reduces the value of the flow of variable capital $V = nv$, which means that s' cannot remain constant in the face of an increase in the technical/organic composition of capital. Marx, however, moved quickly to a second formulation of the law/ tendency. He proposed that a rising composition of capital and a rising rate of surplus value, consistent with a decline in the value of the flow of variable capital, also expressed a declining profit rate (see also *TSV*, volume II, p. 439). Prima facie, this second formulation overcame the problem evident in the first. If the reason for increasing the composition of capital were to increase productivity growth in Department II, then it made little sense to abstract from it.

To evaluate the second formulation, consider a case with 10 per cent productivity growth in wage-goods industries and examine it under the 'same physical output in less time' rubric. Equation 8.5 expands 8.4 to show what happens to total labour time ($L - V = S$) if it takes Department II 100 fewer hours to produce the annual subsistence bundle V. Recall that this time previously was 1,000 (i.e. 2,000–1,000). If there are no productivity changes in Department I, annual surplus value will remain at 1,000 hours (i.e. 1,900–900). The result is interesting:

$$p' = \frac{1,000sn}{11,011.1c + 90v} = \frac{(1,900 - 900)sn}{11,011.1c + 90v} = \frac{1.11s' \times 10n}{122.3c' + 1} = \frac{11.1S'}{123.3(c' + 1)} = 9.008\% \ (8.5)$$

Three points arise from Equation 8.5. The first is that the profit rate remains almost identical to that of Equation 8.4. A rising s' does not seriously counteract the rising technical/value composition. Nor would it matter if s' doubled, trebled or quadrupled. The reasons are simple enough. To begin with, annual surplus value $S = sn$, namely labour hours in Department I, does not change. The fall in V does all the work to increase $s' = S/V$. Moreover, the value of variable capital advanced v must also fall with the reduced production cost in annual labour time of the subsistence bundle $V = nv$. The change in v in the denominator thus works almost in equal proportion to effect an offsetting increase in c'.

The second point is that the necessary fall in the value of variable capital advanced v contradicts Marx's formulation of the law/tendency in terms of a rising organic composition. The value of the organic composition by definition responds only to physical changes in c and v while abstracting from changes in their valuation. The third point is that the change in the rate of surplus value in Equation 8.5 contains the entire effect of increased productivity, the entire increase in relative surplus value. The turnover period has remained constant, despite the decreased value of both V and v. This differs from Engels's chapter 4, which illustrates productivity growth arising from 'a reduction in the turnover time', or an increase in the number of turnovers per year n (Engels, *Capital*, volume III, pp. 163–64; *Capital*, volume I, chapter 16).

Engels's alternative approach is to change (increase) the number of turnovers per annum n to reflect the fact that productivity growth in Department II has reduced the time of the turnover period. It illustrates the 'greater physical output in the same time' case. Here, Equation 8.4 changes as follows:

$$p' = \frac{1,000sn}{11,011.1c + 90v} = \frac{(2,000 - 1,000)sn}{11,011.1c + 90v} = \frac{(\frac{90}{90})s' \times 11.1n}{122.3c' + 1} = \frac{11S'}{123.3(c' + 1)} = 9.008\% \ (8.6)$$

Note that annual surplus value $S = sn$ has not changed. However, because of the increase in the annual number of turnovers from 10 to 11.1, surplus value in each turnover is smaller ($1,000/11.1 = 90$). The rate of surplus value remains as it was in Equation 8.4 ($90/90 = 1,000/1,000 = 1$) because v has fallen in equal proportion to s but S and V have remained unchanged. The effect on the profit rate is the same as in Equation 8.5 because, in the denominator, the stock of v advanced falls and c' rises.

Equations 8.5 and 8.6 have come to the same point because the annual flow of surplus value S is the salient variable. The concept of turnover obscures rather than clarifies Marx's intention. In similar fashion, it makes sense to despatch the complicating abstraction of the organic composition. The technical and value compositions perform all of Marx's conceptual work.

For all that, a more important conclusion is apparent. Equations 8.5 and 8.6 demonstrate that the annual flow of variable capital V has no effect whatsoever on S (annual surplus value, surplus labour, profit). Unless there are productivity changes in Department I, S will still be 1,000, assuming that capitalists desire the same quantity of capital goods. The point has important implications but, for completeness, it is necessary first to deal in the next section with the value of constant capital advanced.

The devaluation of constant capital advanced

Marx thought that productivity growth in Department I would devalue both the stock of constant capital advanced and its flow (depreciation). In so doing, he explicitly denied historical or original cost capital valuation, because 'value depends not on the labour-time that it cost originally, but on the labour-time with which it can be reproduced, and this is continuously diminishing as the productivity of labour grows' (*TSV* II, p. 416; *TSV* II pp. 473–74; *Capital*, volume III, pp. 119, 205–09, 522). This is precisely what the counteracting force on the profit rate of 'cheapening of the elements of constant capital' involves (chapter 14, section 3).

This counteracting force requires the stock of constant capital to decline in value, at year-end, say, by the average annual rate of productivity growth in Department I. That is, devaluation occurs in proportion to the reduced labour time required to produce Department I's output. Using Equation 8.5 as the datum, Equation 8.7 shows the effects of such a 10 per cent productivity increase (dividing by 1.1). Keep in mind that, in aggregate, surplus labour is equivalent to the labour-time valuation of the output of Department I for the year, the quantity of labour time it took to produce that output. Necessary labour, in contrast, is the labour time required to produce the subsistence wage-goods bundle or the output of Department II. Hence, $S = ns$ must also devalue by the same percentage (i.e. by 10 per cent). It is not possible to consider devaluation of constant capital and to abstract from changes in the rate of surplus value.

Recall that this chapter is endeavouring to follow Marx's presentation and his logic. To follow this logic is to focus squarely now on the value composition and the rate of surplus value, as in Equation 8.7. However, this equation shows that the 'double-barrelled' effect of productivity growth in Department I (numerator and denominator) is sufficient to annul any influence on the profit rate. The profit rate is all but back to where it was in Equation 8.4.

$$p' = \frac{(1.11s' \times 10n)/1.1}{(122.3c'/1.1) + 1} = \frac{10.1S'}{112.2(c' + 1)} = \mathbf{9.0008\%} \tag{8.7}$$

This creates a quandary. The above equations show paradoxically that productivity growth, in both departments, singly or in concert, has no effect on the rate of profit. Marx's counteracting forces (increased rate of surplus value and cheapening of the elements of constant capital) do not counteract. The profit rate does not increase above the rate that the increase in the technical composition produced (i.e. from Equation 8.3 to Equation 8.4). Does this mean that Marx's tendency is indeed a foregone conclusion?

The answer is no. To see why, it is helpful to shrink the formula for the profit rate to its simplest form, summarize the above productivity effects symbolically and excise turnover. Using Equation 8.5 as the datum:

$$p' = \frac{S}{c + v} = \frac{\frac{S}{d1}}{\left(\frac{c}{d1}\right) + \left(\frac{v}{d2}\right)} = \frac{S}{c + \left(\frac{d1}{d2}\right)v} \cong \frac{1,000}{11,011.1 + 90} = 9.008\% \tag{8.8}$$

or

$$p' \cong \frac{S}{c} = \frac{1,000}{11,011.1} = 9.082\% \tag{8.9}$$

The symbols $d1$ and $d2$ represent productivity growth $(1 + x\%$ p.a.) for each department. These are valuations by definition, which means that the symbols S, c and v (in normal text not italics) can take the form of physical, technical or real indexes. Multiplying the numerator and denominator by $d1$ groups the index of variable capital advanced v with a trivial term $(d1/d2)$ that it is reasonable for simplicity to ignore. Productivity or valuation effects thus disappear. Apparently, an increase in the technical composition automatically reduces the profit rate.

A fallacy (error) of composition

Now, to show that this cannot be right, consider a different kind of error. It is an easy error to make within Marx's framework, and Marx makes it. Discussing the error will lay the ground for the substantive criticism that follows. It concerns what economists familiarly call the fallacy of composition. Hints of it emerged above in discussing the incapacity of changes in the rate of surplus value to affect the profit rate. Recall how these changes in s' merely reflected decreased necessary labour time, which is the allocation of social labour time to Department II to produce the subsistence bundle. Surplus value is social surplus labour, which is the quite independent allocation of aggregate social labour to Department I to produce capital goods. While changes in relative and absolute surplus value will affect the social rate of surplus value – i.e. the ratio of the time social labour spends working for the employer against the necessary time it spends working to reproduce itself – they will not affect aggregate social surplus value S per se. This was apparent from all of the previous numerical examples.

The error is to abstract from the whole and just take the perspective of a part. For example, to take the working day as given almost inexorably leads to saying something like, 'given a 10-hour day, a reduction in average necessary labour from 6 to 5 hours increases surplus labour from 4 to 5, with the rate of surplus value increasing from 2/3 to 1'. Yet, to make this deduction implicitly abstracts from the number of workers involved. Assume that there are 100 workers in total. Labour time in Department II falls from 600 to 500, and 50 workers not 60 can now accomplish the task in a given 10-hour day. Should capitalists maintain 400 labour hours per day in Department I, 40 workers will remain employed. Total hours will now be 900 per day not 1000. Therefore, the rate of surplus value will be 400/500 = 0.8. Given a 10-hour day, a reduction in average necessary labour time from 6 to 5 hours per day increases the rate of surplus value from 2/3 to 0.8, but it has no effect on social surplus labour. Clearly, total surplus value per day, week, month or year does not change one iota. From a social perspective, the determination of whether or not capitalists increase or decrease the amount of aggregate labour hours allocated to capital goods production is not dependent on the determination of aggregate necessary labour.

This probably over-labours the point, but the imperious logic of what is Kalecki's (e.g. 1971, 1968) imperative that capitalists earn what they spend bears repetition. Its neglect takes us directly to the heart of Marx's law/tendency and to the most serious of the abstraction errors that *Capital*, volume III makes. Recall that Marx formulated the law/tendency as an expression of the rate of surplus value in relation to the composition of capital. He thus fixed his focus on the behaviour of these two ratios, as if it were possible to abstract from one while changing the other. Marx and his readers were then liable to neglect the components of each of the two ratios. It became more difficult to discern that it is impossible to perform this kind of abstraction because the very same variables, in stock and flow incarnations, inhabit both ratios.

Most significantly, Marx falsely abstracted surplus value from constant capital, treating changes in one of these separately from changes in the other. This neglects that they are the same substance: the output of Department I. First, any productivity increase that devalues the stock of constant capital will have the same proportionate effect on its annual flow (i.e. surplus value). Second, annual surplus value *must* equal the growth of the (devalued) capital stock from one year to the next.[13] Put alternatively, it is not possible to conceive of an increase in the composition of capital without a corresponding effect on the mass of surplus value.

The proper focus is now explicit in Equation 8.10, in which I stands for capital investment (spending).

$$p' \cong \frac{S_1}{c_1} = \frac{I_1}{c_1} = \frac{I_1}{c_0 + I_1} = \frac{\left(\frac{I}{d1}\right)}{\left(\frac{c_0}{d1}\right) + \left(\frac{I}{d1}\right)} = or \frac{\Delta c}{c_0 + \Delta c} \tag{8.10}$$

Equation 8.10 has now shown how to correct the error that remained uncorrected in all of the equations from 8.4 to 8.7. That is, the equations treated surplus value independently of constant capital, in the same way that Marx (and Engels) did throughout *Capital*, volume III, especially in formulating the law/tendency. Because the chapter consciously followed Marx's logic and focused largely on the ratios, it deliberately ignored the only correct rendering of Equation 8.4 (following an increase in constant capital from Equation 8.3). It should have been:

$$p' = \frac{1,111.1sn}{11,011.1c + 100v} = \frac{1.11s'x10n}{110.1c' + 1} = \frac{11.11S'}{111.1(c' + 1)} = 10.0\% \tag{8.11}$$

In other words, given this set of magnitudes, it was not at all necessary that the rate of profit should fall. Any increase greater than the above 11.22 per cent in the accumulation of constant capital would have increased annual surplus value by more proportionately than it would have increased the stock of constant capital advanced. The profit rate would have risen had accumulation been greater. Anything less would have seen the profit rate fall. The concluding section will spell out the implications of this arithmetic.

Conclusions

Working faithfully but rigorously through abstraction, profit rate, law and tendency as presented in chapters 13 and 14 of *Capital*, volume III produces unambiguous conclusions. The profit rate will not tend to fall in consequence of relentless productivity-enhancing change that raises the relative value of the stock of constant capital (dead labour) against that required for variable capital (living labour). Rather, periods of strong accumulation are more likely to cause an increase in the rate of profit. Conversely, it will more likely fall in consequence of slowing or weakening investment and growth. These conclusions are contrary to the essence of the theory Marx outlined in chapters 13 and 14 of the third volume of *Capital*.

The implication of the analysis in the chapter, made explicit in Equations 8.8–8.10, is that attention should focus on the real causes that influence the spending decisions of capitalists from year to year. These not only generate profit (surplus value) but also the rate of profit. The rate of profit, the analysis also implies, must lose much of its causal lustre. Capitalists' investment[14] decisions transparently cause it rather than it influencing them. Perhaps of equal importance, the internal critique of Marx's law/tendency the chapter offers should help to dispel technological-deterministic approaches to understanding capitalist dynamics. As Michał Kalecki (1971, pp. 148, 165) explained, the 'theory of investment decisions' constitutes 'the central problem of the political economy of capitalism'. It is this that still 'remains the central *pièce de résistance* of economics'.

Notes

1 With the usual caveat, many thanks for valuable comments on a first draft by Jerry Courvisanos, Geoff Harcourt, John King and Dick Nichols.
2 'As value, [the composition of capital] is determined by the proportion in which it is divided into constant capital, or the value of the means of production, and variable capital, or the means of labour-power, the sum of total wages. As material, as it functions in the process of production, all capital is divided into means of production and living labour-power.... I call the former the value-composition, the latter the technical composition of capital.... I call the value-composition, in so far as it is determined by its technical composition and mirrors the changes in the latter, the organic composition of capital' (*Capital*, volume I, p. 762, see also *Capital*, volume III, p. 244 and Engels's n. 20). That is, Marx defines the organic composition as the form of (i.e. equal to) the value composition obtained by abstracting from (setting aside) *relative* changes in the values of constant and variable capital.
3 Following Engels, this chapter presents annual flow variables in upper case italic, with $S + V$ representing the annual flow of social value added in the forms of profit (surplus value) and the wage equivalent of the value of workers' labour power. Note that later writers have tended not to follow Engels's use of upper case for flows and lower case for stocks. However, the aim here is to make it easier for anyone working through *Capital*. Note also that the social value-added formulation eliminates consumption of raw materials and that gross profit includes depreciation and changes in inventories. In addition, Marx implicitly avoided problems associated with the transformation of surplus value into profit by formulating the law/tendency in terms of the average social capital only and, hence, the general or average rate of profit (*Capital*, volume III, pp. 142, 323, 340).
4 In order for Department II solely to represent industries producing the means of workers' subsistence, assume for the moment that Department I includes use-values consumed by capitalists, i.e. luxury goods. See n. 14.
5 See e.g. chapter 12 of *Capital*, volume I, 'Absolute and Relative Surplus-Value'. Marx wrote and edited this in 1865–67, after he had completed and set aside the draft manuscript of *Capital*, volume III (1864–65). See also *TSV* II, pp. 265–67.

6 Fowkes's Penguin translation, p. 168.
7 Progress Publishers translation, p. 75.
8 See e.g. 'The Method of Political Economy' (*Grundrisse* Introduction, pp. 100–08; *Critique*, pp. 205–14).
9 Despite Engels's valiant efforts, the single-turnover one-year assumption has plagued subsequent Marxian exegesis, analysis and debate, perhaps excluding Dobb (e.g. 1973, p. 156).
10 The reason for this choice of magnitude will become apparent as the chapter steps through Marx's explanation.
11 Refer again to the definitions at n. 2.
12 See n. 2.
13 Not the simplification that Department I includes capitalists' consumption (see n. 4). It is easy to show from Equation 8.10 that the argument holds precisely if capitalists' consumption remains in constant proportion to investment. Furthermore, because capitalists' consumption does not add to the stock of capital advanced, the argument that the direction of the profit rate depends on the direction of capitalists' aggregate spending (investment plus consumption) is stronger.
14 See n. 14.

References

Dobb, M. (1973), *Theories of Value and Distribution since Adam Smith: Ideology and Economic Theory*. Cambridge, UK: Cambridge University Press.

Kalecki, M. (1968), The Marxian Equations of Reproduction and Modern Economics, background paper, International Social Science Council and the International Council for Philosophy and Humanistic Studies symposium, UNESCO, 8–10 May. Published in *Social Science Information* 6(7), pp. 73–79. Republished in J. Osiatyński (ed.) (1991), *Collected Works of Michał Kalecki: Capitalism: Economic Dynamics*, volume II. Oxford: The Clarendon Press, pp. 459–466.

Kalecki, M. (1971), *Selected Essays on the Dynamics of the Capitalist Economy: 1933–1970*. Cambridge, UK: Cambridge University Press.

Marx, K. (1859), *A Contribution to the Critique of Political Economy*. Moscow: Progress Publishers (1970).

Marx, K. (1861–63), *Theories of Surplus-Value*, volumes TSV I (1963), TSV II (1968), TSV III (1971). Moscow: Progress Publishers.

Marx, K. (1867), *Capital: A Critique of Political Economy*, volume I. Harmondsworth, UK: Penguin/New Left Review (1976).

Marx, K. (1894), *Capital: A Critique of Political Economy*, volume III. F. Engels (ed.), translation B. Fowkes. Harmondsworth, UK: Penguin/New Left Review (1981).

Marx, K. (1894), *Capital: A Critique of Political Economy*, volume III. Moscow: Progress Publishers (1959).

Marx, K. (1858–59), *Foundations of the Critique of Political Economy (Rough Draft)*. Harmondsworth, UK: Penguin/New Left Review (1973).

Marx, K. and Engels, E. (1844–95), *Selected Correspondence*, third edition. Moscow: Progress Publishers (1975).

9 The 'Ricardian' theory of rent

A case study in multiple discovery and its mainstream absorption

Michael Schneider[1]

This chapter was inspired in part by my reading the manuscript of John King's book *David Ricardo*, which reminded me that in February 1815 there were no less than four expositions of the differential theory of rent (including one by Ricardo) and led me to realize this curious occurrence of an idea being simultaneously put forward by several apparent discoverers was an event in the history of economic thought that I had never fully investigated. The chapter addresses the following four questions. What is the 'Ricardian' theory of rent? Is it an example of either multiple or chain multiple discovery, or of a singleton? How did the discovery come to be known as 'Ricardian'? How was the discovery absorbed by mainstream economics?

In an article titled 'Merton on Multiples, Denied and Affirmed' George J. Stigler (1980) identified eight history of economic thought candidates for multiple discovery, the 'Ricardian' theory of rent topping the list. The title of Stigler's article reflects the fact that the American sociologist Robert K. Merton wrote a seminal article, published in 1961, on the concept of 'multiple discovery', a concept dating back to a 1922 article titled 'Are Inventions Inevitable? A Note on Social Evolution' by Ogburn and Thomas, who coined the term 'multiple inventions' ('multiple inventions' may be regarded as a sub-set of 'multiple discoveries', the latter including not only new devices but also new ideas). The plural of the term 'multiple discovery' means not multiple discoveries by one person but the same discovery made by multiple discoverers, and Merton coined the simpler (and less confusing) terms 'multiple' and 'multiples' as an alternative, and for the most part it is these terms that will henceforth be used in this chapter, supplemented by Lamb and Easton's subsequently-coined term 'chain multiple', defined by them as a set of related discoveries involving more than one discoverer 'which follow, like links in a chain, each step from the previous one' (1984, p. 53). Discussion of the definitions of 'multiple' and 'chain multiple' is deferred until later, it being suggested at this stage only that the term 'multiple' would seem to require that an idea be hit upon independently by more than one discoverer; there may therefore be a first, second and third, etc., discoverer of an idea. In the realm of ideas a 'discoverer', in turn, may be defined as one who has put forward an idea assuming, rightly or wrongly, that the idea has not been put forward previously.

The body of this chapter first notes that the term 'Ricardian theory of rent' has been used to describe both of two fundamentally distinct though related theories, those based respectively on the 'extensive margin' and 'intensive margin' versions of the law of diminishing returns, and that at least one of these theories was proposed in four papers, each published in February 1815, including three written not by Ricardo but in order of publication by Malthus, West and Torrens. The chapter describes the way in which the theory was presented in each of these three cases. It then discusses whether each of these is an example of a multiple, a chain multiple, or a singleton; it is here that the criteria for both a multiple and a chain multiple are discussed more extensively. The chapter next addresses the question of how this theory became known as 'Ricardian'. It concludes with an examination of how the 'Ricardian' theory of rent became absorbed in mainstream economics.

Expositions of the two 'Ricardian' theories of rent in 1815

The 'Ricardian' theory of rent is alternatively known as the 'differential' theory of rent due to the fact that it depends on the proposition that rent occurs when, as more and more units of a factor of production are used, the product of each additional unit of the factor differs from that of its predecessor, or more specifically, the product per unit of factor added diminishes. As already noted, there are in fact not one but two differential theories of rent, differing from each other fundamentally; one involves a heterogeneous factor of production, and the other homogeneous factors of production. In one of these cases, that where units of one factor are heterogeneous, the use of more units of the factor brings into play less productive units than those previously employed; this will henceforth in this chapter be referred to as the extensive margin law of diminishing returns, with rent resulting from the excess of an assumed uniform unit product price on the one hand, over cost of production in the case of intra-marginal units of the factor on the other (unit price being equal to the cost of production where the marginal unit of the factor is used). In the other case, where units of factors are homogeneous, diminishing returns will set in at some stage if more and more units of one factor of production are applied to a fixed quantity of another factor of production; although this case is commonly termed simply the 'law of diminishing returns', it will henceforth in this chapter be referred to as the intensive margin law of diminishing returns, with rent again resulting from the excess of unit price over cost of production in the case of intra-marginal units of the variable factor. I shall refer to these two differential theories of rent as the 'Ricardian' theory of rent (extensive margin version) and the 'Ricardian' theory of rent (intensive margin version) respectively.

The discussion of rent by Ricardo's classical political economy predecessor Adam Smith was unsatisfactory, the author of the *Wealth of Nations* vacillating between the view that rent is a 'component part' of natural price on the one hand, and the view that 'high or low wages and profit, are the causes of high or low price; high or low rent is the effect of it' (Smith 1776 (1961), p. 163) on the other, and providing no substantial justification for the latter view in particular. The differential theories of rent thus supplied a missing piece in the classical political economy jigsaw. With the exception of an anticipation by Petty, they first appeared in the late eighteenth and early nineteenth centuries, when, with the advent in Britain of the Industrial Revolution, manufacturers were challenging the previous dominance of landowners. As early as the Corn Laws of 1436 and 1463 landowners in Britain had obtained protection from foreign competition in years of plenty and low prices either through the permission or subsidy of the exportation of corn (as in 1436) or through limitation of its importation (as in 1463); by 'corn' was meant any edible grain of a grass, for example wheat, rye, oats or barley. Because manufacturers believed this protection of British agriculture caused labour costs to be higher than they would otherwise be, they opposed proposed increases in agricultural protection and advocated reductions in existing agricultural protection. The discovery of the differential theories of rent can be seen as a by-product of this conflict.

In 1813 committees set up by both the House of Commons and the House of Lords to consider whether, given the prospect of an increase in corn imports following the expected imminent end of the restrictions on trade due to the Napoleonic wars, the existing Corn Laws should be strengthened, published their reports. The House of Commons committee recommended that a high tariff be imposed on corn unless its price exceeded eighty shillings a quarter. The trigger for the publication in February 1815 of four pamphlets setting out a differential theory of rent was the impending parliamentary debate on the Corn Laws in the following month.

By then Malthus had already published, in 1814, a pamphlet titled *Observations on the Effects of the Corn Laws, and of a Rise or Fall in the Price of Corn on the Agriculture and General Wealth of the Country*, in which he discussed the cases for and against the proposed Corn Law. In February of the following year he published two more pamphlets. One, titled *The Grounds of an Opinion on the Policy of Restricting the Importation of Foreign Corn: Intended as an Appendix to 'Observations on the Corn Laws'* (published 10 February, Malthus 1815b), argued that the case for the proposed Corn Law was vastly stronger than that against, partly because of the importance of a thriving agriculture to a country's wealth, and partly because of the importance of self-sufficiency in food production to a country's defence. The other, titled *The Nature and Progress of Rent: An Inquiry* (published 3 February), set out a differential theory of rent. In the 'Advertisement' to this pamphlet Malthus stated that he had hastened the 'appearance' of notes written over the period of time he had spent as lecturer at Haileybury College because of 'the very near connection of the subject of the present inquiry, with the topics immediately under discussion', the latter clause presumably a reference to the Corn Law parliamentary debate scheduled for March.

In the text of this pamphlet Malthus rejected the argument that a high price of corn (relative to prices of other commodities) is due to high rents, an argument he noted had been advanced by both Adam Smith (in some places) and Sismondi, among others, as well as in contemporary debates over recent increases in the price of corn. Exploring the nature and origin of rent, Malthus contended that there was a fundamental difference between an excess of price over cost of production due to rent on the one hand, and an excess due to a natural or artificial monopoly on the other (an example of a natural monopoly being French wines); he thereby became the first to distinguish between what was to become known as 'Ricardian' rent and monopoly rent, a distinction whose importance was subsequently emphasized for example by Alchian in his entry on 'Rent' in *The New Palgrave Dictionary of Economics* (see volume 4, p. 142, Alchian 1987). Malthus saw the cause of high prices in the case of a monopoly as an excess of demand over limited supply, whereas increases in demand for a necessary good such as corn are limited by increases in population, and therefore by increases in the supply of 'the necessary good', i.e. corn – in short, the demand for corn is constrained by the supply of it. Thus by contrast with the case of a monopoly, where there is no such constraint on demand, the cause of a high price of corn is an extension of cultivation and consequent use of capital (both fixed and circulating, the latter being used to pay labour) on land less productive than land currently under cultivation, use of the newly-cultivated less-productive land resulting in an increased unit cost of production. This is an example of the extensive margin law of diminishing returns, diminishing returns being caused by the heterogeneous nature of a factor of production, in Malthus's case land. Rent, Malthus argued, results from the excess of price over cost of production on what we now term intra-marginal pieces of land. This was the first 1815 description of the 'Ricardian' theory of rent (extensive margin version). Malthus, however, came no closer in this pamphlet to the alternative (intensive margin) version of the 'Ricardian' theory of rent than noting that additional land would not be taken into cultivation in response to a fall in the cost of production until the new opportunities for profit by more intensive cultivation of land already under cultivation had been fully taken up.

Malthus believed that rent was due to 'the most inestimable quality in the soil, which God has bestowed on man – the quality of being able to maintain more persons than are necessary to work it' (Malthus 1815a, p. 122).[2] He concluded that the payment of rent 'as a kind of fixture upon lands of a certain quality, is a law as invariable as the action of the principle of gravity' (Malthus 1815a, p. 125), and that such payment occurs regardless of who owns the land, whether a landlord, the crown, or the actual cultivator.

The second pamphlet expounding a differential theory of rent to appear in February 1815 (published 13 February) was that by Edward West, published anonymously (though credited to 'a Fellow of University College, Oxford') under the title *Essay on the Application of Capital to Land*. West began his pamphlet by declaring that his purpose was to make public a principle in political economy that had occurred to him some years previously, and in his view had been confirmed by many of the witnesses whose evidence to recent parliamentary committees on the Corn Laws appeared in published reports. This was the principle that 'in the progress of the improvement of cultivation the raising of rude produce becomes progressively more expensive', or in other words, 'every additional quantity of capital laid out produces a less proportionate return' (West 1815, p. 2), which West illustrated by reference to the occupiers of a new colony cultivating first the richest lands, then lands second in quality, and so on. He contrasted this characteristic of agricultural production with the ability of manufacturing to expand without any increase in unit cost, and adopting the then common assumption that as a country develops the rate of profit falls, concluded that this is explained by the fact that any tendency of the rate of profit to rise as a result of 'improvement', in agriculture as well as manufacturing, will be outweighed by characteristic diminishing returns in agriculture.

West subsequently turned his attention to the consequences of removing restrictions on the import of corn. He argued, first, that removal of such restrictions would not, as some feared, result in the demise of British agriculture, as a reduction in cultivation in Britain would reduce the unit cost of corn produced there, making it more competitive, and the imported corn that replaced it would increase in unit cost as more was produced, making it less competitive. He looked, second, at the consequences for rent, concluding that 'It is diminishing rate of return upon additional portions of capital bestowed upon land that regulates, and almost solely regulates, rent' (West 1815, pp. 49–50). More specifically, given that the farmer will receive the same rate of profit regardless of the productivity of the land he cultivates, compared with corn that is raised at the greatest expense, 'all the additional profit, therefore, on that part of the produce which is raised at a less expense, goes to the landlord in the shape of rent' (p. 51). This was the second 1815 description of the 'Ricardian' theory of rent (extensive margin version). But unlike Malthus, West then went on to expound the 'Ricardian' theory of rent (intensive margin version), which does not depend on a factor of production being heterogeneous. Noting, as Malthus had done, that an increase in the demand for corn will not induce an increase in land brought under cultivation until profit opportunities have been exhausted on land already under cultivation, West illustrated the consequences when more intensive cultivation does occur by means of an example, in which of a capital of £100 applied to land the first £10 generates a profit of 40 per cent, the second £10 a profit of 30 per cent, and so on, concluding that 'The rent of the landlord would ... be all that was made on the whole capital above what the last or least profitable portion of that capital produced' (West 1815, p. 53). This was the first published description of the 'Ricardian' theory of rent (intensive margin version).

The third exposition of a differential theory of rent to appear in February 1815 (published 24 February) appeared in a book titled *An Essay on the External Corn Trade: Containing an Inquiry into the General Principles of that Important Branch of Traffic; an Examination of the Exceptions to which these Principles are Liable; and a Comparative Statement of the Effects which*

Restrictions on Importation and Free Intercourse, are Calculated to Produce upon Subsistence, Agriculture, Commerce, and Revenue, written by Robert Torrens. In the first and second parts of this book Torrens defended at length (in more than 200 pages) what Viner termed the 'eighteenth-century rule', namely 'it pays to import commodities from abroad whenever they can be obtained in exchange for exports at a smaller real cost than their production at home would entail' (Viner 1937, p. 440), which as John King has pointed out 'is absolute advantage in all but name' (King 2013, p. 96). At the beginning of the third part of his book Torrens used this 'rule' to argue against the protection of domestic agricultural production provided by the Corn Laws. He then reinforced his argument against the Corn Laws in two ways.

First, Torrens anticipated in part what was to become known as the law of comparative advantage (itself an example of a chain multiple – see Aldrich 2004), in the following words:

> If England should have acquired such a degree of skill in manufactures, that, she could prepare a quantity of cloth, for which the Polish cultivator would give a greater quantity of corn, than she could, with the same capital, raise from her own soil, then, tracts of her territory, though they should be equal, nay, even though they should be superior, to the lands of Poland, will be neglected; and a part of her supply of corn will be imported from that country.
>
> (Torrens 1815, p. 264)

Torrens justified this statement on the ground that allocation of resources in this way, that is, as we would now say, according to comparative advantage, would maximize England's rate of profit.

Second, in challenging the view, espoused by the House of Commons Committee among others, that cutting off the foreign supply of corn would decrease the price of corn, Torrens argued that instead this 'would, in order to meet the growing demand for corn, and to feed our increasing population, force into cultivation land which could not under free competition, be profitably tilled', adding that 'as such lands afforded the cultivator an adequate profit, better soils would afford a higher rent' (Torrens 1815, p. 211). Here Torrens moved beyond the law of comparative advantage's implicit assumption, in Harry Johnson's words, of 'a static and permanent distribution of comparative advantages and disadvantages' (Johnson 1975, p. 4), to take into account the dynamics of diminishing returns. In the process he hit upon the 'Ricardian' theory of rent (extensive margin version), as the latter part of the above quotation from his *Essay* indicates.

Torrens elaborated on his statement of the 'Ricardian' theory of rent (extensive margin version) by adding that extending cultivation would not lead to higher rent until existing leases expired, but once they did, competition between cultivators for superior land would cause rent on it to rise until the rate of profit fell to its customary rate (Torrens 1815, pp. 219–20). He made the further comment that although the increase in rent resulting from restrictions on the importation of corn would initially benefit landowners, ultimately landowners would suffer because of the adverse effect on manufacturing of the consequent higher price of corn, and hence labour, and the resulting decline in the country's wealth, population, demand for food, and consequently income received in the form of rent.

On the same day as Torrens's book was published, namely 24 February 1815 as already noted, a pamphlet containing Ricardo's first exposition of the differential theory of rent appeared, under the title *An Essay on the Influence of a Low Price of Corn on the Profits of Stock; Shewing the Inexpedience of Restrictions on Importation: With Remarks on Mr. Malthus' Two Last Publications.* In this pamphlet Ricardo, after acknowledging his debt to Malthus's analysis of rent, took as an example a country characterized by neither uncultivated land as well situated as that already under cultivation nor 'improvement' in agriculture over time nor a change in the real wage rate, arguing that to feed an increase in population in such a country, cultivation had to be extended to land less favourably situated than that currently under cultivation, consequently increasing unit transport cost and thereby lowering the rate of profit in agriculture, at the same time creating rent on land more favourably situated. Note that it can be argued that such increasing costs amount to the same thing as diminishing returns, since additional transport costs metamorphose into diminishing returns to a heterogeneous labour factor if one thinks of a labourer on a distant land producing less produce because he has to spend some of his working time in transporting the produce to its market. Ricardo subsequently also used the example to draw the same conclusions in the case of the cultivation of land of worse quality than that previously under cultivation. This led him to conclude that 'by bringing successively land of a worse quality, or less favourably situated into cultivation, rent would rise on the land previously cultivated, and precisely in the same degree would profits fall' (Sraffa 1951b, p. 14); thus unlike Malthus, Ricardo used the differential theory of rent (extensive margin version) to derive his theory that over time the rate of profit would fall. Having outlined the differential theory of rent (extensive margin version), Ricardo then went on to use the same example to draw similar conclusions in the case where alternatively more food was produced by applying additional capital to the fertile land already under cultivation, rent in this case accruing in the case of capital previously employed; he thus also outlined the differential theory of rent (intensive margin version).

Adoption of the differential theory of rent, in both of its forms, enabled Ricardo to conclude (Sraffa 1951b, p. 21):

> the interest of the landlord is always opposed to the interest of every other class in the community. His situation is never so prosperous, as when food is scarce and dear: ... [but h]igh rent and low profits, for they invariably accompany each other, ought never to be the subject of complaint, if they are the effect of the natural course of things.

A very similar account of rent is to be found in Ricardo's *On the Principles of Political Economy and Taxation*, which was published two years after his 'Rate of Profit' pamphlet, and which included an acknowledgment that the differential theory of rent contained in it had been discovered not only by Malthus, but also by 'a Fellow of University College, Oxford' (namely West); as already noted, in the case of Malthus it was in fact only the extensive version of the differential theory of rent that had been put forward.

As a postscript to this section of the chapter, it should be noted that Malthus, West, Torrens and Ricardo were not without predecessors who like them could lay claim to having discovered one or both versions of either the law of diminishing returns or the 'Ricardian' theory of rent. Those meriting examination as having such a claim comprise William Petty (1662), an anonymous French author (1766), Sir James Steuart (1767), A.R.J. Turgot (1977) and James Anderson (1777). Unfortunately, space does not permit discussion of their claims here.[3]

Multiple, chain multiple and singleton discoveries

Now that we have noted the claims of no less than nine economists to have discovered one or both of the differential or 'Ricardian' theories of rent, or at least a key element of them, and examined the claims of four of them in detail, we can turn to the question of whether the 'Ricardian' theory of rent is an example of a multiple discovery, as was implied as early as 1828 by Macaulay, who put its discovery in the same ('multiple') class as the independent discovery of calculus by Leibniz and Newton (see Merton 1963, p. 353).

The term 'multiple' is problematic. For Merton, coiner of the term, only 'similar discoveries' (1973, p. 371) were required to establish the existence of a multiple. However, a serious shortcoming of the sociological literature on multiples is its failure to provide a definition of a 'multiple' precise enough for it to be possible to falsify the proposition that 'x' (say) is an example of a multiple. In particular, given Merton's definition of a multiple, his surprising hypothesis that 'all scientific discoveries are in principle multiples' (Merton 1973, p. 356) would be near-impossible to falsify, even if he had not included the phrase 'in principle'. It is proposed here that a more useful definition of a 'multiple' would require that fundamentally the same idea has been 'discovered' by more than one person; a suggested criterion for 'fundamentally the same' is that the discoveries have essentially the same implications. The best-known examples of a multiple in the realm of ideas, those of the discovery of calculus (integral and differential respectively) by Leibniz and Newton and the discovery of the theory of the origin of species by Darwin and Wallace, are perhaps also the clearest cases, the idea discovered being almost unarguably 'fundamentally the same' (despite being discovered along somewhat different paths).

It is true that there is still an element of subjectivity in the term 'fundamentally the same' as defined above, but whether or not a multiple exists is necessarily to some extent a subjective matter, as the vast number of disputes over discovery priority attests (see in particular Kuhn 1977 and Hall 1980). Nonetheless, compared with 'similar', 'fundamentally the same' requires a closer connection between discoveries, particularly with respect to their implications, and makes a claim of 'multiple' more open to falsification. Whether or not the implications are essentially the same then determines both whether or not two ideas put forward at about the same time can be said to be so 'fundamentally the same' as to comprise a multiple, and whether compared with an idea discovered previously a discovery is so similar that the ideas can be said to be 'fundamentally the same', the two discoveries thus likewise comprising a multiple.

Another problem with the concept of a 'multiple' arises out of the fact that it is often difficult to determine whether or not the same idea has in fact been hit upon independently, for example when the 'discoverers' work at the same time in the same or a nearby institution, or when they are so separated in time that the idea put forward by the earlier discoverer may have filtered through to the later.

Further problems may arise if the concept of 'multiple discovery' is defined even more stringently. For example, Stigler (1980) narrows the definition by requiring that the idea be discovered in the same scientific context, thereby raising the thorny problem of distinguishing one 'scientific context' from another, of which Stigler however claims that 'it is not an easy task but it is not an impossible one' (1980, p. 100), one contentious illustration being the assertion that the discoveries of Keynes and Kalecki do not qualify as a multiple because 'the ruling (Marxian) economics in Poland bore little relationship to that in Britain' (1980, p. 100). Patinkin (1983) also narrows the definition, in his case by requiring that a discovery be part of the discoverer's 'central message', likewise raising a thorny problem, namely that of distinguishing 'central' from peripheral messages. Narrowing the definition enabled Patinkin to strengthen his argument that what became known as Keynesian theory was not an example of multiple discovery, his (again contentious) argument being that the 'central message' of Keynesian theory was not that of either the Stockholm School or Kalecki, on the ground that 'in brief, the Stockholm message was concerned with prices and not output, and that Kalecki's was concerned with investment cycles and not unemployment equilibrium...' (1983, p. 315).

A specific form of multiple is a chain multiple, a term that as already noted was coined by Lamb and Easton and defined by them as a set of related discoveries 'which follow, like links in a chain, each step from the previous one' (Lamb and Easton 1984, p. 53). A chain multiple by definition involves more than one discoverer, the discovery comprising at a minimum an idea put forward by one person being supplemented by a related idea put forward by a second person. By contrast with both 'multiple' and 'chain multiple', a 'singleton' is a discovery made uniquely by an individual, or by a group of individuals working together.

Categorization of the discovery of the 'Ricardian' theory of rent

Since, as already explained, there are in fact both two laws of diminishing returns and two 'Ricardian' theories of rent, there is the possibility that the discoveries of these ideas provide as many as four examples of a multiple, or of a chain multiple.

The discovery of the extensive margin law of diminishing returns can indeed be argued to be an example of a multiple, given that the increasing transport cost version of this law was put forward by both Petty and Ricardo (who taking into account his scrupulousness in acknowledging his debt to Malthus and the priority of West, seems likely to have acknowledged Petty's prior exposition if he had been aware of it), and that the diminishing fertility version of the law was put forward by both Anderson and, apparently independently, by Malthus, West and Torrens, none of whom seems to have been aware of Anderson's 1777 Corn Laws pamphlet. As far as Torrens is concerned, although in the Preface to the book he published in 1815 Torrens made reference to Malthus's *The Grounds of an Opinion*, and might consequently be supposed to have read Malthus's *The Nature and Progress of Rent*, published a week earlier and containing Malthus's exposition of the extensive margin law of diminishing returns, there is no evidence that he had in fact done so, and since in addition his book was self-reportedly written in the previous year, namely 1814 (Torrens 1829, p. ix), one can only assume that he arrived at the extensive margin law of diminishing returns independently also of Malthus.

The discovery of the intensive margin law of diminishing returns is probably also an example of a multiple, with Turgot, West and Ricardo the co-discoverers, it being unlikely that either West or Ricardo knew of Turgot's 'formulation' of it, given that it did not appear in print until 1808–11, during the Napoleonic wars, and not in English. More specifically in the case of Ricardo, although a copy of this edition of Turgot's works was found in the 1930s amongst the books at Gatcombe Park, where Ricardo had lived during the later part of his life, and Sraffa included it in the list of which he wrote that 'There is also little doubt that the following had belonged to him [Ricardo]' (Sraffa 1955, p. 399), given the already-noted generosity of Ricardo in acknowledging predecessors it seems likely that he would have acknowledged Turgot likewise had he known of his (Turgot's) discovery of the extensive margin law of diminishing returns. It should be noted, however, that this case of a multiple does not meet Stigler's stringent stipulation of 'same scientific context', as Stigler himself concluded, because the context for Turgot was Physiocratic and that for West and Ricardo was Smithian. That it meets Patinkin's stipulation of 'central message' is less debatable, given that Turgot, West and Ricardo were all clearly pointing to the inevitability of ultimate diminishing returns if more and more homogeneous doses of capital and labour are applied to a fixed quantity of land.

We turn now to the differential theory of rent. The 'Ricardian' theory of rent (extensive margin version) was initially expounded by Petty, and given the absence of evidence to the contrary, probably independently by Anderson, who based his theory on diminishing fertility as opposed to increasing transport costs, and by Malthus and West, who as already noted seem not to have been aware of Anderson's Corn Laws pamphlet, and by Torrens, who as also already noted seems not to have been aware in addition of the pamphlet Malthus published three weeks before his (Torrens's) book appeared. This surely meets Stigler's stipulation of 'same scientific context', in this case the contemporary culture of Great Britain. It arguably also meets Patinkin's stipulation of 'central message', as all five discoverers primarily sought to demonstrate that the payment of rent does not influence price; though the policy conclusions associated with (as opposed to implied by) the theory differed, Petty not drawing any, Anderson, West and Torrens arguing that the Corn Laws should be either ultimately abolished (in Torrens's case) or weakened (in the cases of Anderson and West) on the ground not that their existence increases rent but that it increases the cost and therefore price of corn (due to extension of cultivation), but Malthus while acknowledging this consequence saw it as outweighed by considerations emanating from what he saw as the greater importance of agriculture and defence.

By contrast, the 'Ricardian' theory of rent (intensive margin version) may be categorized as either a multiple or a chain multiple. Unaware of West's pamphlet when he published his own, Ricardo outlined the differential theory of rent (intensive margin version) independently of West, making this a case of multiple discovery. However, while West and Ricardo were both discoverers, Ricardo's discovery can be regarded as the second link in the chain whose first link was Malthus's extensive margin version of the differential theory of rent, making this a case of a chain multiple.

How the discovery came to be known as 'Ricardian'

When noting the usage of the term 'Ricardian theory of rent' careful commentators have appropriately acknowledged, from the point of view of discovery, its inappropriateness. Marx, for example, in his *Theories of Surplus Value* refers in a chapter-heading to the 'so-called Ricardian law of rent' (Marx 1885, p. 114), detailing in the chapter the prior claim of James Anderson, whom he asserts was plagiarized by Malthus, though first no evidence is provided for this assertion, second Marx is at pains to emphasize the differences in the uses to which Anderson and Malthus put the theory, and third the way in which the theory is developed is completely different in the two cases. The judgement of Jacob Hollander (1815, p. 5) is that:

> The most that can be hazarded is a reasonable likelihood that some part of the clear statement of the law of diminishing [sic: 'increasing'?] costs and of the co-ordination of extensive and intensive cultivation, which appeared in the tract on rent, figures in the Haileybury lectures, and that

James Anderson is to be counted among the influences which may have affected Malthus' academic exposition [of the theory of rent].

Schumpeter, in turn, in his *History of Economic Analysis* refers to 'the "Ricardian" theory of rent' (1954, pp. 476, 490, 933, 934, 936), with both 'Ricardian' in inverted commas, and an accompanying acknowledgement that Edward West's independent discovery of the differential theory of rent and other Ricardian theories justifies reference to 'West-Ricardian doctrines'.

It has been demonstrated above that it is not Ricardo but West who is to be credited with the first discovery of the two versions of the 'Ricardian' theory of rent, which is thus an example of Stigler's Law of Eponymy, formulated in an eponymously titled chapter in *Statistics on the Table* by Stephen M. Stigler (statistician son of economist George J. Stigler) as 'No scientific discovery is named after its original discoverer' (Stigler 1980, p. 277). Tongue in cheek, Stephen Stigler dubbed his Law a 'self-proving theorem', claiming that 'the Law', as he referred to it, is at least implicit in the writings of Merton.

Stephen Stigler added with respect to names given to scientific discoveries that 'they are rarely given and never generally accepted unless the namer (or acceptor of the name) is remote in time or place (or both) from the scientist being honored' (Stigler 1980, p. 280); subsequent chapters in *Statistics on the Table* provide two examples from the area of statistics that generally support this proposition, one case being that relating to Bayes's theorem. As we shall now see, the naming of the 'Ricardian' theory of rent provides an exception to Stigler's assertion, in that it was not remote in either time or place from the 'scientist' being honoured.

Sraffa, in the introductory note to his edition of Ricardo's 'Essay on Profits', observes that

> The popular belief that Ricardo actually invented the theory of rent (whence the phrase 'the Ricardian theory of rent') derives some support from the Note on Rent in McCulloch's 1828 edition of the *Wealth of Nations*: 'The theory of rent ... was first announced to the world in two pamphlets published in 1815, by Mr. West ... and Mr. Malthus ... but, although he [Ricardo] was posterior to the authors above named, in promulgating the doctrine, and less happy in his mode of explaining it than Sir Edward West, it is well known to many of his friends that he was in possession of the principle, and was accustomed to communicate it in conversation several years prior to the publication of the earliest of these works'.
>
> (Sraffa 1951b, p. 6)

If McCulloch's assertion were true it would imply extraordinary generosity on Ricardo's part in trumpeting the primacy of Malthus and West, and Sraffa himself describes the attribution of the discovery of the differential theory of rent to Ricardo as a 'mistaken notion'.

McCulloch was not the first to attribute the differential theory of rent to Ricardo; after an extensive investigation, I have been able to find one even earlier attribution. In 1826 Robert Perronet Thompson published a pamphlet containing a critical review of the differential theory of rent as presented by Ricardo's friend and disciple James Mill in his *Elements of Political Economy* (Mill 1826), under the title *An Exposition of Fallacies on Rent, Tithes, &etc., Containing an Examination of Mr Ricardo's Theory of Rent, in the Form of a Review of Mr Mill's Elements* (Thompson 1826, a second edition of the pamphlet appeared later in the same year, retitled *The True Theory of Rent in Opposition to Mr Ricardo and Others*). Since Thompson's purpose was to criticize the differential theory of rent, it is curious that he went out of his way to associate it with the name of Ricardo. Perhaps he thought doing so would attract attention to his critique.

It is worth noting that one reason why the differential theory of rent has become known as Ricardian in spite of the fact that Ricardo was not its discoverer turns on the distinction between discovery and dissemination, analogous with the distinction between invention on the one hand, and its application, namely innovation, on the other. While, unlike West, Ricardo was not a discoverer of both the differential theories of rent, acknowledging Malthus's and West's priority himself, it was mainly through his writings and the popularization of them by James Mill and McCulloch that these theories were disseminated; naming of a discovery may reflect dissemination, as opposed to discovery.

Mainstream absorption of the 'Ricardian' theory of rent

By 1815, when the 'Ricardian' theory of rent was discovered, the pluralism characterizing economic thought before the publication of Adam Smith's *Wealth of Nations* had given way to a dominant paradigm which later became known as classical political economy. Following the publication of his *Principles of Political Economy* in 1817, Ricardo was quickly acknowledged as the leading exponent of what could be argued to represent the contemporary mainstream economics; Sismondi, for example, dubbed it 'an orthodoxy' (Sismondi 1819, p. 7). At one level, therefore, responsibility for the absorption of the extensive margin version of the 'Ricardian' theory of rent in the economics mainstream at that time lies with Ricardo's endorsement of it (though the intensive margin version was by and large overlooked). At another level, responsibility can be said to lie with the changing balance of power between the landowning and manufacturing classes, referred to earlier in this chapter, providing for the latter an argument against cost-increasing restrictions on the import of corn.

In the 1870s, classical political economy ceased to represent the main-stream, being replaced by neoclassical economics. One of the key assumptions of the new orthodoxy being variable factor proportions, the intensive margin version of the 'Ricardian' theory of rent soon became an integral part of it, notably with the publication of Marshall's *Principles of Economics* in 1890, with the extensive version largely overlooked. Then in articles published in the *Quarterly Economic Review* in 1891, J.A. Hobson and John Bates Clark each extended the 'Ricardian' theory of rent to apply not only to land but also to labour and capital, concluding that both wages and profits may contain an element of rent.

That there is more to the story than the Ricardian theory of rent merely being absorbed into the neoclassical mainstream was subsequently claimed by J. M. Clark. According to Clark, 'The Ricardian theory of rent ... is the first great example of the marginal method, later to become the keystone of the entire Austrian system of economic theory' (Clark 1931, p. 168; cited by Sraffa 1951b, p. 6). In response Sraffa, following his already-noted referral to the 'mistaken notion' that Ricardo was the discoverer of the differential theory of rent, went on to argue that this 'mistaken notion' had an unfortunate consequence, namely 'that of regarding Ricardo as the originator of the whole marginal theory', attributing this view to J.M. Clark. The tiny kernel of truth in this 'view' is that by endorsing the intensive margin version of the differential theory of rent Ricardo lent his support to the idea that factor proportions will be varied so as to maximize profits. But as we have seen, the 'originator' of this theory was not Ricardo but West. And if 'marginal method' is taken to refer to small or infinitesimal changes in such variables as factor proportions, this 'view' is wrong, as in the writings of both West and Ricardo all examples of changes in such variables as factor proportions involve variations that are substantial.

Notes

1 This chapter is an extensively revised version of a paper presented at the History of Economic Thought Society of Australia conference held at the University of Western Australia in July 2013. The chapter has benefited from (1) numerous conversations with John King, (2) suggestions put forward in the discussion of the paper at both the 2013 HETSA conference and the John King Festschrift conference and (3) input from John Pullen on Malthus's alleged plagiarism, but none of those whose assistance is acknowledged should be held responsible for the chapter's deficiencies.
2 Pullen (2014, p. 12) uses a similar statement in Malthus's *Principles of Political Economy* to support his argument that Malthus put forward an absolute, in addition to a differential, theory of rent. Ricardo rejected Malthus's absolute theory of rent, stating in chapter XXXII of his *Principles*, titled 'Mr. Malthus's Opinions on Rent', that 'Rent, it must be remembered, is not in proportion to the absolute fertility of the land in cultivation, but in proportion to its relative fertility' (Sraffa 1951a, p. 403), and by contrast with Malthus's view, approvingly quoted (1951a, p. 76) Adam Smith's statement that 'The labour of nature is paid, not because she does so much, but because she does so little. In proportion as she becomes niggardly in her gifts, she exacts a greater price for her work'.
3 These claims are discussed in a paper of which this chapter is a shortened version.

References

Alchian, A.A. (1987), Rent in, *The New Palgrave: A Dictionary of Economics*. Basingstoke, UK: Palgrave Macmillan.

Aldrich, J. (2004), The Discovery of Comparative Advantage, *Journal of the History of Economic Thought* 26(3), pp. 379–399.

Anderson, J. (1777), *An Enquiry into the Nature of the Corn Laws: With a View to the New Corn-Bill Proposed for Scotland*. Edinburgh: Mrs Mundell.

Clark, J.B. (1891), Distribution as Determined by a Law of Rent, *Quarterly Journal of Economics* 5(3), pp. 289–318.

Clark, J.M. (1931), Distribution, *Encyclopaedia of the Social Sciences*, volumes 5–6. New York: Macmillan, pp. 167–174.

Gieryn, T.F. (ed.) (1980), *Science and Social Structure: A Festschrift for Robert K. Merton, Transactions of the New York Academy of Sciences*, series 2 volume 39. New York: New York Academy of Sciences.

Hall, A.R. (1980), *Philosophers at War: The Quarrel between Newton and Leibniz*. Cambridge, UK: Cambridge University Press.

Hobson, J.A. (1891), The Law of the Three Rents, *Quarterly Journal of Economics* 5(3), pp. 263–288.

Hollander, J.H. (ed.) (1815), *A Reprint of Economic Tracts. Thomas Robert Malthus on the Nature and Progress of Rent*. Baltimore: Johns Hopkins (1903).

Johnson, H.G. (1975), Technological Change and Comparative Advantage: An Advanced Country's Viewpoint, *Journal of World Trade Law* 9(Jan–Feb), pp. 1–14.

King, J.E. (2013), *David Ricardo*. Basingstoke, UK: Palgrave Macmillan.

Kuhn, T.S. (1977), The Essential Tension: Tradition and Innovation in Scientific Research, in C.W. Taylor (ed.), *The Third (1959) University of Utah Research Conference on the Identification of Scientific Talent*. Salt Lake City: University of Utah Press. Reprinted in *The Essential Tension: Selected Studies in Scientific Tradition and Change*. Chicago and London: The University of Chicago Press.

Lamb, D. and Easton, S.M. (1984), *Multiple Discovery*. Avebury, UK: Avebury.

Malthus, T.R. (1814), *Observations on the Effects of the Corn Laws, and of a Rise or Fall in the Price of Corn on the Agriculture and General Wealth of the Country*. London: J. Johnson and Co.

Malthus, T.R. (1815a), *The Nature and Progress of Rent: An Inquiry*. London: John Murray.

Malthus, T.R. (1815b), *The Grounds of an Opinion on the Policy of Restricting the Importation of Foreign Corn: Intended as an Appendix to 'Observations on the Corn Laws'*. London: John Murray.

Marx, K. (1885), *Theories of Surplus Value*, volume II. Moscow: Progress Publishers (1968).

Merton, R.K. (1961), Singletons and Multiples in Scientific Discovery, *American Philosophical Society Proceedings*, 105(5), pp. 470–486. Reprinted as Singletons and Multiples in Science in Merton (1973), pp. 343–369.

Merton, R.K. (1963), Resistance to the Systematic Study of Multiple Discoveries in Science, *European Journal of Sociology* 4, pp. 237–249. Part reprinted as Multiple Discoveries as Strategic Research Site in Merton (1973), pp. 371–381.

Merton, R.K. (ed.) (1973), *The Sociology of Science: Theoretical and Empirical Investigations*. Chicago: University of Chicago Press.

Mill, J. (1826), *Elements of Political Economy*, third edition. London: Baldwin, Cradock, and Joy. Reprinted in D. Winch (ed.) (1966), *James Mill. Selected Writings*. Chicago: University of Chicago Press.

Ogburn, W.F. and Thomas, D. (1922), Are Inventions Inevitable? A Note on Social Evolution, *Political Science Quarterly* 37(1), pp. 83–98.

Patinkin, D. (1983), Multiple Discoveries and the Central Message, *American Journal of Sociology*, 89(2), pp. 306–323.

Petty, W. (1662), *A Treatise on Taxes and Contributions*. London: N. Brooke.

Pullen, J. (2014), Malthus on Causality, *European Journal of the History of Economic Thought*, published online, 30 July 2014 at http://www.tandfonline.com/doi/pdf/10.1080/09672567.2014.916729#.Va99b_mqpBc.

Schumpeter, J.A. (1954), *History of Economic Analysis*. London: Allen and Unwin.

Sismondi, J.-C.-L. Simonde de (1819), *New Principles of Political Economy: Of Wealth in Relation to Population*, translation R. Hyse (1991). New Brunswick, USA and London: Transaction Publishers.

Smith, A. (1776), *An Inquiry into the Nature and Causes of the Wealth of Nation*, J.R. McCulloch (ed.) (1828). London: Adam Black and William Tait.

Smith, A. (1776), *An Inquiry into the Nature and Causes of the Wealth of Nations*, E. Cannan (ed.) (1961). London: Methuen.

Sraffa, P. (ed.) (1951a), *The Works and Correspondence of David Ricardo: On the Principles of Political Economy and Taxation*, volume I. Cambridge, UK: Cambridge University Press.

Sraffa, P. (ed.) (1951b), *The Works and Correspondence of David Ricardo: Pamphlets and Papers 1815–1823*, volume IV. Cambridge, UK: Cambridge University Press.

Sraffa, P. (ed.) (1955), *The Works and Correspondence of David Ricardo, Biographical Miscellany*, volume X. Cambridge, UK: Cambridge University Press.

Steuart, J. (1767), *An Inquiry into the Principles of Political Oeconomy*. London: A. Millar and T. Cadell. Republished with excisions by Andrew S. Skinner (ed.). Edinburgh and London: Oliver and Boyd (1966).

Stigler, G.J. (1980), Merton on Multiples, Denied and Affirmed, in F. Gieryn (ed.). Reprinted in G.J. Stigler (1982), *The Economist as Preacher and Other Essays*. Chicago: University of Chicago Press.

Stigler, S.M. (1980), Stigler's Law of Eponomy, in F. Gieryn (ed.). Reprinted in S.M. Stigler (1999), *Statistics on the Table: The History of Statistical Concepts and Methods*. Cambridge, MA, USA: Harvard University Press.

Thompson, R.P. (1826), *An Exposition of Fallacies on Rent, Tithes, &etc., Containing an Examination of Mr Ricardo's Theory of Rent, in the Form of a Review of Mr Mill's Elements*. London: Hatchard and Son. A second edition of the pamphlet appeared later in the same year, retitled *The True Theory of Rent in Opposition to Mr Ricardo and Others*.

Torrens, R. (1815), *An Essay on the External Corn Trade: Containing an Inquiry into the General Principles of that Important Branch of Traffic; an Examination of the Exceptions to which these Principles are Liable; and a Comparative Statement of the Effects which Restrictions on Importation and Free Intercourse, are Calculated to Produce upon Subsistence, Agriculture, Commerce, and Revenue*. London: J. Hatchard.

Torrens, R. (1829), *An Essay on the External Corn Trade*, fifth edition. London: Longman, Rees, Orme, and Green. Reprinted in Clifton, New Jersey: Augustus M. Kelley.

Turgot, A.R.J. (1977), Observations on a Paper by Saint-Pèravy on the Subject of Indirect Taxation, in *The Economics of A.R.J. Turgot*, edited by P. Groenewegen,

The Hague: Martinus Nijhoff, pp. 109–122 (translation by P. Groenewegen of the original essay written in 1767 published in his complete works 1808–1811 in French).

Viner, J. (1937), *Studies in the Theory of International Trade*. London: Allen and Unwin.

West, E. (1815), *Essay on the Application of Capital to Land, with Observations Shewing the Impolicy of any Great Restriction of the Importation of Corn, and that the Bounty of 1688 Did Not Lower the Price of It*. London: T. Underwood.

10 On Ricardo and Cambridge

G.C. Harcourt and Peter Kriesler[1]

John King's contributions to the history of economic thought are numerous and profound; they take in a wide range of subjects. While his last two decades of work on the history of economic thought have focused 'on the history of more recent economic ideas' (King 2013, p. vii), with a strong emphasis on Cambridge economics, he recently returned to 'nineteenth-century political economy' with his interesting volume on David Ricardo in Tony Thirlwall's 'Great Thinkers in Economics' series (King 2013). Given John's interest in these themes, this chapter on Cambridge interpretations of Ricardo's work constitutes, we hope, an appropriate tribute to him, as a long-time friend and much admired colleague and scholar.

David Ricardo's key place in the history of economic thought is well established. However, both the understanding of his *Principles of Political Economy and Taxation* (Ricardo 1817) and its role in the development of economic analysis are much more controversial. Cambridge economists have contributed significantly to both of these issues. In particular, they have played an important part in two extremely divergent interpretations of Ricardo's place in the development of economic thought. Understanding how Ricardo has been viewed in Cambridge does not result in homogeneity, but in a spectrum of interpretations. In this chapter, we focus on the role of Ricardo's *Principles* in the development of economics as seen by Cambridge economists. At one end of the spectrum is the interpretation by Piero Sraffa and Maurice Dobb, which located Ricardo's work in the surplus approach, which they see as being a quite distinct approach from that of modern neoclassical economics. They argue that the development of neoclassical theory, from the 1870s on, represented an important change in both emphasis and analytical tools used from that of the classical political economists and Marx. In contrast, they argue, the analytical methods of the classical political economists formed the basis of an alternative economic tradition associated with many schools of heterodox economics.

At the other end of the spectrum is Alfred Marshall's interpretation. He argued for continuity from Adam Smith and Ricardo to his own contributions set within the supply and demand approach. Within this view, he argued that Ricardo's theory of value provided some of the essential ingredients of the supply blade of the supply and demand scissors. Together, they mutually determined, he argued, long-period competitive normal prices (and quantities).

The other Cambridge economists whom we consider, and who have contributed to the interpretation of Ricardo include William Whewell, who offered the 'first mathematical formulation of Ricardo's theory' (Campanelli 1982, p. 249; Cochrane 1970), as well as Maynard Keynes, Joan Robinson, Nicholas Kaldor and Luigi Pasinetti.

In a sense, Malthus, Ricardo's contemporary, close friend and great debating partner could be seen as the first Cambridge economist to interpret Ricardo. However, since Malthus did not attempt to provide a systematic account of the Ricardian system, but rather responded to specific aspects of it, the starting point for our account of Cambridge interpretations of Ricardo will be with the much-neglected William Whewell.

Whewell

William Whewell, who has been credited with providing the first mathematical statement of Ricardo's model (Cochrane 1970), was the Master of Trinity College, Cambridge and a University Lecturer in Mathematics, Mineralogy and Moral Philosophy. The question of continuity, which was important for later Cambridge economists, was not relevant for Whewell, as no alternative to classical political economy had yet been fully developed.

His early attempts to provide a mathematical formulation of the Ricardian system were specifically aimed at providing a systematic analysis of political economy in order to avoid errors in logic, arguing that a systematic mathematical formulation would avoid such errors.[2] He likened the principles of political economy to those of mechanics in the importance of mathematics for both. 'It appears I think that the sciences of Mechanics and Political Economy are so far analogous, that something of the same advantage may be looked for from the application of mathematics in the case of Political Economy' (Whewell 1829, p. 5).

Whewell argued that mathematics allowed the logical consequences of postulates to be correctly deduced, and it was this process that he applied to Ricardo's analysis. Nevertheless, the more important task was 'not in reasoning *from* principles, but *to* them: in extracting from a wide and patient survey of facts the laws according to which circumstances and conditions determine the progress of wealth, and the fortunes of men' (Whewell 1829, p. 43: original emphasis).[3]

Whewell provided a mathematical version of Ricardo's system, arguing that 'Ricardian distribution theory was insufficiently supported by empirical evidence' (Cochrane 1970, p. 419). In particular, he took issue with Ricardo's analysis of wages and of rent (Campanelli 1982, p. 254). With respect to wages, he rejected Ricardo's assumption of the iron law of wages, arguing that 'The habitual necessaries and comforts of the labourer may, and do, undergo changes simultaneous and co-ordinate with those of the population' (Whewell 1831, p. 7). He also argued that Ricardo's theory of rent was not a good explanation of the determination of rent owing to the increased importance of '*Auxiliary Capital*' which substantially increases the productivity of agricultural labour (Whewell 1862, pp. 65–72; original emphasis). Rent, according to Whewell, increases not only for the Ricardian reason of extending the margin of cultivation of soil, but also 'by the improvements of methods of culture' and the latter is of much greater empirical significance (Whewell 1862, p. 71).

As a result, Whewell also questioned the validity of the conclusion of Ricardo's model, namely, the tendency towards a stationary state due to the 'extension of agricultural labour to less productive soils'[4] (1862, p. 15). This, he argued, is 'clearly and demonstrably false' due to the 'increase in the power of agriculture', as a result of which 'it is evident that the whole of his assumption of the nature of economic progress of this country, and the views of distribution of wealth arising from this assumption, must fall to the ground' (Whewell 1862, p. 15).

Whewell also modified Ricardo's analysis of prices to incorporate the influence of fixed capital. In doing so, he developed expressions for price which allowed for fixed capital and pre-date the important work in this area by Dmitriev (1904), representing a major breakthrough in the analysis of 'the reduction of fixed capital to dated quantities of labour' (Campanelli 1982, p. 257). Campanelli (1982) emphasizes Whewell's analysis of fixed capital in Ricardo's model, which used the device of reduction to dated labour.

Whewell came neither to praise Ricardo, nor to bury him, but nevertheless to criticize him, first, by criticizing the unreality of the empirical generalizations on which Ricardo's deductions were erected, and, secondly, by providing through mathematical analysis, an internal critique of Ricardo's propositions within Ricardo's own system.

Marshall

Marshall stressed the continuity of economic ideas, with his own analysis being 'a direct linear descent from the classical economists' (Petridis 1998, p. 79). To do so, Marshall had to provide a very generous reading of Ricardo (from his point of view and given his agenda) to justify his interpretation of Ricardo and other classical political economists, including Smith and also Marx. In particular, Marshall defended Ricardo from the criticisms of Walras, Jevons and others by arguing that his contribution can be seen as part of a continuum in the development of economics, with the ultimate emergence of the scissors of supply and demand. In this picture, Ricardo is seen as contributing to the analysis of the supply blade, via his emphasis on cost of production, because, although he understood the demand blade, he did not spend time analysing it because it was intuitively obvious. As Marshall notes:

> Ricardo's theory of cost of production in relation to value occupies so important a place in the history of economics that any misunderstanding as to its real character must necessarily be very mischievous; and

unfortunately it is so expressed as almost to invite misunderstanding. In consequence there is a widely spread belief that it has needed to be reconstructed by the present generation of economists. Cause is shown in Appendix I for not accepting this opinion; and for holding on the contrary that the foundations of the theory as they were left by Ricardo remain intact; that much has been added to them, and that very much has been built upon them, but that little has been taken from them. It is there argued that he knew that demand played an essential part in governing value, but that he regarded its action as less obscure than that of cost of production, and therefore passed it lightly over in the notes which he made for the use of his friends, and himself; for he never essayed to write a formal treatise.

(Marshall 1890, p. 403)

Ricardo and the able business men who followed in his wake took the operation of demand too much for granted as a thing which did not need to be explained: they did not emphasize it, nor study it with sufficient care; and this neglect has caused much confusion, and has obscured important truths.

(Marshall 1890, p. 403; see also p. 525)

The 'cost of production principle' and the 'final utility' principle are undoubtedly component parts of the one all-ruling law of supply and demand; each may be compared to one blade of a pair of scissors. When one blade is held still, and the cutting is effected by moving the other, we may say with careless brevity that the cutting is done by the second; but the statement is not one to be made formally, and defended deliberately.

(Marshall 1890, p. 403; see also p. 820)

In order to demonstrate this position with respect to the idea of continuity in the history of economic analysis, Marshall had to interpret Ricardo in an idiosyncratic way, as has been clearly shown in Bharadwaj (1978a, 1978c) and Groenewegen (2003, 2006):

Irrespective of the interpretation the reader may hold of Ricardo on value, Marshall's views on the subject can be criticised on several grounds. Above all, he can be charged with an anachronistic reading of Ricardo's text, which transforms Ricardo's notions into Marshallian terminology and thereby induces the resemblances Marshall desires his readers to find.

(Groenewegen 2003, p. 37)

The basic thrust of Marshall's comments on Ricardo cannot therefore be accepted as accurate .... Hence Marshall's lengthy, scattered and not very detailed commentary on Ricardo is a good illustration of 'the fact that each generation rewrites its own history of economics [and that] from this perspective an evaluation often tells us more about the commentator than the subject' (Hollander 1979: 4).

(Groenewegen 2003, p. 43)

Most modern commentators accept the argument that 'Marshall read much more into Ricardo's theory of value than any modern reader can now find' (Petridis 1998, p. 82). In particular, Marshall's argument that Ricardo understood the importance of final and marginal utility in determining the demand curve, which played an important role in determining value 'stretche[d] the interpretation of Ricardo ... Either Marshall's imagination or his generosity of interpretation ran out of control' (Petridis 1998, p. 82).

In other words, Marshall's idiosyncratic interpretation of Ricardo served an ulterior purpose in its role of providing evidence for his thesis about the continuity of economics: 'there is something wrong with Marshall's own account. He made astonishing claims for continuity, and he persisted in these claims in the face of contemporary criticism, despite his acute personal sensitivity to criticism' (O'Brien 1990, p. 136).

Keynes

Close to Marshall's interpretation, but putting his main emphasis on the superiority of Thomas Robert Malthus's understanding of the overall workings of the economy relative to Ricardo's, especially in the short period, is Maynard Keynes's interpretation. As he himself admits, in the fundamental debates about the roles of aggregate and effective demand at the heart of his greatest contribution,[5] he had only with difficulty included Ricardo under the rubric of the classical economists.[6] They were represented in Keynes's time by Marshall and especially by A.C. Pigou (he also included F.Y. Edgeworth and John Stuart Mill in his examples). As Keynes (1936, p. xxiii) tells us, he had 'a long struggle of escape' from the ways of thinking on which he was brought up.

In the preface to *A Treatise on Money* (Keynes 1930), Keynes locates one of the most significant contributions of the book in his analysis of the dynamic processes associated with the transition from one position of long-period equilibrium to another.[7] There, Keynes sees the origins of the characteristics of the long-period equilibrium position in Ricardo's work, but, of course, as translated in his analysis into the Marshallian mode of thinking. Ricardo provides evidence both for this interpretation and of why he and Malthus were often at cross-purposes, with his well-known explanation of this lasting gap in their ability to agree or even communicate with one another.[8]

Later, for Keynes, the distinguishing features for his label of the 'classical economists' or the 'Ricardian tradition' are, first, a lack of concern with the determination of total output (Keynes 1936, pp. 4–5), and, second, an adherence to Say's Law 'that supply creates its own demand' (Keynes 1936, p. 18). The result of this is that 'there is no obstacle to full employment' (Keynes 1936, p. 26).

The idea that we can safely neglect the aggregate demand function is fundamental to the Ricardian economics, which underlie what we have been taught for more than a century... The great puzzle of effective demand with which Malthus had wrestled vanished from economic literature. You will not find it mentioned even once in the whole works of Marshall, Edgeworth and Professor Pigou.

(Keynes 1936, p. 32; see also Davis 1998)

In other words, Keynes's discussion of Ricardo, and his analysis of what constitutes 'classical economics', is quite different from that of any of the other Cambridge economists, all of whom concentrate on Ricardo's theories of value, distribution and growth as providing the main basis for differentiation. For Keynes, in contrast, the focus, when labelling schools of economic thought, moves to macroeconomic analysis, particularly the analysis of the determination of output and employment. As a result, all his predecessors in the mainstream of economic thought, with the exception of Malthus, are labelled as classical economists in the Ricardian tradition, and he often laments the dominance of Ricardo's ideas over those of Malthus. 'If only Malthus, instead of Ricardo, had been the parent stem from which nineteenth-century economics proceeded, what a much wiser and richer place the world would be today!' (Keynes 1933, pp. 100–01).

Sraffa

Sraffa's role in the Cambridge interpretation of Ricardo is pivotal. His influence comes from his writings, particularly his editorship with the collaboration of Maurice Dobb of *The Works and Correspondence of David Ricardo*, his preface and appendix on 'References to the Literature' in *Production of Commodities by Means of Commodities* and also through his lectures on 'Advanced Theory of Value' in Cambridge at the end of the 1920s[9] and his discussions with colleagues.

Under Sraffa's influence, there were significant changes in the way Ricardo's work was interpreted. Particularly important was his editorship of *The Works and Correspondence* and his editorial introduction to volume I, *The Principles of Political Economy and Taxation*. It was the introduction which clearly illustrated the unchanging nature of Ricardo's analysis of value. At the same time, it illuminated the differences in method and theory between Ricardo and the classical political economists, on the one hand, and the marginalist school, on the other, restoring the classical notion of the surplus as a key, indeed the core, analytical category.

Sraffa's view of the role of Ricardo and of the development of economic thought represented an important alternative view to that of Marshall which had come to dominate Cambridge thinking. According to Sraffa, there was a fundamental divergence of paths in the development of economic theory as it came out of classical political economy. One path went from the work of the classical political economists into Marx, whom he regarded as the legitimate heir of classical insights, and who criticized, added to and fundamentally transformed this legacy. The other path he identified resulted in the emasculation of the classical insights and approach.[10] 'This standpoint, which is that of the old classical political economists from Adam Smith to Ricardo, has been submerged and forgotten since the advent of the "marginal" method' (Sraffa 1960, p. v).

Such a reading is becoming more and more clear as the riches of the Sraffa archives are brought into the public domain by his hard-working, patient and thorough editors, especially the late Krishna Bharadwaj, Heinz Kurz and Giancarlo de Vivo. Sraffa's literary executor, Pierangelo Garegnani (2008) argues that Sraffa's early interpretation of the development of economics was consistent with Marshall's, but that, in developing his own theoretical ideas, he came to reject the Marshallian interpretation around 1927, while Signorino (2008) traces the change in Sraffa's views from his 'lectures on the advanced theory of value' at Cambridge. Pasinetti summarizes the content of Sraffa's lectures:

> Sraffa is convinced, since the beginning, that an aberrant distortion has taken place in economic theory in the second part of the nineteenth century. From 1870 onwards, dominant (marginalist) economics has caused a change in the contents of the whole subject, with respect to what it used to be previously ... There is an 'abysmal gulf' [Sraffa papers] between the marginal economists' writings since 1870 and those of the economists of the beginning of the nineteenth century ... The change of name itself – from classical 'political economy' to Marshall's 'economics' – is there to 'mark the cleavage' and 'Marshall's attempt to bridge over the cleavage and establish a continuity in the tradition is futile and misguided' [Sraffa papers].
>
> (Pasinetti 2007, pp. 179–180)

Sraffa's view of the place of Ricardo's work in the history of economic thought, as well as his restoration of many of Ricardo's key concepts, became an important foundation for much of heterodox economics, particularly for Post Keynesian and Sraffian economics.

Dobb[11]

Maurice Dobb's interpretation of Ricardo's role in the history of economic analysis is illustrative of the major shift that Cambridge's view underwent as a result of the influence of Sraffa. Bharadwaj has argued that the early Dobb was very much under the influence of Marshall in his interpretation of the history of economic thought.[12] 'Dobb ... was persuaded by the view that Marshall had continued the Ricardo-Mill tradition, rendering their doctrines rigorous and divesting them of some of their obvious "oddities"' (Bharadwaj 1978c, p. 164).

This acceptance of the Marshallian version of the development of economics is apparent from any of Dobb's early writings on the subject. For example, in 1924, he wrote that:

> what the Cambridge school has done is to divest classical political economy of its more obvious crudities, to sever its connection with the philosophy of natural law, and to restate it in terms of the differential calculus. The line of descent is fairly direct from Smith, Malthus, and Ricardo; and Cambridge has remained relatively untouched by the anti-classical doctrines of the German semi-socialists and the Austrian school.
>
> (Dobb 1924, p. 6)

In *Wages*, a Cambridge Economic Handbook, originally published in 1927, he clearly accepts[13] Marshall's demand and supply stream:

> the traditional theories ... can be broadly classified into two main types, according to the type of determining factor on which their emphasis has rested. On the one hand are those theories which have explained wages predominantly in terms of factors which influence the *supply* of labour-power – virtually, costs of production theories of wages. On the other hand are those theories which have treated wages as being determined primarily by certain factors which influence employers' *demand* for labour ... Some economists (most notable, Marshall) have tried to erect a synthesis of the two types of explanation and to hold a balance between the two sets of determining influences; and so have produced a theory of a hybrid type.
>
> (Dobb 1959, pp. 91–92: original emphasis)

In 1931, Dobb, in his entry on 'the Cambridge School' for the *Encyclopaedia of the Social Sciences* (Dobb 1931), argued that 'Marshall imbibed the Ricardian tradition through the medium of J.S. Mill', and that 'he laid the foundations for his theory on the rock of Ricardian conceptions – real cost as the basis of values, the distinctiveness of rent, the concept of a normal rate of profit'. The entry also emphasized Marshall's eclecticism and the incompleteness of his equilibrium analysis.

Throughout these early writings there is a fairly uncritical acceptance of Marshall's view of the classical political economists as providing the explanation of the supply side, and the neoclassical economists, the demand side.

It was a little later, we conjecture mainly as a result of Sraffa's influence, that Dobb became more critical of the essential nature of the Cambridge school and of Marshall's role in it. According to Brian Pollitt, Marshall's influence was only rejected in 1937, with the publication of *Political Economy and Capitalism* (Pollitt 1988, p. 57), despite the fact that intellectual relations between Dobb and Sraffa had begun much earlier, at least by 1926.[14]

In particular, he came to reject Marshall's view of continuity in the development of economic theory, a view which he had accepted before his discussions on the subject with Sraffa. His new interpretation of the development of economic analysis is most apparent in his *Theories of Value and Distribution since Adam Smith* (Dobb 1973), the essential arguments of which were presented in his superb 1972–73 Alfred Marshall Memorial Lectures at Cambridge.[15]

In particular, the way in which Dobb's version of Ricardianism allowed a direct Ricardo–Marx–Sraffa connection to be drawn commands interest, and is indicated in a letter written on board a ship to India by Dobb (in late 1950) to Theodore Prager in Vienna. Dobb wrote:

> Sraffa's edition of Ricardo's works, (on which I think you know he has been engaged since 1930 and on which I have come in since 1948 to help him finish it) is I am glad to say nearing completion at last, at least so far as the first four volumes are concerned …. I think we conclusively establish (in opposition to the traditional Hollander-Marshall-Cannan view) that there was no 'weakening' of Ricardo's enunciation of the labour theory of value as time went on: that in fact he reached at the end of his life a position rather close to that of Marx, so that the true line of descent is certainly from Ricardo to Marx and *not* from Ricardo to the cost-of-production theory au Mill to Marshall as the bourgeois tradition has it.
>
> (quoted in Pollitt 1988, pp. 62–63; original emphasis)

The idea of a 'line of thought' from the *Tableau Economique*'s emphasis on surplus to Ricardo, and on to Marx, influenced Dobb's subsequent thinking profoundly. His review of Sraffa (Dobb 1961), his decade of writings on the Cambridge controversies in capital theory and on Dmitriev, his research for the *Das Kapital* centenary of 1967, his preparations for the 1972–73 Marshall Lectures at Cambridge and for his last major book, *Theories of Value and Distribution since Adam Smith*, all bear witness to the insight expressed in his 1950 letter to Prager.

Dobb's new view was that there were *two* streams in the development of economics. One was that championed by Marshall; the second was brought out by Sraffa's reading of Ricardo. Dobb believed that this latter stream had been 'submerged' between 1870 and 1950. Ricardo's role in opposing Adam Smith on crucial issues (such as the dominant role of agricultural pricing in influencing income distribution and on the 'adding up' problem) led directly to Marx and formed the foundation of this 'second stream'. A precondition of Dobb's acceptance of this two-stream view was his acknowledgement of the strong links between Ricardo and Marx which formed the foundation of the 'second stream'. Similarly, Dobb placed great emphasis on the role of Jevons, not only because of his instrumental role in developing the analysis of 'demand-determination by utility', but also because of his explicit rejection of the Ricardian tradition. For this reason, Dobb referred to the new tradition as the 'Jevonian revolution' (Dobb 1975, p. 330; see also Dobb 1973, chapter 7).[16]

Joan Robinson

Joan Robinson was closer on the spectrum to Sraffa, Dobb and Pasinetti but was more concerned to integrate insights from both Ricardo and Keynes (and, of course, Michał Kalecki) into ongoing developments in Post Keynesian economics. As had Keynes, she too started her analytical life steeped in Marshallian/Pigovian approaches. However, increasingly over her lifetime, the approaches of Keynes and Kalecki and her interpretation of Marx came to the fore.[17] Yet, she never fully threw off the influence of Marshall's method in her own analysis. Nevertheless, she made substantial positive contributions and the final results of her labour are to be found most clearly and consistently expressed in her 1980 article with Amit Bhaduri in the *Cambridge Journal of Economics* (Bhaduri and Robinson 1980). Here, Sraffa's, and through him Ricardo's, as well as Marx's and Kalecki's insights and modes of analysis are integrated, each with their own tasks to perform concerning analysis.

Robinson accepted most of Sraffa's interpretation of Ricardo and of the development of economic thought from an early stage, and her works are full of acknowledgements to this.[18] For her, unlike Sraffa, one of the key distinguishing characteristics of Ricardo, the classical political economists and Marx was their emphasis on growth and accumulation, compared with the neoclassical concern with pricing and distribution of a given output (Robinson 1969, pp. 58–62; 1970, pp. 123–24; 1971, pp. 1, 109; Robinson and Eatwell 1973, chapters 2 and 3). Given the emphasis over her lifetime on the dynamic implications of growth and accumulation, it is unsurprising that these were the main features that, to her, distinguished Ricardo from neoclassical economics: 'Ricardo was observing a historical process of accumulation going on through time' (Robinson 1978, p. 211). 'The central concern of classical political economy was accumulation; the neoclassics substituted equilibrium in a stationary state' (Robinson and Eatwell 1973, p. 37).

Kaldor[19]

Kaldor's position on Ricardo and the classical political economists is very different to that of any of the other Cambridge economists, although the diagram he developed to illustrate Ricardo's analysis has been adopted by many subsequent writers in the area (Kaldor 1950, 1956; King 2013, pp. 64–65; Hicks 1972). His major work on distribution theory (Kaldor 1955–56, p. 209), distinguishes 'four main strands of thought': 'the Ricardian or Classical theory', 'the Marxian', 'the Neo-Classical or Marginalist Theory' and 'the Keynesian'. When discussing Ricardo's analysis, Kaldor distinguished two important principles: 'the "marginal principle" serves to explain the share of rent, and the "surplus principle" the division of the residue between wages and profits'[20] (1955–56, p. 211). 'Marxian theory is essentially an adaption of Ricardo's "surplus theory"' (1955–56, p. 215), while 'neo-classical value and distribution theory derives from … the Ricardian … "marginal principle"'

(1955–56, p. 218), and represents a generalization of this principle.[21] Kaldor distinguished the classical/Ricardian approach from that of the marginalists, as the marginal productivity principle only explained the remuneration of land, those of capital and labour being determined by other factors (see also King, 2015). Kaldor developed a long-period Keynesian theory based on the principle of the multiplier. His conclusion is of interest. 'We have seen how the various "models" of distribution, the Ricardian-Marxian, the Keynesian and the Kaleckian are related to each other. I am not sure where "marginal productivity" comes in, in all this' (Kaldor 1955–56, p. 236). Elsewhere, he distinguishes the classical school which 'started with dynamics', from mainstream economists, whose '"static" economics occupied most of the space in textbooks and in lecture courses' (Kaldor 1996, p. 22).

In his later writings, when he emphasized the importance of increasing returns in the growth process, he in fact criticizes Ricardo, classical political economists and neoclassical economists (though not Marx), treating them as part of the same tradition due to their reliance on constant or diminishing returns at the expense of increasing returns (see e.g. Kaldor 1981; Kaldor 1996, fourth lecture; King 2013, p. 182).

Pasinetti

Luigi Pasinetti accepted Sraffa's view of the two streams of the development of economic thought and located his own contributions within the Ricardo/classical tradition, on which he built and developed, first, in his mathematical model of Ricardo's theory of distribution and growth (Pasinetti 1960; see also 'A Brief Historical Excursus', 1977; 1981), and then as an integral part of the development of his own system of structural dynamics (Pasinetti 1981, 1993, 2007).[22] In fact, in his important overview of what he calls the 'Cambridge Keynesian School', he lists amongst the defining features of that school:

> *Malthus and the Classics (not Walras and the marginalists) as the major inspiring source in the history of economic thought* ... a positive connotation has been the revival of classical economic thought (especially that of Smith, Malthus, Ricardo and Marx). ... It was then Sraffa, with his eleven-volume critical edition of the *Collected Works of David Ricardo*, that provided the crucial path to this revival of classical economics .... The reappraisal of the ideas and methodology of the classical economists seems therefore central to understanding the core contributions of the Cambridge School and to framing them in a 'production' rather than in an 'exchange' paradigm.
>
> (Pasinetti 2007, pp. 222–23; original emphasis)

Passinetti's model tries to overcome the lacuna between Ricardian distribution and growth theory by providing a dynamic model of growth and accumulation. In a mathematical form, he captures the essence of the Ricardian system, showing how the Malthusian principle of population will ensure convergence on the subsistence level of wages as each successive wave of accumulation by capitalists occurs, allowing the economy to grow over 'time' but at a decreasing rate, leading inevitably *in the absence of technical progress* to the stationary state.[23]

According to Joan Robinson, Ricardo used the prospect of the stationary state as 'an awful warning', not as a description of where society was actually going.[24] Of course, Ricardo was well aware that technical advances in agriculture and industry would serve to stave off the approach of diminishing returns in actual historical time. His argument for free trade – repeal the Corn Laws – rested on the proposition that by letting comparative advantage have full play world-wide, it would be 'as if' technical progress caused the total output/input of equal doses of labour and capital relationships in all economies to move up over time. Diminishing returns were still present in the slopes of the total product curves (Harcourt 2006, p. 93) but the entire curves were raised over time both by the effects of free trade (but was that not a once-and-for-all effect?) and technical progress.

What was needed therefore was a theory of endogenous technical progress, which was first provided by Marx (and later by Joseph Schumpeter who, according to Robinson, was 'Marx with the adjectives changed'), then by a few mainstream economists, for example, Charles Kennedy, Paul Samuelson and the Post Keynesians. Of the Post Keynesians, Pasinetti's long-running research project on structural dynamics (e.g. Pasinetti 1981, 1993, 2007) stands out (see also Arena and Porta 2012; Kerr and Scazzieri 2013).

The short period and the long period in economic analysis

Behind these developments and interpretations is a major puzzle which has never been solved by the mainstream, nor fully by the Cambridge School. The puzzle is the lacuna between the short period and the long period in economic analysis, that same gap that led to Ricardo and Malthus not being able to get on the same wavelength in their discussions. Robinson was particularly aware of the relevance of this problem to both Keynes and Ricardo. 'Keynes hardly ever peered over the edge of the short period to see the effect of investment in making addition to the stocks of productive equipment. ... Here it was Ricardo who could have helped him' (Robinson 1978, p. 212).

As long as economists argue that equilibrium positions are strong attractors, akin to magnetic attractors, then, even when path-dependence is taken into account, this incoherence will remain. If we take Ricardo at his word, he tried to overcome this by concentrating on ultimate positions, but he conceded that balance probably required a less extreme position (see note 8). Keynes, on his own initiative and reinforced by Richard Kahn's views and contributions (see Harcourt 1994, 1995), made the short period a subject more than worthy of study in its own right, especially within the context of the trade cycle and historical periods of sustained slumps and high unemployment.

But when Joan Robinson, Nicky Kaldor and Kahn tackled 'generalising *The General Theory* to the long period', they were still under the spell of Marshall and more especially Pigou as the interpreter of Marshall. As Neil Hart (2009, 2011) has shown, Marshall understood that economies and societies were evolving organisms, so that his supply and demand tools for tackling time (which were derived from classical physics) were unsuitable for a full analysis of such processes. Evolutionary theory was needed but was not available in a received form in his lifetime.

This leads us to the lacuna between the short period and the long period to which Robert Solow brought eloquent attention: 'one major weakness in the core of macroeconomics as I have represented it is the lack of a real coupling between the short-run picture and the long-run picture. Since the long run and the short run merge into one another, one feels they cannot be completely independent' (Solow 1997, pp. 231–32; see also Solow 2000). So we have come full circle back to where Ricardo and Malthus, 'the first of the Cambridge economists' (Keynes 1933, p. 71), started off their long debates.

Notes

1 This chapter is based on a lecture given by Geoff Harcourt to the Ricardo Society of Japan at the International Conference on Post Keynesian Economics, September 2011. We would like to thank John King and an anonymous referee for their helpful comments.

2 In particular, Whewell argued that Ricardo had erred in his belief that 'a tax on wages would fall on labourers' (Whewell 1829, p. 2; 1831, pp. 27–30) because he had not investigated the proposition mathematically.

3 These comments are reminiscent of Keynes's description of Malthus's method (Keynes 1933, p. 107).

4 See Pasinetti (1960), Harcourt (2006, chapter 7) and below. Ricardo was aware of the point which Whewell was making, but abstracted from the influence of technical progress in order to bring out the long-term effects of diminishing returns on the distribution of income.

5 That is why Keynes found Pigou's 1933 book on unemployment such a Godsend, because Pigou spelt out explicitly what Keynes previously had deduced about what the classical system must be (see Ambrosi 2003).

6 Having credited Marx with the invention of the name, 'The classical economists', to cover 'Ricardo and James Mill and their *predecessors*', Keynes adds: 'I have become accustomed, perhaps perpetrating a solecism, to include ... the *followers* of Ricardo, those ... who adopted and perfected the theory of Ricardian economics' (Keynes 1936, n. 3; original emphasis).

7 'My object has been to find a method which is useful in describing, not merely the characteristics of static equilibrium, but also those of disequilibrium, and to discover the dynamical laws governing the passage of a monetary system from one position of equilibrium to another' (Keynes 1930, p. xvii).

8 'It appears to me that one great cause of our differences in opinion ... is that you have always in your mind the immediate and temporary effects of particular changes – whereas I put these immediate and temporary effects quite aside, and fix my intention on the permanent state of things which will result from them. Perhaps you estimate these temporary effects too high, whilst I am too much disposed to undervalue them. To manage the subject quite right they

should be carefully distinguished, and the due effects ascribed to each' (Sraffa ed. 1952, p. 120).

9 For a discussion of the role of the lectures in shaping Sraffa's views on Ricardo and the classical economists and his shifting view of Marshall, see Signorino (2008).

10 A case made convincingly by Krishna Bharadwaj in her wonderful 1976 Dutt Lectures, published in 1978 (Bharadwaj 1978a). In them she followed the same intellectual pilgrim's progress as Sraffa, and she arrived at the same end point. This is witnessed by her remarkable review article of Sraffa (1960), 'Value through Exogenous Distribution' (Bharadwaj 1963). This article first brought her to Sraffa's attention and resulted in the start of their close friendship and subsequent collaboration.

11 This section is very much influenced by McFarlane and Kriesler (1993).

12 See also Holt (1998).

13 This acceptance is kept throughout the various editions of the Handbook, even though the sixth edition was published as late as 1959 (see Bharadwaj 1978b, pp. 164–65).

14 In a letter written in 1928, Dobb wrote: 'I believe that I have gained more by intellectual contact with him in the last year than from any single person' (quoted in Pollitt 1988, p. 62).

15 Dobb forbade Sraffa from attending the lectures. Piero asked me (GCH) to take notes and tell him what Maurice said, a daunting task, I can tell you.

16 It is interesting to note that in Dobb (1973) and in his Marshall Lectures, Dobb argues that Jevons misinterpreted Ricardo by levelling the accusation that, in his value theory, Ricardo was trying to determine two unknowns with one equation. That this charge, which originated with Walras, was not made by Jevons has been argued elsewhere (see Kriesler 1984). However, some related points should be noted. First, Dobb only seems to have made the charge in his 1973 book and Marshall Lectures. It is not referred to elsewhere. In particular, there is no reference to the charge in Dobb (1975). Second, in his Marshall Lectures, Dobb uses the argument to contend that Jevons's misunderstanding of Ricardo indicated that he had absorbed Ricardo through J.S. Mill rather than the original, a charge which is not made elsewhere. Finally, Dobb's error would seem to undermine his strong contention that Jevons intentionally changed the nature of economic analysis. If Jevons did not correctly comprehend Ricardo, as Dobb argues, then his 'revolution' was against ideas which he did not fully understand.

17 Her interpretation is limited and unsupportable, as Prue Kerr has convincingly documented in her account of the debates between Dobb and Joan Robinson as the latter was writing her 1942 *Essay* (Robinson 1942). See Harcourt and Kerr (2009, chapter 4). The book is a joint work but Prue wrote the first draft of chapter 4 drawing on her prior research on these issues.

18 She calls Marshall's version of classical economics and of Ricardo a 'travesty' (Robinson 1978, p. 212). See also Robinson (1967; 1972, pp. 32–35; 1979b, pp. 21–24).

19 John King has recently written an interesting paper on 'Kaldor, Nicholas, and Ricardo' (King, 2015).

20 See also King (2013, p. 182).

21 For a different view see King (2013, p. 182).

22 There is a Cambridge irony here. Bob Rowthorn (1974) criticized Sraffa's interpretation in the Sraffa/Dobb introduction to volume one of the Ricardo volumes (Sraffa ed. 1951) for being set too much in a static setting at the expense of Ricardo's own emphasis. Rowthorn argued for the priority of accumulation, growth and development. The irony is that the emphasis in Pasinetti's model of production and expenditure interrelationships is ultimately also on the processes of growth.

23 Pasinetti's views are also to be found in Kaldor's account of Ricardo's theory of distribution, in his 1955–56 article 'Alternative Theories of Distribution' (Kaldor 1955). It is my (GCH) understanding that Kaldor may have been influenced in his account by notes Sraffa lent him when Kaldor, though at the LSE, was in Cambridge with the LSE during the war. Kaldor gave the lecture on Ricardo in a 'circus' on great economists organized by Pigou. Pigou had asked Sraffa to do the lecture but because Sraffa loathed lecturing, he asked Kaldor to do it for him and gave him some background notes for the task.

24 '[Ricardo's] stationary state was not an equilibrium, but an awful warning. If … the Corn Laws [were not abolished] so as to reduce the real cost of wages, which were fixed in terms of bread, the rate of profit[s] would go on falling as employment in agriculture increased with "diminishing returns" until … accumulation would be brought to an end' (Robinson 1978, p. 213).

References

Ambrosi, G.M. (2003), *Keynes, Pigou and Cambridge Keynesians: Authenticity and Analytical Perspective in the Keynes-Classics Debate*. Basingstoke, UK: Palgrave Macmillan.

Arena, R. and Porta, P.L. (eds.) (2012), *Structural Dynamics and Economic Growth*. Cambridge, UK: Cambridge University Press.

Arestis, P., Baddeley, M. and McCombie, J.S.L. (eds.) (2007), *Economic Growth: New Directions in Theory and Policy*. Cheltenham, UK and Northampton, MA, USA: Edward Elgar.

Bhaduri, A. and Robinson, J. (1980), Accumulation and Exploitation: An Analysis in the Tradition of Marx, Sraffa and Kalecki, *Cambridge Journal of Economics* 4(2), pp. 103–115.

Bharadwaj, K. (1963), Value through Exogenous Distribution, *Economic Weekly* 15, pp. 1450–1454.

Bharadwaj, K. (1978a), *Classical Political Economy and Rise to Dominance of Supply and Demand Theories*. New Delhi: Orient Longman.

Bharadwaj, K. (1978b), Maurice Dobb's Critique of Theories of Value and Distribution, *Cambridge Journal of Economics* 2(2), pp. 153–174.

Bharadwaj, K. (1978c), The Subversion of Classical Analysis: Alfred Marshall's Early Writing on Value, *Cambridge Journal of Economics* 2(3), pp. 253–271.

Campanelli, G. (1982), W. Whewell's Contributions to Economic Analysis: The First Mathematical Formulation of Fixed Capital in Ricardo's System, *The Manchester School* 50(3), pp. 248–265.

Cochrane, J. (1970), The First Mathematical Ricardian Model, *History of Political Economy* 2(2), pp. 419–431.

Davis, J.D. (1998), Keynes, John Maynard, as an Interpreter of the Classical Economists, in H. Kurz, and N. Salvadori (eds.) (1998), *The Elgar Companion to Classical Economics A–K*. Cheltenham, UK and Northampton, MA, USA: Edward Elgar, pp. 449–452.

Dmitriev, V.K. (1904), *Economic Essays on Value, Competition, and Utility*, translated into English and edited by D.M. Nuti. Cambridge, UK: Cambridge University Press (1974).

Dobb, M.H. (1924), The Entrepreneur Myth, reprinted in M.H. Dobb (1955), *On Economic Theory and Socialism*. London: Routledge and Kegan Paul Ltd.

Dobb, M.H. (1931), The Cambridge School, in E.R.A. Seligman (ed.), *Encyclopaedia of the Social Sciences*, volume 5. New York: Macmillan, pp. 368–371.

Dobb, M.H. (1959), *Wages*, sixth edition. Cambridge, UK: Cambridge University Press.

Dobb, M.H. (1961), An Epoch Making Book, *Labour Monthly*, pp. 487–491.

Dobb, M.H. (1973), *Theories of Value and Distribution since Adam Smith: Ideology and Economic Theory*. Cambridge, UK: Cambridge University Press.

Dobb, M.H. (1975), Ricardo and Adam Smith, in A.S. Skinner and T. Wilson (eds.), *Essays on Adam Smith*. Oxford: Clarendon Press, pp. 324–335.

Garegnani, P. (2008), On a Turning Point in Sraffa's Theoretical and Interpretative Position in the Late 1920s, in H. Kurz, L.L. Pasinetti and N. Salvadori (eds.) (2008), *Piero Sraffa: The Man and the Scholar*. London and New York: Routledge, pp. 79–118.

Groenewegen, P. (2003), Marshall on Ricardo, in P. Groenewegen, *Classics and Moderns in Economics: Essays on Nineteenth and Twentieth Century Economic Thought*, volume II. London and New York: Routledge, pp. 29–49.

Groenewegen, P. (2006), Interpreter of the 'Classics', in T. Raffaelli, G. Becattini, and M. Dardi (eds.), *The Elgar Companion to Marshall*. Cheltenham, UK and Northampton, MA, USA: Edward Elgar, pp. 111–115.

Harcourt, G.C. (1994), Kahn and Keynes and the Making of *The General Theory*, *Cambridge Journal of Economics* 18(1), pp. 11–23, reprinted in Harcourt (1995), pp. 47–62.

Harcourt, G.C. (1995), *Capitalism, Socialism and Post-Keynesianism: Selected Essays of G.C. Harcourt*. Cheltenham, UK and Northampton, MA, USA: Edward Elgar.

Harcourt, G.C. (2006), *The Structure of Post-Keynesian Economics: The Core Contributions of the Pioneers*. Cambridge, UK: Cambridge University Press.

Harcourt, G.C. and Kerr, P. (2009), *Joan Robinson*. Basingstoke, UK: Palgrave Macmillan.

Harcourt, G.C. and Kriesler, P. (eds.) (2013), *The Oxford Handbook of Post-Keynesian Economics: Theory and Origins*, volume 1. Oxford: Oxford University Press.

Hart, N. (2009), Marshall's Equilibrium and Evolution: Then and Now, unpublished PhD Dissertation, School of Economics, University of New South Wales.

Hart, N. (2011), *Equilibrium and Evolution: Alfred Marshall and the Marshallians*. Basingstoke, UK: Palgrave Macmillan.

Hicks, J.R. (1972), Ricardo's Theory of Distribution, in M. Peston and B.A. Corry (eds.), *Essays in Honour of Lord Robbins*. London: Weidenfeld and Nicholas, pp. 160–167.

Hollander, S. (1979), *The Economics of David Ricardo*. London: Heinemann.

Holt, R. (1998), Dobb, Maurice Herbert, as an Interpreter of the Classical Economists, in H. Kurz and N. Salvadori (eds.) (1998), *The Elgar Companion to Classical Economics A–K*. Cheltenham, UK and Northampton, MA, USA: Edward Elgar, pp. 227–229.

Kaldor, N. (1950), Distribution, Theory of, in *Chambers' Encyclopaedia*, sixth edition. Edinburgh: Chambers, pp. 359–382.

Kaldor, N. (1955–56), Alternative Theories of Distribution, *Review of Economic Studies* 23(2), pp. 83–100, reprinted in N. Kaldor (1980), *Essays on Value and Distribution* second edition. London: Gerald Duckworth and Co. Ltd., pp. 209–236.

Kaldor, N. (1981), The Role of Increasing Returns, Technical Progress and Cumulative Causation in the Theory of International Trade and Growth, *Economie Appliquée* 34(4), reprinted in F. Targetti and A.P. Thirlwall (eds.) (1989), *Further Essays on Economic Theory and Policy*. London: Gerald Duckworth and Co. Ltd., pp. 201–223.

Kaldor, N. (1996), *Causes of Growth and Stagnation in the World Economy*. Cambridge, UK: Cambridge University Press.

Kerr, P. and R. Scazzieri (2013), Structural Economic Dynamics and the Cambridge Tradition, in Harcourt and Kriesler (eds.) (2013), *Handbook of Post-Keynesian Economics: Theory and Origins*, volume 1. Oxford: Oxford University Press, pp. 257–287.

Keynes, J.M. (1930), *A Treatise on Money: The Pure Theory of Money*, volume 1, reprinted in J.M. Keynes (1971), *Collected Writings*, volume V. London: Macmillan.

Keynes, J. M. (1933), Thomas Robert Malthus: The first of the Cambridge Economists, in J.M. Keynes, *Essays in Biography*, reprinted in J.M. Keynes (1972), *Collected Writings*, volume X. London: Macmillan, pp. 71–103.

Keynes, J.M. (1936), *The General Theory of Employment, Interest and Money*, reprinted in J.M. Keynes *Collected Writings* (1973), volume VII. London: Macmillan.

King, J.E. (2013), *David Ricardo*. Basingstoke, UK: Palgrave Macmillan.

King, J.E. (2015), Kaldor, Nicholas, and Ricardo, in H. Kurz and N. Salvadori (eds) (2015), *The Elgar Companion to David Ricardo*. Cheltenham, UK and Northampton, MA, USA: Edward Elgar, pp. 225–230.

Kriesler, P. (1984), On Dobb's Interpretation of Jevons on Ricardo, *Cambridge Journal of Economics* 8(4), pp. 403–405.

Kurz, H.D., Pasinetti, L.L. and Salvadori, N. (eds.) (2008), *Piero Sraffa: The Man and the Scholar*. London and New York: Routledge.

Kurz, H. and Salvadori, N. (eds.) (1998), *The Elgar Companion to Classical Economics A–K*. Cheltenham, UK and Northampton, MA, USA: Edward Elgar.

McFarlane, B. and Kriesler, P. (1993), Maurice Dobb's Re-interpretation of Ricardo: Critical Notes, paper presented at the Seventh History of Economic Thought Society of Australia Conference, July, Wollongong University.

Marshall, A. (1890), *Principles of Economics*, ninth (variorum) edition, edited by C.W. Guillebaud (ed.) (1961). London: Macmillan.

O'Brien, D.P. (1990), Marshall's Work in Relation to Classical Economics, in J.K. Whitaker (ed.), *Centenary Essays on Alfred Marshall*. Cambridge, UK: Cambridge University Press, pp. 127–163.

Pasinetti, L.L. (1960), A Mathematical Formulation of the Ricardian System, *Review of Economic Studies* 27(2), pp. 78–98.

Pasinetti, L.L. (1977), *Lectures in the Theory of Production*. London: Macmillan.

Pasinetti, L.L. (1981), *Structural Change and Economic Growth: A Theoretical Essay on the Dynamics of the Wealth of Nations*. Cambridge, UK: Cambridge University Press.

Pasinetti, L.L. (1993), *Structural Economic Dynamics: A Theory of the Economic Consequences of Human Learning*. Cambridge, UK: Cambridge University Press.

Pasinetti, L.L. (2007), *Keynes and the Cambridge Keynesians: A 'Revolution in Economics' to be Accomplished*. Cambridge, UK: Cambridge University Press.

Petridis, R. (1998), Marshall, Alfred, as an Interpreter of the Classical Economists, in H. Kurz and Salvadori, N. (eds.) (1998), *The Elgar Companion to Classical Economics A–K*. Cheltenham, UK and Northampton, MA, USA: Edward Elgar, pp. 79–83.

Pigou, A.C. (1933), *The Theory of Unemployment*. London: Macmillan.

Pollitt, B.H. (1988), The Collaboration of Maurice Dobb in Sraffa's Edition of Ricardo, *Cambridge Journal of Economics* 12(1), pp. 55–65.

Ricardo, D. (1817), *The Principles of Political Economy and Taxation*. Reprinted in P. Sraffa (ed.) (1951). Cambridge, UK: Cambridge University Press.

Robinson, J. (1942), *An Essay on Marxian Economics*, second edition. London: Macmillan (1966).

Robinson, J. (1967), Growth and the Theory of Distribution, *Annals of Public and Cooperative Economy* 38(1), pp. 3–7, reprinted in J. Robinson (1979a), *Collected Economic Papers*, volume V. Oxford: Basil Blackwell, pp. 71–75.

Robinson, J. (1969), The Theory of Value Reconsidered, *Australian Economic Papers* 8(12), pp. 13–19, reprinted in J. Robinson (1973), pp. 59–66.

Robinson, J. (1970), Economics Today, *Basel Wirtschaftswissenschaftliche Vortage, 2*, reprinted in J. Robinson (1973), pp. 123–128.

Robinson, J. (1971), *Economic Heresies: Some Old-Fashioned Questions in Economic Theory*, London: Macmillan.

Robinson, J. (1973), *Collected Economic Papers*, volume IV. Oxford: Basil Blackwell.

Robinson, J. (1978), Keynes and Ricardo, *Journal of Post-Keynesian Economics* 1(1), pp. 12–18, reprinted in J. Robinson (1979a), pp. 210–216.

Robinson, J. (1979a), *Collected Economic Papers*, volume V. Oxford: Basil Blackwell.

Robinson, J. (1979b), *Aspects of Development and Underdevelopment*. Cambridge, UK: Cambridge University Press.

Robinson, J. and Eatwell, J. (1973), *An Introduction to Modern Economics*, revised edition. Maidenhead, UK: McGraw-Hill.

Rowthorn, R. (1974), Neo-Classicism, Neo-Ricardianism and Marxism, *New Left Review* 86, pp. 63–87, reprinted in R. Rowthorn (1980), *Capitalism, Conflict and Inflation*. London: Lawrence and Wishart, pp. 14–47.

Signorino, R. (2008), Piero Sraffa's Lectures on the Advanced Theory of Value 1928–1931 and the Rediscovery of the Classical Approach, in H. Kurz, L.L. Pasinetti and N. Salvadori (eds.) (2008), *Piero Sraffa: The Man and the Scholar*. London and New York: Routledge, pp. 195–216.

Solow, R.M. (1997), Is There a Core of Usable Macroeconomics We Should All Believe In? *American Economic Review* 87(2), pp. 230–232.

Solow, R.M. (2000), The Neoclassical Theory of Growth and Distribution, *Banca Nazionale del Lavoro Quarterly Review* 53(215), pp. 349–381.

Sraffa, P. (ed., with the collaboration of M.H. Dobb) (1951), *The Works and Correspondence of David Ricardo: On the Principles of Political Economy and Taxation*, volume I. Cambridge, UK: Cambridge University Press.

Sraffa, P. (ed., with the collaboration of M.H. Dobb) (1952), *The Works and Correspondence of David Ricardo: Letters 1816–1818*, volume VII. Cambridge, UK: Cambridge University Press.

Sraffa, P. (1960), *Production of Commodities by Means of Commodities: Prelude to a Critique of Economic Theory*. Cambridge, UK: Cambridge University Press.

Whewell, W. (1829), Mathematical Exposition of Some Doctrines of Political Economy, *Cambridge Philosophical Society Transactions* 3, pp. 1–38, reprinted in Whewell (1968).

Whewell, W. (1831), Mathematical Exposition of Some of the Leading Doctrines in Mr. Ricardo's *Principles of Political Economy and Taxation*, *Cambridge Philosophical Society Transactions* 4, pp. 1–44, reprinted in Whewell (1968).

Whewell, W. (1862), *Six Lectures on Political Economy*. Cambridge: Cambridge University Press. Reprinted New York: Augustus M. Kelley (1967).

Whewell, W. (1968), *On the Mathematical Exposition of Some Doctrines of Political Economy*. London: Gregg International Publishers.

Theme IV

Pluralism develops – twentieth-century alternatives

What can alternative twentieth-century views of capitalism offer to the pluralist vision for the twenty-first century? The authors in Chapters 11 to 15 examine principles and ideological structures that can provide pluralist agendas both for research and for learning economics. First, in Chapter 11, Jan Toporowski examines how both Keynes and Kalecki questioned the mainstream view that a fall in money wages would result in increased employment. The inability of free markets to attain equilibrium where resources are fully utilized is central to both analyses, exposing the neoclassical myth that money wages can be reduced without affecting total demand in the economy. Toporowski then shows how Marxist concepts of monopoly capital and class distribution of income are core to Kalecki's analysis, providing an effective approach that can synthesize different heterodox economic traditions.

In contrast, Neil Hart and Peter Kriesler in Chapter 12 discuss 'serious and irreconcilable methodological differences' that make it impossible for a 'broad Post Keynesian church' to be built that includes both the Sraffian research programmes and the evolving Keynesian-Kaleckian alliance. The former acts primarily as a constructive critique of neoclassical theory, while the latter provides a historically-situated model of critical aspects of the real world. Nevertheless, pluralism allows such divergent agendas to co-exist, to be researched and fathomed for what they offer a new generation of economists.

A pluralist approach allows Harry Bloch in Chapter 13 to explicate an extension of Post Keynesian price theory using Schumpeter's theory of innovation. This enables a more realist price theory to emerge. Bloch explores the implications of enhancing the roles of 'history and expectations' in Post Keynesian price theory via this 'Schumpeterian twist', namely 'having a mark-up factor with dynamics that flow from innovation and creative destruction'. A similar theme emerges in Therese Jefferson's chapter on George Katona's contribution to behavioural macroeconomics. Katona's work on decision-making (inspired by psychology) identifies the importance of macroeconomic insights related to social processes in 'framing' economic actions: insights like group dynamics, institutions and societal changes over time, as well as standard neoclassical individual rationality. This raises the role of macroeconomics, negating the neoclassical primacy of microfoundations. It also means that heterodox economists need to apply wider methodological forms of enquiry, such as those adopted by Katona. This opens up avenues of research, which are pluralist in tradition, that can uncover broader patterns of behaviour.

Tim Thornton in Chapter 15 explains the role complexity science can play in economics. His principal argument is that neoclassical economics can only offer a limited mathematical and computing role for complexity within the tight setting of market-driven individualistic principles. A corollary to this critique offers complexity as a synthesis across divergent schools of economic thought through the identification of ontological commonalities in its open-systems non-instrumental approach. Thornton is pessimistic concerning the ability of neoclassical economics to embrace complexity, reinforcing his argument that 'political economists should seek institutional independence and disciplinary differentiation'. This raises the question as to whether a new pluralist economics can be inclusive of orthodox, as well as heterodox, economics in a traditional political economy context. The concluding chapter will examine this issue.

11 Kalecki on wages

An alternative to Keynes[1]

Jan Toporowski

Neither Keynes nor Kalecki was a pluralist, in the sense of acknowledging that there is more than one approach to economic theory. Their perspective was that accepted views in economics need to be probed and challenged. An important part of this challenge was checking the consistency of economic theories with observed economic phenomena. This is very apparent in their respective evaluations of the proposition advanced by proponents of the 'Treasury View' in the 1920s and 1930s – and of the Walrasian general-equilibrium approach – that persistent unemployment was the result of a failure of the wage rate to adjust to bring about full employment. Keynes's and Kalecki's respective approaches to wage theory established disequilibrium in the labour market as a key part of the new macroeconomic analysis that is associated with their names.

In his masterly analysis of the economic theory of Rosa Luxemburg, Tadeusz Kowalik, the great Polish political economist and historian of economic thought wrote that 'Socialist theorists only became capable of analysing the contradictions of capitalism and its place in history after they had overcome the one-sided pamphleteering and accusation that was characteristic of the early critical as well as socialist literature' (Kowalik 2012, p. 239). Although written in the 1960s and about Rudolf Hilferding, this characterization of reasoned, rather than romantic, Marxism could just as easily have been written about John King. He was one of the first Marxists to realize that the traditional Marxist analysis based around exploitation in a factory system of production is inadequate for late twentieth century capitalism. This led him to embrace Post Keynesian economics, while rejecting its inability to engage with the class and social nature of capitalism (Howard and King 1992, pp. 394–95). This sensible opening to a more sophisticated understanding of contemporary capitalism is not, however, unqualified: he has followed the Marxist mainstream in placing Kalecki in a 'Left Keynesian' category of economists (King 2002, pp. 49–52). For obvious reasons, John King could not have read the late Tadeusz Kowalik's earlier scholarly work, which, with the exception of his contributions to the *festschriften* dedicated to Oskar Lange and Michał Kalecki, exists only in Polish, Spanish and Italian. Tadeusz Kowalik showed that Kalecki correctly belongs to a Marxist stream opened up by Luxemburg (Kowalik 2012, chapter 3). Only in the framework of that analysis, rather than the marginal-cost approach that Keynes inherited from Marshall or the underconsumptionist interpretation of Marx that characterizes Sweezy's earlier Marxism (Sweezy 1942), does Kalecki's analysis of wages make sense.

Real and money wages according to Keynes

Despite his doubts over Kalecki's statistical work for the Cambridge Research Scheme in 1939 (Toporowski 2013, pp. 129–37), Keynes was decidedly taken with Kalecki's ability to draw theoretical conclusions from his statistics on an aspect of the argument in the *General Theory* that even he, its author, admitted was unclear and even confused. This was Keynes's explanation in chapter 19 of his book of the relationship between real and money wages. As Kalecki had pointed out (in Polish, so Keynes would not have been aware of this criticism), the chapter itself fits uneasily into an analysis in which the basic unit of analysis is given as the 'wage-unit', which should, by definition, stay constant if money wages change (Kalecki 1936). In that chapter, Keynes set out to challenge the doctrine commonly held among economists, and, in the 'Treasury View' expounded by Ralph Hawtrey, the foundation of government policy in the inter-war period (and since the 1980s), that a fall in money wages would result in increased employment. Behind this doctrine, Keynes rightly pointed out, was an assumption that money wages could be reduced without affecting total demand in the economy. In Keynes's view (1936, p. 10), this was wrong because

> in the short period, falling money wages and rising real wages are each, for independent reasons, likely to accompany decreasing employment; labour being readier to accept wage-cuts when employment is falling off, yet real wages inevitably rising in the same circumstances on account of the increasing marginal return to a given capital equipment when output is diminished.

Soon after the publication of Keynes's book, John T. Dunlop (1938) and Lorie Tarshis (1939) published articles pointing out that, historically, real wages tend to rise with employment.

Keynes responded to Dunlop and Tarshis with a paper that came out, together with the paper by Tarshis, in the March 1939 issue of *The Economic Journal*. The article (Keynes 1939) marks the high point of Keynes's regard for Kalecki.[2] In the paper, Keynes sought to recover his essential argument about wages and employment by distinguishing between changes in real wages that are associated with changes in output, and changes in real wages that are the outcome of changes in prices. He wanted to show that the latter are unimportant in determining the level of employment: 'The conclusion, that changes in real wages are not usually an important factor in short-period fluctuations until the point of full employment is approaching, is one which has already been reached by Dr. Kalecki on the basis of his own investigations' (Keynes 1939, p. 43).

The whole issue, in Keynes's view, turned on the question of whether 'marginal real costs', that is the real cost of producing additional output with a given productive apparatus, increase or decrease. For if they decrease, then increasing output with that given productive apparatus should result in falling profit per unit of output. Here, Keynes stated, 'Dr Kalecki is inclined to infer approximately constant marginal real cost' (1939, p. 44), that is that the resource cost of increasing output is constant when productive capacity is underutilized. Kalecki inferred from this that real profits too would not decrease (or increase) in response to changes in output. This would be reflected in a fairly constant share of labour income relative to profits. The 'undisputed facts' (Keynes 1939, p. 48) seem to confirm this. Keynes put forward figures showing the share of manual labour in the national income of Great Britain (figures for 1911, and then 1924–1935) and then the same share in the United States (1919–1934). In both countries, fluctuations in this share were small and apparently random. But there was no evidence of any reduction in the share of labour in years when output increased.

Keynes therefore concluded that 'these facts do not support the recently prevailing assumptions as to the relative movement of real wages and output, and are inconsistent with the idea of there being any marked tendency to increasing unit-profit with increasing output'. That tendency was essential if falling wages were to result in higher employment, as the conventional view supposed. For Keynes the absence of any marked change in the share of labour income 'remains a bit of a miracle' that implies that changes in prices almost exactly offset increases in marginal costs (1939, pp. 48–49).

> The only solution was offered by Dr. Kalecki in the brilliant article which has been published in *Econometrica*. Dr. Kalecki here employs a highly original technique of analysis into the distributional problem between the factors of production in conditions of imperfect competition, which may prove to be an important piece of pioneer work .... His own explanation is based on the assumptions that marginal real costs are constant, that the degree of the imperfection of the market changes in the opposite direction to output, but that this change is precisely offset by the fact that the prices of basic raw materials (purchased by the system from outside) relatively to money wages increase and decrease with output. Yet there is no obvious reason why these changes should so nearly offset one another ... It may be noticed that Dr. Kalecki's argument assumes the existence of an opposite change in the degree of the imperfection of competition (or in the degree to which producers are taking advantage of it) when output increases from that expected by Mr. R.F. Harrod in his study on *The Trade Cycle*. There Mr. Harrod expects an increase; here constancy or a decrease seems to be indicated. Since Mr. Harrod gives grounds for his conclusions which are *prima facie* plausible, this is a further reason for an attempt to put the issue to a more decisive statistical test.
>
> (Keynes 1939, pp. 49–50)

Harrod's '*prima facie* plausible' grounds were that consumers and firms become much more selective in their buying in a slump, and less so in a boom. The demand that firms face therefore becomes much more price-elastic, and this would make markets more competitive in a slump (Harrod 1936, pp. 86–87). Kalecki's (1938) reasoning about competition was not based on the variable scruples of consumers and firms, but on the pricing policy of firms. He had argued in his *Econometrica* article that firms try to hold prices stable and form cartels in a slump, when they have less fear that new producers will enter the market, while in a boom cartels are more likely to be dissolved, and new firms enter the market so that competition increases.

Keynes was therefore unconvinced by Kalecki, but he knew what he wanted out of the discussion. Pending more statistical work

> it is evident that Mr. Dunlop, Mr. Tarshis and Dr. Kalecki have given us much to think about, and have seriously shaken the fundamental assumptions on which the short-period theory of distribution has been based hitherto ... Meanwhile I am comforted by the fact that their conclusions tend to confirm the idea that the causes of short-period fluctuation are to be found in changes in the demand for labour, and not in changes in its real-supply price.
>
> (Keynes 1939, p. 50)

Thus, aggregate demand and not the wage rate determined employment in the short run.

Kalecki on wages, real and money

Kalecki's approach to the subject was much clearer, and free of Marshallian dilemmas applied to historical data. The wage share year by year that Keynes was using as evidence for his conclusions about the short period indicated the phase of the business cycle rather than changes in output with the capital stock held constant. Until May 1939, when he saw, and was disconcerted by, the results of the industrial studies in the Cambridge Research Scheme, Keynes would not have been aware of the evidence underlying Kalecki's reasoning (Toporowski 2013, pp. 127–33). The circulation of Kalecki's evidence, and his interpretation of that data, occurred at around the same time that his detailed analysis of the wages question appeared – not in England, but in the country from which he was trying to distance himself, Poland. Of course, it also appeared in Polish rather than in English. The English-speaking world had to wait three decades before the translation of Kalecki into English appeared, with a volume of his earliest essays, *Studies in the Theory of Business Cycles: 1933–39* (Kalecki 1969).

Despite his falling out, in 1936, with the Institute for the Study of Business Cycles and Prices and its patron, the Polish Finance Minister Eugeniusz Kwiatkowski, Kalecki was not altogether considered an outcast in the Polish political establishment. On 30 August 1938, the Polish Ministry of Labour and Social Welfare wrote to Kalecki with a request for a study of wages policy. The study was 'to emphasize from the economic point of view the positive effects of the tranquillizing of social relations through collective labour agreements and through the work of mediatory institutions' (Osiatyński 1991, p. 517; editorial notes). The Ministry was, however, equivocal about publishing a study whose precise conclusions were not yet known. The letter went on:

> The Ministry of Labour and Social Welfare believes that if the point of view of the author agrees completely with the views of the Ministry, the Ministry itself will publish the said work. If there are some differences of opinion, the Ministry will publish it at its own expense and effort, handing over the task to one of the scholarly institutions affiliated with the Ministry.
>
> (See Osiatyński 1991, p. 517; editorial notes)

In the event, the study was published by the Institute of Social Economy (*Instytut Gospodarstwa Społecznego*) as an essay titled 'Money and Real Wages'. In January 1939, Kalecki wrote to Joan Robinson referring to

> some work for the Polish Ministry of Labour which I accepted last summer. It consists in writing a paper on the wage cuts being not the way to fight unemployment. (That being what they want may seem, I guess, strange to you, but may be easily explained. From 'professional' point of view the officials of the Ministry are frightened by the prospect of being compelled by the Government to assist the wage reductions which naturally causes a lot of trouble. And in some of them, this professional interest may be unconsciously shaped into a sincerely progressive ideology.)
>
> (Kalecki quoted in Osiatyński 1991, pp. 517–18; editorial notes)

The 'progressive ideology' of the Ministry's officials was also due to strong representation in the Polish Government apparatus of many of Józef Piłsudski's former comrades from the Polish Socialist Party, as well as the growing political significance of wages policy in nearly all European countries as mass unemployment appeared to resist a slow economic recovery from 1936. In Poland more than one-third of the labour force employed in 1929 had been laid off work by 1933 and, while most of those laid off had been employed again, nearly half-a-million remained registered as unemployed (and many more unregistered), more than one-quarter of the urban labour force. Nominal wages had fallen by more than one-fifth since their peak in 1930, but prices had fallen even more. For those who remained in employment, real wages had risen although, as Kalecki was to note later on, household real incomes fell because of the rise in unemployment.

In 1938, a booklet had been published titled 'Rigid Wages as a Source of Unemployment' (*Sztywne płace źródłem bezrobocia*), by Jan Wątecki, urging reductions in real wages as a way of combatting unemployment and encouraging employers to take on more workers. The proposal, and similar ones in other countries (including the 'Treasury view' in the UK, the 'liquidationist' or Austrian view associated with the University of Chicago in the United States or the view of Jacques Rueff in France[3]), found favour with many economists and some employers. Although it was widely seen as 'unfair' and regressive, there was, despite Keynes's efforts, no clear and systematic exposition of the relationship between wages and employment. Kalecki set out to explain that relationship in his essay.

Kalecki's essay was an extended version of chapter 3 of *Essays in the Theory of Economics Fluctuations* (Kalecki 1939b). That chapter had considered a closed economy (one with no foreign trade), that being, in Kalecki's view, 'the only case to which the Keynesian argument fully applies' (1939b, p. 274). The original essay was divided into two parts. The first was headed 'I. Theory' and commenced with an exposition of 'The "classical" theory of wages'. In Kalecki's view, the 'classical' theory rested on two assumptions. The first was an 'assumption of' perfect competition and of the so-called "law of increasing marginal costs".' The latter supposes that firms face increasing marginal costs (including labour costs) as they increase output. Given a certain price level for finished goods, increasing marginal costs determine how much firms will produce, and how much labour they will employ. From this, it follows that if real wages are reduced, firms will increase output and employment, so that there is an inverse relationship between real wages and employment. The second assumption was that there is a given price level, or a certain value of aggregate demand, that does not change when wages change. It follows that a change in money wages will result in a proportional change in real wages (Kalecki 1939a, p. 21).

However, Kalecki pointed out that it cannot be concluded from this that a fall in *money* wages can lead to an increase in production

> since no relation between changes in money and real wages has been established yet. The 'classical' theory, in order to deal with this problem, makes additional assumptions of a different type. It is sometimes assumed that the general level of prices depends on the credit policy of the banks (in particular on that of the central bank). Assuming, moreover, that this policy, and thus the general level of prices, is given, the conclusion is arrived at that the reduction in money wages is identical with that of real wages. Frequently, however, a more sophisticated assumption is made that it is the value of aggregate demand or – what amounts to the same – the value of aggregate production that is determined by the credit policy.
>
> (Kalecki 1939a, pp. 22–23)

In both cases, the reduction in money wages is not supposed to change the general price level, because aggregate demand or credit policy remains unchanged. The reduction in money wages then reduces marginal costs opening up a gap between the price of output and its marginal cost. Profit-seeking firms will then eliminate this gap by expanding output and employment. Kalecki's judgement on this kind of reasoning is clear:

> The assumption of a given general price level or a given aggregate demand is totally unfounded. We know only too well that in the course of the business cycle both magnitudes are subject to violent swings. Why then should we assume that they remain unaltered in the aftermath of a wage reduction? If, however, we reject these assumptions a quite new theoretical construction is required in order to enable us to appreciate the consequences of changes in money wages.
>
> (Kalecki 1939a, p. 24)

This 'new' theoretical construction, Kalecki proposed (in his Introduction) to build on 'on the basis of Keynes's theory of wages and of my own theory published in Poland and abroad' (Kalecki quoted in Osiatyński 1991, p. 517; editorial notes[4]).

In a section on 'Reduction of wages on the assumption of perfect competition', Kalecki laid out his essential three-sector model (sectors producing workers' consumption goods, capitalists' consumption goods and investment goods, respectively), in which income equals expenditure, workers do not save but consume their incomes and there is no foreign trade. Dividing income between capitalists and workers, he showed how capitalists' income is equal to investment and capitalists' consumption in a given period. This equation (later to be put forward as the foundation of his theory of profits) turns out to be the key to the analysis.

> It enables us to explain the fluctuations of production. Let us consider investment, capitalist consumption, and workers' consumption in a certain period. In which of these three items of national income may spontaneous changes occur? It is first obvious that workers' consumption cannot be subject to such a change. Indeed, it can neither exceed nor fall short of their earnings. But the position is quite different as far as capitalist expenditure is concerned. In the next period they may increase their consumption or their outlay on investment above their present income, drawing on bank credits or on reserves of their own. The capitalists also may reduce their expenditure on consumption and investment below their present income, paying off credits or increasing their reserves. Once they have done it, however, the above equation shows clearly that the income of the capitalists as a whole will increase or diminish precisely by as much as their expenditure was increased or diminished. The aggregate production is bound to reach the level at which the profits derived from it by the capitalists are equal to their consumption and investment ... Therefore, the capitalists as a class

determine by their expenditure their profits and in consequence the aggregate production.

(Kalecki 1939a, p. 25)

In the three-sector model, capitalists' profits are therefore equal to the sum of profits in the three sectors and also to the value of production in the investment goods and capitalists' consumption goods sectors. Wages are equal to the sum of wages in the three sectors, as well as (by assumption) the value of output in the workers' consumption goods sector. The sectoral equalities make up the components of the overall identity between income and expenditure.

Kalecki also showed a remarkably advanced understanding of the credit relations that allow capitalists to spend in a manner unconstrained by income: 'The question is frequently asked about the wherewithal for financing the increase in investment if capitalist consumption does not decrease simultaneously and does not "release" some purchasing power for investment. It may sound paradoxical, but ... investment is "financed by itself" ' (Kalecki 1939a, p. 27).[5] He explained this as follows:

> If, for instance, an entrepreneur is gradually drawing on his bank deposit for [the] construction of plant, he is increasing by the same amount (on the assumption of stable capitalists consumption) profits of other entrepreneurs (through an increase in the production), and as a result, along with the dwindling of his bank deposit the deposits of other entrepreneurs are rising *pro tanto* and therefore the banks are not forced to reduce credits.

(Kalecki 1939a)

This view is 'advanced' because, even in the twenty-first century, it is commonly thought that the amount of credit in the economy (that is, excluding inter-bank transactions) is determined by the central bank, or by commercial banks' lending decisions, and that the lending capacity of banks is reduced by the amount of credit advanced. By contrast, Kalecki argued that the amount of credit in the economy was determined by the management of their debts and reserves by the capitalists (Sawyer 1985, pp. 91–107; Sawyer 2001; Toporowski 2013, pp. 63–64).

So much for transactions between capitalists who pay each other with bank deposits. However, payments are also made to workers and petty capitalists, who are paid in cash and use cash in their exchange transactions:

> in line with the increased turnover the demand for cash in [non-bank] circulation rises. Consequently the bank deposits would diminish and thus the banks would lose a part of their cash reserves. This in its turn would cause an increase in the rate of interest which would adversely affect investment activity. For it is, indeed, the difference between the expected

rate of profit and the rate of interest that stimulates investment. However, the situation is relieved by the expansion of credits of the central bank which increases the quantity of money in circulation and in this way either prevents any rise in the rate of interest or at least limits its scope.

(Kalecki 1939a, p. 27)

What would happen if the central bank did not 'accommodate' the increased demand for cash? According to Kalecki, 'This is the assumption behind the "classical" theory mentioned in the preceding chapter.' As far as economic activity is concerned, such monetary restraint is likely to be ineffective: 'changes in the rate of interest are in general much too weak to halt an incipient upswing resulting from an increase in investment or to prevent a depression brought about by its collapse' (Kalecki 1939a, pp. 27–28).

The reason for this ineffectiveness of monetary policy is that it is not the central bank rate of interest that influences investment. Business investment is unresponsive to this short-term rate of interest because it is not that rate of interest but 'the long-term rate of interest that is relevant to investment in fixed capital.' However, the long-term rate of interest does not change very much in response to changes in short-term rates.

This results in the following set-up: the increase in investment activity causes a rise in the aggregate output and thus in the demand for cash; this tends to push up the short-term rate of interest, which, however, is only slightly reflected in the level of the long-term rate of interest. Thus the expansion of investment is not much hampered by the reaction of the money and capital market.

(Kalecki 1939a, p. 28)

Kalecki's rejection of the rate of interest as an influence on investment and the trade cycle was also featured in 'The Long-Term Rate of Interest' in his 1939 volume of *Essays* (Kalecki 1939b). It marks out an unusual point on which Kalecki's monetary analysis was, if not more sophisticated, at least more in touch with reality than that of Keynes. In his *General Theory* Keynes had argued for a permanently accommodating monetary policy on the grounds that low central bank interest rates would keep long-term interest rates low, thereby encouraging high rates of investment. In particular he was very critical of the tendency to operate monetary policy in a cyclical fashion, raising (central bank or short-term) interest rates in the boom (Keynes 1936, pp. 315–26). However, Keynes's presumed relationship between short-term and long-term interest rates, in which long-term rates were supposed to rise with short-term rates, met with widespread scepticism. In his 1937 Marshall Lectures in Cambridge, Ralph Hawtrey, Keynes's rival who had, before the Great Depression, championed the short-term rate of interest as the regulator of the business cycle, pointed out, in advance of Kalecki, that long-term interest rates were relatively unaffected by changes in short-term interest rates

(Hawtrey 1938, pp. 187–88).[6] Even before those lectures, John Hicks had enunciated his 'pure expectations' theory that arbitrage in the money market would make long-term interest rates the average of the short-term rates expected over that long term (Hicks 1939, chapter 11). The relative stability of long-term interest rates made them a weak predictor or cause of much more volatile changes in investment. Even Harrod, whose views on competition and the accelerator principle in the business cycle had been criticized by Kalecki, recognized that large shifts in short-term rates resulted in only small changes in long-term rates. In his *Essays*, Kalecki cited Harrod's observations on interest rates and investment as supporting his own analysis (Kalecki 1939b, p. 297; citing Harrod 1936, p. 112).

Having explained the structure of the economy, its essential relations, and its monetary and financial arrangements, Kalecki went on to consider how such an economy would be affected by a fall in money wages. Given the essentially passive nature of workers' consumption (passive in the sense that the amount of workers' consumption is wholly determined by their income), the effect of a reduction in wages depended on how capitalists would alter their consumption and investment in response to the wage reduction. Should the capitalists increase their consumption and investment in anticipation of higher profits, then indeed the fall in wages would give rise to higher output and employment, 'and the "classical" theory would be vindicated' (Kalecki 1939a, p. 28).

Kalecki pointed out that capitalists would have to increase their consumption and investment immediately after the fall in wages for any expansion in output to arise. It was far more likely that capitalists would wait for any increase in profits to materialize before spending more money on consumption and investment. If there is no immediate change in consumption and investment then, in accordance with the reflux theory of profits outlined above, profits will stay the same. Under conditions of perfect competition, the fall in expenditure by workers, due to the cut in wages, will cause competing firms to lower their prices in proportion to the reduced wages. Real output and employment will therefore stay the same.

Kalecki then considered what came later to be known as the 'Keynes effect': the possibility that, with the fall in wages and prices, less money would be needed in circulation, banks would find themselves with excess cash in their tills, and this would cause (short-term) interest rates to fall. The fall in interest rates would then stimulate investment. As he had already argued, Kalecki pointed out that the rate of interest has only a weak effect on investment. Moreover, the fall in prices would reduce incomes in relation to debts incurred under the previous higher prices. Difficulties in servicing debts would arise, undermining confidence in the solvency of firms.[7] The loss of confidence may even lead to an increase in long-term interest rates, despite the fall in short-term rates.

In a footnote to this brief consideration of the effect of wage reductions on corporate finance, and with insights that anticipate his later views on economic development, Kalecki (1939a) introduced a summary digression on the relations between rentier capitalists, who derived their incomes from profits but did not organize production, and the capitalist 'entrepreneurs', who organize production. He noted that

> when prices decline in the same proportion as wages, this will be also true of profits. But the money income of rentiers consisting of the interest on 'old' debts does not change and, therefore, their relative share in profits increases. If the entrepreneurs are 'poorer' than the rentiers, this kind of shift will result rather in a decrease of total capitalist consumption. Should the reverse be the case [a shift in profits from rentiers to entrepreneurs], the result would be an increase in capitalist consumption. The first pattern applies usually to societies where the concentration in industry is not too far advanced, the second to developed capitalist economies. In the latter case... capitalists' consumption is likely to increase, and this in turn will have a favourable effect on production and employment. But the final outcome is by no means certain even in this case, because quite a number of firms are in a precarious financial position, as a result of the decline in income while their 'old' debts remain unchanged, and this discourages any investment activity on their part. In any case should an increase in employment take place at all, it would be on a small scale.
>
> (Kalecki 1939a, p. 30)

Thus, the assumption of perfect competition merely ensures that prices fall in proportion to the fall in the marginal cost, or money wages, while profits remain more or less constant, depending on their distribution between money capitalists and entrepreneurs. Output and employment will therefore stay more or less the same. However, under imperfect competition, firms form cartels to resist falling prices. As a result of the fall in money wages, real wages are reduced and, with a smaller market, output and employment in the wages goods sector falls.

In the case of an open economy, the effect of a reduction in money wages on output and employment depends on the elasticity of demand for exports. With tariffs, this elasticity is likely to be small and, with imperfect competition, any increase in employment in the export industries will be offset by the reduction in employment in the wages goods sector. As with a currency depreciation, the expansion of the foreign market is offset by the contraction of the domestic market.

In this way, Kalecki laid out the structure of the capitalist economy, the key relations of which were: capitalists determining output (and employment) by their expenditure on their own consumption and fixed capital investment; and the degree of competition between capitalists determining the real wage in relation to the wages agreed in money terms. Foreign trade then is, according to Kalecki, marginally affected by changes in wages. His conclusion from this theoretical exposition is that reduced wages either make no difference at all to the volume of output and employment or else, if there is imperfect competition, they reduce output and employment as well.

Kalecki then went on to part II of his essay (Kalecki 1939a), his statistical analysis. This covered the same questions as Keynes's statistical analysis, namely do the statistics on wages and employment show that lower wages coincide with, or lead to, higher employment? However, unlike Keynes, Kalecki distinguished two elements in the marginal cost, namely the real wage and the cost of raw materials. Kalecki came to this from a criticism of the statistical analysis of Jacques Rueff, the French monetary economist. In a study that was much quoted and emulated, outside Britain, Rueff (1925) had claimed to show that the enormous rise in unemployment that had occurred in Britain in the wake of World War I was caused by a rise in real wages. Kalecki remarked:

> He starts from the generally correct premisses that, when the problem of the relation between real wages and employment in industry is examined, by real wages should be meant the ratio of money wages of the industrial workers to the prices at which the respective products are sold, i.e., wholesale prices. In the realization of this approach, however, Rueff committed gross statistical errors. He simply divided the index of industrial money wages by the general index of the wholesale prices and considered the fact that the ratio increased during the slump and declined during the boom to be proof of the 'classical' theory.
>
> (Kalecki 1939a, p. 39)

Kalecki pointed out that the wholesale prices indices were based largely on the prices of raw materials and semi-manufactured goods. The indices that Rueff was using reflected more the costs of domestic and imported raw materials than finished industrial products.

> No wonder, then, that the ratios received [obtained] by Rueff increased in the slump and declined in the boom, as it is generally known that the prices of raw materials fluctuate more strongly than wages (and prices of manufactured goods). But it is also clear that the ratio of wages of the British worker to the price of Brazilian coffee is rather irrelevant to the conditions of industrial production in Great Britain. Thus Rueff's method applied by Mr. J. Wątecki ... is far from being a pattern worth following.
>
> (Kalecki 1939a, p. 39)

Kalecki resolved the dilemma of the estimation of real wages by decomposing the marginal costs of production into the costs of raw materials and wages. He drew on his extensive studies of commodity markets and cartels at the Warsaw Institute for the Study of Business Cycles and Prices and, since then, in Paris and Cambridge to show that, during a boom, raw materials prices rise more rapidly than wages and, in a slump, those prices fall more strongly than wages. But this rise in marginal costs is offset by increased competition in a boom and reduced competition in the recession (Toporowski 2013, chapter 5, pp. 96–97, chapter 13). In any case, at any given time, in Kalecki's view, marginal costs were constant in relation to the output of an individual firm so that, up to full capacity operation, raw materials costs and wages would not vary (Toporowski 2013, pp. 130–31). If Rueff and the 'classical' theory were correct then the ratio of wages to the prices of finished goods should rise in the recession and fall in a boom. But if, as Kalecki argued, the ratio of the prices of finished goods to the prime costs (raw materials and wages) falls in the boom (because the more rapid rise of raw materials prices cannot be passed into the market due to increased competition) and rises in the slump (because the more rapid fall in raw materials prices is not passed into the market due to reduced competition), 'the direction of changes in real wages cannot be foreseen' (1939a). In addition, he pointed out, there would be an upward trend in real wages, excluding cyclical changes, due to technical progress.

Kalecki's way of 'testing' statistically the 'classical' theory against what he called the 'Keynesian' theory (in fact Kalecki's own theory) was to examine annual data for wages and prices over the period from 1928 to 1939. The data revealed no evidence that the prices of finished industrial goods fell in relation to wages during the slump of 1929 to 1933, or rose during the weak recovery that started in 1934. In fact, the prices of finished industrial goods rose, in relation to wages, during the slump, and fell during the recovery. Kalecki attributed the recovery not so much to the fall in real wages that had occurred during the slump, but to the dollar depreciation in 1933, which stimulated the expenditure of hoarded dollars (principally on residential construction and stock accumulation, notably of textiles). The expenditure caused an increase in private investment that, combined with an increase in government investment, was the main factor in the recovery. He concluded:

> the 'classical' theory is wrong in maintaining that the prices of finished industrial products increase in relation to prime costs when production expands and vice versa. In fact the reverse is true. This is in complete agreement with our theoretical analysis which rejects the law of increasing marginal costs and assumes that the degree of monopoly increases in the depression and declines in the boom. It appears also most unlikely that the considerable cuts in money wages which took place in Poland during the downswing had any mitigating effect upon the latter. This again is in accord with our approach to the problem of reduction of money wages.
>
> (Kalecki 1939a, p. 50)

Conclusion

In the abbreviated version of this analysis, which appeared in his *Essays in the Theory of Economic Fluctuations*, Kalecki drew out the political implications of his analysis:

> There are certain 'workers' friends' who try to persuade the working class to abandon the fight for wages in its own interest, of course. The usual argument used for this purpose is that the increase of wages causes unemployment, and is thus detrimental to the working class as a whole.

The Keynesian theory undermines the foundation of this argument .... If viewed from this standpoint, strikes must have the full sympathy of 'workers' friends'. For a rise in wages tends to reduce the degree of monopoly, and thus to bring our imperfect system nearer to the ideal of free competition. On the other hand, it tends to increase the thriftiness of capitalists by causing a relative shift of income from rentiers to corporations. And 'workers' friends' are usually admirers both of free competition and of thrift as a virtue of the capitalist class.

(Kalecki 1939b, p. 284)

Kalecki's study for the Polish Government of the effects of changes in real and money wages placed the theory of distribution at the centre of his business cycle theory. By contrast, Keynes struggled to get out of the partial equilibrium analysis of the labour market. Discreetly, in Polish, as he had done in English in his 1939 *Essays*, Kalecki challenged Keynes's belief that monetary policy was a factor in the business cycle. The key role of monopoly capital in the business cycle places Kalecki in the discussions initiated by Rudolf Hilferding and Rosa Luxemburg, rather than those of John Maynard Keynes. This discussion thus shows how Post Keynesian economics can benefit from a more pluralist perspective, by attempting to synthesize Keynes's work with significant Marxist perspectives on monopoly capital and class distribution of income.

Notes

1 John King has been a stimulating and cultured interlocutor, editor and friend to the author. I am especially grateful to John King for his kindness in reading through some of the draft chapters for the first volume of my intellectual biography of Kalecki. Jerry Courvisanos and anonymous reviewers have greatly improved the present chapter.
2 See also Kaldor's 'Personal Recollections on Michał Kalecki' (Kaldor 1989).
3 See below.
4 Kalecki's Introduction is included in the editorial notes.
5 The original Polish title of his study (1939a) is 'Nominal and Real Wages' (*Płace nominalne i realne*). In translating this as 'Money and Real Wages', Kalecki introduced, probably unawares, a suggestion that his study would also consider money and credit, which indeed it does.
6 Hawtrey, it should be noted, was the principal exponent of the 'Treasury view' in Britain, which urged the wisdom of lowering money wages as a remedy for mass unemployment (see e.g. Hawtrey 1931, pp. 44–48).
7 Kalecki (1944) was to reiterate this in his later criticism of the monetarist notion that lower prices would stimulate expenditure through increasing the value of money balance.

References

Dunlop, J.G. (1938), The Movement of Real and Money Wage Rates, *The Economic Journal* 48(191), pp. 413–434.

Harrod, R. (1936), *The Trade Cycle*. Oxford: Oxford University Press.

Hawtrey, R. (1931), *Trade Depression and the Way Out*. London: Longmans Green and Co.

Hawtrey, R. (1938), *A Century of Bank Rate*. London: Longmans Green and Co.

Hicks, J.R. (1939), *Value and Capital*. Oxford: The Clarendon Press.

Howard, M.C. and King, J.E. (1992), *A History of Marxian Economics: 1929–1990*, volume II. Basingstoke, UK: Macmillan.

Kaldor, N. (1989), Personal Recollections on Michał Kalecki, in M. Sebastiani (ed.), *Kalecki's Relevance Today*. New York: St. Martin's Press.

Kalecki, M. (1936), Some Remarks on Keynes's Theory, in J. Osiatyński (ed.) (1990), *Collected Works of Michał Kalecki: Capitalism: Business Cycles and Full Employment*, volume I. Oxford: Clarendon Press, pp. 223–232.

Kalecki, M. (1938), The Distribution of the National Income, *Econometrica* 6(2), pp. 97–112.

Kalecki, M. (1939a), Money and Real Wages, in J. Osiatyński (ed.) (1991), *Collected Works of Michał Kalecki: Capitalism: Economic Dynamics*, volume II. Oxford: Clarendon Press, pp. 21–50.

Kalecki, M. (1939b), *Essays in the Theory of Economic Fluctuations*. London: George Allen and Unwin Ltd. Reprinted in J. Osiatyński (ed.) (1990), pp. 65–108.

Kalecki, M. (1944), Professor Pigou on 'The Classical Stationary State': A Comment, *The Economic Journal* 54(213), pp. 131–132.

Kalecki, M. (1969), *Studies in the Theory of Business Cycles: 1933–39*. Oxford: Basil Blackwell.

Keynes, J.M. (1936), *The General Theory of Employment, Interest and Money*. London: Macmillan.

Keynes, J.M. (1939), Relative Movements of Real Wages and Output, *The Economic Journal* 49(193), pp. 34–51.

King, J.E. (2002), *A History of Post-Keynesian Economics since 1936*. Cheltenham, UK and Northampton, MA, USA: Edward Elgar.

Kowalik, T. (2012), *Róża Luksemburg Teoria Akumulacji i Imperializmu*. Warszawa: Książka i Prasa.

Osiatyński, J. (ed.). (1990), *Collected Works of Michał Kalecki: Capitalism: Business Cycles and Full Employment*, volume I. Oxford: Clarendon Press.

Osiatyński, J. (ed.) (1991), *Collected Works of Michał Kalecki: Capitalism: Economic Dynamics*, volume II. Oxford: Clarendon Press.

Rueff, J. (1925), Les variations du chômage en Angleterre, *Revue Politique et Parlementaire* 32(décembre), pp. 425–437.

Sawyer, M. (1985), *The Economics of Michał Kalecki*. Basingstoke, UK: Palgrave Macmillan.

Sawyer, M. (2001), Kalecki on Money and Finance, *The European Journal of the History of Economic Thought* 8(4), pp. 487–508.

Sweezy, P.M. (1942), *The Theory of Capitalist Development*. New York: Oxford University Press.

Tarshis, L. (1939), Changes in Real and Money Wages, *The Economic Journal* 49(193), pp. 150–154.

Toporowski, J. (2013), *Michał Kalecki: An Intellectual Biography: Rendezvous in Cambridge 1899–1939*, volume 1. Basingstoke, UK: Palgrave Macmillan.

12 Keynes, Kalecki, Sraffa
Coherence within pluralism?

Neil Hart and Peter Kriesler[1]

The first notion to be discarded ... must be 'equilibrium in the long run'
(Robinson 1985, p. 160)

The title of this chapter corresponds to that of a chapter in John King's (2002) *A History of Post Keynesian Economics Since 1936*, where the question of coherence amongst the members of the congregation of the 'broad church' known as Post Keynesian economics is being discussed. The notion that Post Keynesian thought could be defined inclusively in terms of the Keynesian, Kaleckian and Sraffian strands emerged strongly from Geoff Harcourt and Omar Hamouda's well-known survey article on Post Keynesian economics (Hamouda and Harcourt 1988). There the question of coherence between the three strands is not pursued in the context of the possibility of synthesizing the strands into a coherent whole, but rather as a 'horses for courses' approach in which the various strands differed from one another because they were concerned with different issues and often different levels of abstraction of analysis. Intuitively, the basis for such a coalition would include a shared critique of the mainstream 'neoclassical' approaches, a closely aligned intellectual history, and the search for alternative methodological and theoretical foundations that reflect shared ambitions and histories.

Subsequent developments would suggest, as King (2002, p. 205) observed, that the rather optimistic conclusion reached by Harcourt and Hamouda seems to have underestimated the degree of hostility between the three proposed Post Keynesian groups and exaggerated the possibility of peaceful coexistence between them. These conclusions would appear to apply most directly with respect to the Sraffians and the evolving Keynesian-Kaleckian alliance. Initial attempts by Joan Robinson in particular to establish meaningful linkages between the work of her close intellectual companion Piero Sraffa and those involved in the early development of a Keynesian-Kaleckian approach that she had advocated proved to be rather unfruitful and were largely discarded by Robinson with some reluctance.[2] Nevertheless, as described by Gary Mongiovi (2012, p. 502), from 1960 until the mid-1980s, the affinities between the Keynes-Kalecki effective demand mechanism and Sraffa's work were not generally considered to be a matter of dispute; however, since then something of a rift has developed between the Sraffian camp and many of those who identify themselves with the Post Keynesian movement. The battle lines seem to have been drawn following the rather infamous Trieste summer school of 1985, where the intention had been to forge a unified methodological and analytical foundation for the Post Keynesian movement. Consequently, there has been very little constructive dialogue between the two groups, and text-book expositions of Post Keynesian economics rarely allude to the positive contributions that may be associated with the Sraffian research programmes.

Despite these widely perceived divisions, an entry on Sraffian economics is to be found in *The Elgar Companion to Post Keynesian Economics*, with Mongiovi (2012, p. 502) arguing that despite the existence of 'genuine differences of perspective', these do not render the Sraffian and Post Keynesian traditions incompatible with each other, with at least some Post Keynesian resistance to the Sraffian view being 'based on a misunderstanding of it'. Similarly, three of the first four chapters in the first volume of the recently published *Oxford Handbook of Post Keynesian Economics* (Harcourt and Kriesler 2013c) are devoted to Sraffian economics and what are perceived to be its constructive connections with Post Keynesian economics and to a potential Sraffa-Keynes synthesis.[3] However, all three papers start from a position that Sraffians are essentially distinct from Post Keynesians. Kurz's chapter in that volume locates a strong bond between Sraffa and Post Keynesians in 'their opposition to the marginalist or neoclassical theory' (Kurz 2013, p. 51), but sees them as being essentially different. The Arena and Blankenburg chapter considers possible approaches to derive a synthesis, but is critical of the Sraffian approach which utilizes the 'long-period interpretation of Sraffa's production prices'. Concluding that 'it is difficult to see why gravitation theory would be fundamentally different from the theory of *tâtonnement* in general equilibrium theory' (Arena and Blankenburg 2013, p. 84). So it would appear that the question of coherence between Sraffian economics and the Keynesian-Kaleckian strand of Post Keynesian economics continues to attract considerable interest. This spirit of reconciliation also features prominently in a recent paper by Marc Lavoie (2011), where the question contained in the title 'Should Sraffian economics be dropped out of the Post Keynesian school?' is answered strongly in the negative:

> Thus in contrast to what has been claimed repeatedly, Sraffians and other Post Keynesians are brought together more than by their dislike of neo-classical economics. This dislike, as reflected in their critique of neoclassical economics, is more a source of tension than a source of unison. Despite appearance to the contrary, Sraffians and other Post Keynesians are brought together by their similarities in their positive contributions.
>
> (Lavoie 2011, p. 1039)

An important attempt to reconcile the analysis of Post Keynesians and Sraffians, and to make a case for 'the coherence of a complete system of post-Keynesian principles' (Harcourt and Kriesler 2013c, p. 2) is the work of Henrich Bortis (see Bortis 2013 for the most recent statement). In his synthesis, there are three layers: 'a long-period set of growth relations ... a Robinsonian theory of the cycle, and short-period problems' (Harcourt and Kriesler 2013c, p. 230). However, many of the incompatibilities identified below between the groups remain unsolved in this attempt. In particular, the problem of the coherence between the short-run and long-run analysis is not adequately addressed.[4] In addition, the assumption of given technology means that the competitive processes discussed below, associated with investment in research and technology as well as with investment in the most recent techniques of production, is problematic in the Bortis analysis.

It is argued in this chapter that recent optimism concerning the establishment of coherence between the Keynesian-Kaleckian and Sraffian perspectives is misplaced, largely because of a failure to understand the substantial methodological issues which divide the two traditions. Much of this results from an unwillingness on the part of the Sraffians to embrace the implications arising from the Kaleckian insights that have displaced much of the 'Marshallian' (or, more accurately, Pigouvian) structure that came to be associated with Keynes's *General Theory*. The most significant implication arising from this relates to the different conceptions of competitive processes in modern capitalist economies, together with the question as to whether these forces can be associated with the generation of long-period equilibrium configurations. Indeed, from the Keynes-Kalecki perspective, it is the illegitimacy of drawing inferences from comparisons of long-period equilibrium positions which represents the most significant point of dispute between themselves and those working in the Sraffian tradition. In this respect, the Post Keynesian critique of the Sraffian analytical approach is not dissimilar to that which has been mounted against the more orthodox long-run equilibrium approaches founded on marginalist principles.

The arguments presented in the remainder of this chapter are organized as follows. The next section will describe the various components that have come together to form the Keynes-Kalecki strand of Post Keynesian economics. The substantive differences between this perspective and the Sraffian research programmes are then discussed. The central conclusions of the chapter are briefly re-stated in the final section.·

The Keynesian-Kaleckian Post Keynesian perspective

Before proceeding with an indicative summary of the nature of the Keynesian-Kaleckian Post Keynesian perspective, it is important to consider the 'critique' element flowing from this school of thought. The critique has as a starting point objections to the usage of long-period equilibrium analysis to investigate real world economies, and instead to place the analysis firmly within the realms of historical time. This line of thinking has links back to the Cambridge controversies over capital theory, and in particular to Robinson's perspective on these debates:

> The long wrangle about 'measuring capital' has been a great deal of fuss over a secondary question. The real source of trouble is the confusion

between comparisons of equilibrium positions and the history of the process of accumulation ... We might suppose that we can take a number of still photographs of economies each in a stationary state; let us suppose that the 'measurement' problem can be solved by calculating all values in terms of labour time, and that it happens that the economies can be arranged in a series in which a larger value of capital per man employed is associated with a higher net output per man of a homogeneous consumption good, as on Professor Samuelson's 'Surrogate production function'. This is an allowable thought experiment. But it is not allowable to flip the stills through a projector to obtain a moving picture of a process of accumulation.

(Robinson 1974, p. 135)[5]

As had been emphasized earlier by Harcourt (1969, p. 398), it is the *general methodology* of neoclassical analysis, rather than any particular result, which basically is under attack. From this perspective, to the extent that equilibrium analysis finds any place within the analytical core of Post Keynesian economics, it is only short-period equilibrium that sometimes has an analytical role as a state of rest, and even then the significance of its propositions is largely in what they deny, rather than what they affirm (Robinson 1956, pp. 57–60; Harcourt 1981). Therefore, questions relating to the determination of economic aggregates cannot be usefully confronted within long-period equilibrium-based analytical frameworks. Equally, a 'long-period' position cannot be contemplated as existing independently from 'short-run adjustments' in a world in which change is cumulative in nature. This theme is most directly reflected in the ·dynamic analysis developed in the tradition of Richard Goodwin and (later) Michał Kalecki, where the inseparability of the cycle and the trend in terms of changes in aggregate output is emphasized. When considering the dynamics of economic change, it is the cumulative causation approach as championed by Nicholas Kaldor, following in the footsteps of Smith, Young, Myrdal and Veblen, that replaces the equilibrium-based theories that have dominated both 'old' and 'new' neoclassical models of economic growth. The implications for an evaluation of the Sraffian research programme arising from this perspective are considered directly in the next section.

Following Robinson's (1979, p. xviii) characterization, 'Post Keynesian theory has taken over, in the main, the hypotheses suggested by Keynes and Kalecki, and refined and enlarged them to deal with recent experience', with the assimilation of the ideas of Keynes and Kalecki very much orchestrated through Robinson's interpretative accounts of both of these seminal thinkers (Robinson 1964). The influence of Keynes is centred on his emphasis on the role of effective demand and the non-neutrality of money, decision-making under conditions of uncertainty and the associated role of subjective and volatile expectations, all of which represent an attack on the validity of Say's law of markets. Within the modern Post Keynesian literature, the role of uncertainty has been accentuated in the writings of Paul Davidson (whose treatment of uncertainty followed in the tradition of George Shackle), where it was argued that Keynes's description of uncertainty matches technically with what mathematical statisticians call a non-ergodic stochastic system, in which one can never expect whatever data set exists today to provide a reliable guide to future outcomes (Davidson 2002, p. 187). Importantly, in such a world, markets cannot be efficient, and the non-ergodic dimension of the economic environment calls into question the validity of the assumption of rational expectations that plays a central role in a variety of mainstream macroeconomic frameworks (Davidson 1982–3).

Post Keynesian economics is therefore concerned with understanding how economic processes function in the real world through historical time. Some of the underlying features are the:

1   denial of the validity or the usefulness of general theory,
2   view of the economy as being an historical process, with the unchangeable past influencing the present, hence the key role of uncertainty,
3   concern with historical time, the future is uncertain and expectations have a significant and unavoidable impact on economic events,
4   importance of institutions, social and political forces in shaping economic events, and
5   central role of effective demand and of money/finance in determining the levels of employment and output.

Post Keynesian economists see the economy as being an historical process, and they attempt to understand how economic processes function in the real world in historical time. Their theory is anchored in the real world, attempting to understand some specific aspect of capitalism. Because they are concerned with historical time, the future is uncertain and expectations have a significant and unavoidable impact on economic events.

Apart from his theoretical legacy, Keynes's influence on the Post Keynesians extends to an embrace of the general methodological position that Keynes had taken from Alfred Marshall. Keynes fully embraced Marshall's inclination to forgo analytical rigour in pursuit of increased realism, and adopted Marshall's partial (or 'particular') framework. Marshall had justified this on the grounds that economic problems needed to be treated 'a bit at a time', both by market participants and also by those who were seeking to analyse their behaviour. Keynes applied the partial analysis to reduce the complexities of time and uncertain knowledge in economics to manageable proportions. The role of money and the indeterminacy of expectations associated with uncertainty could not have been effectively portrayed within a general equilibrium framework. For these reasons, partial analysis remains the chief analytical technique used by Post Keynesian economists, who emphasize mutual determination, with causality playing a key role (Kriesler and Nevile 2002).

Keynes's theoretical structure has been refined and extended in a number of different directions by the Post Keynesians, perhaps most importantly in relation to the representation of financial markets and institutions. In the tradition of Keynes, the existence of uncertainty is re-emphasized as the key rationale for holding money as a store of value, playing a vital role in connecting the irreversible past and uncertain future. Following from Kaldor's (1982) critique of the monetarist doctrines, the endogeneity of the money supply is stressed; with the money supply increasing as financial institutions make more loans available, leading to increased deposits in financial institutions and/or purchase of financial assets. These borrowing and lending decisions are based on expectations about the future and the cost of funds. Changes in the volume and composition of financial assets depend critically on the subjective perceptions on the part of lenders of the balance sheet positions of potential borrowers. The collective manner in which these perceptions are formed leads to alternating episodes of optimism and pessimism within financial markets, which may well amplify similar shifts in confidence within the real sectors of the economy. As was demonstrated emphatically in Hyman Minsky's (1982, 1985) financial instability hypothesis, real and financial sector instability are interconnected and inevitable characteristics of capitalist economies. Countervailing forces to endogenous instability are to be found in the operations of central banks and fiscal stabilization policies (combined with the operation of automatic stabilizers).

As stated by Robinson, within the Post Keynesian literature, the conclusions derived from Keynes's macroeconomics are combined with similar conclusions flowing from Kalecki's work. Significantly, unlike Keynes's *General Theory*, Kalecki's theory of effective demand was constructed in the setting of conditions that explicitly departed from competitive markets and which emphasized links between short-period nominal output determination and the more dynamic questions of capital accumulation, income distribution and economic growth.[6] The Post Keynesian alternative to equilibrium-based demand and supply theories of price is based on Kalecki's contributions. Following Kalecki, the industrial structure of an economy can be conveniently divided into two sectors. On the one hand, there is the 'flexible price' sector consisting mainly of primary products and raw materials, where price determination does resemble Marshall's short-period analysis, with prices to a significant extent 'demand determined' due to a variety of factors that limit the capacity of supply to react to demand variations. On the other hand, the majority of goods and services are produced and traded in the 'fixed price' sector, characterized by imperfect competition and oligopolistic markets. The assumption of myopic profit-maximizing behaviour is replaced with a notion of mark-up pricing where prices are depicted as being a 'mark-up' on expected average costs of production. The mark-up pricing principle generates a wide variety of alternative theories, each with different specifications of 'prime costs' and emphasizing various factors that determine the mark-up applied to these costs. Kalecki's (1937) consideration of a corporation's internal and external financing requirements, and the role of the mark-up in influencing cash flows for the firm, establishes important linkages between pricing behaviour and investment decisions. In general, therefore, the mark-up pricing principle can be seen as a 'rule of thumb' pricing routine adaptable to the variable and uncertain environment in which corporations seek to survive and grow. The 'full-cost' prices emerging from Post Keynesian theory should be viewed conceptually as non-equilibrium prices, playing the more dynamic role of reflecting and promoting change in the economy (Robinson 1961).

Kalecki's (1954, 1971) contributions in particular emphasize the importance of oligopolistic-type markets for the analysis of the industrial sector, characterized by the existence of excess capacity. Importantly, excess productive capacity is seen to be a characteristic of production within firms. This does not reflect 'sub-optimal' decisions but instead the realities of decision-making under uncertainty. For given input prices, average costs of production are seen as being constant until full capacity is approached, and as a result demand pressures do not have a direct effect on prices, unless this situation is encountered. The shift away from an emphasis on demand and supply determined equilibrium prices and quantities means that the macroeconomic analysis of output, employment and general prices changes substantially, as is most cogently argued in Kalecki's contributions. In the absence of demand pressures associated with the proximity of full capacity utilization, inflationary pressures emerge largely from 'cost factors' such as raw material costs, import prices and wages. Importantly, it is the level of effective demand, rather than real wages, which determines the level of employment. Real wages are not primarily determined by market forces, but instead by the pricing behaviour outlined above and the bargaining processes related to the struggle between wages and profits over shares in national income (see Chapter 11 by Toporowski). The outcomes of these processes depend very much on the institutional setting that has evolved through time, and also reinforce the classical and Kaleckian emphasis on the importance of income distribution in economic analysis. In more general terms, Kalecki's writings accentuate the significance of ideology and class in shaping economic thinking and behaviour, aspects which clearly are closely related to perceptions of the evolving nature of economic and social organization.

As King (2002) observes, there have been some pockets of resistance within the Post Keynesian camp, from what could be termed the 'fundamentalist Keynesians', to some elements of the evolving Keynes-Kalecki synthesis described above. These reservations were expressed most openly by Paul Davidson and were more widely communicated in Davidson's (2003–2004) review of King's historical accounts. This review fuelled reactions by the likes of Lavoie (2005).[7] The origins of Davidson's indifference towards the Kaleckian elements of Post Keynesian thought have been expressed in the following terms:

> I believe it is useless, if not senseless, to attack the mainstream's core propositions such as the assumption of maximizing behaviour of self-interested agents that result in equilibrium outcomes as unrealistic, and then urge a disequilibrium analysis instead. After all ... even if Keynes accepted this basic belief in maximization by self-interested decision-makers

as a theoretical framework, he could nevertheless demonstrate that such a (fictional) market system would not (and could not) automatically adjust to a full employment equilibrium.

(Davidson 2003–4, p. 269)

Post Keynesians readily accept the fact that Keynes's attack on Say's law and the prevailing orthodoxy was not founded on any particular assumptions about the nature of competitive forces and market structure. As Keynes (1937, p. 213) emphasizes, the methods of classical economics were rendered unsuitable because of the fact that 'our knowledge of the future is fluctuating, vague and uncertain'. However, the point is that the simplistic and logically challenged 'Marshallian microeconomic foundations' that were (strategically) employed in Keynes's critique[8] have to be abandoned and replaced with observations that more closely reflect the realities of contemporary capitalist economies. In this respect, the insights developed by Kalecki and his followers have played an indispensable role in the development of Post Keynesian economics.

The Sraffian research programmes and Post Keynesian economics

As is identified in the subtitle 'Prelude to a Critique of Economic Theory', the major objective of Sraffa's (1960) *Production of Commodities* was to provide the ingredients for a more fully developed *critique* of the marginalist approach to value and distribution theory. While there are few direct attacks on the marginalist theories that were the subject of debate in the Cambridge controversies over capital theory, those that were made were emphatic.[9] As observed by Heinz Kurz (2013, p. 63), perhaps the most important conclusion that follows from Sraffa's analysis of the problem of the choice of technique is that Say's Law of markets, as envisaged by the marginalists, cannot be sustained, because if we cannot rely upon the principle of substitution in production expressing the monotonic prejudice, then there is no reason to presume that the economy, if left by itself, will bring about a tendency to the full employment of all productive factors. This leads the Sraffians and Post Keynesians to reach agreement on fundamental issues such as the rejection of the notion that flexible money wages have the capacity to generate full employment, and also agree that it is variations in output rather than the rate of interest through which investment and saving may be equated.

The source of 'tension' between the Sraffians and Post Keynesians is identified by Lavoie (2011) as arising from different views as to why a lack of deterministic results prevails. As noted above, and flowing directly from Keynes, the Keynesian-Kaleckian perspective rests on notions of radical uncertainty and non-ergodicity. Sraffians tend to emphasize the lack of clear results that can be obtained outside of the core (which deals with the determination of 'normal prices'). Similarly, the existence of uncertainty and volatile expectations highlights the key role played by money and finance within the Keynesian-Kaleckian coalition, while the attack on Say's Law of markets associated with the Sraffian tradition holds whether or not the economy utilizes money (Mongiovi 2012, p. 503).

Given the fundamental importance of the analysis of money for Post Keynesian economists, the lack of a significant role for it within the Sraffian framework is a major difference with Post Keynesian economists who consider money as a central feature of capitalist economies (Minsky 1990, pp. 368–71). Mongiovi (2012) argues that the Sraffian treatment of money is enough for it to be compatible with the Post Keynesian approach. This position is firmly rejected by Minsky, who argues that the Post Keynesian 'analytical framework ... is one in which money, in the sense of the money that emerges within a full-bodied capitalist financial system, is there at the beginning. Money is not added onto an analysis that derives its essential propositions in a framework that abstracts from money and hopes that these propositions have some relevance for a monetary economy' (Minsky 1990, p. 370).

As is well known, Sraffa proceeded to develop his analysis in what he perceived to be the classical tradition, beginning with the meticulous edition of Ricardo's collected works (with the collaboration of Maurice Dobb). Subsequently, a group of economists have been working in the Sraffian tradition in order to provide models of modern capitalist economies. Central to this argument is the view that the tendency to a uniform rate of profits dominates other tendencies in contemporary capitalist economies, and that this tendency underlies the forces which allow for the establishment of long-period equilibrium positions (King 2002, p. 209). As summarized by Tony Aspromourgos (2004), the contemporary Sraffian research programmes investigate themes such as income distribution, relative commodity prices, output levels and employment and monetary phenomena and the real economy. These programmes 'posit a set of solutions to the relationship between distribution and "*equilibrium*" (or more appropriately, "normal") prices in production systems subject to competition', and that it is 'long-period distribution and value theory, which is at the heart of the Sraffian project' (Aspromourgos 2004, pp. 181, 191; emphasis added). This clearly reflects Sraffa's endeavour to establish the relationships that must hold between commodities, wages and profits in capitalist economies in a long-period equilibrium configuration. Sraffa's analysis is founded on the 'classical' notion of 'free' competition with its associated principle of the tendency towards profit-rate equalization in the long period, and assumes that the level and composition of production is given for the purpose of his analysis. Within this setting, long-period positions could be characterized as corresponding to a situation where the structure of capacity has been adjusted to the structure of demand, and hence in which there is a uniform rate of profit in each line of production (Eatwell and Milgate 1983, preface). Essentially, it is the tendency towards a uniform rate of profits which provides the adjustment process of the economy to its long-period position, and of market prices towards production prices.

The force of competition which established the uniform rate of profits and which brings market prices back to their natural values is the movement of capital in response to profit rate differentials. Sectors or industries which earn (for example) profits above those earned elsewhere attract additional investment by existing firms and the entry of new firms in order to take advantage of those higher profits. The resulting increase in output pushes market prices towards natural values, and profits in that sector back to the normal profit rate earned elsewhere in the economy. However, in a modern capitalist economy, investment does not simply increase output of commodities. Rather it is associated with research and development, and with the introduction of the latest techniques of production. As a result, processes of cumulative causation may lead to those sectors (or industries) increasing their competitive advantage and to associated structural change as these sectors grow and develop, with increased technical progress leading to the emergence of new sectors and products as a result of that growth (Young 1928). The forces which are supposed to push the economy to its long-period equilibrium are likely to, in fact, lead to greater and greater changes in the economy as these cumulative processes generate cumulative change. This suggests that path dependency rather than long-period equilibrium positions is the appropriate way to analyse competitive processes.

The central objections to the method of analysis employed within the Sraffian research programmes can be best understood in terms of concerns expressed by Robinson on the usefulness of the Sraffian framework to investigate actual economics processes. This is largely because the arguments are seen to be constructed in terms of comparisons of logically possible positions without the consideration of causation or change, as opposed to processes taking place in actual history:

> Sraffa habitually uses the language of change but, properly speaking, there are no events in his world except for the cycle of self-reproduction and the flow of net output to wages and net profits ... there is no movement from one position to another, merely a comparison of positions corresponding to different levels of the rate of profits.
>
> (Robinson 1980a, p. 139)

> All of this is a purely logical structure – an elaborate thought experiment. There is no causation and no change. At each moment, in any one system, the stock of inputs required for its technology and its growth rate has already come into existence, which implies that in the past, when stocks were being replaced, there must have been correct foresight of what 'today' would be like, so that the profit-maximizing variety of technology has been installed – in short the distinction between the future and the past, as viewed from 'today', has been abolished.
>
> (Robinson 1980b, p. 132)

Robinson (1985, p. 165) later proposed a slightly more sympathetic evaluation of Sraffa's analytical framework by suggesting that 'we have a broad frame within which detailed studies of actual history can be carried out'. However, she concludes that 'there does not seem to be much point in making further systematic generalizations', and that 'this is where Sraffa leaves us and hands us back to Keynes.[10]

In his survey of Sraffian economics, Aspromourgos argues that 'the Sraffian project [is] open to "history" in a substantial sense' (Aspromourgos 2004, p. 183), but this only seems to relate to how the exogenously determined distributive variable (the so-called 'closure' issue) is determined. In contrast to Post Keynesian economics, history is not fundamental to Sraffian economics.

Sraffa's (classical) regime of free competition neglects the 'obstacles' to competition which Sraffa (1926, p. 522) had on a previous occasion argued 'are not of the nature of "frictions", but are themselves active forces which produce permanent and even cumulative effects'. As Richard Arena and Stephanie Blankenburg (2013, p. 94) argue, these effects cannot simply be accounted for by replacing Sraffa's initial assumption of a uniform rate of profits with differential intra- and inter-sectoral rates of profits. Monopoly capitalism is characterized by barriers to entry and the existence of excess capacity due to (*inter alia*) uncertainty regarding future demand. These forces cannot be considered to be transitory in nature. Within this setting, prices in most sectors of the economy are determined as a mark-up on (expected) unit costs, where these mark-ups are influenced by prevailing and potential competitive pressures and the strategic goals of the firm, including those associated with financing investment decisions. Firms are primarily concerned with survival and growth as opposed to profit maximization.

Clearly, therefore the departures from free competition which characterize contemporary capitalist economies challenge the mechanisms through which market prices can be seen to gravitate towards production prices. Moreover, the influence of monopolistic elements on the pricing decisions of the firm has important implications for the realization of the surplus. The problem of effective demand in modern capitalist economies requires a consideration of the effects of increases in the concentration of capital and economies of scale. Moreover, the capital flows that may occur between sectors are not simply associated with changes in the composition of output, as they also embody new techniques of production. It is not surprising, therefore, that as Paolo Sylos-Labini (1985) observes, it is in the sphere of the growth process, particularly in the presence of technical progress, that the proposed extensions to Sraffa's framework have been least forthcoming. This is the result of Sraffian economists considering the central economic problem to be the analysis of inter-sectoral prices with a given output:

> Price theory is the core of the analysis, and is perceived as being important in its own right. ... The classical [and Post Keynesian] dynamic concerns with accumulation and growth cannot be readily incorporated into the analysis, and pose insurmountable problems for the Sraffian analysis of price ... The Sraffa framework cannot incorporate changes in output or technology into its analysis of prices.
>
> (Kriesler 1992, pp. 163–4)

In Sraffa's depiction of the determination of an economy, the system of production has already been determined in all possible spheres, with no role for individuals to influence the methods of production that are being used. The nature and transfer of knowledge between individuals and institutions are not considered, and the ever-present forces that shape innovation and structural change have no place in Sraffa's system. These issues challenge the Sraffian notion that market interaction is derived essentially from the structure of technology, with the subjective 'mental determinants' playing only a relatively insignificant role (Marchionatti 2001, p. xxi).

The above discussion clearly raises fundamental questions relating to path dependency in the attainment of hypothesized long-period equilibrium price configurations. As writers such as Joseph Halevi and Peter Kriesler (1991) and Arena and Blankenburg (2013) argue, steady-state balanced growth appears to be implied by any adjustment mechanism associated with the Sraffian system. However, Lavoie (2011, pp. 1047–9) claims that Sraffians have been unfairly criticized for neglecting the possibility of path-dependency, pointing to two (footnoted) references in the Sraffian literature where the possibility of path-dependency is recognized. However, as Arena and Blankenburg (2013, p. 96 n. 4) observe, 'to our knowledge neither of these authors has gone beyond the mere recognition of the possibility'. Until some coherent dynamic adjustment process can be specified which describes the 'traverse' from one equilibrium position to another in a manner that ensures that the traverse itself does not influence the final equilibrium point, the notion of a long-run equilibrium configuration that is determined independently from short-period adjustments and fluctuations will remain an elusive concept.[11] Instead, the Keynesian-Kaleckian-Robinsonian coalition embraces Kalecki's (1971, p. 165) view that 'In fact the long-run trend is but a slowly changing component of a chain of short-period situations; it is not a separate entity'. In order to develop an understanding of the dynamics that link these short-period situations, the institutional framework of a social system must be recognized as a fundamental element of the analysis. A consideration of these issues may be superfluous to the derivation of long-period equilibrium prices within the simplistic world constructed by the Sraffians; however, the purpose of economic analysis within the Keynesian–Kaleckian–Robinsonian tradition is to develop an understanding of actual economic processes embodied within modern capitalist societies.

Concluding comments

As emphasized above, Sraffian economists draw inferences about accumulation from comparisons of long-run equilibrium positions, using comparative static methodology. Underlying this is an implicit assumption that the path the economy takes between these equilibria will not influence the final position. However, this is the equivalent of placing the analysis in what Joan Robinson called logical time, and not in the historical time that Post Keynesian economists believe is the appropriate method to use. By doing so, they ignore at least three of the propositions which we earlier argued are the foundation of Post Keynesian analysis, namely: that accumulation should be viewed as a historical process, with the unchangeable past influencing the present and hence the key role of uncertainty; that this concern with historical time means that, because the future is uncertain, expectations have a significant and unavoidable impact on economic events; and, finally, they ignore the importance of institutions and of social and political forces in shaping economic events.

For Sraffian economists, uncertainty remains a peripheral issue, with Mongiovi even arguing that its central role in Post Keynesian analysis is due to methodological errors: 'One of the reasons the post Keynesian literature relies so heavily on the pervasiveness of uncertainty is that it is not solidly grounded in a theory of value and distribution' (Mongiovi 2012, p. 503). This statement both misunderstands the importance of the analysis of price and distribution for Post Keynesian economists, and it also lacks any insight into what Post Keynesian economists see as the essential elements of capitalist economies. Certainly in a world where there is a strong tendency towards long-period equilibrium which is independent of the path that the economy takes to get there, and which economic agents may be aware of, there is no room for uncertainty as the potential outcome is determined, and there is also little room for money (Bortis 2013, p. 328). However, in any realistic model, such as Keynes and Post Keynesians prefer, uncertainty permeates all decision-making. In fact, the essence of Post Keynesian models of pricing, investment and distribution stress the importance of these processes occurring as an historical process, with uncertainty permeating all aspects of the decision-making process (for an excellent survey of the Post Keynesian approach to pricing see Coutts and Norman 2013). The unimportance of uncertainty for Sraffian economists, on the other hand, is strongly related to the long-period method and the lack of path dependency in their models. Related to this is the role of money, which occupies a central position for Post Keynesian economists, as reflecting an essential element of capitalist economies. For Sraffian economists, money, like history, mainly enters in the question of exogenous closure. As Minsky (1990) argued, money is not part of their essential vision of capitalist economies – it is an afterthought.

For these reasons, Lavoie's conclusion that Sraffians and other Post Keynesians are brought together by their similarities in their positive contributions cannot be supported in the setting of the Post Keynesian perspectives described in this chapter. In this context, the following observations presented by Maurice Dobb are pertinent:

> to my mind, the whole issue has been misrepresented by the critics through their failure to appreciate the specific design and intention of Sraffa's work (as represented, *e.g.*, in the sub-title of his book, 'Prelude to a Critique of Economic Theory') .... The design and intention was, in effect, to answer certain major critiques of Marx (and by implication of

the whole Ricardo-Marx approach) from Böhm-Bawerk onwards .... In this sense his work is to be regarded as primarily constructive *anti-kritik*, and not as a new theoretical system, replacing or mediating between its predecessors.

(Dobb 1975–76, p. 468; original emphasis)

Notes

1 We would like to thank Geoff Harcourt and John King for their helpful comments on an earlier draft.
2 The reasons for Robinson's reservations about formalizing positive linkages between the work of Sraffa and the early Post Keynesians are discussed in the section on Sraffian research programmes below. An example of such an attempt can be found in Bhadhuri and Robinson (1980). Particularly interesting discussion of the intellectual connections between Sraffa and Robinson can be found in Harcourt (1986) and Marcuzzo (2005), while Robinson's (1961) review of Sraffa (1960) underlines the importance she placed on Sraffa's critique of the marginalist approach.
3 It should be noted that the Introduction to Harcourt and Kriesler (2013c, p. 4) states: 'we need to point out that the inclusion of [Sraffa's contributions] as part of the core of post-Keynesian economics is not a universal view', and it is clear that one of the editors (PK) sees 'no role for ... Sraffians ... in post-Keynesian developments'.
4 This point was made to us by Geoff Harcourt.
5 For further discussion of the significance of this line of argument to the development of the strand of Post Keynesian analysis under discussion see Setterfield (1995) and Harris (2005).
6 A summary of the similarities and points of departure between the theories of effective demand developed by Keynes and Kalecki is presented in Kriesler (1997), with some interesting comparisons also found in Robinson's (1966) observations. See also Kalecki's review of Keynes's *General Theory* in Targetti and Kinda-Hass (1982).
7 See, for example, Davidson's reported statement that 'I don't think that Kalecki adds anything to the system' (King 1995, p. 29) and lack of reference to the work of Kalecki in the formal statement of his work, such as Davidson (1972). No connections between the work of Keynes and Kalecki are to be found in Davidson's (2007) extensive account of Keynes's contributions and lasting legacy. As King (2002, p. 212) also suggests, a further reason for Davidson's 'hostility' to Kaleckian economics relates to political considerations, with Davidson (1972, pp. 3–4) associating himself and the 'Keynes school' with the political centre, while the 'Kaleckians' were seen as being 'left of centre' and being overly concerned with class divisions and allied policy issues.
8 Keynes was being tactical in showing that unemployment could still result, even allowing for the main assumptions of the prevailing orthodoxy.
9 No more so was his summary of the substantive 'capital reversal' conclusion: 'The reversals in the direction of relative prices, in the face of unchanged methods of production, cannot be reconciled with *any* notion of capital as a measurable quantity independent of distribution and prices' (Sraffa 1960, p. 38; original emphasis). However, it is interesting to note that this passage was placed within parenthesis aside from the main text.
10 In this respect, Kalecki, who inspired much of Robinson's later work, was critical of Sraffa's price theory because it neglected aggregate demand (Nuti 1989, p. 319; Kowalik 2009, p. 114). As King (2002, p. 209) highlights, this perspective is stated more forcefully by the prominent Post Keynesian, Hyman Minsky (1990, p. 363), who argued that 'Sraffa says little or nothing about effective demand and Keynes's *General Theory* can be viewed as holding that the long run is not a fit subject for

study ... At the arid level of Sraffa, the Keynesian view that effective demand reflects financial and monetary variables has no meaning, for there is no monetary or financial system in Sraffa.'

11 More general discussion of the significance of the traverse and path dependency in the Post Keynesian literature can be found in Halevi et al. (2013).

References

Arena, R. and Blankenburg, S. (2013), Sraffa, Keynes, and Post-Keynesians: Suggestions for a Synthesis in the Making, in G.C. Harcourt and P. Kriesler (2013a), *Handbook of Post-Keynesian Economics: Theory and Origins*, volume 1. Oxford: Oxford University Press, pp. 74–100.

Aspromourgos, T. (2004), Sraffian Research Programmes and Unorthodox Economics, *Review of Political Economy* 6(2), pp. 179–206.

Bhaduri, A. and Robinson, J. (1980), Accumulation and Exploitation: An Analysis in the Tradition of Marx, Sraffa and Kalecki, *Cambridge Journal of Economics* 4(2), pp. 103–115.

Bortis, H. (2013), Post-Keynesian Principles and Economic Policies, in G.C. Harcourt and P. Kriesler (2013b), *Handbook of Post-Keynesian Economics: Critiques and Methodology*, volume 2. Oxford: Oxford University Press, pp. 326–365.

Coutts, K. and Norman, N. (2013), Post-Keynesian Approaches to Industrial Pricing: A Survey and Critique, in G.C. Harcourt and P. Kriesler (2013a), *Handbook of Post-Keynesian Economics: Theory and Origins*, volume 1. Oxford: Oxford University Press, pp. 443–466.

Davidson, P. (1972), *Money and the Real World*. London: Macmillan.

Davidson, P. (1982–83), Rational Expectations: A Fallacious Foundation for Studying Critical Decision-Making Processes, *Journal of Post Keynesian Economics* 5(2), pp. 182–196.

Davidson, P. (2002), *Financial Markets, Money, and the Real World*. Cheltenham, UK and Northampton, MA, USA: Edward Elgar.

Davidson, P. (2003–2004), Setting the Record Straight on a History of Post Keynesian Economics, *Journal of Post Keynesian Economics* 26(2), pp. 245–272.

Davidson, P. (2007), *John Maynard Keynes: Great Thinkers in Economics Series*. Houndmills, UK: Palgrave Macmillan.

Dobb, M. (1975–76), A Note on the Ricardo-Marx-Sraffa Discussion, *Science and Society* 39(4), pp. 468–470.

Eatwell, J. and Milgate, M. (1983), *Keynes's Economics and the Theory of Value and Distribution*. Oxford: Oxford University Press.

Gibson, B. (ed.) (2005), *Joan Robinson's Economics: A Centennial Celebration*. Cheltenham, UK and Northampton, MA, USA: Edward Elgar.

Halevi, J., Hart, N. and Kriesler, P. (2013), The Traverse and Equilibrium Analysis, in G.C. Harcourt and P. Kriesler (2013b), *Handbook of Post-Keynesian Economics: Critiques and Methodology*, volume 2. Oxford: Oxford University Press, pp. 175–197.

Halevi, J. and Kriesler, P. (1991), Kalecki, Classical Economics and the Surplus Approach, *Review of Political Economy* 3(1), pp. 71–92.

Hamouda, O. and Harcourt, G.C. (1988), Post Keynesianism: From Criticism to Coherence? *Bulletin of Economic Research* 40(1), pp. 1–33.

Harcourt, G.C. (1969), Some Cambridge Controversies in the Theory of Capital, *Journal of Economic Literature* 7(2), pp. 369–405.

Harcourt, G.C. (1981), Marshall, Sraffa and Keynes: Incompatible Bedfellows? *Eastern Economic Journal* 7(1), pp. 39–50.

Harcourt, G.C. (1986), On the Influence of Piero Sraffa on the Contributions of Joan Robinson to Economic Theory, *Economic Journal* 96(381), pp. 96–108.

Harcourt, G.C. and Kriesler, P. (eds.) (2013a), *The Oxford Handbook of Post-Keynesian Economics: Theory and Origins*, volume 1. Oxford: Oxford University Press.

Harcourt, G.C. and Kriesler, P. (eds.) (2013b), *The Oxford Handbook of Post-Keynesian Economics: Critiques and Methodology*, volume 2. Oxford: Oxford University Press.

Harcourt, G.C. and Kriesler, P. (2013c), Introduction, in G.C. Harcourt and P. Kriesler (eds.) (2013a), *Handbook of Post-Keynesian Economics: Theory and Origins*, volume 1. Oxford: Oxford University Press, pp. 1–44.

Harris, D.J. (2005), Robinson on 'History versus Equilibrium', in B. Gibson (ed.), (2005), *Joan Robinson's Economics: A Centennial Celebration*. Cheltenham, UK and Northampton, MA, USA: Edward Elgar, pp. 81–108.

Kaldor, N. (1982), *The Scourge of Monetarism*. Oxford: Oxford University Press.

Kalecki, M. (1937), The Principle of Increasing Risk, *Economica* 4(16), pp. 440–447.

Kalecki, M. (1954), *The Theory of Economic Dynamics*. London: Allen and Unwin.

Kalecki, M. (1971), *Selected Essays on the Dynamics of the Capitalist Economy: 1933–1970*. Cambridge, UK: Cambridge University Press.

Keynes, J.M. (1937), The General Theory of Employment, *Quarterly Journal of Economics* 51(2), pp. 209–223.

King, J.E. (1995), *Conversations with Post Keynesians*. London: Macmillan.

King, J.E. (2002), *A History of Post Keynesian Economics since 1936*. Cheltenham, UK and Northampton, MA, USA: Edward Elgar.

Kowalik, T. (2009), Luxemburg's and Kalecki's Theories and Visions of Capitalist Dynamics, in R. Bellofiore (ed.), *Rosa Luxemburg and the Critique of Political Economy*. London: Routledge.

Kriesler, P. (1992), Answers for Steedman, *Review of Political Economy* 4(2), pp. 163–170.

Kriesler, P. (1997), Keynes, Kalecki and *The General Theory*, in G.C. Harcourt and P. Riach (eds.), *A 'Second Edition' of Keynes's General Theory*. London and New York: Routledge.

Kriesler, P. and Nevile, J. (2002), IS-LM and Macroeconomics after Keynes, in P. Arestis, M. Desai and S. Dow (eds.), *Money, Macroeconomics and Keynes: Essays on Honour of Victoria Chick*, volume 1. London and New York: Routledge, pp. 115–123.

Kurz, H.D. (2013), Sraffa, Keynes, and Post-Keynesianism, in G.C. Harcourt and P. Kriesler (2013a), *The Oxford Handbook of Post-Keynesian Economics: Theory and Origins*, volume 1. Oxford: Oxford University Press, pp. 51–73.

Lavoie, M. (2005), Changing Definitions: A Comment on Davidson's Critique of King's History of Post Keynesianism, *Journal of Post Keynesian Economics* 27(3), pp. 371–376.

Lavoie, M. (2011), Should Sraffian Economics be Dropped Out of the Post-Keynesian School? *Economies et Sociétés* 44(7), pp. 1027–1059.

Marchionatti, R. (2001), Sraffa and the Criticism of Marshall in the 1920s, in T. Cozzi and R. Marchionatti (eds.), *Piero Sraffa's Political Economy: A Centenary Estimate*. London and New York: Routledge.

Marcuzzo, M.C. (2005), Robinson and Sraffa, in B. Gibson (ed.), (2005), *Joan Robinson's Economics: A Centennial Celebration*. Cheltenham, UK and Northampton, MA, USA: Edward Elgar, pp. 29–42.

Minsky, H.P. (1982), *Can It Happen Again? Essays on Instability and Finance.* Armonk, NY: M.E. Sharpe.

Minsky, H.P. (1985), The Financial Instability Hypothesis: A Restatement, in P. Arestis and T. Skouras (eds.), *Post Keynesian Economic Theory.* Brighton, UK: Wheatsheaf, pp. 24–55.

Minsky, H.P. (1990), Sraffa and Keynes: Effective Demand in the Long Run, in K. Bharadwaj and B. Schefold (eds.), *Essays on Piero Sraffa: Critical Perspectives on the Revival of Classical Theory.* London: Unwin Hyman.

Mongiovi, G. (2012), Sraffian Economics, in J.E. King (ed.), *The Elgar Companion to Post Keynesian Economics*, second edition. Cheltenham, UK and Northampton, MA, USA: Edward Elgar, pp. 499–505.

Nuti, M.D. (1989), Michal Kalecki's Contributions to the Theory and Practice of Socialist Planning, in M. Sebastiani (ed.), *Kalecki's Relevance Today.* London: Macmillan.

Robinson, J. (1956), *The Accumulation of Capital.* London: Macmillan.

Robinson, J. (1961), Prelude to a Critique of Economic Theory, *Oxford Economic Papers* 13(1), pp. 53–58.

Robinson, J. (1964), Pre-Keynesian Theory after Keynes, *Australian Economic Papers* 3(1–2), pp. 25–35.

Robinson, J. (1966), Kalecki and Keynes, in P.A. Baran et al. (eds.) *Problems of Economic Dynamics and Planning: Essays in Honour of Michał Kalecki.* Oxford: Pergamon Press. Reprinted in J. Robinson (1978), pp. 53–60.

Robinson, J. (1974), History vs. Equilibrium, *Thames Papers in Political Economy*, in J. Robinson (1978), *Contributions to Modern Economics*, Oxford: Basil Blackwell, pp. 126–136.

Robinson, J. (1978), *Contributions to Modern Economics.* Oxford: Basil Blackwell.

Robinson, J. (1979), Foreword, in A.S. Eichner (ed.), *A Guide to Post Keynesian Economics.* London: Macmillan.

Robinson, J. (1980a), Misunderstandings in the Theory of Production, in J. Robinson (1980c), *Contributions to Modern Economics.* Oxford: Basil Blackwell, pp. 135–140.

Robinson, J. (1980b), Retrospect: 1980, in J. Robinson (1980c), *Contributions to Modern Economics.* Oxford: Basil Blackwell, pp. 131–134.

Robinson, J. (1980c), *Further Contributions to Modern Economics.* Oxford: Basil Blackwell.

Robinson, J. (1985), The Theory of Normal Prices and Reconstruction of Economic Theory, in G.R. Feiwel (ed.), *Issues in Contemporary Macroeconomics and Distribution.* London: Macmillan.

Setterfield, M. (1995), Historical Time and Economic Theory, *Review of Political Economy* 7(1), pp. 1–27.

Sraffa, P. (1926), The Laws of Returns under Competitive Conditions, *Economic Journal* 36(144), 535–550.

Sraffa, P. (1960), *Production of Commodities by Means of Commodities: Prelude to a Critique of Economic Theory.* Cambridge, UK: Cambridge University Press.

Sylos-Labini, P. (1985), Sraffa's Critique of the Marshallian Theory of Prices, *Political Economy: Studies in the Surplus Approach* 1(3), pp. 51–71.

Targetti, F. and Kinda-Hass, B. (1982), Kalecki's (1936) Review of Keynes's *General Theory*, *Australian Economic Papers* 21(39), pp. 244–260.

Young, A.A. (1928), Increasing Returns and Economic Progress, *Economic Journal* 38(152), pp. 527–540.

13 Post Keynesian price theory with a Schumpeterian twist

Harry Bloch

Price theory is at the core of neoclassical economics. It provides the linkages among the analyses of production, consumption and distribution as well as the basis for welfare theorems about the efficiency of competitive markets. Yet, it is based on the achievement of general equilibrium with assumptions of individual optimization and perfect information that are acknowledged as unrealistic. Nonetheless, neoclassical economists insist on the relevance of the theory for understanding economic development and for the formulation of public policy.

Post Keynesian (PK) price theory rejects the neoclassical assumptions as unrealistic and instead starts from assumptions of imperfect competition, incomplete information and bounded rationality, which leads to a focus on rule-based behaviour, especially in large and complex firms. Two of the widely adopted rules for product-pricing are mark-up pricing and full-cost pricing. Among other things, application of these rules implies that demand shocks lead to less short-run price adjustment and more quantity adjustment than occurs in neoclassical analysis of the same shocks.

Schumpeter accepts the neoclassical model of general equilibrium as appropriate for the analysis of a stationary economy. However, he then argues that a stationary economy is unsustainable under capitalism because a stable economy enhances the ability of entrepreneurs to seek profit from innovations. Innovations disrupt equilibrium, as does the process of creative destruction that ensues as new ways of doing things drive out established products and firms through aggressive competition. The stationary analysis of general equilibrium is supplanted by an evolutionary analysis of innovation and creative destruction.

PK price theory generally ignores the impact of technological change by focusing on analysis of the short run. Exceptions are provided in Sylos-Labini's (1962) *Oligopoly and Technical Progress* and in Steindl's (1952) *Maturity and Stagnation in American Capitalism*. Sylos-Labini includes technological discontinuities in a full-cost pricing model, while Steindl adds dynamic competition among firms with different technologies to Kalecki's (1971) exposition of the mark-up pricing model. However, the treatments of technology by both Sylos-Labini and Steindl are highly restrictive.

PK theory correctly focuses on the behaviour of large corporations and oligopolies, especially the use of pricing rules that provide some buffer against the vagaries of market supply and demand. However, the analysis is generally static and only suitable for short-run analysis. Adding insights from Schumpeter's evolutionary theory can extend the theory to include the impact of innovation, which is an essential characteristic of the long-run development of modern economies. These insights include a cyclical pattern of movements in unit direct cost and the mark-up factor as well as the need to allow for the impact of obsolescence due to technological change.

The remainder of this chapter is organized in the following way. The next section reviews the content of PK price theory in some detail, particularly the full-cost model of Sylos-Labini and the mark-up model of Kalecki. This is followed by an analysis of the impact of innovation and creative destruction on the dynamic adjustment of the average unit direct cost and average mark-up factor within an industry. The penultimate section discusses extending the full-cost model to include prospective obsolescence as a part of fixed costs. The final section summarizes the modifications to PK price theory to incorporate the Schumpeterian twist.

Post Keynesian price theory

PK price theory has been developed to apply to the large corporate enterprises that dominate many sectors of the modern economy, particularly the industrial sector. These enterprises are taken to have different organizational drivers and face different market conditions than competitive or monopolistic firms, leading to the need for a price theory that takes these differences into account. Neoclassical oligopoly theory is rejected as appropriate for this purpose as it leads to indeterminate solutions and imposes unrealistic assumptions about optimization with perfect information. PK price theory recognizes the need of large and complex enterprises for pricing rules that can be applied across the organization and monitored centrally. It also recognizes that smaller firms operating in the same industries will set their prices in relation to those of the dominant firms, so that the pricing rules of dominant firms will directly or indirectly apply across the industry.

Lee (1998, p. 10) identifies three PK pricing procedures: mark-up, normal cost and target rate of return. The latter two procedures involve different ways of adding an allowance for profits to the average direct and fixed costs of production. They are subsumed under the umbrella of full-cost pricing in the discussion below. Mark-up pricing and full-cost pricing are discussed separately below, but they also have a formal correspondence that is noted as part of the discussion.

Kalecki (1971) distinguishes between 'cost-determined' prices of finished goods (essentially manufacturing products) and 'demand-determined' prices of raw materials. The 'cost-determined' prices are calculated using a combination of the producer's own unit prime cost (expenditure per unit for raw materials and production labour) and the average price charged by producers of similar goods, with

$$p = mu + n\bar{p} \tag{13.1}$$

where p is the firm's price, u is unit prime cost, $\bar{p}$ is the weighted average price of all firms, m is a positive coefficient and n is positive coefficient with a value less than one (Kalecki 1971, p. 45). For Kalecki, the m and n coefficients capture the degree of monopoly for the firm. Aggregating over an industry consisting of firms producing similar products yields

$$\bar{p} = \bar{u}\left(\frac{\bar{m}}{1 - \bar{n}}\right) \tag{13.2}$$

where the bar over each variable and coefficient indicates an appropriately weighted average for the industry. The average price in Equation 13.2 is equal to average unit prime cost times a mark-up factor, $\bar{m}/(1 - \bar{n})$, which captures the degree of monopoly for the industry.[1]

Kalecki argues that the degree of monopoly is given in the short run, so the average price for the industry is proportional to average prime unit cost. Over the longer run, the degree of monopoly is subject to change. Factors mentioned by Kalecki as operating on the degree of monopoly in the US during the period from the late 1800s through the 1930s include increased industrial concentration, increased strength of trade unions and increased ratios of overheads to prime costs. Technological progress is mentioned as a factor that affects unit prime cost, but its influence on the degree of monopoly is only acknowledged as possibly operating through the level of overheads in relation to prime costs.

Kalecki's pricing equation as given in Equation 13.2 has a fairly direct formal correspondence to the simplest version of Sylos-Labini's (1962, p. 40) full-cost pricing equation, which is

$$p = v + qv \tag{13.3}$$

where p is product price as before, v is variable cost per unit and q is a margin to cover overheads and profit. Sylos-Labini deals formally only with the case of homogenous products, for which $p = \bar{p}$. Furthermore, Kalecki's unit prime cost and Sylos-Labini's unit variable cost are essentially the same concept of unit direct cost, and neither puts much emphasis on differences in unit cost across firms, so it is appropriate to set $\bar{u} = v$. With these two equalities, substituting for p in 13.3 with the expression for $\bar{p}$ in 13.2 and rearranging terms yields

$$1 + q = \bar{m}/(1 - \bar{n}) \tag{13.4}$$

Thus, when the equalities hold, one plus Sylos-Labini's margin equals Kalecki's mark-up factor.

As noted above, Kalecki's mark-up factor is treated as constant in the short run but changes with factors influencing the degree of monopoly in the long run. Similarly, with Sylos-Labini there is a distinction between pricing with a fixed margin (applying to small changes in cost in the short run) and an analysis appropriate for more substantial cost changes or for the longer period. In particular, capital costs and changing competitive conditions have an explicit role in determining full cost for the longer period. Sylos-Labini's (1962, p. 40) most complete formula for the calculation of the full-cost price takes the form:

$$p = \left(v + \frac{k}{x} \right)(1 + r_m) \qquad (13.5)$$

where p is the product price, v is unit variable (or direct) cost, k is total fixed cost per period, x is output per period (normally taken to be capacity output) and r_m is the minimum rate of profit acceptable to the firm.

Combining Equations 13.3 and 13.5 leads to a formal equivalence between the mark-up factor and the variables that enter into the full-cost price as follows:

$$1 + q = \frac{\left[\left(v + \frac{k}{x} \right)(1 + r_m) \right]}{v} \qquad (13.6)$$

Sylos-Labini then argues that the factors that determine the mark-up factor, at least in the long run, are the levels of fixed cost, normal output and the minimum rate of return. In this interpretation the full-cost and the mark-up pricing rules are but different ways of relating pricing behaviour to the same underlying theory, with the left-hand side determining the relation between price and unit variable cost in the short run and the right-hand side applying in the long run.

When firms employ heterogeneous technologies, as assumed by Sylos-Labini, applying the pricing formula in Equation 13.5 leads to a variety of possible prices for a group of products. The question then arises of how these prices are reflected in the market. The basic case considered by Sylos-Labini is that of concentrated oligopoly, dominated by a few large firms producing homogenous products. After considering the prospects for expansion of existing firms and entry of new firms, Sylos-Labini concludes that the most efficient firm or firms will act as price leader and that the long-run equilibrium price for the industry is the full-cost price for the least efficient (highest average total cost) firms in operation.[2] More efficient (lower-cost) firms then earn a profit rate above their minimum acceptable level.

Sylos-Labini acknowledges that there may be several different possible long-run prices associated with different configurations of technologies in use.

Technologies with even higher average total cost may exist and the absence of firms employing such technologies depends in part on the past pricing behaviour of the group of remaining firms, particularly whether they have been aggressive in eliminating high-cost competitors. This leads him to extend the list of elements of price determination to include the absolute size of the market and the elasticity of demand, as well as those elements that determine the average total cost of all firms, namely the set of available technologies along with the prices of machines and variable inputs.

Changes in technology are considered by Sylos-Labini (1962, pp. 63–66) as a possible influence on price changes. He cites Schumpeter (1939) in arguing that changes in production technology, at least major changes, involve construction of new plant and equipment. Applying full-cost pricing, cost reductions are then reflected in price reductions to the extent that the technology is available to the least efficient firms. If the innovations are only available to large firms, they 'will simply sit back and enjoy the larger profits they can get at the existing price, after the cost reduction' (Sylos-Labini 1962, p. 64). Thus, Sylos-Labini concludes that concentrated oligopoly leads to a tendency for cost reductions from technological progress to be only partially passed through to price reductions. This conclusion is criticized in the section below as failing to recognize the ongoing nature of technological change and the implications of this for the movement of costs and prices through time.

The role of direct unit cost as a determinant of price is clear in both the mark-up and full-cost variants of PK price theory, while the influence of other factors is generally indirect and differs across variants.[3] Among the factors that have an occasional indirect role in influencing price, particularly in the long run, are overhead costs per unit, industry concentration, strength of trade unions and technology. Notably, demand does not feature as a determinant in PK price theory, aside from in the extreme boom conditions mentioned by Kalecki (1971, p. 54). This provides a clear contrast to neo-classical price theory in which demand changes normally lead to price changes in the same direction.

Creative destruction and dynamics of the mark-up factor

Both Kalecki and Sylos-Labini acknowledge a role for technological progress in changing the direct cost element in their pricing equations. They also allow for the possibility that technological progress may affect the ratio of price to unit direct cost, but generally only in qualified circumstances.[4] However, neither explicitly considers the adjustment to innovations, which can affect the relation between prices and costs in both the short run and the long run.

In contrast, Steindl (1952) provides a PK analysis of pricing that focuses on the process of adjustment to heterogeneity in cost levels across firms, where such heterogeneity can arise from technological innovation.[5] He argues that firms expand their production capacity through internal accumulation (reinvestment of retained profits). Low-cost (progressive) firms have an advantage in this internal accumulation as they have higher profits arising from their lower costs.[6] The advantage is cumulative, as expanding output can yield economies of scale or allow firms to introduce more advanced technology, further enhancing the cost advantage of the low-cost (progressive) firms.

In Steindl's 'ideal' pattern of competition, the advantages of progressive firms tend to lead to their increasing domination and to relative concentration of the industry without any change in price. However, given the cumulative impact of internal accumulation, there is a tendency for excess capacity to emerge. When the progressive firms respond by engaging in aggressive sales and price competition, high-cost (marginal) firms are eliminated and absolute concentration of the industry occurs.

According to Steindl, once there is absolute concentration, progressive firms become more aware of their interdependence and also of the limits to eliminating further competitors through aggressive competition. In this stage of industry development, which Steindl identifies as maturity, progressive firms refrain from both aggressive competition and investment in further capacity beyond the industry growth rate, even though some high-cost (marginal) producers remain.[7] The industry cost structure is thus similar to that associated with equilibrium for Sylos-Labini's concentrated oligopoly.

Indeed, Sylos-Labini's analysis can be viewed as starting where Steindl leaves off, namely with a mature concentrated industry. Sylos-Labini acknowledges the possibility of aggressive competition by low-cost firms to eliminate marginal firms but does not provide detail for the process and its implications for price dynamics. When the analyses of Sylos-Labini and Steindl are combined, Sylos-Labini's full-cost pricing equation applies to mature concentrated industries, while Steindl's price dynamics apply during the process of relative and absolute concentration that gives rise to the mature industry.

Relative concentration through growth of progressive firms leads to a fall in average unit direct cost for the industry in Steindl's analysis, which implies a rising average mark-up factor given the presumption that short-run price rigidity prevails. Once the progressive firms turn to aggressive price competition to eliminate marginal firms, there is a further fall in average unit direct cost (due to elimination of high-cost firms) along with a decline in the average price for the industry. Whether the average mark-up factor rises or falls depends on the severity of the price decline required to eliminate the marginal firms with their higher-than-average unit direct cost. In all cases, after the cessation of aggressive competition, there will be a higher mark-up factor for the industry as a whole than prevailed before the process of relative and absolute concentration began.

The dynamics of the mark-up over the course of the 'ideal' pattern of competition are consistent with Kalecki's argument that the mark-up factor reflects the degree of monopoly in the industry, albeit with a short-run analysis added to Kalecki's long-run analysis. The industry starts with a low level of concentration and with a relatively low level of the mark-up factor. The mark-up then rises with relative concentration reflecting the lack of direct competition between old and new technologies. The mark-up factor may drop with aggressive competition between the technologies, even though industry concentration keeps rising. This is an anomaly from a long-run perspective, but it reflects the importance of aggressive strategies adopted by the progressive firms in the short run. Once the process of absolute concentration has run its course, the industry concentration and the average mark-up factor are higher than at the beginning in accord with Kalecki's long-run analysis.[8]

In Steindl's analysis, the pattern of 'ideal' competition is an emergent property of industry evolution. The dynamics of differential investment and further widening of cost differentials make the continuation of price rigidity unsustainable. Aggressive competition is an increasingly likely outcome of the growing structural imbalance, while the end of aggressive competition is a likely outcome of the greater homogeneity of unit costs that results from removal of marginal firms in maturity. However, the timing of aggressive competition and the transformation to cooperative price leadership is uncertain. Indeed, institutional structures, such as regulation, might even prevent the dynamics that are emergent in the dynamics of capacity and unit cost.

Emergence is central to Schumpeter's analysis of pricing. His price theory, as laid out in *Business Cycles* (Schumpeter 1939, especially chapters 8 and 10), is primarily about the forces that potentially operate on the movement of prices following the introduction of innovations. A successful innovation generates entrepreneurial profits, meaning that price exceeds full cost, encouraging investment to expand operations by the innovator and also the entry of imitators. Rapid expansion of the innovator and imitators creates structural imbalance in the economy, eventually leading to creative destruction of established producers that have not adopted the innovation as prices fall, mark-up factors decline and profits disappear. Importantly, this analysis applies to all forms of disruptive innovation, not just to the case of technical change leading to cost heterogeneity that is dealt with by Steindl.

Schumpeter starts and ends the pattern of motion in his price theory in a stationary state with competitive equilibrium. This provides a nice analytical anchor for Schumpeter, who was a great admirer of Walrasian general equilibrium theory, but is clearly inconsistent with the realist orientation of PK price theory. In *Capitalism, Socialism and Democracy*, Schumpeter (1942) acknowledges the growing domination of large corporations and imperfect competition in industry, but he does not address the implications of the rise of large corporations and oligopolies for his price theory.

Steindl's 'ideal' pattern of competition can be viewed as a specific example of how Schumpeter's price theory might work without assuming perfectly competitive general equilibrium at the start and finish of the process. Price rigidity and cost heterogeneity across firms characterize the situation at the start of Steindl's 'ideal' pattern. The heterogeneity of unit cost is a possible result of the introduction of a cost-saving process innovation by the progressive firms, which leaves the marginal firms using older technologies with higher unit direct cost. The process of absolute concentration is then the particular form taken for the working of the perennial gale of creative destruction as conceived by Schumpeter. At the end of the process, older technologies with higher direct cost of production have been substantially eliminated from the industry.

Neither Steindl nor Sylos-Labini considers the possibility of further innovation disrupting the structure of a concentrated industry. However, Schumpeter (1942) argues forcefully that these large corporations had become the key agents of research and development (R&D) and of innovation in modern economies. There is considerable debate about whether this argument is valid and consistent with Schumpeter's earlier analysis of capitalist development, but it is nonetheless useful to consider how disruptive innovations might affect prices in a concentrated industry.[9]

Suppose that a new substantially lower cost technology is introduced by a new entrant into a concentrated oligopoly with a number of operating technologies. If the output of the innovator is small relative to established firms, there is unlikely to be any change in price following its entry and the innovator has a higher than average mark-up factor thereby increasing the industry average. The industry is characterized by price rigidity as in Steindl's process of relative concentration. Expansion by the innovator and by imitators will continue to increase the average mark-up factor, but eventually further growth is limited by the unwillingness of established firms to cede sales at the pre-entry price. Price reductions or other forms of aggressive competition, such as advertising, by the innovator and the imitators induce the exit (creative destruction) of the old production technologies. Depending on the form of the competition, the mark-up factor may fall or rise but the profit rate certainly falls toward the level associated with the full-cost price.

These dynamics of price and the mark-up factor following the introduction of a cost-reducing technological change into a concentrated industry are very similar to those in Steindl's 'ideal' pattern of competition.[10] The main difference is that it is no longer clear that the mark-up factor and the profit rate at the end of the process of creative destruction are higher than before the introduction of the new technology. The industry is highly concentrated at both the beginning and end of the process, so the degree of monopoly may increase, decrease or remain unchanged depending on changes to industry concentration, product differentiation and other influences on the degree of monopoly.

Sylos-Labini argues that if a cost-reducing innovation is available only to large firms (the technological leaders), they 'will simply sit back and enjoy the larger profits they can get at the existing price, after the cost reduction' (Sylos-Labini 1962, p. 64). This argument might have some validity for a single modest innovation, but it ignores the gap that emerges between the leading firm and others after a disruptive innovation or after a prolonged series of modest innovations. With such a gap, Schumpeter's analysis is compelling. In practice, concentrated oligopolies worldwide have simply not been able to insulate themselves fully from the perennial gale of creative destruction.

From the above discussion, it is seen that adding the Schumpeterian twist of the price dynamics from innovation and creative destruction to the PK pricing rules makes the theory applicable to episodes of disruptive cost-reducing technological change. The price and mark-up dynamics are shown to be similar whether the initial industry structure is competitive or concentrated oligopoly, although the mark-up factor and profit rate in the initial industry structure differ along the lines suggested by PK price theory. Thus, Schumpeterian price theory and PK price theory are shown to be complementary, at least in parts.

Expanding the range of disruptive innovations for which the Schumpeterian twist is added to PK pricing rules extends the circumstances to which PK price theory provides a realist foundation for analysing modern economies. In addition to innovations in production technology, Schumpeter (1934, p. 66) identifies the following as categories of disruptive innovations that are important in capitalist development: opening up new sources of supply of inputs to production, introduction of new products, opening up of new markets and changes in the organization of an industry. Each category of innovation introduces a potential dynamic to unit direct cost, the mark-up factor and product price for the innovator and for the industry.

In the case of opening a new source of supply for a raw material or intermediate input, the dynamics of unit direct cost, the mark-up factor and product price are likely to be similar to those for the introduction of new production technology. Assuming that a single producer is responsible for the innovation, it achieves a lower direct unit cost than its competitors do and this gives the innovator a higher mark-up factor, as with an improvement in production technology, assuming that prices remain rigid. The high mark-up factor and corresponding profit rate encourage the innovator to expand market share through aggressive competition. As with cost-reducing technological innovation, competitors will seek to adopt the innovation to reduce their own costs, leading to declining average unit direct cost for the industry, further lifting the industry mark-up factor. However, aggressive competition eventually leads to falling mark-up factors putting further downward pressure on price.[11]

In the case of major successful product innovations, the mark-up factor on the new product is likely to be high, representing the high value of such innovations to the buyer and the monopoly position of the seller. Subsequently, unit direct cost for the new product is likely to fall substantially as production increases due to both economies of larger production runs and learning by doing. Product price falls even if the innovator maintains its high mark-up factor. Price falls further once imitators enter into competition with reduced mark-up factors to gain market share, even more so if the innovator responds by reducing its own mark-up factor.

Generally the new product competes most directly with the products of some existing industry and, at least initially, is classified as part of that industry. Thus, television sets were initially classified as part of the radio and television receivers industry. Where the qualities of the new product are substantially superior, as in the radio and TV example, both unit direct cost and the mark-up factor for the new product are likely to be relatively high. The average unit direct cost, mark-up factor and product price for the industry then rise with the innovation. As indicated above, the new product generally experiences first a pronounced fall in unit direct cost and then in the mark-up factor. Producers of the older products in the industry are under extreme pressure to reduce costs and prices to maintain market share or be eliminated. The combined effect across new and old products for the overall industry is declining average product price over a prolonged period.

Innovations involving opening of new markets have similar effects to the introduction of new products in that the product is new in the market, but are likely to happen within a different time frame. Patterns of use of the product have been established in the old markets, presumably aiding in the diffusion of the new product. Also, there are generally existing competitors in the old market for the innovator that opens up the new market, so the process of entry of competitors into the new market should be quicker once the profitability of the market is established. Overall, the dynamics of unit direct cost, the mark-up factor and product price are similar to that of introduction of a new product, but with shorter time lags.

Schumpeter's (1934, p. 66) example of innovation in the organization of markets is establishment of a monopoly position (as with merging production and distribution through a cartel trust) or the breaking up of a monopoly position. This example has become less relevant since the introduction of antitrust and competition regulation in modern economies. However, important innovations in market organization continue, such as franchising, retail chain stores, mass media marketing, outsourcing and supply chain management.

The diversity of characteristics of innovations in market organization means it is not possible to provide a general characterization of the dynamics of direct unit cost, the mark-up factor and product price, unlike the other categories of innovation discussed above. Separate analysis of each innovation is required, preferably in the specific historical context in which it occurs. These analyses are beyond the scope of the present chapter but would add to the range of circumstances covered by a realist PK price theory for analysing modern economies.

One complication with some innovations in market organization is that they are not primarily industry specific, but extend to the relationship between industries. For example, innovations in supply chain management integrate activities, but not ownership, across firms in vertically related industries. The analysis of cost, mark-up and price dynamics would need to account for these vertical relationships. Of course, most innovations have at least some indirect impact on vertical relationships across industries, but these have been ignored in the discussion of the dynamics associated with the categories of innovation discussed above. A full analysis of the impact of innovation on prices needs to account for these secondary effects.[12]

Excluding the case of innovations in market organization, two general patterns of cost, mark-up and price dynamics following disruptive innovations are identified in this section. First, for the categories of innovations in production technology and opening up new sources of supply of inputs, there is an initial tendency for price rigidity followed by declining product price. The price decline is driven first by declining average direct unit cost and then by a declining average mark-up factor. Whether the final mark-up factor is greater than the initial level depends on changes to the degree of monopoly along lines suggested in Kalecki's (1971) and Steindl's (1952) pricing analyses. However, a decline in product price is assured by the decline in average direct cost.

Second, for the categories of product innovation and opening of new markets, there is an initial tendency for product price to rise followed by a long period of price decreases that leaves price well below the initial level. Average direct unit cost, the mark-up factor and price are all high when a new product is introduced or a market opened up. Average direct unit cost is likely to fall first with increased scale of production, followed by declining mark-up factors as competitors enter production and creative destruction eliminates older competing products.

The price dynamics as outlined above suggest modifications to PK pricing rules. In particular, they suggest that the competitive dynamics following from a disruptive innovation and its diffusion through creative destruction impart a dynamic pattern to the average mark-up factor in the industry most affected by the innovation. Such dynamics are conceptually consistent with the realist foundation of PK price theory and should be viewed as useful complements in analysing modern economies where disruptive innovations are common. However, a degree of contingency is introduced into the analysis as creative destruction is an emergent property of an industry experiencing innovation, the timing and extent to which it affects prices being uncertain.

Innovation, obsolescence and the determinants of full cost

The previous section analyses dynamics of unit direct cost, the mark-up factor and product price following disruptive innovations. These are treated as modifying the PK pricing rules that prevail before the introduction of the innovation and after its diffusion. In this section, further implications of Schumpeter's analysis of disruptive innovations and creative destruction are developed, especially the need to add allowances for technological obsolescence to the calculation of costs in full-cost pricing and the need to make corresponding adjustments to the margin in mark-up pricing.

One of the virtues of PK pricing rules is that they can be implemented with readily available and reliable accounting information, so that price calculations are transparent. This allows disparate parts of large organizations to set prices that accord with central policy and allows management to monitor conformance with that policy. Unfortunately, standard accounting conventions do not adequately deal with technological obsolescence or with R&D expenditures. While adjustments to accounting treatments are conceptually possible, in practice these adjustments are difficult and imprecise. Applying PK pricing rules thus becomes problematic in circumstances of disruptive innovation.

In an economy that is repeatedly experiencing innovations and their diffusion, there is a reasonable expectation that further innovations will be introduced and lead to creative destruction. Production often requires long-lasting investments that embody existing technology, such as machinery. The development of new machines that use less input, particularly labour, to produce the same level of output undermines the value of the old machinery. Similar concerns extend to labour skills that are specific to the current technology of production, such as training in the operation of machinery using a specific technology.

The threat from creative destruction to the value of investments in embodied technology is substantial. In the case of plant and equipment, this loss of value is recognized in the concept of technological obsolescence. In the case of labour skills, there is the corresponding concept of technological unemployment. There may be alternative uses for the obsolete equipment or skills, but generally only at substantially lower prices or wages. Commitments to the current technology will not occur if the expected revenues in the absence of creative destruction are only sufficient to cover the full cost of production over the physical lifetime of the investment. An extra allowance for the potential loss from creative destruction is required.

Accounting methods sometimes recognize the potential loss of value to production equipment through depreciation charges for plant and equipment that exceed the rate of physical deterioration. The expected useful life in these cases is based on the length of time for which the plant and equipment is expected to remain profitable to operate rather than the time at which the plant and equipment wears out. For example, the accounting lifetimes for computers and communication devices are generally shorter than their physical operating lifetimes due to the rapid rate of technological change in equipment capabilities.

At one extreme, an innovation may cause an investment in older embodied technology to become obsolete before it goes into production, thereby rendering the investment worthless from the start. The appropriate *ex post* charge for obsolescence is the full expenditure on the investment less any scrap value. At the other extreme, no changes in technology occur to reduce the value of the investment during its planned lifetime and no charge for obsolescence is due.

There is no great difficulty in accounting for possible losses *ex post*, with a write down in asset value occurring when there is a decline in operating profit from the use of the equipment. However, *ex ante* it is not known if and when innovations will occur. The example of computers and communication devices is exceptional. Generally there is no relevant historical experience on which to base a probability distribution for calculating an expected value of the loss from obsolescence. Yet, if the product price is to cover the full cost of production on average in a world of rapid technological change, *ex ante* charges for obsolescence need to be included in the calculation of fixed cost.

Accounting treatment of R&D provides an interesting counterpoint in terms of dealing with uncertain outcomes. Expenditures on R&D are generally expensed in the current period, even though they are undertaken to have long-lasting positive impacts on operating profits. The result of expensing in the current year is that there is no asset created corresponding to the R&D activity.[13] One rationale for expensing is that the returns to these expenditures are too uncertain to be recognized as investments that create assets that are then amortized over the economic life of the asset.

Treating R&D expenditures as current expenses leads to systemic differences between accounting cost measures and an economic concept of full cost. Relative to the economic cost measure, the accounting cost measure is over-stated in the year of initial expenditure but then understated in following years. The opposite pattern of misstatement occurs when investments in fixed assets are depreciated based on physical lifetimes without any allowance for potential obsolescence. This is not to say that the treatments are in any way offsetting, rather that uncertainty prevails in both treatments and that opposing approaches to dealing with the uncertainty have come to be accepted conventions.

The mark-up pricing rule does not require measurement of fixed costs and, hence, seemingly avoids the difficulties associated with uncertainty regarding obsolescence and returns to R&D. However, in the analysis of Sylos-Labini, the full-cost pricing rule is used to determine the size of the mark-up factor in the long run, as indicated in the relationship shown in Equation 13.6 above. Kalecki's analysis of the long-run determinants of the mark-up factor loosely relates the size of the mark-up to the ratio of fixed costs to total costs.

Where does this leave the PK price theory when applied to industries exposed to rapidly changing technology? Prices determined by applying the pricing rules to historical accounting data without adjustment would be unreliable in pro-ducing the intended profit outcomes. Adjustments to the calculation of full costs based on guesses about the likely future gains to R&D expenditures or losses from obsolescence could improve reliability, although only within limits and at the cost of undermining the transparency of the rules.

The essential difficulty for the PK mark-up and fixed-cost pricing rules is that they work well only when the past is a good guide to the future. Rapid technological change breaks the link between past and future and reduces the ability of the rules to generate the results built into the calculations. In the most extreme cases of disruptive innovation, application of the pricing rules becomes untenable and alternatives are required.[14]

Wood (1975), Eichner (1976) and Harcourt and Kenyon (1976) provide a variant of PK price theory that relates price determination to the future as well as the past. In these models, the mark-up factor is determined to yield profits that are sufficient to allow financing of the level of capacity expansion required to meet demand at the mark-up price. The financing requirement replaces depreciation as a determinant of the margin, thereby obviating the need to determine the adjustments required for technological obsolescence and expensing of R&D.

Ong (1981) suggests that this type of price determination based on financing investment is applicable to industries that are mature rather than stratified.

A mature industry is one that is dominated by a small number of relatively homogenous firms, such as an industry that has gone through Steindl's 'ideal' pattern of competition. A stratified industry is one with heterogeneous firms, as exist in Steindl's analysis when an industry is going through relative or absolute concentration. In a mature industry, a price set to finance growth in capacity can meet the strategic objectives of all the homogenous firms. However, in a stratified industry the progressive firm or firms as price leader decide on a price within a wide range with implications for the speed of relative or absolute concentration. The price and the extent of capacity expansion are related but neither is uniquely determined in the way suggested by the analyses of Wood (1975), Eichner (1976) and Harcourt and Kenyon (1976).

Ong (1981) also discusses the case of price-setting in a newly developing industry. In an industry undergoing rapid growth due to product development, the financing needs for capacity expansion (and for new product development, etc.) are likely to be substantial, suggesting very high margins if investment is to be financed out of profits. Such margins might also be appropriate from the Schumpeterian perspective of covering the high threat of creative destruction. However, Ong notes that a low mark-up factor may be in the interest of the dominant innovator as it allows building the market, as well as enhancing the firm's relative cost advantage due to learning and scale economies. This aggressive pricing by the dominant innovator may require access to external financing of investment during the period of rapid structural change. Thus, the finance-oriented variant of PK price theory may yield sustainable pricing outcomes, but only after the Schumpeterian process of creative destruction has done its work.

Some PK economists have used the link from investment to pricing as a microeconomic foundation for their macroeconomic analysis (e.g. Eichner 1985). Ong's analysis argues against this approach. The link is applicable only to mature industries and, as argued by Ong (1981) and in the discussion above, maturity should not be treated as a permanent characteristic of an industry, much less a complete economy. The perennial gale of creative destruction that is emergent in capitalism threatens maturity, providing further justification for a Schumpeterian twist to PK price theory.[15]

Conclusion

PK price theory provides a realist foundation for analysing economies that are dominated by large corporations and oligopolies. It recognizes mark-up and full-cost pricing rules as mechanisms for insulating prices from the vagaries of market supply and demand shocks. However, the disruptive impact of innovation in products, production processes and market organization is generally neglected. It is precisely these disruptive impacts that are at the core of Schumpeter's theory of capitalist development. Given the importance of innovation to the workings of modern capitalism, providing PK price theory with a Schumpeterian twist extends the applicability of the theory in the modern context. In particular, this twist can help transform what is largely a static and short-run analysis into an evolutionary theory suitable also for studying the long-run development of advanced capitalist economies.

With regards to full-cost pricing, the Schumpeterian twist involves adding an allowance for technological obsolescence to the measure of full cost to account more fully for the impact of innovation on the economic viability of equipment and modes of production that embed current technology. Innovation and the ensuing process of creative destruction have made continued operation of much equipment unprofitable sooner than would have occurred otherwise. The occurrence of such obsolescence is uncertain and its timing unknown. Yet, investors are keenly aware of the possibilities of obsolescence (especially in areas of rapidly changing technology), so they are unwilling to undertake investments unless prices are more than high enough to cover wear and tear on equipment. Similar considerations apply to individuals making investments in skills and to organizations making investments in brand image, product development and the like.

With regard to mark-up pricing, the Schumpeterian twist involves having a mark-up factor with dynamics that flow from innovation and creative destruction. In particular, the mark-up factor rises after the introduction of an innovation and then falls in the perennial gale of creative destruction. Steindl's (1952) PK analysis of the 'ideal' pattern of competition fits the working of this process, at least in part. Full incorporation of the Schumpeterian twist into mark-up pricing extends to innovations beyond the case of cost heterogeneity considered by Steindl. All of this fits Kalecki's (1971) argument that the mark-up factor is determined by the degree of monopoly, but with the degree of monopoly as a dynamic concept compared to the static version in Kalecki's analysis.

Adding a Schumpeterian twist to PK price theory brings two characteristic features of PK theorizing to greater prominence. These are history and expectations. History is of increased importance because successful innovations are historical events that alter the path of prices and outputs for the related group of products over long periods of time. This path is not reversible, so history matters. Expectations are of increased importance because obsolescence allowances are included in the fixed cost component in full-cost pricing. These allowances are based on expectations and subject to surprise as obsolescence occurs in the aftermath of future innovations, which are inherently unpredictable events.

Enhancing the role of history and expectations in PK price theory through adding the Schumpeterian twist raises the degree of contingency in the theory.[16] This is a mixed blessing. More complex price dynamics can be explained, but contingency undermines the realist character of the theory. A fixed pricing rule that is based on relatively stable variables yields precise predictions, while theory incorporating dynamic competition through innovation and creative destruction along with relatively volatile (and unobservable) expectations of obsolescence yields imprecise predictions. Arguably, the latter is more appropriate to providing an evolutionary analysis of the modern capitalist economy, while the former provides a historically specific basis for short-run forecasting and demand management.

Notes

1 Kalecki (1971, pp. 46–47) shows that the magnitude of the ratio of price to unit direct cost for an individual firm depends on the ratio of the industry average price to the firm's unit direct cost as well as on the firm's m and n coefficients. This introduces an influence from prices of other firms directly into determination of each firm's mark-up factor, which is absent from other PK formulations of mark-up pricing. There has been considerable discussion of the relation of Kalecki's pricing equation to the other PK formulations of mark-up pricing and to full-cost pricing, as well as its relation to marginalist pricing (see e.g. Kriesler 1987; Lee 1998).

2 Higher prices would attract entry and result in price falling until the long-run price is re-established, but with a lower output for the price leader.

3 This remains the case in modern treatments of PK price theory (e.g. Lee 1998, especially chapter 11). However, Shapiro and Sawyer (2003) make an important distinction between cost-determined prices and cost-based prices. The former suggests a rigid relationship between price and cost, as in having a fixed mark-up factor in Equation 13.2, as well as a clear externally determined definition of cost. Shapiro and Sawyer argue instead that the size of the mark-up is influenced by strategic factors, and the level of cost attributable to a particular product or group of products, especially overhead costs, are to a substantial degree administered by the firm to achieve its strategic objectives, thereby resulting in cost-based prices. Even Lee acknowledges that prices are not always cost determined (see Lee 1998, p. 203 n. 7). The Schumpeterian twist to PK pricing developed below clearly is in the category of cost-based rather than cost-determined prices.

4 For example, Sylos-Labini (1962, pp. 63–66) suggests that a new technology available only to large firms can lead to a higher margin.

5 Bloch (2006) discusses how various characterizations of technological change as the source of heterogeneity in firm costs fit with Steindl's analysis.

6 Use of the term progressive for the low-cost firms suggests quickness in responding to technological opportunities. In this way, Steindl's progressive firms bear a similarity to Schumpeter's entrepreneurs, although Steindl does not specifically refer to entrepreneurship or to Schumpeter.

7 Where absolute concentration is widespread through the economy, a situation Steindl associates with the 'mature' American economy of the 1930s depression era, investment falls and the economy stagnates.

8 Asimakopoulos (1975) provides an adaptation of Kalecki's model to the context of price leadership. In the adapted model m is strictly larger than 1 for the price leader and equal to 0 for the followers, while n is 1 for followers and 0 for the leader. Bloch (1990) uses this model to show how the rise in the average mark-up factor occurs without any change in value of m for the leader or n for the followers, depending instead in changes in the average values of u (decreasing), m (increasing) and n (decreasing) as the market share of the leader expands at the expense of followers.

9 See Andersen (2012) for a discussion as to whether Schumpeter's position in *Capitalism, Socialism and Democracy* (1942) contradicts his earlier views in *The Theory of Economic Development* (1934) on the dominant role of entrepreneurs and new firms in the innovation process. Also, see Acs and Audretsch (1988) for

evidence on the relative importance of large and small firms as generators of innovation in modern economies. Neither debate denies the vulnerability of highly concentrated industries to disruptive innovations that are introduced from within or without the industry.

10 See Bloch (2000) for a discussion of the parallels and differences between the analysis of the dynamics of competition in Schumpeter and the corresponding analysis by Steindl.

11 If the lower priced inputs are available to all producers in an industry, the fall in unit direct cost occurs across the board. With a fixed mark-up factor as in Equation 13.2, a proportional fall in product price results. With the more elaborate full-cost pricing formula in Equation 13.5, the fall in price is somewhat less than proportional because direct cost falls as a proportion of total cost.

12 Secondary impacts do play an important role in Schumpeter's (1939) discussion of price movements over the course of the business cycle.

13 This often leads to a gap between market value and book value of firms that have inputs committed to marketing, research, distribution and internal organization. However, when the intangibles are acquired through the merger or acquisition by another firm, the gap between market value and book value generally becomes recognized under the asset category of goodwill. In these cases, a write down in goodwill occurs if the expected future income stream is eroded through the competitive impact of innovations.

14 Some cases are clearly beyond the scope of the historically grounded PK pricing rules. Consider, for example, the pricing of new pharmaceuticals. The use of accounting information on the production cost of the drug in small batches or the amortization of development cost over an unknown quantity of future sales does not provide a suitable basis for the application of mark-up pricing or full-cost pricing. Some estimate of the future therapeutic value of the drug, especially if there are alternative treatments available, is a more plausible basis for pricing. Also, see Lee (1998, p. 203 n. 7) for the example of a strategic radical price cut by Ford Motors in 1922.

15 In keeping with the theme of this volume, it is appropriate to note King's (2012) generic argument against insisting on microfoundations of macroeconomics. One of John's specific arguments is that the microfoundations dogma ignores emergence within capitalism. Innovation and creative destruction clearly fall within the examples of emergent forces whose importance he notes.

16 Shapiro and Sawyer (2003) make a related point regarding incorporating firm strategy more fully into PK price theory. They note that strategic considerations can undermine the rigidity in mark-up factors and the clarity of the allocation of overhead costs across products and time, thereby converting cost-determined prices into cost-based prices. While firm strategy is not emphasized in Schumpeter's analysis, it adds to innovation and creative destruction as processes that are emergent in modern capitalism.

References

Acs, Z.J. and Audretsch, D.B. (1988), Innovation in Large and Small Firms: An Empirical Analysis, *American Economic Review* 78(4), pp. 678–690.

Asimakopoulos, A. (1975), A Kaleckian Theory of Income Distribution, *Canadian Journal of Economics* 8(3), pp. 313–333.

Andersen, E.S. (2012), Schumpeter's Core Works Revisited: Resolved Problems and Remaining Challenges, *Journal of Evolutionary Economics* 22(4), pp. 627–648.

Bloch, H. (1990), Price Leadership and the Degree of Monopoly, *Journal of Post Keynesian Economics* 12(3), pp. 439–451.

Bloch, H. (2000), Schumpeter and Steindl on the Dynamics of Competition, *Journal of Evolutionary Economics* 10(3), pp. 343–353.

Bloch, H. (2006), Steindl on Imperfect Competition: The Role of Technical Change, *Metroeconomica* 57(3), pp. 286–302.

Eichner, A.S. (1976), *The Megacorp and Oligopoly*. Armonk, NY, USA: M.E. Sharpe (1980).

Eichner, A.S. (1985), *Toward a New Economics: Essays in Post-Keynesian and Institutionalist Theory*. Armonk, NY, USA: M.E. Sharpe.

Harcourt, G.C. and Kenyon, P. (1976), Pricing and the Investment Decision, *Kyklos* 29(3), pp. 449–477.

Kalecki, M. (1971), *Selected Essays on the Dynamics of the Capitalist Economy*. Cambridge, UK: Cambridge University Press.

King, J.E. (2012), *The Microfoundations Delusion*. Cheltenham, UK and Northampton, MA, USA: Edward Elgar.

Kriesler, P. (1987), *Kalecki's Microanalysis: The Development of Kalecki's Analysis of Pricing and Distribution*. Cambridge, UK: Cambridge University Press.

Lee, F.S. (1998), *Post Keynesian Price Theory*. Cambridge, UK: Cambridge University Press.

Ong, N.P. (1981), Target Pricing, Competition and Growth, *Journal of Post Keynesian Economics* 4(1), pp. 101–116.

Schumpeter, J.A. (1934), *The Theory of Economic Development*, translation second German edition, R. Opie. London: Oxford University Press (1961).

Schumpeter, J.A. (1939), *Business Cycles*. New York: McGraw Hill.

Schumpeter, J.A. (1942), *Capitalism, Socialism and Democracy*, third edition. New York: Harper and Row (1950).

Shapiro, N. and Sawyer, M. (2003), Post Keynesian Price Theory, *Journal of Post Keynesian Economics* 25(3), pp. 355–365.

Steindl, J. (1952), *Maturity and Stagnation in American Capitalism*, second edition. New York: Monthly Review Press (1976).

Sylos-Labini, P. (1962), *Oligopoly and Technical Progress*. Cambridge, MA, USA: Harvard University Press.

Wood, A. (1975), *A Theory of Profits*. Cambridge, UK: Cambridge University Press.

14 Adding a deeper behavioural perspective to macroeconomics

The role of George Katona in framing and method

Therese Jefferson[1]

In 2010, a symposium in the *Journal of Post Keynesian Economics* considered the question of whether Post Keynesians could make better use of behavioural economics (Davidson 2010–11; Fung 2010–11; Jefferson and King 2010–11). One conclusion reached by Jefferson and King was that behavioural macro-economics was an 'almost' empty set. Since publication of that small symposium, a number of publications have emerged which suggest that it was lucky that the descriptor 'almost' was used (Edwards 2012; Hosseini 2011; Pietrykowski 2009). These publications suggest that George Katona's work provides an important example of a major research project to develop behavioural macroeconomics.

The purpose of this chapter is to revisit Katona's work and, in doing so, to argue that Katona's arguments are of continuing relevance for heterodox and behavioural economists. This is particularly the case because his approach to behavioural economics was informed by his background in Gestalt psychology, and thus he viewed institutions, groups and individuals as part of a 'whole' in which economic behaviour took place. This approach is not based on neoclassical assumptions of individual rationality, nor does it take market equilibrium as a starting point for analysis. His approach contrasts with major strands of recent literature within behavioural economics, particularly those which focus on experimental approaches to exploring individual decision-making and departures from 'rationality'.

This exploration of Katona's work produces two conclusions that were unexpected at the start of this project. First, his discussions demonstrate the importance of pluralism in the methods used in applied economic research. Second, Katona's arguments about the 'framing' of economic decisions are important additions to arguments about whether 'microfoundations' form a sensible basis for developing macroeconomic insights. These conclusions are consistent with calls from Post Keynesian scholars for pluralism in economic research (King 2012, 2013).

A brief account of Katona's contributions to psychology and economics

George Katona was born in Budapest, Hungary 1901 and died in West Berlin in June 1981. His formal education was initially experimental psychology and he attained a doctoral degree in 1921 from the University of Gottingen. Upon graduating, he worked as a researcher at the University of Frankfurt, supplementing his earnings as a *privatdozent* by working within a bank. The experience of hyperinflation prompted his move to Berlin to further his knowledge of Gestalt psychology under the mentorship of Max Wertheimer (Pietrykowski 2009, p. 55). During this period he also worked as an economic journalist for *Der Deutsche Volkswirt*, under the editorship of Gustav Stolper (Wärneryd 1982), a publication banned by Hitler's government in 1933. He immigrated to the US and together with Stolper founded an advisory service for those seeking to invest in Europe (Hosseini 2011, p. 979). After contracting and recovering from tuberculosis between 1936 and 1939, Katona returned to academia. He worked at the New School for Social Research, the Cowles Commission and the Department of Agriculture in Washington and, following World War II, founded the Survey Research Center (SRC) at the University of Michigan. He was appointed professor of economics and psychology at the University of Michigan in 1950 and retired from this position in 1972 (Wärneryd 1982).

Wärneryd (1982) attributes Katona's early interest in the intersections between psychology and economics to his experiences of hyperinflation in 1920s Germany. Pietrykowski (2009) also attributes Katona's interest in economics to his experiences prior to World War II and notes that his first extended foray into economics was his publication of *War Without Inflation* (Katona 1942). In this book, Katona considers the different ways in which consumers can respond to policies and propaganda aimed at curtailing consumption and increasing savings and identifies a range, including spending as usual, saving or spending differently. For Katona these were issues to be investigated empirically not predicted on an a priori basis by the use of assumptions that implied the mechanistic causes and effects embedded in economic theory. In *War Without Inflation* Katona strongly rejects the form of the argument that 'given stimulus A the response B will follow necessarily and invariably' (Katona 1942, p. 6) and this is a theme that can be found throughout much of his later work.

The following exploration of Katona's work has three main purposes. First, it summarizes Katona's key criticisms of economics, including Keynes's *General Theory*, as they relate to psychological aspects of decisions made by consumers and producers. These criticisms are instructive for understanding Katona's approach to identifying the potential contribution of psychology to macroeconomics. Second, Katona's methods for developing psychological insights relevant to macroeconomics are outlined. His methods provide an important example of behavioural macroeconomics and reflect a methodological approach that has been largely neglected in more recent approaches to behavioural economics, which have largely focused on individual decision-making processes. Third, it is argued that Katona's work provides an example of methods that address two issues of ongoing discussion among heterodox economists: microfoundations and the need for pluralism in economic research.

Katona's criticisms of 'psychological laws' in economics

Katona's studies in economics occurred alongside the development of Keynes's *General Theory*. However, Katona was firmly of the opinion that there were deficiencies in the psychological aspects of Keynes's *General Theory* and that economics could benefit from a closer alliance with psychology. He acknowledged that psychologists' focus on behaviourism and psychoanalysis during the 1920s did not necessarily assist collaboration between the two disciplines. He agreed with Frank Knight that the focus of psychology throughout the 1920s had led to 'an increasing emphasis on unconscious motivation and on prejudice and caprice in the conscious motives of men' (Katona 1946, pp. 44–45) which he viewed as unhelpful for contributing to economic theory.

While the apparent mismatch in the interests of psychologists and economists may have provided a reason for a lack of engagement between the disciplines, Katona expressed specific criticism of Keynes's neglect of empirical research by psychologists. This view is clearly evident in 1946 when he commented on Keynes's neglect of psychological insights into consumer and producer behaviour:

> J.M. Keynes, in describing 'psychological characteristics of human nature,' did not borrow from psychologists but proposed, without their aid, what he called 'a fundamental psychological law' referring to the propensity to consume under the influence of changes in income. Keynes also ignored the work of psychologists in describing certain subjective factors that contribute to the formation of producers' expectations.
>
> (Katona 1946, p. 45)

Katona's criticisms were not reserved for Keynes's *General Theory*. He was similarly critical of other examples of theorizing based on psychological assumptions that were not well grounded in psychological research and the rational expectations hypothesis was one such example. He made particularly unflattering comments about Milton Friedman's apparent approval of rational expectations and his approach to theorizing in general (Katona 1978, p. 75). Also, some of Kenneth Arrow's work on the listing of criteria for rationality Katona found to be at odds with observed human behaviour (Katona 1953, pp. 311–12).

Despite criticisms of Keynes's approach to invoking psychological 'laws', Katona does not argue against or reject Keynesian theory and most of his major research agenda is complementary to Keynesian economics, broadly defined. His focus on empirical research gives insights into individual decisions to save, spend or invest and the links these decisions have with events at a macroeconomic level of analysis. He demonstrates the extent to which Keynes's assumptions on consumption and savings were supported (or otherwise) by empirical research and, if so, the conditions in which the assumptions might be an appropriate basis for theory or policy. Further, he acknowledges the achievements of Keynesian economics with respect to the important role it played in framing discussions about public debt, an issue which did not invoke a direct appeal to psychological assumptions.[2]

Katona's work is sufficiently distinctive to have been identified as one of the eight specific research traditions within the umbrella term of 'behavioural economics' by John Tomer, a founding member, former president and executive director of the Society for the Advancement of Behavioral Economics (Tomer 2007, pp. 476–77). The discussion below focuses on Katona's arguments about the appropriate methods for integrating psychological insights into macroeconomic research and their continued relevance for heterodox economics.

Katona's approach to economics and psychology

Katona's approach to psychology was informed by the Gestalt school founded by Max Wertheimer (Katona 1951, p. 31; Pietrykowski 2009, p. 55). Katona studied with Max Wertheimer in Berlin, worked at the New School in New York at the same time and lived next door to him for a period when first emigrating (American Psychological Association 1978, p. 70). Wertheimer's Gestalt approach varies considerably from the 'stimulus-response' approach associated with Ernest Fechner and influential among some neoclassical economists (Pietrykowski 2009). Gestalt psychology is generally understood in terms of holistic frames:

> Wertheimer was against the narrow application of an arbitrarily analytical, 'and summative,' mechanical mode of thought in scientific work – indeed in any area. Viewing wholes as the mere sum of their component parts, he argued vehemently, does violence to the true nature of these wholes; parts must be seen in their place, role, and function in the whole of which they are parts ... In the great majority of cases, the whole does not equal the sum of the parts, nor is it merely more than the sum of its parts – the typical whole is so different from a sum of its parts that thinking in such summative terms yields only a distorted, impoverished caricature of genuine reality. One of his favourite examples of Gestalt was a soap bubble. Its 'component parts' are not indifferent to each other. A tiny alteration such as a pinprick in one minute part produces a dramatic change in the whole.
>
> (King et al. 1994, pp. 910–11)

Katona's approach to psychology, economics and empirical research must be viewed within the holistic approach of Gestalt psychology. This means that a key step for Katona is to 'define the field' or 'whole' of his particular areas of study. In keeping with Gestalt psychology, Katona argues that a 'whole', as defined by a behavioural field, is different from its parts and can be affected by any of its parts. A change in one part may or may not affect other parts of the whole. The whole has some degree of closure and is organized so that it is unified and delineated from other items which do not belong to it.

In Katona's view individuals, groups, their environment and their perceptions form part of the field to be studied when researching economic behaviour. Behaviour, by individuals, is organized within a field and this behaviour in turn can exert influence on that field. Individuals' perceptions provide the basis for how stimuli within the field are understood, appropriate responses identified and behaviour organized. Katona argues that it is not sufficient only to relate the environment (including, for example, social practices and institutions) to economic behaviour. It is also necessary to study the relationship between individuals' *perception* of the environment and the *perception of changes* in the environment to the organization of behaviour (Katona 1951, p. 31).

Of crucial importance to Katona's arguments is the observation that, faced with apparently identical environments, different people will not respond in identical ways. This is because the individuals themselves form part of the 'whole'. The way in which they perceive their environment and organize their perceptions will differ. These differences in perception can lead to differences in the organization of their behaviour. In turn, their behaviour can alter the 'whole'. Behaviour thus takes place within a field, is influenced by the field and in turn, influences the field (Katona 1951, p. 32).

Katona uses some simple examples to illustrate his argument and these are reproduced below in Figure 14.1; where the dots in example (a) could be perceived as three rows, three columns or a square with a central point. The dots in example (b) are more likely to be considered solely as three rows because of the proximity of the horizontal lines of dots compared with the vertical columns. The dots in the centre horizontal line of example (c) could be perceived as a 'short' row because of the fewer dots compared with the top and bottom horizontal lines. In each case our perception of single dots is organized and influenced by the way in which we organize our perceptions. We tend to see the dots in (a) as a distinct figure that is separate from (b) and (c).

Katona's chief concern is with changes in perception, learning and purposeful decision-making as opposed to habitual behaviour (Katona 1951, p. 49). True decision-making in Katona's view is associated with higher order thinking, learning and problem-solving. These processes commence with a given

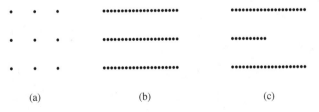

(a)   (b)   (c)

Figure 14.1 Examples of simple perceptual organizations
Katona (1951, p. 32)

perceptual organization and then proceed with reorganizing or restructuring perceptions in order to understand and solve a particular problem.

Within this approach there are many relevant and related concepts which can be briefly mentioned here, including: 'situations', which consist of tasks and a willingness to solve particular tasks; the recognition that tasks have direction, and there may be forces within a field that push towards one specific organization of the task rather than another; motives, attitudes and emotions as part of a field; and 'frames of reference' which influence the organization of perceptions as well as responses. In total, this approach to defining a field of organization is based on the premise that human actions as a response within a field are not automatic or mechanical reactions to stimuli. An understanding of how people might respond can be gained by careful exploration of their perceptions and expectations in particular fields at particular points in time.

Katona firmly views psychology as an empirical discipline and asserts that understanding behaviour within a field can only be achieved through observation, as opposed to 'armchair considerations and what is believed to be common sense' (Katona 1951, p. 29). Maintaining that empirical results must be related to one another, Katona argues that the purpose of empirical research is not to describe or accumulate isolated pieces of evidence but to identify patterns and give coherence through the formation of hypotheses or theory.

From Katona's work, changes in behaviour are evidence that behaviour is not merely repetitive and that learning is important. Actions like buying, selling, pricing and producing as learned behaviour can develop and change with experience (Katona 1951, p. 30). His research focuses on the role that changing perceptions and expectations play in the decision-making process of both consumers and firms. Katona argues that changing perceptions and expectations occur prior to actions. Thus, by empirically assessing the expectations of consumers or producers it is possible to gain insights into important lead indicators of economic activity.

There are three important aspects of this chain of reasoning. First, adequate resources (such as income) as well as expectations are required for actions such as consumption or investment. Second, while Katona is interested in expectations, which by necessity are held by individual consumers or business people, his interest is embedded in a concern for understanding the outcomes and relationships between economic aggregates. His main concern is macroeconomic theory and policy, not the decision-making processes of individual economic units. Individual decisions are of interest to Katona because they are a source of data about distributions of resources and expectations that give insights into broader patterns of behaviour and causal relations that can be theorized and explored at an aggregate level. Third, expectations are likely to be informed by the 'field' in which individual behaviour occurs. That is, expectations and economic behaviour are influenced and can be altered by changes in the economic environment and changes in the perception of that environment.

Katona's approach to studying behavioural economics

Katona views microeconomics as a process of describing and classifying the actions and responses of economic agents. For him, microeconomic data should be used to provide information on the distribution of income, profit and savings and the decisions and actions by different groups of actors. The purpose of analysing microeconomic data, however, is to identify relevant constituent groups and social processes that can provide a basis for a dynamic analysis of the macroeconomy.

For reasons of space and clarity, the following discussion will focus on Katona's approach to studying consumer behaviour, although it is important to acknowledge that he also conducted empirical research in the area of firms' investment decisions. As outlined at the start of this chapter, Katona rejected the assumption that consumption was merely a function of income. This was partly because, as explained above, he rejected a mechanistic approach to explaining behaviour as an 'automatic' response to specific stimuli. However, he also recognized that in a context of rising incomes and greater discretionary consumption, it was possible that the nexus between income and expenditure could vary. This was particularly the case with respect to durable consumer goods because their purchase was part of a deliberative planning process and the timing of a purchase could, in many cases, be implemented or postponed depending on consumers' perceptions of their economic context.

With this in mind, his key approach to data collection and analysis was to conduct large-scale surveys of a representative sample of consumers. On the basis that perceptions precede expectations and behaviour, he instigated a programme of consumer surveys to explore perceptions of the economic environment and expectations about future expenditure.

Katona, microfoundations and pluralism in economic research

Katona provides detailed arguments about the appropriate design and implementation of a macroeconomic behavioural research agenda. His approach and methods appear relevant to a wide range of interests among heterodox economists and a few examples illustrate this argument. First, his approach is consistent with arguments that assumptions required for closed-system modelling and neglect of ontological uncertainty are misplaced (Lawson 1997; Dow 2004). This might be related to his concern with developing his agenda within a broad approach of realism: 'resources both of economics and psychology need to be used to arrive at a realistic analysis of economic behaviour' (Katona 1951, p. v). Second, his focus on the interaction of individuals and groups has some areas of commonality with arguments about the social construction of institutions (Searle 1995; Hodgson 1998). Third, his interest in perceptions of the environment and reflexivity intersects with areas of interpretive epistemology. These are all broad areas of intersection with contemporary heterodox economic discussions that remain to be further explored. In the following discussion, however, I would like to focus on two key areas of Katona's work that link with themes in some of John King's recent contributions: microfoundations and pluralism in economic research (King 2012, 2013).

In *The Microfoundations Delusion*, King (2012) identifies two insurmountable problems with the proposition that macroeconomics can be reduced to statements about individuals as economic agents. The first is the fallacy of composition, which refers to incorrect inferences that derive from the assumption that what is true for one part of a *whole* is true for the whole. A simple example is that one person at a sporting event may get a better view if they stand rather than sit. The same proposition is not true however, if every spectator decides to stand. There are many examples of this fallacy within the field of economics and King (2012) lists various examples, including the well-known paradox of thrift: if one person saves an increased proportion of their income then their savings will increase but if everyone saves a higher proportion of their income then aggregate demand will decline with the result that incomes (and savings) will decrease. He argues, therefore, that the proposition that macroeconomic events should reflect microeconomic assumptions of individual motivations and behaviour is logically and methodologically flawed.

King (2012) also identifies the major problem posed by the causal links assumed in arguments that microeconomics should form the basis of macro-economic theory and analysis. Research has repeatedly demonstrated that the motivations and actions of economic agents are shaped by their institutional context. Similarly, social institutions are shaped by the actions of economic agents. The causation is not only complex but also multidirectional. This is a key aspect of many theories about the nature of social reality (see e.g. Searle 1995; Hodgson 1998) but is neglected in calls for microfoundations.

Katona's work provides an instructive example of integrating research on individual motivations and actions with a macroeconomic approach to theory and policy. It demonstrates an approach to investigating individual behaviour that does not invoke a fallacy of composition or assume a one-way causation from individual decisions to macroeconomic outcomes. Two key elements of Katona's approach are particularly relevant to King's arguments about microfoundations. The first is the link between individual perceptions, action and group dynamics and the second is the importance of frames of reference for decision-making.

Individual perceptions, actions and group dynamics

Katona maintained that in order to understand human behaviour, it is necessary to study both individual and group life. This is because thoughts and behaviour are embedded within individuals but are influenced by groups. Individuals may belong to more than one group and their behaviour may change depending on which group is most relevant at a particular time. In addition, individuals can play different roles within groups and this will also influence their behaviour. Groups can be relatively strong or weak and this can be assessed in terms of their behaviour requirements. For example, a group of military personnel may have stronger behaviour requirements than a book club. It is also possible for groups to influence the behaviour of non-members, in which case they form the function of a 'reference group'. Thus, non-members might mimic the behaviour of group members because they aspire to join that group or to be considered as having traits similar to the reference group members.

As noted above, Katona's work is critical of economists' approach to exploring or assuming particular approaches to individual decision-making and then using this is a basis for describing aggregate behaviour. He notes that this is often justified by appeal to the 'law of large numbers' in which it is assumed that variations between individuals would 'cancel out'. Katona argues that the 'law of large numbers' is only appropriate when the events under consideration are independent. For example, one toss of a coin is an independent event from the second toss of a coin. The decisions of individuals, however, can be influenced by the decisions of others. It cannot be assumed that individual decisions are independent events and that a law of large numbers will apply:

> Group belonging and group reinforcement play a substantial role in changes of behavior due to problem solving. Many people become aware of the same events at the same time; our mass media provide the same information and often the same interpretation of events to groups of people (to businessmen, trade union members, sometimes to all Americans). Changes in behavior resulting from new events may therefore occur among very many people at the same time. Some economists (for instance, Lord Keynes ...) argued that consumer optimism and pessimism are unimportant because usually they will cancel out; in the light of sociopsychological principles, however, it is probable, and has been confirmed by recent surveys, that a change from optimistic to pessimistic attitudes, or vice versa, sometimes occurs among millions of people at the same time.
>
> (Katona 1953, p. 310)

In addition, aggregate data could disguise important issues of difference and distribution within a relevant population. Katona provides a range of examples to illustrate his argument:

> Aggregative statistics may tell us, for example, that national income ... rose from 200 to 220 billion in a certain year. This is an increase of 10 per cent of total income, or a 10 per cent increase of the average family income. It is possible – but very improbable – that in this case, the income of every family rose by 10 per cent. It is also possible that the income of half the families rose by 20 per cent and that of the other half remained unchanged ... Information about the distribution of aggregates and of the changes in aggregates can serve to correct misleading impressions and to avoid false conclusions.
>
> (Katona 1951, p. 18)

In Katona's view microeconomic data provide the link between individual perceptions, expectations and behaviour which together with psychological variables can facilitate a dynamic analysis of changes in aggregate levels of variables such as savings, consumption and investment. The purpose in collecting microeconomic data from individuals or firms is not to describe or understand individual cases but to identify possible regularities in the attitudes or behaviour of different groups of agents. While it is individual agents who enact particular decisions, it is groups that can inform or motivate particular actions. Further, they may inform a range of different motivations for specific behaviour, with the implication that behaviour may not reflect a single or dominant motivation. The groups to which an individual belongs are part of the relevant field for studying behaviour and individual actions may vary from those observed at an aggregate level.

In the absence of independent events, the link between individual decisions and group outcomes requires something different from simple assumptions that a 'representative' agent will reflect, on average, events at a macroeconomic level. Groups play a key role in individual behaviour and the outcomes that occur at an aggregate level. The relevant 'group' in Katona's approach was highly dependent on the area of study. However, the relevant groups might be defined by their role as business investors or household consumers as well as by factors such as their level of income or employment status. So, for example, he might find that research into expectations about consumption or saving might exhibit a pattern where expectations varied with income levels or employment status. At an aggregate level, therefore, expected consumption or saving would be affected not only by individual expectations but also by the distribution of income or employment among potential consumers or savers. This approach does not assume that what is true for individuals is necessarily true for the national economy. Katona summarizes this approach in the following terms:

> Since the objective of microeconomic analysis is not the description of individual cases, microeconomic data will be presented as 'distributions'. Data about aggregated national income must be supported by facts concerning the distribution of income, that is, by information on the proportion of those who receive high, medium and low incomes ... Analysis of economic behaviour, then, will be undertaken here from a specific point of view. First, negatively, this study will exclude certain forms of economic analysis. It will not seek to arrive at dogmatic statements or general principles that are valid under ideal circumstances ... Its aim will be to determine the probable types of behaviour under different conditions. For that purpose it will analyse the distributions of economic position and the behaviour of individual consumers and firms.
>
> (Katona 1951, p. 24)

In this context 'economic position' need not only refer to income but could also include other characteristics that affect the socio-economic position of individuals and the groups to which they belong, including for example age or ownership of assets. Individual decisions and actions are then, at a their most fundamental level, inescapably affected by factors that are intrinsically a function of social role and position, a proposition strongly at odds with the notion of autonomous, individual decision-makers.

Katona's approach makes no assumptions that individual decisions would be rational or formed with any particular access to information. One of his successors at the SRC at Michigan University articulates the methodological differences between the methods developed by Katona and the implications of later theories of rational expectations and information asymmetries (Curtin 2004). Despite the inclusion of factors such as expectations and information in mainstream models of individual decision-making there remain significant and irreconcilable differences between Katona's empirical approach and deductive mainstream models.

Frames of reference

As noted above, Katona's interests centred on deliberative decision-making (rather than habits) and learning. This means he was interested in how decisions by an individual can change over time rather than being endlessly repetitious.

Katona gives savings decisions during World War II as one example of the importance of framing for individual decision-making. He notes that in the process of collecting survey data it became apparent that, 'there were many people who appeared to believe literally that they were buying war bonds to provide ammunition for the boys abroad, that planes, tanks, and ships could not be built if they did not provide the money in bonds' (Katona 1951 p. 79). In addition, many people were aware that their neighbours and friends were either buying war bonds or saving part of their income. It was an accepted pattern of behaviour which Katona describes as climbing on the bandwagon. Understanding these motivations helped to explain how mass behaviour of saving occurred during a specific time in history and why these motivations may not be relevant to behaviour at other times.

Katona argues that the source of behavioural change that is most relevant for economics is learning. He distinguishes learning by rote or repetition from problem-solving or understanding and argued that we invoke a problem-solving approach only when we 'see' a problem: 'a gap, a question, something puzzling or new must confront us' (Katona 1951, p. 48). In the absence of a problem, we tend to repeat actions that have been sufficiently successful in previous similar situations. Genuine decisions are defined as those that require perception of a new situation and formation of a solution.

Time plays an important role in genuine decision-making because it is our past experiences that organize our perceptions and thus the structure of the relevant behavioural field at any given moment. However, the future is also important because expectations, plans, fears and aspirations also shape behaviour (Katona 1951, p. 52). Expectations are formed on the basis of past learning, through either repetition or understanding. A change in expectations occurs if changes in the environment occur which lead to the identification of a problem or task to be addressed, and a reorganization of perceptions is required to identify appropriate actions.

Katona's approach suggests that 'changes' in the environment provide a further reason for rejecting methodologies based on microfoundations. The causal link between individual decisions and macroeconomic events can occur in either direction. For example, macroeconomic events can prompt changes in expectations and perceptions, both of which can result in a change of individual behaviour. It therefore makes little sense to suggest on an a priori basis that individual decisions take theoretical precedence and should form the basis of macroeconomic theorizing. It is just as logical to assume that individual decisions are an outcome of macroeconomic events. Katona's approach, however, reflects the complex, iterative processes through which individual decisions and the field of behaviour can each exert causal influences on the other.

Katona's arguments on perceptions of the decision environment have been reflected in many subsequent studies showing the importance of framing for economic decision-making. Among the most well-known studies are those by Kahneman and Tversky (1979, 1984) which demonstrate the importance of prospects being defined as potential gains or losses. The type of framing considered by Katona is, however, more general than the deliberate manipulation of surveys or experiments undertaken in many behavioural economics studies. His discussions are more closely aligned with the approach outlined by Dow (2013), who considers broader sociological concepts of framing, drawing on the work of Searle (1995), among others, and discusses not only the effects of framing but also which individuals or groups have the capacity to frame particular decision contexts. The common thread in all these areas of work is, however, the relatively simple proposition that individual decisions reflect perceptions and expectations that are closely linked with their decision context or field.

Katona's approach continues to be implemented today in the data-gathering and analysis that is used to develop the index of consumer sentiment in the US and which has been applied in varying forms in many other countries (Curtin 2004, 2008). As Richard Curtin notes: 'Rather than macro data, people's decisions are typically based on a different information set, namely the strength of the local economy, the change in the prices they actually face, and job prospects for people with their same skills and abilities' (Curtin 2008, p. 154).

Curtin's research demonstrates that while consumers may have little knowledge of official economic indicators such as GDP or inflation rates, their expectations about their financial circumstances, general economic conditions and likely purchase of major household items form accurate lead indicators of aggregate consumer demand (Curtin 2008). To a large extent the data and analysis accumulated by the SRC are consistent with Katona's argument that willingness to spend (or save or invest) are not simple functions of income but are linked with changing perceptions of the decision context. Perceptions of asset values appear to be emerging as an important link with consumption plans and it is predicted that changing perceptions of government approaches to economic stimulus are likely to pose challenges for US economic policy in coming years (Curtin 2013).

Pluralism and behavioural approaches to macroeconomics

The linking of individual data to macroeconomic events and outcomes required Katona to employ methods that were rarely used by economists and which, it could be argued, remain underutilized. The main challenge for Katona was to develop a method in which decisions by individual decision-makers (such as consumers or firms) could be linked with macroeconomic theory. This is a point worth repeating because it is a key point of difference with 'new' behavioural economics, which largely focuses on individual decision-making and treats systematic departures from a defined, rational or optimal decision as anomalies.

Katona linked individual decisions with macroeconomic variables by collecting data from individuals and then analysing their perceptions or expectations with reference to particular groups to which they might belong. For example, groups may be defined in terms of their income level or asset holdings. Thus changes in aggregate consumption, for example, might be analysed on the basis of the different expectations of low, medium and high income earners or owners of different classes of assets. These are just possible examples. Another might be to analyse the different motivations for expected savings between say, dissavers and savers, to draw conclusions about possible changes in aggregate savings. The data thus provides insight into expectations and motivations for future decisions from which lead indicators of change in a dynamic economy can be developed.

In general terms Katona's method utilizes survey data-collection methods from relatively large, random samples of consumers, savers or producers. A sample of 3,500 'spending' units formed the basis of early surveys into consumer finances (Katona 1951), although smaller, regular samples of 500 respondents per month are commonly used in the US today, giving a sample of 1,500 for the development of quarterly indices (Curtin 2013). Katona paid particular attention to survey design and he considered that the capacity of the data-collection process to provide insights into relatively complex and nuanced answers to be particularly important. For this reason he largely rejected mail questionnaires as a preferred form of data collection in comparison with face-to-face interviews. His preference was for survey questions to focus not only on the decisions or expectations of the particular survey participants but also on questioning why the participant had made a particular decision or held a specific expectation. While the survey questions were well-defined and consistent for all participants, the possible answers were not tightly restricted to pre-defined measures. Rather, participants could answer using their own words and express their own opinions. In addition, it provided a capacity for interviewers to use follow-up questions or prompts such as 'Would you tell me more about it?' or 'What do you have in mind?' (Katona 1951, p. 313).

Katona readily acknowledged that this form of survey data collection required interviewers with considerable skill. The key advantage of this approach to data collection was, however, the capacity to develop a nuanced understanding of possible causal relationships and for issues to 'emerge' from the responses given by survey participants. These are now relatively well known and understood advantages of interview data collection frequently cited in social research methods handbooks, although still largely underutilized within economic research projects (Bewley 2002). Katona argued that 'free-answer interviewing' is particularly important when interviewing business owners or managers because individual businesses often use language and processes that may differ from the terms included in a particular survey document. Issues of clarity and meaning can be addressed readily in an interview and improve the quality of data collected. Today, surveys of this nature are typically conducted by phone and, while the questions remain similar to those developed by Katona, they appear to be more tightly formatted with regard to some possible responses (Survey Research Center 2013).

One of the key purposes of this approach to data collection is to explore changes in expectations or perceptions of the economic environment in which decisions are being made. That is, the purpose was not to test the accuracy of consumer or producer expectations about the economy against official data but to compare differences in expectations between one period and another. The open-ended nature of the questions provide an opportunity for changes in expectations to be linked with specific events or factors in the environment, thus allowing for analysis of the conditions in which particular relationships between, say consumer demand and investment, may hold.

While the above overview gives an indication of Katona's preferred approach, he expressed openness to other forms of research, including case studies and experiments. The main overall goal from Katona's perspective is, however, to provide an empirical basis for economic theorizing and the development of new theoretical insights. Of particular importance to current debates about economic methods is the absence of an *a priori* commitment to methods that assume or assign a particular priority to concepts such as equilibrium or rationality. The key driver for Katona appears to be the careful collection and analysis of data, using multiple methods and data sources, to develop a dynamic picture of a specific economy changing through time. This again is an approach consistent with many recent heterodox discussions of research methodology and methods and appears entirely consistent with the type of pluralism discussed by King (2013).

Conclusions and future directions

While Katona's name is not prominent in recent economic scholarship, he contributed to a large and ongoing research agenda which continues at the

SRC at Michigan University and is reflected in regular data-collection and indicators such as the index of consumer sentiment released regularly in Australia by the Melbourne Institute of Applied Economic and Social Research. The relative lack of engagement of heterodox scholars with these data sets and, more generally with Katona's research and methods, remains something of a puzzle for future investigation. Katona's project is consistent with recent methodological discussions in several areas of heterodox economics and his data and analysis appear particularly relevant to many aspects of Post Keynesian theory, in particular. At the very least, the commonly used and widely reported indices of consumer sentiment based on Katona's research are at odds with much of mainstream economic theory (Curtin 2004). However, Katona's project also provides support for arguments against any need for prioritizing deductively derived microfoundations as a worthwhile research agenda within economics (King 2012).

It is relatively easy to conclude that Katona is an important contributor to a research agenda that might be considered to be a genuine form of behavioural macroeconomics that is consistent with Keynesian theory. His work is a challenge to any claims that behavioural macroeconomics is an empty set, although his research agenda, now pursued by others, stands as a relatively unique contribution to a set that has relatively few members.

Notes

1 I am indebted to anonymous reviewers who gave very helpful suggestions about the structure and argument of this chapter. An earlier version was presented at the Society for Heterodox Economics annual conference at the University of New South Wales in December 2013. I am grateful for the suggestions and comments of participants.
2 On this matter, Katona commented: 'Limitations of space make it impossible to analyze the reorganization of a frame of reference which has been recently accomplished by some experts with regard to the proper function of government deficits and taxes and which likewise should result in flexible and adaptable knowledge. Because public debt was considered in the same light as private debt, deficits were traditionally held to be un-sound and dangerous. The accomplishment of Keynesian economists in this respect is not the discovery of the principle that "government borrowing is sound" but rather the enlargement and reorganization of the context within which public debt must be appraised' (Katona 1944, p. 344 n. 7).

References

American Psychological Association (1978), Distinguished Professional Contribution Award for 1977, *American Psychologist* 33(1), pp. 69–74.

Bewley, T. (2002), Interviews as a Valid Empirical Tool in Economics, *Journal of Socio-Economics* 31(4), pp. 343–353.

Curtin, R.T. (2004), Psychology and Macroeconomics, in J.S. House (ed.), *A Telescope on Society: Survey Research and Social Science at the University of Michigan and Beyond*. Ann Arbor, USA: University of Michigan Press, pp. 131–155.

Curtin, R.T. (2008), What US Consumers Know About Economic Conditions, in OECD, *Statistics, Knowledge and Policy 2007: Measuring and Fostering the Progress of Societies*, Paris: OECD, pp. 153–176.

Curtin, R.T. (2013), *Consumer Behavior Adapts to Fundamental Changes in Expectations. Surveys of Consumers*. Michigan: Thomas Reuters and University of Michigan.

Davidson, P. (2010–11), Behavioral Economists Should Make a Turn and Learn from Keynes and Post Keynesian Economics, *Journal of Post Keynesian Economics* 33(2), pp. 251–254.

Dow, S.C. (2004), Structured Pluralism, *Journal of Economic Methodology* 11(3), pp. 275–290.

Dow, S.C. (2013), Framing Finance: A Methodological Account, Post Keynesian Economics Study Group, Working Paper 1308.

Edwards, J.M. (2012), Observing Attitudes, Intentions, and Expectations (1945–1973), *History of Political Economy* 44(5), pp. 137–159.

Fung, M.V. (2010–11), Comments on 'Can Post Keynesians Make Better Use of Behavioral Economics?' *Journal of Post Keynesian Economics* 33(2), pp. 235–249.

Hodgson, G.M. (1998), The Approach of Institutional Economics, *Journal of Economic Literature* 36(1), pp. 166–193.

Hosseini, H. (2011), George Katona: A Founding Father of Old Behavioral Economics, *Journal of Socio-Economics* 40(6), pp. 977–984.

Jefferson, T. and King, J. (2010–11), Can Post Keynesians Make Better Use of Behavioral Economics? *Journal of Post Keynesian Economics* 33(2), pp. 211–249.

Kahneman, D. and Tversky, A. (1979), Prospect Theory: An Analysis of Decision under Risk, *Econometrica* 47(2), pp. 263–291.

Kahneman, D. and Tversky, A. (1984), Choices, Values, and Frames, *American Psychologist* 39(4), pp. 341–350.

Katona, G. (1942), *War Without Inflation*. New York: Columbia University Press.

Katona, G. (1944), The Role of the Frame of Reference in War and Post-War Economy, *American Journal of Sociology* 49(4), pp. 340–347.

Katona, G. (1946), Psychological Analysis of Business Decisions and Expectations, *American Economic Review* 36(1), pp. 44–62.

Katona, G. (1951), *Psychological Analysis of Economic Behavior*. New York: McGraw-Hill.

Katona, G. (1953), Rational Behavior and Economic Behavior, *Psychological Review* 60(5), pp. 307–318.

Katona, G. (1978), Discussion, in Papers and Proceedings of the Ninetieth Annual Meeting of the American Economic Association, *American Economic Review* 68(2), pp. 75–77.

King, D.B., Wertheimer, M., Keller, H. and Crochetiére, K. (1994), The Legacy of Max Wertheimer and Gestalt Psychology, *Social Research* 61(4), pp. 907–935.

King, J.E. (2012), *The Microfoundations Delusion: Metaphor and Dogma in the History of Macroeconomics*. Cheltenham, UK and Northampton, MA, USA: Edward Elgar.

King, J.E. (2013), A Case for Pluralism in Economics, *Economic and Labour Relations Review* 24(1), pp. 17–31.

Lawson, T. (1997), *Economics and Reality*. London and New York: Routledge.

Pietrykowski, B. (2009), *The Political Economy of Consumer Behavior: Contesting Consumption, Routledge Advances in Social Economics*. London and New York: Routledge.

Searle, J. (1995), *The Construction of Social Reality.* Harmondsworth, UK: Penguin.

Survey Research Center (2013), *Survey of Consumers Questionnaire.* Institute for Social Research: University of Michigan.

Tomer, J.F. (2007), What Is Behavioral Economics? *The Journal of Socio-Economics* 36(3), pp. 463–479.

Wärneryd, K.-E. (1982), The Life and Work of George Katona, *Journal of Economic Psychology* 2(1), pp. 1–31.

15 The 'Complexity Revolution' seen from a historical and heterodox perspective

Tim Thornton

It has recently been claimed that the science of complexity is in the process of bringing about a revolution in economics (Colander 2000b; Colander, Rosser and Holt 2011). It is argued that complexity science is being increasingly incorporated into economics, particularly orthodox (neoclassical) economics. In this chapter this view is examined and is found to be misconceived. The argument fails to appreciate that complexity's fundamentally different conception of economics is likely to continue to be very confronting to neoclassical economists; therefore imminent revolution of this wing of the discipline seems unlikely. In regards to the social-science wing of the discipline (political economy[1]) the story is somewhat different. Political economists are more likely to be open to developments in complexity science. However, even here complexity seems unlikely to be a revolutionary force: first, because many of the key ideas of complexity have long been part of political economy; second, because complexity ultimately faces constraints in how it can be applied to social-science analysis. Nonetheless, despite its lack of revolutionary implications, complexity may still be of some use to political economists. Obvious uses are in promoting synthesis between political economy's constituent schools and in supporting the case for economic pluralism.

What is complexity economics?

Complexity economics is a branch of the science of complexity whose origins largely lie in recent developments in the natural sciences and mathematics. Much of the early work in complexity economics originated at the Santa Fe Institute. As is often the case with particular approaches or schools of thought, complexity science is actually somewhat of an umbrella term and its exact boundaries are not clear-cut. However, at the core of complexity economics is a conception of an economic system characterized by evolutionary processes of change that are, to some extent, adaptive and self-organizing. Such systems are characterized by emergence, path-dependence and positive feedback loops. They exist in historical time, and it is the path-dependent connections between elements that define the essence of the system (rather than the elements themselves). Complex systems are also characterized by non-linearities and can be highly dependent on initial conditions. Following Beinhocker (2006), it is useful to define the science of complexity into five key aspects: evolution, emergence, networks, dynamics and agents (see Table 15.1).

The right-hand column 'traditional economics' is neoclassical economics; in other words, complexity economics is exactly what neoclassical economics is not. This dualistic relationship between complexity economics and neoclassical economics raises immediate doubts about the capacity for neoclassical economists to embrace complexity given their generally strong record of fealty to the core tenets of neoclassicism.

While complexity economics can be defined as what neoclassical economics is not, it has substantial common ground with political economy. Indeed, a lot of concepts in complexity are not really new or cutting-edge to political economists. For example, explicit evolutionary theorizing within economics goes back as far as Veblen, who long ago made the case that economics should be completely recast on an evolutionary foundation (Veblen 1898). Furthermore, the concepts of increasing returns, historical time and path-dependence that

Table 15.1 Complexity economics versus traditional economics

	Complexity economics	*Traditional economics*
Dynamics	Open, dynamic, non-linear systems, far from equilibrium	Closed, static, linear systems in equilibrium
Agents	Modelled individually; use inductive rules of thumb to make decisions; have incomplete information; are subject to errors and biases; learn to adapt over time; heterogeneous agents	Modelled collectively; use complex deductive calculations to make decisions; have complete information; make no errors and have no biases; have no need for learning or adaptation (are already perfect); mostly homogeneous agents
Networks	Explicitly model bilateral interactions between individual agents; networks of relationships change over time	Assume agents only interact indirectly through market mechanisms (e.g. auctions)
Emergence	No distinction between micro/macroeconomics*; macro patterns are the emergent result of micro-level behaviours and interactions	Micro and macroeconomics remain separate disciplines
Evolution	The evolutionary process of differentiation, selection and amplification provides the system with novelty and is responsible for its growth in order and complexity	No mechanism for endogenously creating novelty, or growth in order and complexity

Beinhocker (2006, p. 97)

* This particular assertion by Beinhocker is misconceived. Macro and micro remain distinct entities (see King 2012).

are often associated with complexity are established concepts within Post Keynesian and old institutional economics. Herbert Simon's pioneering work in the 'old' behavioural economics stressed the limitation of the human brain in processing information accurately and the consequent reliance on rules of thumb to arrive at satisfactory, rather than optimum, outcomes. Given that there is this common ground between complexity and political economy, and given the long-standing indifference and hostility to political economy from neoclassical economists, this further adds to doubt about neoclassicism's capacity to embrace complexity in any meaningful way.

It has been argued that what complexity does bring to both neoclassical economics and political economy is the better capacity to capture concepts and theories that have previously only been described in discursive form (Colander 2000a). Previously, in the absence of modern computing, economic model-building could only be undertaken via algebraic analytical solutions. This was very limiting. However, advances in computer software and hardware mean that numerical simulations can now be undertaken, and thus a much broader range of equations can be incorporated into economic modelling.

Do these developments in computing greatly extend the capacity for economics to be a model-building and model-testing science? Some have argued they do (Colander 2008). Yet some caution on this point is in order. A complex system is generally characterized by non-linear relationships, and this is suggestive of a compatible match between the new mathematical tools available and the underlying nature of the object of inquiry. However, the very nature of a complex system (its potentially vast range of non-linear interactions, its evolutionary and path-dependent dynamics) mean that modelling it accurately is highly dependent on specifying all the initial conditions accurately. For applied work this will seldom be possible. The initial conditions will be many in number, some will be hard to measure, some will be hard to quantify and some will quickly change. Some of those who are forecasting a coming 'complexity era' really appear not to acknowledge these very familiar constraints to the building of applied models:

> In agent-based modelling one essentially studies the economy by creating a virtual economy, which is then used to simulate policies. These simulations are used to guide policy-makers. No equilibrium needs to be imposed on the system; *all one needs to do* is specify the characteristics of the agents and the environment they operate in.
>
> (Colander 2008, p. xiv; emphasis added)

Economic modelling using dynamic numerical simulations can be useful and interesting (see e.g. Epstein and Axtell 1996), and mathematics can be useful in clarifying and communicating ideas long associated with political economy (Chick 1998; Keen 2009). However, it would be a mistake if complexity gave even further impetus for economics to be beholden to Kelvin's dictum that 'when you cannot express it in numbers, your knowledge is of a meagre and unsatisfactory kind' (Thomson 1883, p. 73). Such a mind-set is likely to limit the scope for complexity to contribute to the development of economics and to the other social sciences.

There is nothing about the nature of a complex system that dictates the increased use of complex mathematics, with the exclusion of other more discursive methods such as fieldwork, interviews and case studies. Furthermore, being open to advances in psychology, anthropology or sociology might be far more productive to economics than developing more complex numerical simulations. In fact, a complex system is actually supportive, not only of pluralism of method and interdisciplinarity, but also of theoretical and epistemological pluralism. Why so? Conceiving of a complex system is essentially the same as conceiving of the economy as an open system. As Dow points out, it is an open-system ontology that is the basis for pluralism in all its forms (Dow 2007), an open system being one in which:

> not all the relevant variables can be identified, and where the external boundaries of the system are therefore not knowable. The system is subject to outside influences which cannot be accounted for in advance (where 'account for' includes knowledge that an outside influence, or relationship, is random). Further, within the system, there is scope for change in the relationships between variables which cannot be identified in advance, and indeed for change in the nature of the constituent variables themselves. Since the system in reality cannot be understood in terms of constituent parts of a fixed nature, it is pluralist.
>
> (Dow 2007, p. 28)

If one compares the characteristics of complexity given in Table 15.1 and Dow's description of complex systems given above, then a good case can be made that an open system is an example of a complex system. On this basis, a complex system is, more than anything, just an ontological starting point. To make theory operational, one is faced with the familiar challenges of where to make the provisional closures and abstractions. Of course, this is when all the familiar methodological schisms and debates open up.

It is useful at this point to dig a little further into the five core ideas of complexity economics presented in Table 15.1. In each instance, the core idea will be examined and the relationship with political economy, and the (non) relationship with neoclassical economics will be made more explicit. The scope for these ideas to fall prey to being ignored or distorted will also be analysed.

Evolution

The concept of evolution has been much misunderstood and misapplied in economics and the social sciences in general (Hodgson 2004). It is thus necessary to define what is meant by the term. Darwin, drawing on an idea of

Malthus, explained evolution as a three-step process of variety, replication and selection. Generating of variety is the first step in the evolutionary process. Variety creates a range of choices from which the environment can select. The variation in the population can result from chance mutation (for example, to the DNA of a particular organism), though it should be stressed that it can also involve a degree of intentionality. For example, individuals may change their behaviour or thinking on the basis of their personal motivations, intentions or hunches based on induction (Beinhocker 2006). In summary, both the intentional and unintentional can be consistent with an evolutionary process (Nelson and Winter 1982).

Replication is the second step of the evolutionary process. Replication is required so that successful variations can pass on their characteristics through time. In the biological sphere, replication is achieved via the passing on of DNA during sexual reproduction. In the social sphere, institutions can reproduce themselves because they are relatively stable and can be replicated by the coming generation via a process of emulation that occurs through socialization (Hodgson 2008).

Selection is the final stage of the evolutionary process. Selection becomes inevitable because of super-fecundity: more variations exist than the environment can support. This means that variations that are more environmentally fit persist, and the variations that are less so die out (Hodgson and Knudsen 2010). Note that it is critical to understand that 'environmentally fit' simply means 'fit enough to survive for the moment', rather than the fittest (or optimum) of all possible designs.

Darwinian evolution is compatible with many ideas that have long been important in political economy such as path-dependency, lock-in effects, increasing returns, learning and adaptation. Because an evolutionary ontology is particularly able to nest these established political-economy concepts and theories it increases the scope for synthesis between the various schools of political economy.

Darwinian evolution would also appear to offer a pathway forward through some long-established problems with theorizing in economics and the social sciences. For example, by combining biological and social evolution, it allows us to formulate theories that can transcend cultural or biological determinism (Hodgson 2004; Thornton 2013). Furthermore, an evolutionary framework need not be trapped in either methodological individualism or methodological holism (Hodgson and Knudsen 2010).

Darwinian evolution has been subject to much confusion and misuse, and there is no guarantee that similar confusions will not arise again. Evolution has a very unfortunate history of being twisted to support racist and anti-egalitarian ends (Hodgson 2006a). Such confusion and misuse has given evolutionary theorizing in the social sciences a bad name and contributed to its marginalization (Hodgson 2004). As mentioned previously, a key interpretive error is that evolutionary processes produce optimum outcomes. Gould and Lewontin have also made the point that evolutionary processes can produce features (so called 'Spandrels') that have arisen as a side consequence of the selection of other features, and are not actually an object of environmental selection themselves (Gould and Lewontin 1979).

Confused use of evolutionary ideas can be seen in Spencer's concept of Social Darwinism or, more recently, among some on the far right, who justify extreme *laissez-faire* public policy – so called bio-babble (Krugman 1997). One could also point to Friedman's confused resort to evolution to try to defend the use of unrealistic 'as-if' assumptions in the neoclassical theory of the firm. This is a good example of how neoclassical economics has a striking ability to distort a useful idea to defend its hard-core beliefs. There is a plausible risk of evolutionary and complexity concepts being misused in this way again, particularly by neoclassical economists who have a tendency only to absorb new ideas in a manner that supports their existing frameworks of analysis.

In general, the current scope to utilize evolutionary concepts in economic analysis needs to be kept in some perspective. While current evolutionary theorizing is useful in prompting lines of inquiry and providing guidance to empirical analysis (Hodgson and Knudsen 2010), evolutionary theorizing in the social sciences is still only at an early stage of development (Hodgson 2004). Furthermore, if one wants to move to applied analysis, this requires the addition of more context specific (mid-range) theorizing (Hodgson 1998, 2006b). For applied analysis, evolution will never be enough, and other established and new concepts and theories will nearly always be necessary.

To move away from a simple mechanistic view of economic phenomena and to see the economy as an evolutionary system is also an invitation for modesty and caution, rather than hubris about some bold new era in economics. As Nelson explains, the evolutionary approach leads to a more modest, cautious and idiographic economic analysis:

> There is no question that, in taking on board this complexity, one often ends up with a theory in which precise predictions are impossible or highly dependent on particular contingencies, as is the case if the theory implies multiple or rapidly shifting equilibria, or if under the theory the system is likely to be far away from any equilibrium, except under very special circumstances. Thus an evolutionary theory not only may be more complex than an equilibrium theory. It may be less decisive in its predictions and expectations. To such a complaint, the advocate of an evolutionary theory might reply that the apparent power of the simpler theory in fact is an illusion.
>
> (Nelson 1995 p. 85)

An evolutionary system is not one that is amenable to easy prediction or explanation. There are temporal differences between the different levels in the system, non-linearities and co-evolution between the components which would be difficult to capture fully in any model or simulation. Evolutionary systems may be gradual and orderly for a time, yet they are also prone to periods of punctuated equilibrium: sudden great leaps which interrupt periods of slow change. The sudden leaps might be caused by external disturbances outside the system or, more probably, evolutionary processes within the environment that lead to a tipping point that then prompts radical change within the system.[2]

Evolutionary systems are not like the gearbox of a car (or like the general equilibrium of Walras). Evolution, despite being a simple three-step process, can generate complex outcomes that are difficult to predict. Temporal differences within the system are important in explaining why this is so. In economic and social systems, instincts evolve biologically over a very long period of time, while habits evolve more slowly, and institutions more slowly still (Hodgson 1998). A further complication is that there can be co-evolution between levels (for example, the co-evolution of instincts and institutions). Such characteristics will not be captured easily, even with advanced computing software and hardware, particularly when all the initial conditions may need to be estimated with near-complete accuracy.

All these aspects of an evolutionary economics do not fit well with the neoclassical view of the world. As such, they are confronting to habits of mind and institutions that exist within traditional centres of economics teaching. It is hard to imagine neoclassical economists embracing what, for them, is such a radically different conception of economic and social processes.

Emergence

Complex systems are usually understood to be characterized by emergence.[3] Put most simply, the idea of emergence is that entities are more than the sum of their parts. An emergent entity is composed of its constituent parts, but also the interaction of its constituent parts. The novel properties that emerge from the interaction of the constituent parts (whether these are novel structures, novel properties or novel patterns) could not have been foreseen by simply examining the constituent parts. What results from an emergent process is not reducible to, or explicable in terms of, the underlying component parts (Goldstein 1999). Attempts at such reductionism run up against the fallacy of composition problem.

Emergence suggests a layered ontology. A layered ontology posits that there are succeeding levels of reality: the physical, molecular, organic, mental, individual, human and the social. The interaction at the preceding level of reality is central in giving rise to the next level of reality (Hodgson 2004). Within economics, the most crucial levels of reality are between microeconomic and macroeconomic phenomena. While microeconomic phenomena give rise to macroeconomic phenomena, macroeconomics is not reducible to microeconomic foundations. Macroeconomics is understood as a distinct entity in its own right that has its own properties and characteristics. Indeed, there is clear scope for macroeconomics to exert downward influence on microeconomic phenomena (King 2012).

Over the last two decades, the concept of emergence has become a fashionable topic in the philosophy of science. However, it is far from a revolutionary idea that has only recently been discovered via complexity science: it goes back as far as Aristotle, who argued in chapter 6 of his Metaphysics that 'the whole is not, as it were, a mere heap, the totality is something besides the parts' (Aristotle; cited by Ackrill 1986, p. 320). Emergence has also been advocated (albeit, often in fragmented form) by economists such as Friedrich List, John Stuart Mill, Thorstein Veblen, John Hobson and Friederich von Hayek, sociologists such as Talcott Parsons and Emile Durkheim and philosophers of biology such as Lloyd Morgan (Hodgson 2000, 2004; King 2012).

Emergence has very direct relevance to issues of structure and agency, as it is antithetical to the idea of methodological individualism, which is at the very centre of neoclassical economics. If methodological individualism's central premise is 'the doctrine that *all* social phenomena (their structure and their change) are in principle explicable *only* in terms of individuals – their properties, goals, and beliefs' (Elster 1982, p. 453; emphasis added), then it is at loggerheads with emergence, which argues that the properties of group phenomena may be quite different to the properties of the individuals that make up a group.

Emergence also has clear implications for the structure-agency problem because it provides support for the idea of downward causation in social and economic explanation. Specifically, emergence allows for something new to emerge from the interaction of the constituent parts that can then potentially affect the constituent parts. The idea of downward causation becomes harder to countenance if nothing new has emerged from the interaction of the constituent parts.

Emergence, particularly in a strong form that allows for downward causation, would appear more easily applicable to the social sciences than to the natural sciences. As Gordon (1991) has pointed out, when hydrogen and oxygen combine to form water, new properties do indeed emerge, yet the properties of hydrogen and water are not dependent on the existence of water (Gordon 1991; King 2012). By contrast, in the social world, the nature of individuals is very dependent on the society in which they are enculturated. Hodgson's idea of reconstitutive downward causation is relevant here: social institutions do not just change what we do, they change who we are. The chief mechanism whereby this occurs is by heavily influencing the formation of preferences. One could also point out that our basic cognitive processes and the acquisition of language are also strongly socially constructed. On this basis to start all social explanation from the perspective of individual agency is unsustainable.

It is difficult to imagine how emergence will be accepted by the neoclassical economists because it conflicts so dramatically with traditional notions of what science is. On this point, it is worth noting that even within the philosophy of science, emergence, particularly in its strong form, has been criticized as being mysterious, somewhat mystical or even magical and non-scientific (Gordon 1991; Kim 1999; King 2012). Whilst there are many philosophers of science and many natural scientists who are actively engaged with the issue of emergence, it will require a lot of neoclassical economists to follow suit. The challenge it presents to their view of economic phenomena being mechanical and simple, their belief in microfoundations and their general commitment to methodological individualism is very substantial and should not be underrated.

Networks

A chief distinguishing feature of a complex system is that every element of the system is not connected to every other element of the system. This contrasts with a simple system where all the elements of the system are fully connected to each other. Work undertaken by Potts (2000) has shown that political economy, and the social sciences in general, presuppose a complex system whilst neoclassical economics presupposes a simple system. In other words there is a profound ontological difference that resides in the geometry of economic space. This difference in the geometry of economic space provides perhaps the strongest basis for arguing that neoclassical economics is fundamentally different to complexity economics, to political economy and to the social sciences in general.

In neoclassical economics, the economic system exists as an integral field (the concept of a field is taken from graph theory). The components of the system are all connected to each other in a manner that means responses to change are fully determined and predictable. In such a system, it is the agents themselves (rather than the connections between them) that hold centre stage. Such a system can be quite complicated (the many pages of equations that comprise general equilibrium theory are a good example of this). However, beyond this surface complexity, the consistent nature of the connections between agents means that, in essence, the system is simple (see e.g. Foster 2005). Certainly, for all its superficial complication, it is a fully determined system and exhibits the type of event regularities that make it well suited for the deployment of formal methods to gain knowledge of its workings and to generate precise predictions. Furthermore, economic change is also rather simple: it is about substitution that is driven by changes in relative prices, with such prices being driven by changes in supply and demand (Earl 2006).

Political economy, and the social sciences in general, conceive of social and economic reality as being nested inside a complex (rather than complicated) system. In this system it is the connections between the agents, rather than just the agents themselves, that define much of the economic system. It is changes in the connective structure of the system that actually create the dynamics of the system. For example, technology is understood as being a set of connections between materials and institutions. Organizations are understood as connections between people. Furthermore, learning and knowledge are understood as emergent properties of new connections (Schmid 2003). The lack of full connectivity is not only because of fundamental uncertainty and bounded rationality, but also due to organizational, spatial, temporal, market and social structures (Schmid 2003). The connections that do exist are the product of path-dependent historical time. The system is not entirely deterministic, as agents are rule followers and have a degree of latitude in their responses.

Structure and agency co-evolve and there is both change within the system and change in the nature of the overall system. While formalism and computer simulations may be useful to analyse such a system, they are not necessarily the only method, or even the dominant method.

A complex system's ontology is generally compatible with political economy, particularly the Post Keynesian, institutionalist, Austrian and Marxian schools. This common ontological foundation suggests the capacity for greater synthesis between these schools (Potts 2000), as well as suggesting further reasons why synthesis with neoclassical economics will be very difficult. This idea of an economic system that is an evolving partially-connected network does provide an underlying foundation that is compatible with so many important heterodox ideas. For example, a long-standing feature of much heterodox work is the assumption that the economy is an evolving and historical entity. It is also generally recognized that we do not have full information about our choices before we choose, nor do we have the cognitive powers to optimize our choices with the information we do have. We are rule followers (and rule creators) rather than rational calculators. In this view of reality, the human agent is not the mindless and isolated prisoner of an exogenously given preference function: human beings are social beings who carry knowledge and create new knowledge via their interaction with others (Potts and Nightingale 2001).

Agents

Complexity economics shuns the perfectly informed and rational actor of neoclassical economics. Again, this is not revolutionary. We have known since the 1950s that fully rational calculation on most matters is well beyond the computational abilities of the human mind. Often the information we most need resides in a fundamentally uncertain future. We cannot generally compute the optimum solution, and therefore opt to satisfice, which is to find a good-enough solution, usually arrived at via a rule-based procedure that is itself deemed 'good enough' on the basis of historical experience (Simon 1957).

This view of the human mind is generally consistent with the political-economy perspective, particularly with its branches of old institutionalism and old behavioural economics pioneered by Herbert Simon. Whilst orthodox economists may claim they have some affinity with this view of agency via the 'new' behavioural economics that has arisen since about 1980, such a claim is problematic. Much of the new behavioural economics that is palatable to neoclassical economics still eschews the idea of satisficing and is still wedded to the maximizing calculator of *homo economicus* – albeit with the acknowledgement of various biases and heuristics (Earl 2010).

Dynamics

As set out in Table 15.1, dynamics in a complex system are non-linear and non-equilibrium based. This is incompatible with neoclassical economics, which is fundamentally static, linear and equilibrium orientated. The essential difference in dynamics is tightly related to the basic difference in network structure previously discussed: particularly the point that it is changes in the connective structure of the system that create the dynamics of the system. Because the connections in a complex system arise from history, complexity economics also operates in historical rather than logical time. Again this conception of dynamics, whilst foreign to neoclassical economics, is broadly compatible with political economy.

Conclusion

The overview of complexity undertaken in this chapter suggests that it is mistaken to talk of a coming complexity era: neoclassical economics is likely to continue largely to ignore complexity, while political economy has long incorporated many of the supposedly new ideas of complexity. Complexity offers little scope for bridge-building or the creation of a common ground with neoclassical economics. It is one more reason why political economists should seek institutional independence and disciplinary differentiation from neoclassical economics: institutional independence in basing themselves out-side traditional centres of economics teaching (usually in social science faculties), and disciplinary differentiation in referring to themselves as poli-tical economists rather than economists (for a detailed case for this strategy see Thornton 2013).

The science of complexity is interesting and worth monitoring. However, rather than seeing it as offering a mathematical and computer driven great leap forward, it might be better to see it as just an interesting addition to the political-economy tool box. As such, complexity may be best deployed in much the same manner as other political-economy theories and concepts: offering some general guidance, prompting questions to ask, and suggesting batteries of possibilities to look for and lines of inquiry that may be fruitful. Rather than superseding established schools within political economy, com-plexity may simply offer one particular means to assist in their refinement. In particular, its identification of ontological commonalities may promote synthesis between the schools. Furthermore, its conception of economy and society as open systems provides further support to those who argue for greater economic pluralism.

Notes

1 'Political economy' is defined here to encompass the term 'heterodox economics'. For a detailed discussion of both terms, see Thornton (forthcoming).
2 The cyclical growth models of Goodwin (1990) and Kalecki (1937) are good examples of attempts to come to terms with an economy characterized by these features.
3 This section on emergence was greatly improved by reading King (2012) and the associated literature on emergence that it drew upon.

References

Ackrill, J.L. (ed.) (1986), *A New Aristotle Reader*. Oxford: Oxford University Press.

Beinhocker, E.D. (2006), *The Origin of Wealth: Evolution, Complexity, and the Radical Remaking of Economics*. Boston: Harvard Business School Press.

Chick, V. (1998), On Knowing One's Place: The Role of Formalism in Economics, *The Economic Journal* 108(451), pp. 1859–1869.

Colander, D.C. (2000a), *The Complexity Vision and the Teaching of Economics*. Cheltenham, UK and Northampton, MA, USA: Edward Elgar.

Colander, D.C. (2000b), The Death of Neoclassical Economics, *Journal of the History of Economic Thought* 22(2), pp. 127–143.

Colander, D.C. (2008), Foreword , in C. Arnsperger (ed.), *Critical Political Economy: Complexity, Rationality, and the Logic of Post-Orthodox Pluralism*. London and New York: Routledge, pp. xviii–xxiii.

Colander, D.C., Rosser, J.B. and Holt, R.P.F. (2011), The Complexity Era in Economics, *Review of Political Economy* 23(3), pp. 357–369.

Dow, S.C. (2007), Pluralism in Economics, in J. Groenewegen (ed.), *Teaching Pluralism in Economics*. Cheltenham, UK and Northampton, MA, USA: Edward Elgar, pp. 22–39.

Earl, P.E. (2006), *Capability Prerequisites and the Competitive Process*. St Lucia, Australia: Department of Economics, University of Queensland.

Earl, P.E. (2010), Economics Fit for the Queen: A Pessimistic Assessment of Its Prospects, *Prometheus* 28(3), pp. 209–225.

Elster, J. (1982), Marxism, Functionalism, and Game Theory, *Theory and Society* 11(4), pp. 453–482.

Epstein, J.M. and Axtell, R.L. (1996), *Growing Artificial Societies: Social Science from the Bottom Up*. Washington, DC: Brookings Institution Press.

Foster, J. (2005), From Simplistic to Complex Systems in Economics, *Cambridge Journal of Economics* 29(6), pp. 873–892.

Goldstein, J. (1999), Emergence as a Construct: History and Issues, *Emergence: Complexity and Organization* 1(1), pp. 49–72.

Goodwin, R.M. (1990), *Chaotic Economic Dynamics*. New York: Oxford University Press.

Gordon, S. (1991), *The History and Philosophy of Science*. London and New York: Routledge.

Gould, S.J. and Lewontin, R. (1979), The Spandrels of San Marco and the Panglossian Paradigm: A Critique of the Adaptationist Programme, *Proceedings of The Royal Society of London* 205(1161), pp. 581–598.

Hodgson, G.M. (1998), The Approach of Institutional Economics, *Journal of Economic Literature* 36(1), pp. 166–193.

Hodgson, G.M. (2000), From Micro to Macro: The Concept of Emergence and the Role of Institutions, in L. Burlamaqui, A.C. Castro and H-J. Chang (eds.), *Institutions and the Role of the State*. Cheltenham, UK and Northampton, MA, USA: Edward Elgar, pp. 103–126.

Hodgson, G.M. (2004), *The Evolution of Institutional Economics: Agency, Structure, and Darwinism in American Institutionalism*. London and New York: Routledge.

Hodgson, G.M. (2006a), *Economics in the Shadows of Darwin and Marx: Essays on Institutional and Evolutionary Themes*. Cheltenham, UK and Northampton, MA, USA: Edward Elgar.

Hodgson, G.M. (2006b), Why We Need a Generalized Darwinism: And Why a Generalized Darwinism Is Not Enough, *Journal of Economic Behavior and Organization* 61(1), pp. 1–19.

Hodgson, G.M. (2008), How Veblen Generalized Darwin, *Journal of Economic Issues* 42(2), pp. 399–406.

Hodgson, G.M. and Knudsen, T. (2010), *Darwin's Conjecture the Search for General Principles of Social and Economic Evolution.* Chicago: The University of Chicago Press.

Kalecki, M. (1937), A Theory of the Business Cycle, *Review of Economic Studies* 4(2), pp. 77–97.

Keen, S. (2009), Mathematics for Pluralist Economists, in J. Reardon (ed.), *The Handbook of Pluralist Economics Education.* London and New York: Routledge, pp. 150–168.

Kim, J.E. (1999), Making Sense of Emergence, *Philosophical Studies* 95(1–2), pp. 3–36.

King, J.E. (2012), *The Microfoundations Delusion: Metaphor and Dogma in the History of Macroeconomics.* Cheltenham, UK and Northampton, MA, USA: Edward Elgar.

Krugman, P. (1997), New-Age Market Theory Is Bio-Babble: Pseudo-Economics Meets Pseudo Evolution, *Ottawa Citizen,* 1 November.

Nelson, R.R. (1995), Recent Evolutionary Theorizing About Economic Change, *Journal of Economic Literature* 33(1), pp. 48–90.

Nelson, R.R. and Winter, S.G. (1982), *An Evolutionary Theory of Economic Change.* Cambridge, MA, USA: Belknap Press of Harvard University Press.

Potts, J. (2000), *The New Evolutionary Microeconomics: Complexity, Competence, and Adaptive Behaviour.* Cheltenham, UK and Northampton, MA, USA: Edward Elgar.

Potts, J. and Nightingale, J. (2001), An Alternative Framework for Economics, *Post-Autistic Economics Review* 10, article 3.

Schmid, A.A. (2003), Review of the New Evolutionary Microeconomics by Jason Potts, *Economic Record* 79(244), pp. 140–142.

Simon, H.A. (1957), *Models of Man: Social and Rational: Mathematical Essays on Rational Human Behavior in a Social Setting.* New York: Wiley.

Thomson, W. (1883), *Popular Lectures,* volume 1. New York: Macmillan.

Thornton, T.B. (2013), The Possibility of a Pluralist Economics Curriculum in Australian Universities: Historical Forces and Contemporary Strategies. PhD thesis, La Trobe University, Melbourne.

Thornton, T.B. (forthcoming), *From Economics to Political Economy: The Promise, Problems and Solutions of Pluralist Economics.* London and New York: Routledge.

Veblen, T. (1898), Why is Economics Not an Evolutionary Science? *Quarterly Journal of Economics,* 12(4), pp. 373–397.

Theme V

Mainstream economics and neoliberalism – resistance to pluralism

The major resistance to reclaiming pluralism in economics is the overwhelming hostility to it by the dominant mainstream of economists, who claims allegiance to the monistic neoclassical paradigm. Moreover, the theoretical authority of market-driven processes (whether valid or not) in capitalist societies has ushered in a period of broadly neoliberal public policies across all spheres. This means, as Michael Howard makes clear in Chapter 18, that political agencies act as financiers and regulators of markets on a grand scale by extending the role of the market into all aspects of human activity and interaction.

Three aspects of this dominant terrain are examined by the authors in Chapters 16 to 18, aspects that create significant hurdles on the path to reclaiming pluralism for research, teaching and public policy implementation. First is the nature of mainstream economists' antipathy to any diversity, such as exemplified by heterodox economists. Second is how the neoliberal agenda has extended outside of the arcane world of general equilibrium econometric modelling. Third is how resilient this dominant monistic economic position is, despite the global financial crisis of 2008.

Arnaldo Barone identifies the one major theoretical resistance to pluralism which prevents young economists from studying alternative economic approaches. It is the fierce dismissal of all heterodox economics strands by the mainstream as 'bad' economics, with only certain 'worthy' elements being absorbed without undermining the basic neoclassical theoretically 'pure' model. Barone effectively dismantles this good/bad dichotomy using Veblen's powerful critique of 'neoclassical' economics as 'pre-Darwinian': the term having been coined by Veblen himself. As Barone says, 'mainstream economics is built (ironically) on the same foundations as the astrology and creationism it equates with the heterodox schools. The replacement of the alphabet of language with the alphabet of mathematics as its mode of discussion may give it a veneer of scientific method and respectability, but closer inspection suggests that, at its core, the very stuff that mainstream economics is made of is pre-Darwinian.'

In Chapter 17, Patrick O'Leary conducts a detailed case study of how the dominant neoliberal political agenda in the US and Australia has sponsored significantly greater employer discretion in industrial relations strategies. The discretion to hire and fire workers and destroy existing collective agreements and conciliation regimes has intensified since neoclassical economics achieved its monistic dominance in the mid-1970s. O'Leary uses the meat industries of both countries to illuminate the loss of workers' rights. He concludes by discussing recent calls for 'neo-pluralism' reform along the lines of 'associational' social relations and workplace partnerships.

Fittingly, the final chapter in this theme is by John King's long-time collaborator, Mike Howard. Fitting, too, is that the chapter reflects upon their 2007 book, *The Rise of Neoliberalism in the Advanced Capitalist Economies.* The book was launched only a few months before Lehman Brothers' bankruptcy brought on the global financial crisis. The chapter provides a penetrating evaluation of 'the effects of the financial crisis on neoliberalism and mainstream macroeconomic theory'.

16 Veblen and the pretensions to 'science' of mainstream economics

Arnaldo Barone

Perhaps as a sign of our age, one of my favoured pastimes has become to trawl through the blogosphere. On one occasion, I happened upon a blog written by an author purporting to be a mainstream[1] economist with an entry devoted to heterodox economics. More precisely, the blog entry was devoted to 'chastising' the heterodox schools of economics, arguing that they represent in economics what astrology is to astronomy, or creationism to evolution.

The dismissive charge laid by the blogger is by no means new, nor are such charges limited to the blogosphere. Indeed, similar dismissals have been made by some of the discipline's most eminent and celebrated practitioners. As an example, consider this response from John H. Cochrane to Paul Krugman's suggestion that economics turn to the writings of Maynard Keynes for cues on how to deal with the recent Global Financial Crisis: '[Paul Krugman] calls for a return to the eternal verities of a rather convoluted book written in the 1930s, as taught to our author in his undergraduate introductory courses. If a scientist, he might be an AIDS-HIV disbeliever, a creationist, a stalwart that maybe continents don't move after all' (Cochrane 2009, paragraph 2).

Other exponents of this view exist, such as Harald Uhlig from the University of Chicago, who likens teaching heterodox approaches to the teaching of mystical Mayan beliefs to would-be astronomers: 'The Mayans have thought about the origins of the universe, but I don't think ... [one] needs to learn what they thought ... [instead] one would learn the modern astrophysicist's perspective' (in Alberti 2012, pp. 3–4). And it seems the divide between so-called 'Saltwater' and 'Freshwater' economics falls to naught on this matter, with the economist Gene Grossman of Princeton University arguing that giving voice to heterodox ideas is akin to 'science departments ... [giving] equal weight to flat-earth theories or creationist approaches' (in Alberti 2012, p. 4).

Whether astronomy versus astrology, creationism versus evolution or, indeed, any other such analogy, the mainstream's point is a simple one: heterodox economics represents the discipline's embarrassing, pre-scientific past, while the mainstream represents the discipline's break from pseudo-science and mumbo-jumbo towards a form of economics that can finally claim to be scientific.[2]

Two questions immediately arise from these assertions. To begin with, a considered analysis of the propositions outlined above would recognize that heterodox economics encompasses a number of schools, some of which operate at cross-purposes and have diametrically different approaches and methods. Thus to treat heterodox economics in monolithic terms is to fail to recognize the diversity of approaches that fall under the heterodox tag. Therefore, to test the proposition thoroughly, one would need to determine the scientific bona fides of individual heterodox schools. Herein lies the first question: which particular heterodox school, tradition or approach is unscientific? All of them? Some of them? To be sure, whether all or some, testing this could prove a Herculean task, and it is certainly beyond the scope of this chapter.

The other implication arising from the mainstream charge is that their own approach is scientific. It seems that much of the mainstream claim to science is rooted in its adoption of the language of 'formal mathematical model[s]' (Colander 2007, p. 4). Indeed, before his 2009 claim that the 'economics profession went astray because economists, as a group, mistook beauty, clad in impressive-looking mathematics, for truth' (Krugman 2009), Paul Krugman wrote that attacks on the mainstream mathematical approach represented a:

> strong desire to make economics less like a science and more like literary criticism … [W]hen it comes to economics I speak English as a second language: I think in equations and diagrams, then translate. The opponents of mainstream economics dislike people like me not so much for our conclusions as for our style: They want economics to be what it once was, a field that was comfortable for the basically literary intellectual.
>
> (Krugman 1996, paragraphs 5, 7)

This brings us to the second question: how valid is the mainstream's claim to science? Does mainstream economics represent the discipline's scientific triumph, or have mainstream economists deluded themselves and confused the language of mathematical formalism with science?[3] To be sure, this proposition is, relatively speaking, a less burdensome task than the former, and so this chapter will focus on the claims made by mainstream economists to the title of 'true' scientists of the economics discipline.

The approach that will be taken in this chapter is to base the analysis on the arguments made by one of the discipline's earliest agitators, the American economist Thorstein Veblen. Veblen's argument was with the mainstream's forebears, to whom he referred by the term he coined, the hyphenated 'neo-classical' (Colander 2000, p. 131). His criticism focused on the discipline's pre-Darwinian[4] nature, and it is my contention that many of the criticisms Veblen levelled at the mainstream's neoclassical progenitors continue to hold currency. If his criticisms do still have relevance, then rather than being a paragon of scientific virtue, mainstream economics represents an adherence to a pre-Darwinian method that has more in common with the ideas that drive creationism and its tenets of a designed universe than with the methods of modern, post-Darwinian science.

Pre-Darwinian science and the Darwinian challenge

Pre-Darwinian science had three defining characteristics. The first is the idea that the world (and universe) is designed by a Creator, invariably a Creator of Christian (or monotheist) complexion. Drawing authority from the Biblical story of creation, it was considered that the Creator, in His wisdom, had ordered the universe in such a way as to be optimal to man's existence. Such a designed world is unchanging (static) and could not possibly be any other, for if it were subject to change it would nullify the idea that it had been supremely ordained as the best of all possible worlds by a perfect and omniscient Providence, or worse yet, admit the possibility for chaos (Wilson 1967, p. 3).

The second defining characteristic is that of teleology. The designer, in His wisdom, has set in place laws that ensure that the universe and all within it move according to a plan, that there is a pre-determined optimal goal towards which things move. Another way to consider this is to say that things move to fulfil the supremely ordained plan; that they move with a purpose.

The third defining characteristic is the inability to fulfil the plan, or move away from a predestined course. Such inability is due to some disturbance, to an unnatural force, or an element that is barring the proper teleological finality from taking hold.

Given the Darwinian nomenclature used thus far in the introduction, the best exposition of this mind-set is to consider thinking in the biological and natural sciences before Charles Darwin's discoveries. Prior to Darwin, our biological conception was made through the Biblical story of Creation and the Aristotelian idea of the Great Chain of Being, alternately referred to as the 'Ladder of Life', or *Scala Naturae* (Oldroyd 1980, p. 2). The Great Chain's two latter names perhaps give a better indication regarding its operation. In essence, the Great Chain organized all living and non-living matter in an order and rank (a ladder) that reflected its degree of perfection. Solipsism dictated that man be found at its peak (although Christian interpretations would place God at the summit, with man immediately beneath), while 'lower' animals such as bugs or worms were near its base, with the base itself composed of non-living matter such as air, earth and metals (Oldroyd 1980, pp. 6–10). Further, there are no gaps or 'missing steps' in the Chain, so that the creatures that inhabit the Earth are 'linked' to one another, ensuring the continuity of the Chain (Lovejoy 1936). For example, man could be considered to be connected to apes, which are in turn connected to monkeys.

One can see how the Great Chain manifests two characteristics of the pre-Darwinian mind-set. To begin with, it marries with the idea that the natural world operates according to a design set in place by a Creator. The Great Chain of Being is such a design, it tells us how the natural world is ordered. The Great Chain also tells us that things move towards an end, which, in the case of the Great Chain, is from the lowliest of creatures to those that are mighty and closer to perfection. In other words, the Great Chain is teleological, it moves in a pre-determined way until we reach that most perfect of Earthly beings, man.

In the pre-Darwinian world, movements away from the pre-ordained plan were viewed as the result of some disturbance or element that has barred the natural order from obtaining. An example of how this operated in the construct of the Great Chain is its treatment of mass species extinction.[5] 'Naturally' occurring mass species extinction was not fathomed or even considered possible by pre-Darwinian thinkers for a number for reasons (Ruse 1979, p. 4). To begin with, the possibility for natural mass species extinction meant that breaks could occur in the Great Chain, which would contradict the notion of continuity and the idea that the universe is God's perfect creation. Secondly, if natural species extinction were possible, it suggested that the universe was not static, but rather a place of change, including change that could lead to man's own extinction, invalidating both the Great Chain and the story of Genesis.[6] Because of this, it was generally considered that there could not be natural species extinction, and what extinction is witnessed is an aberration caused by unnatural forces, such as the actions of man. Thus we see the third characteristic of pre-Darwinian thought, that which requires deviations from the plan to be explained in terms of an aberration or unusual disturbance: in this instance, to the special case of man's destructive powers (Ruse 1979, p. 6).

The discussion above presents an implication regarding the role of scientists. Consider that if the laws that govern the universe are given, and if we are armed with information on where things will ultimately settle, then as scientists, we need not concern ourselves with the discovery of said laws. Instead, we can be comfortable knowing that our world is designed and moves to achieve some end. In the case of the biological world, knowledge of the Great Chain of Being meant the laws were such that they ordered living matter according to the already mentioned degree of perfection. Armed with this knowledge, the scientist avoids expenditure of time on futile activities such as the discovery of laws, like those that explain impossible phenomena like species extinction (or appearance), and instead devotes his time to classifying living (and non-living) matter in such a way as to fulfil and fit within the given construct of the Great Chain of Being. The scientist's role is reduced to that of taxonomist and classifier, but it is a taxonomy drawn in terms of the pre-determined construct, so that our classification is one that is struck in such a way as to be congruent with the Great Chain.

In time, a number of discoveries helped to shift this mind-set. First, it was discovered that the world was much older than had previously been thought. Previous ageing of the Earth was based on work by Biblical scholars like Bishop Ussher that had suggested its age was in the order of thousands of years. New analyses found that the world was far older than this, in the millions, if not billions of years. Second, the appearance of the fossil record served to challenge the idea of a static and designed universe. It implied that the universe was a place of change, where animals both appear and disappear (Ruse 1979, p. 4).

Many pre-Darwinian scientists, unhappy with these conclusions, scrambled to find explanations for the fossil record that would ensure the continued integrity and use of the Great Chain. For example, some explained fossils as manifestations of forms in the inorganic world, or as the remains of extant but as yet undiscovered animals, which presumably, when discovered, could be placed within the construct of the Great Chain (Ruse 1979, p. 4). The French Naturalist Jean Baptiste Lamarck developed an explanation for the fossil record as the remnants of existing animals that through the process of so-called 'Lamarckian evolution' (see Oldroyd 1980; Ruse 1979; Gray 1860) changed their appearance by such proportions as to be rendered impossible to recognize (Ruse 1979, p. 7; Mayr 1991, p. 16). However, Lamarck's version of 'evolution' was still teleological and relied heavily on the idea of the Great Chain (Oldroyd 1980, p. 35).

For Charles Darwin, explaining the fossil record lay not in the direction of the Great Chain of Being but elsewhere. With the help of the economist Robert Malthus and his essays on population, Darwin learned to appreciate the hunt that all organisms make for scarce resources and the resulting struggle for existence (Oldroyd 1980, p. 66; Ambirajan 1959, pp. 200–01). From this, he discovered the force that determined species' appearance and disappearance, which he called *natural selection* (Darwin 1859, p. 48).

Through natural selection, species that possessed attributes that gave them an advantage in the hunt for resources would flourish, while those that did not would struggle and eventually die out or, at least, diminish markedly in number or in the territories in which they could be found. Natural selection meant that it could no longer be said that the world was a static place designed by a benevolent God to be both favourable to and under man's dominion. Such 'argument[s] of design in nature ... which formerly seemed to be so conclusive' were roundly rebutted in the face of natural selection (Darwin in Mayr 1991, p. 57). On the contrary, rather than ordered, designed and moving to fulfil some purpose, natural selection cast the world around us as 'haphazard and opportunistic' (Mayr 1991, p. 66). It could no longer be said that things move towards a particular point or along a pre-determined path; rather, natural selection told us that there is no pre-determined path, no fated end to be made real. Nor was the direction necessarily one of progress. With natural selection, we simply do not know which direction life will be taken: forward or backward; upward or downward; or towards a dead end. Importantly for man, natural selection meant that his own appearance came not from a breath of life from the Almighty into the mouth of Adam but from a chance outcome of natural selection, an accident of history. But further, it meant that man too might also fall prey to the inescapable forces of natural selection and become extinct.

Clearly, Darwin's discoveries were a challenge, forcing man to see (and admit) that there is 'no more design in the variability of organic beings in the action of natural selection, than in the course which the wind blows' (Darwin in Mayr 1991, p. 57; see also Hodgson 2004, p. 87). Darwin's discoveries made it folly to continue with constructs built in terms of aberrations, inter- ferences or disturbances that barred the attainment of an otherwise fated Arcadia. The implications for science were marked. While pre-Darwinian scientists took the 'laws' that govern nature for granted, as the province of theology or philosophy and outside their own scope of activity, Darwin showed that it was now possible for scientists to discover said laws, setting science on the process away from teleology, classification and taxonomy and towards the unravelling of causal explanations (Hodgson 2004, p. 87).

Veblen's criticisms of neoclassical economics and their challenge to the mainstream

Between 1898 and 1900, Thorstein Veblen published 'Why is Economics not an Evolutionary Science?' and 'The Preconceptions of Economic Science'. These works, perhaps more than any other, encapsulate Veblen's objections to the then fledgling neoclassical school of economics, which would later become the foundation for today's mainstream economics.

Veblen's first criticism of neoclassical economics was that it was not a *modern* science. By modern science, Veblen meant that economics was not an evolutionary science, in the Darwinian sense. Modern, Darwinian scientists insist on 'an answer in terms of cause and effect' which is their 'last recourse' (Veblen 1898, p. 377); but for pre-Darwinian scientists this is insufficient, and instead they 'seek a higher ground for their ultimate syntheses' and impute a design or purpose in the phenomena within their scope of study (Veblen 1898, p. 378). In classical economics, this 'higher ground' was 'natural law', an 'analogue' to the Great Chain of Being that 'exercise[s] ... a coercive surveil- lance over the sequence of events' to ensure a 'consistent propensity tending to some spiritually legitimate end' (Veblen 1898, p. 378).

The Physiocrats presented this in terms of a '*loi naturelle*' and '*ordre naturel*' that was 'immutable and unerring' and worked to achieve the 'ordained goal of supreme human welfare' (Veblen 1899, pp. 126, 127). Later, Adam Smith famously took the Physiocratic notion and transformed it into an 'invisible hand', where each worked to 'promote an end which was no part of his intention' but that results in the 'greatest value' for society (Smith 1776, p. 364; see Veblen 1900, p. 397). For the neoclassical economists, natural law was transformed into 'Laws of Equilibrium' that saw markets as tending towards an optimal, market equilibrium (Jevons 1871, p. vii). Each is a case of pre- Darwinian teleology in economic thinking, an example of Veblen's 'higher ground', where things are envisaged as moving towards some predestined end.

But consider for a moment the implications of economic teleology in practice, more specifically in the case of neoclassical economics. To begin with, teleology means that we can speak of an economic world as it *should* be, which naturally is that which mimics the pre-determined market-equilibrating end. Conversely, we can determine from this how the economic world *should not* be, which would be a state where the given 'legitimate' end (the market equilibrium) is not obtained. Armed with this knowledge, the economic investigator need not bother with pointless exercises like the discovery of underlying laws of economic and social development. Like pre-Darwinian biologists who adhered to the Great Chain and for whom notions of mass species extinction were unthinkable, economists imbued with pre-Darwinian thinking need give no consideration to understanding the forces that have shaped and created the economic system. There is no point, since the economic system and its ultimate trajectory are a 'given'. Indeed, it could be argued that such economists, at least implicitly, did not consider the possibility that the economic system might become 'extinct', or that it could be subject to forces that could change it or lead to its demise.

Instead, with the implicit notion that the economic system is so designed[7] as to achieve the inevitability of optimal market equilibrium, the economist focuses his efforts on examining and listing the various movements, activities and actions that lead to this end. And since this end is the one that leads to the optimal equilibrium outcome, his role could be said to be to develop a 'code of ideal economic conduct':

> [Economic theory] is a projection of the accepted ideal of conduct. This ideal of conduct is made to serve as a canon of truth, to the extent that the investigator contents himself with an appeal to its legitimation for premises that run back of the facts with which he is immediately dealing, for the 'controlling principles' that are conceived intangibly to underlie the process discussed, and for the 'tendencies' that run beyond the situation as it lies before him .... By this method the theory of an institution or a phase of life may be stated in conventionalized terms of the apparatus whereby life is carried on, the apparatus being invested with a tendency to an equilibrium at the normal, and the theory being a formulation of the conditions under which this putative equilibrium supervenes.
>
> (Veblen 1898, pp. 382–83)

The lack of 'modernity' in neoclassical economics meant that economic analysis amounted to 'taxonomy'. For neoclassical economists, confident in a world that would (barring unnatural barriers) always lead to the optimal equilibrium, devoted their time to classifying, identifying and categorizing the behaviour that corresponds with this legitimate end. Veblen would refer to this as a system of economic taxonomy: 'The agencies or forces causally at work in the economic life process are neatly avoided. The outcome of the method, at its best, is a body of logically consistent propositions concerning the normal relations of things – a system of economic taxonomy' (Veblen 1898, p. 384).

The economists of Veblen's time were like the naturalists and biologists of old. For the naturalists and biologists, the classification process centred on flora and fauna and then placing them on the Ladder of Life; for economists, the focus was on matters such as wages, rent and prices at the market equilibrium. But while they were busying themselves classifying wildly different phenomena, their actions both were in essence those of the taxonomist.

The implications of such thinking in terms of practical application are profound. Our knowledge of the pre-determined legitimate end and the actions that correspond with it enable us to identify the unnatural or disturbing factors in operation at an illegitimate state of being. By excising (or at the very least attenuating) these 'distorting' factors we can ensure that things 'right themselves' (Veblen 1900, p. 398) and set the market back towards equilibrium (or at the very least come closer to achieving it). The job of the economist therefore is to ensure that the world imitates that of his model, or at the very least to try hard to ensure that it does. The resulting effect is that economists (both in Veblen's time and now) learn to appreciate so-called market failures not as an innate part of the economy but as something that is extrinsic or unnatural to it. In other words, market failures in economics are akin to the pre-Darwinian treatment of mass species extinction, which Darwin of course showed was not an aberration or unnatural but an inherent part of the operation of nature.

I once recounted Veblen's criticisms to a colleague who practised mainstream economics. He found Veblen's arguments very interesting but suggested that they would surely not be relevant to the economics of today, since in his mind the discipline had done much since Veblen's time to ensure that it was a closer representation of reality. It is true to say that much has happened in the economics discipline since Veblen's passing in 1929 to include features that are intended to ensure that its models resonate with the real world. Examples include George Akerlof's (1970) consideration of the operation of markets with imperfect information; New Keynesian notions of markets operating with imperfect competition and sticky wages or prices; the adoption of bounded rationality in recognition that man is invariably anything but a 'lightning calculator' (Veblen 1898, pp. 389–90); and work to determine if the market equilibrium 'proven' to exist by Arrow and Debreu continues to do so with relaxed assumptions.[8] Another way to describe each of these is to say that the mainstream of the discipline has steadily shed the strict and unrealistic assumptions that underlie their paradigm to determine how the market functions after such a change.[9]

But does the relaxation of these underlying assumptions and the embedding of 'real world' manifestations into mainstream economic models represent an embrace of modern scientific thought, in the form of the Darwinian paradigm? In my view, the answer is no, so that Veblen's charge that 'economics is helplessly behind the times' (Veblen 1898, p. 373) still has some validity.

How can this be so? It is because, at their core, the 'realistic' inclusions from modern mainstream economists are the responses of a discipline still casting its analyses in terms of a pre-Darwinian 'ideal': the fêted market equilibrium. It is a point highlighted by the American economist Edward

Lazear, who proudly proclaimed the centrality of the concept in economics (Lazear 2000, p. 101). Ironically, Lazear made this point in a paper titled 'Economic Imperialism', which asserted the scientific credentials of the economics discipline, a feature he claims has enabled it increasingly to enter and take over intellectual domains once considered outside the discipline's scope or interest. While 'broader-thinking sociologists, anthropologists and ... psychologists may be better at identifying issues' they are 'worse at providing answers'. Economics, by contrast, may sometimes be limited in view but can provide 'concrete solutions' which, he claims, gives it a 'major advantage in analysis' (Lazear 2000, p. 103).

However, in each of the examples highlighted above, the 'real world' additions to economics are examined in terms of the deleterious effect they have on the attainment of the ideal. In other words, each is built on a teleological construct that considers the role of these 'realisms' in barring the market equilibrium that would, in their absence, occur.[10] The discipline may have excised overt references to design or to supernatural Providence and adopted a more 'detached' and algebraic language, but while the language may have been stripped of 'embellishments' and 'spiritual' references, its essential structure remains pre-Darwinian.

Conclusion

Edmund Burke once said that 'the age of chivalry is gone. That of sophisters, economists, and calculators, has succeeded' (Burke 1790, pp. 212–13). Today, to be sure, the economics profession, particularly its mainstream, holds a position of power few disciplines could rival (Lazear 2000).

The authority held by the mainstream economics profession is at least partly built upon the notion that it has developed an understanding of the economy built in the strictest of scientific terms. It is upon this foundation that the mainstream marginalizes and dismisses the thought and ideas of the so-called heterodox traditions. But as the discussion above shows, mainstream economics is built (ironically) on the same foundations as the astrology and creationism it equates with the heterodox schools. The replacement of the alphabet of language with the alphabet of mathematics as its mode of discussion may give it a veneer of scientific method and respectability, but closer inspection suggests that, at its core, the very stuff that mainstream economics is made of is pre-Darwinian.

If this is the case, mainstream economics has a markedly lessened claim to the scientific label, and the confidence that the mainstream's adherents hold in terms of its unimpeachable scientific credentials should be abandoned. When (or if) the mainstream realizes this, perhaps it will abandon the hubris that colours the statements made by some of its most renowned practitioners, recognize the pre-Darwinian nature of its methods and admit that it struggles to pass the very test to science by which it derides and belittles its heterodox cousins.

Notes

1 Coase (1998, p. 72) defines mainstream economics as microeconomics. This view resembles the 'economic family tree' produced by Samuelson and Nordhaus (2010), which shows the modern mainstream to be direct descendants of the neoclassical school, which built their analyses on microeconomic foundations. Therefore, the term mainstream economics as used here follows these approaches and refers to a form of economics that insists on an analysis built on microeconomic foundations, such as New Keynesian, Keynesian (neoclassical synthesis) and New Classical economics.

2 Some mainstream economists have recognized that there may be elements within heterodox traditions that warrant further consideration. But, often, the approach is to take these 'positive' elements and subsume them within the mainstream paradigm. A famous example of this attitude comes from Milton Friedman, who once said that there is 'only good economics, and bad economics' (in Dolan 1976, paragraph 4). Friedman was referring to the Austrian strand of heterodox economics, and his suggestion was that the worthy elements of that school be 'smoothly incorporated into the mainstream of economic theory' (Dolan 1976, paragraph 4). The suggestion that economics be made up of a plurality of schools (including Austrian economics) each with their differing approaches was, to Friedman, an invalid pursuit. The mainstream represents 'good' economics, while heterodox approaches represent 'bad' economics.

3 On this point, Friedrich von Hayek argued that what many economists use as their badge of science is in reality 'scientistic', a term he used to describe the 'mechanical and uncritical application of habits of thought to fields different from those in which they have been formed' (Hayek 1974, paragraph 2). The 'scientistic as distinguished from the scientific view is not an unprejudiced but a very prejudiced approach which, before it has considered its subject, claims to know what is the most appropriate way of investigating' (Hayek 1942, p. 269). Therefore, the insistence on mathematical formalism at the expense of all other forms of analysis, even though others may be more appropriate, represents not science, but 'scientism'.

4 Pre-Darwinian refers to the period before the discoveries made by Charles Darwin.

5 Another example would be that of species 'appearance', also considered impossible by pre-Darwinian scientists because it implied the possibility for change and challenged the idea of a static and Providentially ordered creation. A consequence is that 'appearances' were also treated as an aberration (Wilson 1967, p. 5).

6 The possibility that man could become extinct challenged the Biblical notion that the world in which we live was so created by God to be under man's dominion, for his use and benefit. If the world was created *for* man, then it makes little sense to think that it could go on *without* man, acting against the possibility for the extinction of man.

7 The American economist James Galbraith contends that 'Economists ... have been Intelligent Designers since the beginning' and that the discipline's modern mainstream incarnation had not 'escaped its pre-Darwinian rut' (Galbraith 2005, paragraphs 4, 9).

8 Among the assumptions made by Arrow and Debreu are competitive and complete markets with zero transaction costs and consumers who exhibit convex preferences (for a fuller description see Arrow and Debreu 1954).

9 The American economist and Nobel laureate Ronald Coase was less magnanimous in his assessment of mainstream economics, suggesting while it 'purports otherwise', mainstream economics 'has become more and more abstract over time ... [and] is in fact little concerned with what happens in the real world' (Coase 1998, p. 72).

10 The Australian economist Steve Keen has likened the 'realisms' added by mainstream economists to the addition of epicycles by Ptolemaic astronomers to address and make workable a model of the universe that was increasingly confounded by reality (Keen 2012).

References

Akerlof, G. (1970), The Market for 'Lemons': Quality Uncertainty and the Market Mechanism, *Quarterly Journal of Economics* 84(3), pp. 488–500.

Alberti, M. (2012), Mainstream Economics on the Defensive, *Remapping Debate*, 21 March. At http://www.remappingdebate.org/sites/all/files/Mainstream%20economists%20on%20the%20defensive.pdf, accessed 11 September 2013.

Ambirajan, S. (1959), *Malthus and Classical Economics*, Bombay, India: Popular Book Depot.

Arrow, K. and Debreu, G. (1954), Existence of an Equilibrium for a Competitive Economy, *Econometrica*, 22(3) pp. 265–290.

Burke, E. (1790), *Reflections on the Revolution in France: In a Letter Intended to Have Been Sent to a Gentleman in Paris*, in The Harvard Classics. New York: P.F. Collier and Son (1937), pp. 143–378.

Coase, R. (1998), The New Institutional Economics, *American Economic Review* 88(2), pp. 72–74.

Cochrane, J.H. (2009), How Did Paul Krugman Get it So Wrong?16 September. At http://faculty.chicagobooth.edu/john.cochrane/research/Papers/krugman_response.htm, accessed 10 October 2013.

Colander, D. (2000), The Death of Neoclassical Economics, *Journal of the History of Economic Thought* 22(2), pp. 127–143.

Colander, D. (2007), Pluralism and Heterodox Economics: Suggestions for an 'Inside the Mainstream' Heterodoxy, Middlebury College Economics Discussion Paper No. 07–24, Middlebury, Vermont USA. At http://sandcat.middlebury.edu/econ/repec/mdl/ancoec/0724.pdf, accessed 11 December 2013.

Darwin, C. (1859), *The Origins of Species by Means of Natural Selection*. London: Watts and Co. (1929).

Dolan, E.G. (1976), Austrian Economics as Extraordinary Science, originally in The Foundations of Modern Austrian Economics. At http://oll.libertyfund.org/?option=com_staticxt&staticfile=show.php%3Ftitle=104&chapter=23583&layout=html&Itemid=27, accessed 10 January 2014.

Galbraith, J. (2005), Smith vs. Darwin, *Mother Jones*, December. At http://www.motherjones.com/politics/2005/12/smith-vs-darwin, accessed 10 December 2013.

Gray, A. (1860), Review of Darwin's Theory on the Origin of Species, in R.J. Wilson (ed.) (1967), *Darwinism and the American Intellectual: A Book of Readings*. Homewood, Illinois, USA: The Dorsey Press, pp. 20–37.

Hayek, F.A. (1942), Scientism and the Study of Society, *Economica* 9(35), pp. 267–291.

Hayek, F.A. (1974), The Pretence of Knowledge, Nobel Prize Lecture, 11 December. At http://www.nobelprize.org/nobel_prizes/economic-sciences/laureates/1974/hayek-lecture.html, accessed 2 December 2013.

Hodgson, G.M. (2004), *The Evolution of Institutional Economics: Agency, Structure and Darwinism in American Institutionalism*. London and New York: Routledge.

Jevons, W.S. (1871), *The Theory of Political Economy*, fifth edition. New York: Sentry Press (1957).

Keen, S. (2012), Ptolemaic Economics in the Age of Einstein, *Steve Keen's Debtwatch*, 2 April. At http://keenomics.s3.amazonaws.com/debtdeflation_media/2012/04/PtolemaicEconomicsInTheAgeOfEinstein.pdf, accessed 30 January 2014.

Krugman, P. (1996), Economic Culture Wars, *Slate*, 25 October. At http://www.slate.com/articles/business/the_dismal_science/1996/10/economic_culture_wars.single.html, accessed 12 August 2013.

Krugman, P. (2009), How Did Economists Get It So Wrong? *The New York Times*, 2 September. At http://www.nytimes.com/2009/09/06/magazine/06Economic-t.html?pagewanted=all&_r=0, accessed 2 December 2013.

Lazear, E.P. (2000), Economic Imperialism, *Quarterly Journal of Economics* 115(1), pp. 99–146.

Lovejoy, A.O. (1936), *The Great Chain of Being: A Study of the History of an Idea*. New York: Harper and Row (1960).

Mayr, E. (1991), *One Long Argument: Charles Darwin and the Genesis of Modern Evolutionary Thought*. Cambridge, USA: Harvard University Press.

Oldroyd, D.R. (1980), *Darwinian Impacts: An Introduction to the Darwinian Revolution*. Milton Keynes, UK: The Open University Press.

Ruse, M. (1979), *The Darwinian Revolution*. Chicago and London: University of Chicago Press.

Samuelson, P.A. and Nordhaus, W.D. (2010), *Economics*, nineteenth edition. Boston: McGraw-Hill Irwin.

Smith, A. (1776), *An Inquiry into the Nature and Causes of the Wealth of Nations*, two volumes, in R.H. Campbell and A.S. Skinner (eds.) (1976), *The Glasgow Edition of the Works and Correspondence of Adam Smith*. Oxford: Oxford University Press.

Veblen, Thorstein (1898), Why is Economics Not an Evolutionary Science? *Quarterly Journal of Economics* 12(4), pp. 373–397.

Veblen, Thorstein (1899), The Preconceptions of Economic Science, part 1, *Quarterly Journal of Economics* 13(2), pp. 121–150.

Veblen, Thorstein (1900), The Preconceptions of Economic Science, part 3, *Quarterly Journal of Economics* 14(2), pp. 240–269.

Wilson, R.J. (ed.) (1967), *Darwinism and the American Intellectual: A Book of Readings*. Homewood, Illinois, USA: The Dorsey Press.

17 Neoliberal policy and employer industrial relations strategies in the United States and Australia

Patrick O'Leary[1]

Neoliberalism emerged as a dominant doctrine of political and economic practice in the US and Australia during the late 1970s. Its influence over the last three or four decades on economic and social policy in both western developed economies and in developing economies has been widely analysed, but its influence on business-level industrial relations strategy is less well-known. Despite this limited understanding, its influence over management strategies cannot be ignored. Therefore, this chapter aims to explore what might be regarded as neoliberal management strategies and practices, particularly in an industrial relations framework. While this is a very broad canvas, the focus will be specifically on management industrial relations strategies and practices in the US and Australian meat processing industries, as a case example of how neoliberalism has affected the world of work.

Meat processing ('meatpacking' in the US) has long been fertile ground for labour historians, sociologists and industrial relations researchers. Over the last three decades, meat processing industrial disputes have received considerable attention. The perspectives and roles of labour unions and workers have been a dominant focus. Employers have attracted far less attention. In particular, there has been little discussion of how employer decision-making processes may generate different courses of action and outcomes. Therefore, the aim is to explore the strategy and behaviour of meat processing companies in two economies heavily influenced by neoliberal policy-making. It does this by first engaging with the broader theoretical literature on employer strategy and behaviour.

A comparative examination is undertaken of a number of employer strategies through several case examples and disputes and some more general, industry-wide examples in the US and Australia. The case examples are two plants, the Hormel plant in Austin, Minnesota, USA, and the Australia Meat Holdings (AMH) plant at Portland, Victoria. The disputes are notably those in Victoria 1989–1991, and in Queensland with AMH in the mid-1990s and at the G. and K. O'Connor plant in Pakenham, Victoria. All these cases share a number of elements that make comparison useful, while their differences help us identify salient aspects useful for engagement with the relevant literatures.

The main neoliberal industrial relations strategies in both the US and Australia provide the context to investigate the links between neoliberal political policy developments at the national and international level, as well as changes in firm-level industrial relations strategies in the meat industry, by exploring employer strategy and behaviour during the 1980s and 1990s and into the twenty-first century. Comparative ideological developments and industrial relations have been widely studied in a variety of contexts, but this research looks at a specific industry across two countries where neoliberal policies dominate. What is also unique about this research is the linking of national and international ideological developments to industrial relations strategy at the firm and industry levels, analysing these concerns in a comparative way. What emerges is an identifiable set of strategies, some unique to each country and others that cross national boundaries.

Neoliberal industrial relations

Neoliberalism has had undeniable influences on the industry case studies presented later. This influence is analysed using a framework based on the literature expounded in this section that explains employer initiative in generating and managing outbreaks of large-scale conflict. Combining strategic choice theory and neoliberalism provides this framework.

Pioneering strategic choice theory in industrial relations by Kochan et al. (1984) examines the competitive pressures on employers, workers, unions and governments in the US in the late 1970s. In moving from more mechanistic systems theories, long dominant in industrial relations, they argue for viewing these industrial relations actors as active agents with some degree of choice over their preferences and behaviours. This is particularly important where these choices alter an actor's role or relationship with other actors. According to this strategic choice model, the decisions these actors make can be categorized into three levels within an industrial relations system: the macro or corporate level, the employment relationship or plant level and the workplace or individual and group level.

In a refinement of this model, Kochan et al. (1986) link the institutional structure of industrial relations at the firm level with the external environment, particularly the product market. They argue that product market challenges contribute to fundamental changes in the values and strategies of American employers and managers, and that these lead them, in turn, to choose strategically to alter their industrial relations policies and practices. The aggregate outcome of these individual company-based changes is a significant shift in formal American industrial relations activity from the macro and workplace levels to the industrial relations level, where union influence was least effective.

While this is a very useful explanatory model, it fails to account for the outcomes of these strategic choices. Kochan et al. (1984, p. 21) offer the important corollary that 'strategic decisions can only occur where the parties have discretion over their decisions; that is, where environmental constraints do not severely curtail the parties' choice of alternatives'. Lewin (1987) suggests that, where environmental constraints leave either party with only one realistic option, the notion of 'strategic choice' does not apply.

This leaves open the question of what shapes those environmental constraints: in particular, to be aware that management decisions can shape organizational contexts as well as be shaped by them. More importantly, national industrial relations policy initiatives can both constrain employer strategy-making but also create opportunities for redirecting employer strategy and behaviour. In this context, neoliberalism created a new landscape in the US and Australia within which employers could exercise greater discretion over their industrial relations strategic choosing and, therefore, strategy-making.

Important to note is that the former Australian Prime Minister, Kevin Rudd (2009), raised the whole concept of neoliberalism as an important factor in national policy development in an article published in a number of leading national print media circulations. Rudd (2009) effectively denigrated neoliberalism, but it is possible to place his administration and the subsequent Labor Government of Prime Minister Julia Gillard within this broad ideological tradition. So what is neoliberalism and why is it important for this study?

In purely industrial relations terms, a neoliberal environment could be thought of as, 'one in which the state and leading managers share a common ideology which precludes unions playing a significant role in national economic management or workplace governance' (Boxall and Haynes 1997). This is important, because the meat industry is characterized by high levels of union density and militancy, as well as strong union ties to local communities and social structures (O'Leary and Sheldon 2012). Neoliberal strategies in such a context strike at the very heart of the community in these locations. Here, these issues are identified in a way not developed before. Given the very strong links between Australian and US meat processors, as well as some similarities between the rise of neoliberalism in the two economies, a comparative study distils the significance of neoliberalism outside the domain of strictly economic models.

While Boxall and Haynes (1997) offer a rather monolithic view of neoliberalism, there is now a growing literature from political economy, as well as industrial relations perspectives, that broadens our understanding of the term. There are, for example, scholars who categorize neoliberalism purely in political-ideology terms, where the state must largely withdraw from interventions that support older, 'outmoded' notions of the Keynesian welfare state in favour of structures consistent with the free market (Chang 2002; Peck and Tickell 2007). Cahill (2004) argues that neoliberalism, in Australia at least, is more a movement that relies on a particular set of almost utopian ideals about the 'self-interested individual' and the role of markets and the state. Cahill (2004, p. 68) goes on to suggest that 'the individual is conceived of as a rational, calculating, self-interested utility maximiser'. In terms of the role of the market and the state, Cahill (2004, p. 72) argues that neoliberals hold that the Keynesian welfare state does not work, as it, in economic terms, 'is unable to achieve its aims of providing goods and services to all through the redistribution of income via taxation and the public provision of services'. This is because it has been captured by special interests, such as bureaucrats, politicians and other powerful lobby groups. Also, in ethical terms, 'the welfare state inevitably infringes individual liberty [and] ... is therefore an evil' (Cahill 2004, p. 73). In political-economy terms, neoliberalism is an ideologically driven perspective that advocates individual self-interest within a free market, free from the constraints of state intervention.

In industrial relations terms, neoliberals advocate deregulation of the labour market in favour of individual 'freedom to choose one's own job and negotiate one's own conditions of work' (Cahill 2004, p. 73). This deregulation not only refers to the receding of the state but also freedom from collective organizations, such as trade unions and employer associations (Bray and Underhill 2009). Rather ironically, many neoliberals advocate the state legislate and develop policies designed to destroy existing collective regimes (the so-called 'industrial relations club') or labour regulation (decollectivization), and introduce individualized forms of regulation (individualization) (Bray and Underhill 2009, p. 374). The paradox with neoliberal policy-making, particularly in industrial relations, is that creating the conditions for the destruction of existing collective regimes often requires significant state intervention.

Thus, in general terms, there are a number of key elements about neoliberalism from an industrial relations perspective. First, Cahill (2004) suggests it is more a 'movement' than a political ideology. Second, Harvey (2007) demonstrates that this 'movement' is often geographically determined, that is, it is unevenly developed across both time and space. For example, neoliberalism in the US or China will look very different from neoliberalism in Australia. Third, as stated above, creating the conditions for a neoliberal regime often requires significant state intervention, rather than a receding state, as suggested by the movement's main advocates. Thus, if neoliberalism is a movement which rhetorically advocates shrinking state intervention in the economy as well as in other institutional relations, such as the employment relationship, then what factors are important for the meat processing industries in the US and Australia, and are there employer strategies that have specifically emerged in the industry under successive neoliberal administrations in both countries?

During the early 1980s in the US, for example, the first Reagan administration emboldened employer anti-unionism both through direct intervention in the air traffic controllers' dispute, through intervention in state agencies and through legislative reforms to corporate power, particularly over hiring and firing. Reagan's smashing of the air traffic controllers' strike in 1981 was an important turning point, but his appointment of strongly pro-employer officials to the National Labor Relations Board had more enduring consequences for the tenor of collective industrial relations (Farber and Western 2002). Reagan invoked the law that striking government employees forfeit their jobs, an action that unsettled those who believed no President would ever uphold that law. Reagan prevailed but, far more importantly, his action gave weight to the legal right of private employers, previously not fully exercised, to use their own discretion both to hire and to discharge workers. This activism was motivated by the prevailing neoliberal assumptions concerning the individual, freed from the constraints of collectivist regulation and state intervention. The Reagan initiatives emboldened, among others, employers in the meat-processing industry in the US to attempt to decollectivize their workplaces, as is discussed later.

In Australia, successive neoliberal government administrations, particularly from the mid-1980s, attempted to liberalize or 'decentralize' the economy, including public sector reforms and deregulation of the labour market. The core elements of these national restructuring projects were an overarching economic liberalization, public sector management reforms and privatization; each of which was justified by the perceived need to increase the international competitiveness of the Australian economy. Indeed, internationalization has vested restructuring with a sense of inevitability and irrefutability. Public sector management reform involved reductions in employment levels, divestment of functions and implementation of a private sector model of management variously described as 'managerialism' (Considine and Painter 1998) or the 'new public management' (NPM) (Osborne and Gaebler 1992; Hood 1991, 1995).

The labour market has been an important component of these restructuring projects in Australia and, as with other areas of reform, there has been a substantial measure of political bipartisanship. The general thrust of these changes has been to reduce the role of institutions (industrial tribunals, unions and employer associations) and shift the focus of employment regulation to the workplace. Underlying this shift has been an abiding preoccupation with increasing labour flexibility, particularly in relation to utilization and payments. Advocates of these neoliberal ideas suggest the need for employment conditions that are consistent with profitability, that is: labour market flexibility; employees that are more productive; high productivity growth from the decentralized determination of wages and conditions; and, more importantly, the decline in centralized trade union power. Thus, in industrial relations terms, an Australian neoliberal environment would be 'one in which the state and leading managers share a common ideology which precludes unions playing a significant role in national economic management or workplace governance' (Boxall and Haynes 1997).

This shift in legislative emphasis in Australia, first on decentralized wage-fixing (enterprise bargaining) and then to Australian Workplace Agreements (AWAs) or individual contracts and greater restrictions on union activity,[2] emboldened many employers to choose radically altered industrial relations strategies. These employer strategies vary markedly: from adhering to the status quo (particularly at the state level), to shifting to enterprise bargaining in co-operation with resident unions and all the way to radical employer militancy through lockouts, deunionization and individualization of employment contracts. The Australian neoliberal experience, while very different to the neoliberal agenda in the US, nonetheless, reveals some stark similarities, with some trade unionists referring to these restructuring projects as the

Americanization of the Australian labour market (O'Leary 2008). It is on the industrial implications of neoliberalism that the case studies below focus.

The United States

While the industry's political economy varied markedly over time, by the 1970s, meat processing in the US was undergoing dramatic change (Perren 2006). Industry-level change in the US meat processing industry had been in train since the 1960s, although, during the 1980s and 1990s, many of the older firms in the industry merged or were acquired, resulting in a level of concentration in beef- and pork-processing not seen since the so-called 'Beef Trust' at the turn of the twentieth century (Azzam 1998). During the 1960s and 1970s, there was a radical shift to rural and regional based processing, away from the 'traditional' industrial centres such as Chicago. This was driven by the shift away from the belief that 'it was more efficient to slaughter cattle near their source and ship the carcasses' to the guiding economic principle that 'it is even more efficient to ship cattle as "boxed beef" than to ship carcasses' (Azzam and Anderson 1996, p. 23). This shift in the structure of the industry during the 1960s and 1970s had far-reaching consequences for the political economy of the industry and its labour process – initially in the 1970s, but more so during the 1980s and 1990s.

The old meat processing companies, located in 'Corn-Belt' states of the northern mid-west increasingly suffered competitive disadvantages – in terms of product market and labour market control – to newer, independent firms located in 'right-to-work' states in the south where employers' union avoidance strategies received support from sympathetic state legislatures (Craypo 1994). These competitive pressures intensified during the 1980s, particularly in the wake of the Reagan administration's interventions in industrial relations and corporate governance, encouraging senior managements of the older, more established meat processors to respond with more aggressive labour management strategies. Meat processing was thus a good example of the transformational processes that Kochan and his colleagues were exploring.

One of the key leaders in emergent anti-union, neoliberalism in the US meat processing industry was the George A. Hormel Company. Established in 1891, Hormel is a large US meatpacking and smallgoods[3] company, with SPAM one of its most recognized brands. Hormel's international head office is in Austin in Minnesota's rural south-east, some 110 miles south of the Twin Cities (Minneapolis/St Paul). During the 1980s, Austin was essentially a single-industry town. Workers at the Austin plant had established a union in 1915 and the plant had a history of militant 'IWW-inspired' unionism from the 1930s (Schleuning 1994).

By the 1970s, Hormel had established other plants across the US, giving it significant labour market and product market control – in hog-slaughtering at least. From then on, with the aim of generating major concessions from its unionized workforce, Hormel senior management began to use the general shifts underway in the industry to issue open threats that it would mothball its ageing Austin plant and shift production to one of the 'right-to-work' states (Rachleff 1993, 1997). The United Food and Service Workers' Union (UFCW), the organizing union across the Hormel organization, responded. In exchange for a company promise to maintain employment in Austin by building a new plant there, they accepted lower wages for Austin workers. Thus, in 1978, the union and workforce agreed to wage reductions to underwrite, through an escrow loan to the company, a new plant in Austin. Hormel opened this new, more efficient plant in 1982 (Horowitz 1997; O'Leary and Sheldon 2009).

For its part, despite Hormel building one of the most efficient meat processing plants in the US in the newly opened Austin plant – in the wake of Reagan's pro-employer industrial relations policies – senior management unilaterally reduced the size of its Austin workforce and cut wages and conditions by 23 per cent in 1984 (Schleuning 1994, p. 7). It also acted similarly at its other plants, playing off its employees in one plant against those in others for concessional bargaining outcomes. This strategy was common throughout the industry during this period and the UFCW leadership seemingly collaborated as a means of defending its position in the industry. When Local P-9 (at Austin) moved to resist the new round of concessions, the UFCW leadership effectively sided with management. By the end of 1984, six of the eight plants in the Hormel group had signed the new, low-wage contract, with the seventh signing in early 1985. Austin remained the only plant where employees actively resisted management's plans (Schleuning 1994; Rachleff 1993, 1997).

Hormel's unionists at Austin rejected the company offer and struck on 17 August 1985. Despite Local P-9 having set up a picket – illegal under Minnesota state law – Hormel reopened the plant with 'scab' (non-unionized) workers in January 1986. By the end of June 1986, the UFCW had disendorsed Local P-9 and re-established a union presence (Local 9) at the plant among the strike-breakers. Despite widespread support, most strikers lost their jobs and the plant returned to full operations, with the 23 per cent pay cut and other lost entitlements firmly in place (Rachleff 1993; Schleuning 1994; Horowitz 1997; O'Leary and Sheldon 2009). While these legal, labour market and product market conditions were specific to Hormel during the Reagan administration, other key developments illustrate the impact of neoliberalism in the wider industry.

In other parts of the US meat processing industry, the major shifts in the political economy had a major, far-reaching impact on industrial relations strategies. One significant strategy, directly stemming from the shift in processing capacity from urban to rural areas and from the so-called 'Corn Belt' states in the northern mid-west to so-called 'right-to-work' states in the south, was the replacement of well-paid, unionized domestic workers in the meat-processing plants with low-paid, entirely immigrant workers, principally from Mexico (Champlin and Hake 2006). The importance of this strategy is revealed by the fact that, historically, the plants employing entirely immigrant workforces were in rural locations with non-existent Mexican populations.

These workers were imported into these communities for one purpose only, to replace well-paid, unionized domestic workers otherwise employed in other locations (Champlin and Hake 2006).

Australia

The political economy of the meat processing industry in Australia had, like its counterpart in the US, varied markedly over time, but in a quite different way. Until the early 1960s, Australian meat processing had been economically marginal, often going through long periods of poor profitability. However, export demand, particularly for beef, entered a boom cycle between 1975 and 1979, before collapsing in 1980 (O'Leary 2007, 2008; O'Leary and Sheldon 2012). During this five-year boom, meat processing capacity grew by more than 60 per cent. This expansion resulted in an under-utilization (over-capacity) of meat processing capacity once the boom had ended in the early 1980s. Over-capacity in Australian meat processing has been a chronic problem for much of its history but, this time, the problem re-emerged as a direct result of management decisions during the late 1970s.

Production over-capacity has also been a constant source of conflict between labour and capital, because shortages of cattle supply have exacerbated meatworkers' traditional lack of job security. To rationalize this over-capacity, in 1986, a group of larger Queensland meat industry companies formed a joint venture, Australia Meat Holdings (AMH). Although AMH was based predominantly within the Queensland beef sector, in 1988 it purchased another large meat processing company, Borthwick, which had several plants in Queensland and another plant at Portland in the south-western district of Victoria (O'Leary 2008; O'Leary and Sheldon 2009, 2012).

Running parallel with these labour market and product market shifts was the emerging, neoliberal inspired trend towards decentralization in industrial relations in Australia in the late 1980s. This, in turn, encouraged a number of employers to experiment with decollectivist strategies. One such example was AMH, particularly at its newly acquired plant in Portland, Victoria.

The Portland plant, with its strong exposure to beef-processing, became AMH senior management's priority, as an attempt to respond to the critical problem that over-capacity represented in the beef sector. A dispute occurred in a very tight product and labour market environment. The aim was to drive down labour costs and regain control of the labour process at the Portland plant. AMH's specific strategic objectives were to regain control of the labour process by killing off the local union structure and destroying worker militancy. While Borthwick's management had informally allowed the union to gain some degree of control of the labour process at Portland, AMH was determined to take back control (O'Leary and Sheldon 2009, 2012).

AMH successfully drove down wages and conditions at the Portland plant. AMH achieved this through a campaign fought partly at the community level through official support and the use of strike-breakers, partly by shifting slaughtering capacity to its Queensland plants and partly at the state level through a new, low-wage award from the Australian Industrial Relations Commission (referred to as the 'Commission'). The new award resulted in a $100 per week pay cut, increased workloads and decreased job security. The dispute ended with union acceptance of the new award and removal of the picket in July 1989. So, AMH, like Hormel several years earlier, successfully defeated significant local union solidarity through a strategy that reduced its dependence on the plant by shifting capacity to its other plants during the dispute. Both companies reduced their dependence on their respective plants, while isolating the dispute to their on-site workers, thus increasing the workers' dependence on the plant (O'Leary and Sheldon 2009, 2012).

Within weeks of the end of the Portland dispute, in 1989, all major meat processors in Victoria moved to duplicate the successes of AMH. What the employers in the Victorian industry were attempting to do was overturn the existing award, which provided for high wages and significant union control over the labour process. After two-and-a-half years of union resistance and significant processing time lost to wildcat strikes and retaliatory lockouts, the employers began to reach out to the union, as a result of the introduction of enterprise bargaining by the neoliberal state in 1991. This neoliberal decentralization strategy gave hard-pressed employers an opportunity to settle this protracted, costly and, ultimately, futile dispute. The focus on enterprise-based bargaining throughout the mid-1990s, encouraged by the more extensive neoliberal agenda of the conservative Government of Prime Minister John Howard, via the more extreme aspects of the WRA 1996, enabled management to contain labour costs and supply problems.

Following the success of AMH at Portland, Victorian exporters and domestic processors alike were concerned by the Portland outcome, for it reset the wage-effort bargain to their disadvantage. To achieve a similar outcome, and thus to remove their new competitive cost disadvantage, the other meat industry employers refused to honour or renegotiate all unregistered over-award agreements. They chose to carry out this strategy through their employer association, the Meat and Allied Trades Federation of Australia (MATFA) (O'Leary 2008).

Prior to 1989, most employers in Victoria had practised a type of active acquiescence to workplace-level union demands by including resulting improvements in wages and conditions in unregistered agreements (O'Leary 2008; O'Leary and Sheldon 2012). Companies such as Gilbertson in Altona North had handed over much of their primary bargaining responsibilities to the MATFA during the 1970s and 1980s. During a bitter and protracted dispute in Victoria between 1989 and 1992, this delegation of responsibility to their association intensified. This Victoria-wide dispute therefore intensified employer reliance on their association and the way this translated into new industrial relations objectives, policies and strategies (O'Leary 2008; O'Leary and Sheldon 2008). It also produced a highly confrontational approach to the union.

The Victoria-wide dispute started in July 1989, but followed in the wake of decisions by MATFA, meat employers and the Commission from late 1986 to mid-1989. Issues in this dispute included a claim by MATFA to return to a disused 1982 award, which would have resulted in a loss of $70 a week in pay by workers. MATFA also opposed registration of so-called S. 28 agreements under the 1904 Act, whereby the union had won wage increases for its members through variations in the award (O'Leary 2008). The union, for its part, sought a reduction in the working week to 38 hours, which had become standard in much of the private sector (O'Leary and Sheldon 2012). It initially secured a victory when the Commission agreed to vary the award to include a 38-hour week and what was called a 'second tier' pay increase, but it rejected the S. 28 agreement in March 1989 (O'Leary and Sheldon 2012). MATFA, with support from other employers, appealed against this decision to Full Bench of the Commission, applying for a minimum rates award containing bans clauses against industrial action. In September 1989, the Full Bench upheld MATFA's appeal against the 38 hour week, continued hearings into the minimum rates award and the bans clause and refused to register the S. 28 agreement (O'Leary and Sheldon 2012). The union responded by instituting rolling stoppages on a weekly basis at most export plants. The result was an unprecedented wave of strikes on 23 per cent of available working days over a period of two-and-a-half years (O'Leary and Sheldon 2012). MATFA applied to the Federal Court for the deregistration of the Australasian Meat Industry Employees' Union (AMIEU). However, in 1990, it agreed to a conditional stay of proceedings, mainly because the Commission had established a Meat Industry Enquiry a month earlier (O'Leary and Sheldon 2012). Nevertheless, the industrial campaign continued.

The actual breakdown of MATFA's campaign came, as in most sustained multi-employer campaigns, through key individual members reassessing and changing their strategy and other members following suit. In this particular campaign, the first member to reassess its strategy was G. and K. O'Connor at Pakenham. In October 1990, the union approached the company to discuss potential productivity-based agreements as a way to end the dispute and secure a pay rise for its members. MATFA had advised its members that they should not correspond with the union, so O'Connor's resigned from MATFA and began discussions with the union (O'Leary 2008; O'Leary and Sheldon 2008, 2012).

The first real breakthroughs came at Gilbertson's in Altona North and, a little later, O'Connor's in Pakenham. Within a matter of months, facing up to the enormous losses they had incurred during the long struggle, and with no immediate sign of victory in sight, almost every other Victorian meat processor had abandoned the MATFA model and adopted the Gilbertson's model. Thus, the vast majority of agreements that the Commission certified in the weeks and months after the Gilbertson's agreement were very similar to it. By the middle of 1993, there were some twenty-seven separate registered enterprise agreements in the Victorian meat processing industry. MATFA had

had little or no input into any of them (O'Leary 2008; O'Leary and Sheldon 2008, 2012). The industry in Victoria subsequently experienced very low levels of industrial conflict until the late 1990s, when another dispute, again inspired by the outcome of an AMH dispute, seriously disrupted the industry. It would therefore appear that, indeed, MATFA might have been the single greatest contributing factor to the protracted nature of the Victoria-wide dispute.

In the mid-1990s, AMH initiated another significant industrial dispute, this time at its four major plants in Queensland. The final settlement of this dispute, resulting in significant improvements in AMH's cost structures and, therefore, its competitive advantage in the labour and product markets, drove many of its competitors to seek alternative dispute resolution strategies (O'Leary 2007, 2008; O'Leary and Sheldon 2012). In the late 1990s, for example, due to significant supply constraints, some employers, including O'Connor's in Pakenham, attempted to deunionize their plants, drive down wages and conditions there and ultimately to individualize the employment relationship through AWAs. This strategy, inspired by the neoliberal policies of the Howard Government, resulted in the decollectivization of the O'Connor Pakenham plant and the significant reduction in labour costs but also significant labour-supply problems and the eventual engagement of refugee workers via the special 457-visa process (O'Leary 2008; Jerrard 2000; Tham and Campbell, 2011).

Conclusion

The neoliberal focus on the individual and the free market, has, when adopted by various governments around the world, rarely resulted in state withdrawal from the market, particularly from the labour market. In the US, for example, successive neoliberal administrations, starting with the Reagan presidency, intervened in the labour market supposedly to create a freer market. Reagan directly intervened in the air traffic controllers' strike in 1981 and subsequently intervened in labour market regulation, particularly through increased rights of employers to hire and fire, and through the appointment of strongly pro-employer officials to the National Labor Relations Board. These interventions encouraged employers in that country to decollectivize their workplaces. In meat processing, for example, this led to significant, direct attacks on union contract conditions, major employer industrial action, union concessional bargaining in the face of highly aggressive anti-union employer behaviour, the wholesale shifting of large parts of the meat processing industry to the so-called 'right-to-work' anti-union states in the south, and significant engagement of immigrant workers which avoided union wage rates and other long-fought-for working conditions. While these examples are particular to US meat processing, the meat industry in Australia experienced similar industrial pressures, particularly during the early 1980s.

In Australia, successive neoliberal Labor and Coalition Governments intervened in the labour market to create the conditions for a more decentralized system. The Hawke-Keating Labor Federal Government in the 1980s shifted the bargaining regime from collective national bargaining to work-place union and non-union bargaining. The Howard Coalition Government in the 1990s more actively intervened in the labour market to shift bargaining towards the individual, through AWAs, and through strongly anti-union regulations. These interventions encouraged some employers in this country to decollectivize their workplaces. In meat processing, for example, this led to significant, direct attacks on union bargaining arrangements, major employer industrial action, widespread workplace bargaining with the unions and even the shifting of the wage-effort bargain to the individual, through AWAs and the engagement of low cost immigrant workers via 457 visas.

Neoliberalism, as a political economy movement, has largely failed to live up to its utopian ideals of the withdrawal of the state from the market, including the labour market. Despite this, neoliberal programmes have significantly shifted the bargaining arrangements in industries such as meat processing, creating opportunities for redirecting employer strategy and behaviour. In this context, it could be suggested that neoliberalism created a new landscape within which employers could exercise greater discretion over their industrial relations strategic choosing and, therefore, strategy-making. What this chapter argues is that active neoliberal intervention in the labour market in both the US and Australia has significantly affected the 'wage-effort bargain', the labour process and the bargaining arrangements in the meat processing industry in both countries.

In line with the focus of this book as a whole, one should say something about a way forward from here, one that can both advance political ideas, as well as advance worker collective rights. In light of the all-pervasive and stubborn nature of neoliberalism within the modern political discourse in the US and Australia, among other countries, there is a need to think in more contemporary ways about industrial relations and not long for the old industrial relations institutions and the old, seemingly outdated, notions of pluralism which underpinned them. Ackers (2002, 2014) and Kahn and Ackers (2004) argue that a way through this confusion is to reframe industrial relations (employment relations) through the lens of neo-pluralism. They suggest that state policy focus on regulating the labour market, rather than act as a night-watchman, as espoused by neoliberals. They go on to reject the neoliberal notions of market domination and managerial unitarism in favour of 'associational' social relations and workplace partnerships, which include references to the so-called 'old institutions' and to trade unions. These prescriptions need further development at an industrial relations and societal level.

Notes

1 The author acknowledges that sections of the chapter are derived from research associated with the author's PhD thesis, which was also the basis for O'Leary and Sheldon (2012). The author also acknowledges the significant contribution of Associate Professor Peter Sheldon, PhD supervisor and co-author, to this body of research.

2 Successively through the *Industrial Relations Act 1988*, the *Industrial Relations Reform Act 1993*, the *Workplace Relations Act (WRA) 1996* and the *Workplace Relations (WorkChoices) Act 2005*.
3 Smallgoods is a generic Australian term for processed and edible meat by-products, such as ham, bacon, sausages and salami, etc.

References

Ackers, P. (2002), Reframing Employment Relations: The Case for Neo-Pluralism, *Industrial Relations Journal* 33(1), pp. 2–19.

Ackers, P. (2014), Rethinking the Employment Relationship: A Neo-Pluralist Critique of British Industrial Relations Orthodoxy, *International Journal of Human Resource Management* 25(18), pp. 2608–2625.

Azzam, A. (1998), Competition in the US Meatpacking Industry: Is it History? *Agricultural Economics* 18(2), pp. 107–126.

Azzam, A. and Anderson, D. (1996), *Assessing Competition in Meatpacking: Economic History, Theory, and Evidence*. Washington, DC: United States Department of Agriculture.

Boxall, P. and Haynes, P. (1997), Strategy and Trade Union Effectiveness in a Neo-liberal Environment, *British Journal of Industrial Relations* 35(4), pp. 567–591.

Bray, M. and Underhill, E. (2009), Industry Differences in the Neoliberal Transformation of Australian Industrial Relations, *Industrial Relations Journal* 40(5), pp. 372–392.

Cahill, D. (2004), *The Radical Neo-liberal Movement as a Hegemonic Force in Australia, 1976–1996*. Wollongong, Australia: PhD thesis, University of Wollongong.

Champlin, D. and Hake, E. (2006), Immigration as Industrial Strategy in American Meatpacking, *Review of Political Economy* 18(1), pp. 49–69.

Chang, H. (2002), Breaking the Mould: An Institutionalist Political Economy Alternative to the Neo-liberal Theory of the Market and the State, *Cambridge Journal of Economics* 26(5), pp. 539–559.

Considine, M. and Painter, M. (1998), *Managerialism: The Great Debate*. Melbourne: Melbourne University Press.

Craypo, C. (1994), Meatpacking: Industry Restructuring and Union Decline, in P. Voos (ed.), *Contemporary Collective Bargaining in the Private Sector*. Madison, WI, USA: Industrial Relations Research Association, pp. 63–96.

Farber, H. and Western, B. (2002), Ronald Reagan and the Politics of Declining Union Organization, *British Journal of Industrial Relations* 40(3), pp. 385–401.

Harvey, D. (2007), *A Brief History of Neoliberalism*. Oxford, UK: Oxford University Press.

Hood, C. (1991), A Public Management for all Seasons? *Public Administration* 69(1), pp. 3–19.

Hood, C. (1995), Emerging Issues in Public Administration, *Public Administration* 73(3), pp. 165–185.

Horowitz, R. (1997), *Negro and White, Unite and Fight: A Social History of Industrial Unionism in Meatpacking, 1930–1990*. Chicago: University of Illinois Press.

Jerrard, M. (2000), Dinosaurs Are Not Dead: The AMIEU (Qld) and Industrial Relations Change, *Journal of Industrial Relations* 40(1), pp. 5–28.

Kahn, A.S. and Ackers, P. (2004), Neo-Pluralism as a Theoretical Framework for Understanding HRM in Sub-Saharan Africa, *International Journal of Human Resource Management* 15(7), pp. 1330–1353.

Kochan, T., McKersie, R. and Cappelli, P. (1984), Strategic Choice and Industrial Relations Theory, *Industrial Relations* 23(1), pp. 16–39.

Kochan, T., Katz, H. and McKersie, R. (1986), *The Transformation of American Industrial Relations*. New York: Basic Books.

Lewin, D. (1987), Industrial Relations as a Strategic Variable, in M. Kleiner, R. Block, M. Roomkin, and S. Salsburg (eds.), *Human Resources and the Performance of the Firm*. Madison, WI, USA: Industrial Relations Research Association, pp. 1–43.

O'Leary, P. (2007), Strategic Choice in the Australian Meat Processing industry: A Case Study Analysis, in *Proceedings of the 15th conference of the International Employment Relations Association, Canterbury*. Canterbury, UK: Canterbury Christ Church University.

O'Leary, P. (2008), *Employers and Industrial Relations in the Australian Meat Processing Industry: An Historical Analysis*. Sydney: PhD thesis, University of New South Wales.

O'Leary, P. and Sheldon, P. (2008), Strategic Choices and Unintended Consequences: Employer Militancy and Industrial Relations in Victoria's Meat Industry, 1986–1993. *Labour History* 95 (Nov), pp. 223–242.

O'Leary, P. and Sheldon, P. (2009), Multi-plant Capacity, Employer Strategy and Industrial Conflict in Meatpacking: Hormel, US (1985–1986) and Portland, Australia (1988–1989), in *Proceedings of the 23rd Association of Industrial Relations Academics in Australia and New Zealand (AIRAANZ) Conference*. Newcastle, Australia: Newcastle Business School, Faculty of Business and Law, The University of Newcastle.

O'Leary, P. and Sheldon, P. (2012), *Employer Power and Weakness: How Local and Global Factors Have Shaped Australia's Meat Industry and its Industrial Relations*. Ballarat, Australia: VURRN Press.

Osborne, T. and Gaebler, T. (1992), *Reinventing Government: How the Entrepreneurial Spirit is Transforming Government*. Reading, MA, USA: Addison Wesley Publishing Co.

Peck, J. and Tickell, A. (2007), Conceptualizing Neoliberalism, Thinking Thatcherism, in H. Leitner, J. Peck and E. Sheppard (eds.), *Contesting Neoliberalism: Urban Frontiers*. New York: The Guildford Press.

Perren, R. (2006), *Taste, Trade and Technology: The Development of the International Meat Industry since 1840*. Aldershot, UK: Ashgate Publishing.

Rachleff, P. (1993), *Hard-Pressed in the Heartland: The Hormel Strike and the Future of the Labor Movement*. Boston, MA, USA: South End Press.

Rachleff, P. (1997), Cram Your Spam: Remembering the Hormel Strike, *The Baffler* 9. At http://thebaffler.com/salvos/cram-your-spam, accessed 13 September 2015.

Rudd, K. (2009), The Global Financial Crisis: The End of Neo-liberalism. *The Monthly*, February, pp. 20–29.

Schleuning, N. (1994), *Women, Community and the Hormel Strike of 1985–86*. London: Greenwood Press.

Tham, J. and Campbell, I. (2011), Temporary Migrant Labour in Australia: The 457 Visa Scheme and Challenges for Labour Regulation, Working Paper No. 50. Melbourne: Centre for Employment and Labour Relations Law, University of Melbourne.

18 Neoliberalism after the global financial crisis

A reconsideration

M.C. Howard

In this chapter I will evaluate the effects of the financial crisis on neoliberalism and mainstream macroeconomic theory, and will do so through the analysis provided in *The Rise of Neoliberalism in Advanced Capitalist Economies* (*RONACE*[1]). I will emphasize what the book said about neoliberal finance, and will concentrate mainly on the US and the UK, which are the most developed neoliberal capitalisms and homes to the two principal financial centres. Of course, the majority of the economies of the European Union and Japan are all advanced capitalist economies (ACEs) and some have large financial sectors, but they are less amenable to analysis at the present time or of secondary relevance to the concerns of this chapter. The EU may well be undergoing a collapse, and if it does survive it will have to constitute basic financial institutions, including a union fiscal centre, a banking union and a proper European central bank, all of which are integral to *all* capitalist finance and not only to its neoliberal forms (Lapavitsas 2013, pp. 300–5). Therefore, the fate of finance in the EU is especially uncertain. And because of its development model, Japan has played a relatively minor role in global finance in the neoliberal era, and especially during the period since the beginning of its long stagnation in the early 1990s, which resulted from a large financial crisis nearly twenty years in advance of the other ACEs (Eichengreen 2011, pp. 44–45, 127).

The manuscript of *RONACE* was delivered to the publisher in mid-2007 and the book was published in mid-2008, several months before the financial crisis began in the US with the bankruptcy of Lehman Brothers.[2] However, the book argued that a serious financial crisis was likely in the near future, and would also bring a reversal of neoliberalism in the ACEs, and it is this claim that will be evaluated in this chapter. Before doing so, though, I will outline the type of theory employed in *RONACE* to explain neoliberalism, and then focus on one crucial aspect of this type of capitalism; namely, financialization.

The theory used in *RONACE* to explain neoliberalism in all the ACEs was historical materialism, and it was embraced as a general account of economic, political and ideological systems, not only as a theory of neoliberal capitalism. Since historical materialism is often regarded as the grandest of grand narratives, it is important to stress that neither John King nor I wholly abandoned scepticism in favour of allegiance to a teleology. We were very well aware of the many criticisms of the doctrine, and indeed added a few of our own (Howard and King 1985, 1989, 1992, 1994). Moreover, we were cognizant of the great difficulties faced in explaining anything conclusively. All theory is underdetermined by the facts (Gellner 1974), and there are special difficulties in explaining human behaviour. A key point was made by Karl Popper – it is impossible to know the trajectory of social development without knowing future knowledge, which is logically impossible (Popper 1957). And the results of social theorizing can affect the material that is the subject of theorizing in ways unknown in the natural sciences (McCloskey 1990). Similarly, laboratory experiments allowing the separation of causal forces, and thereby grounding conditional forecasts, are not possible for historical processes. These three obstacles are reinforced by a variety of other considerations, including those stressed by heterodox economists regarding the importance of radical uncertainty in human decision-making. Furthermore, while human nature is such as to allow a structuralist account of behaviour, the shorter the time frame and the more concentrated is power the greater are the degrees of freedom allowing decisions to be at variance with systemic imperatives (Mills 1959). There are also the pervasive forces of randomness and opportunism to contend with (Taleb 2004, 2007; Williamson 1985, 1996).

These difficulties had long been a concern to us before we published *RONACE* but what weighed most was the fact that leading economists of all major schools proved to be completely wrong about the development of neoliberal capitalism. Marxians, Austrians, Keynesians, neoclassicals and institutionalists all stressed that the trends of modernity included the decline of the market. Since none of these people was known to be stupid or ignorant, it was an especially sobering reminder to anyone attempting to explain neoliberalism, and most of all for those who would seek to do so in terms of a grand narrative. In consequence, while we sought a high degree of explanatory determinism, we were cautious. I will endeavour to continue in this vein in this reconsideration.

The nature of neoliberal capitalism

However, one matter on which we were very definite was that neoliberalism was not a return to the world of classical liberalism. By contrast, neoliberalism involves political agencies acting as financiers and regulators of markets on a grand scale, and extending marketization into their own operations and programmes, many of which originated in the era of the 'mixed economy' after World War II.[3] Thus neoliberal capitalism does not entail a reduced presence for states and their activities. Most of what is financed by states, including health and education services, along with the 'safety net', are crucial to the efficient functioning of other sectors of the economy. However, the hallmark of neoliberalism is that they are supplied more by private corporations that are contracted to do so by public authorities, and delivered more through markets and market-mimicking mechanisms. It is only those parts of the 'welfare state' most at variance with maintaining market dependence of the able-bodied poor that have significantly contracted in the ACEs.[4]

Classical liberal concepts of the autonomous individual, the negative conception of freedom, the minimal state and market competition are still employed ideologically. But typically they are joined to displacements reflective of neo-liberal realities. Neoliberal capitalism tends to rationalize, instrumentalize, commodify and monetize all human attributes and social relationships. Thus new conceptions of individuals as consumers, embodied skill sets and commercial innovators have emerged. Culture has become a matter for the entertainment industry, education is seen as the acquisition of human capital and states are frequently thought of as businesses or corporations. Today there are no liberal political parties that are not neoliberal, and their main competitors have similarly moved. During the twentieth century social democrats made their peace with capitalism and conservatives accommodated themselves to mass democracy and the welfare state. And with the development of neoliberalism since the 1970s, they too have transitioned to new categories suited to neo-liberal realities. So far as economists are concerned, neoclassical orthodoxy has converged to neoliberalism. We documented this at various points in *RONACE*, but other examples are easily given. For instance, Eugene Fama, the originator of the modern version of the 'efficient market hypothesis', and Robert Shiller, his principal critic, are both neoliberal, differing only as to the specific marketizations and regulatory structures that are most appropriate for neoliberal finance.

Explaining neoliberal capitalism

RONACE sought to understand neoliberal capitalism in the terms of historical materialism.[5] This theory claims that the character of the productive forces (including technology) determines the productive relations (economic system), which determines the superstructure (political and legal regime), to which correspond particular forms of social consciousness (ideology). Moreover, we claimed, tentatively, its relevance to pre-modern history and, with more con-fidence, its explanatory power for modernity. However, we utilized historical materialism in a restructured form which disabled some criticisms of the doctrine. The teleology of liberation in terms of realizing 'species being' makes no appearance, the role of class struggle was minimized in explaining neoliberalism and there was a great deal of conceptual renovation.

During the previous half century, analytic philosophers have redefined the basic concepts of historical materialism in ways that protect the main propo-sitions from the logical problems inherent in earlier formulations (Cohen 1978; Torrance 1995). For example, this involved clarifying that the produc-tive forces included productive knowledge as well as labour power and the skills of labour, so that the antonym of material is 'social', not 'mental'. The productive relations are social relations, conceived as 'powers', or 'roles', not 'rights', which fall into the domain of the superstructure. And, social consciousness is understood non-reductively in terms of Weber's concept of 'elective affinity', in which ideas express the interests defined by the productive relations and their superstructural analogues (Gerth and Mills 1948, pp. 62–63, 284–85). Moreover, when it is said that the productive forces determine the productive relations, or the productive relations determine the superstructure, the causal relations are deemed to be 'functional', so that, for instance, the economic system is as it is because it is most appropriate for the development of the productive forces at the current state of their development. Similarly, the superstructure is as it is because it is most appropriate for securing the productive relations.

Obviously, even if all logical criticisms are thereby refuted, this does not establish the empirical truth of the theory. For that to be substantiated the links of functional causation have to be supplemented with 'selection mechanisms', operating on the basis of a transhistorical human nature, and which correctly explain the functional correspondences in terms of human actions. *RONACE* referred to five such mechanisms: human rationality, competition, disruptions occasioned by exogenous shocks, group conflicts and geopolitical rivalries. All operate on the basis of a human nature which includes being intelligent, somewhat rational and orientated to overcoming scarcity, so humans possess both the motivation and the capacities to develop the productive forces. But we also recognized this drive toward increasing productive power is constrained by a human nature that also seeks security (safety) and identity (meaning), and explain why these two constraints do not normally operate wholly to counter the drive to overcome scarcity.[6] Any such prioritization of the need for security and meaning will tend to be episodic because these non-economic needs can be satisfied in a multitude of ways compared with overcoming scarcities, and therefore can more easily adapt to the economic in the long run compared to the economic adapting to the dictates of security and identity. Thus, the historical materialism we utilized is not a philosophic materialism which treats human activity and consciousness as epiphenomenal. The 'material' in historical materialism includes some human knowledge, some human capabilities and some human needs, and the historical process is seen as one involving human actions and creativity.[7] And the historical materialism of *RONACE* was inherently pluralistic in recognizing a place for multiple perspectives and theories that concern how the determinants of human action work out over time.

Much of *RONACE* was devoted to explaining how changes in the productive forces during the twentieth century, and especially from the 1970s, promoted change in capitalist relationships in a neoliberal direction. In some cases the cause was direct, when new technologies made market provision more efficient. In other cases the cause was more roundabout, as with rising productivity in pre-neoliberal forms of capitalism bringing about changes in consumer behaviour that promoted neoliberal capitalism. There was also an extensive discussion of the historical trajectory in which neoliberal changes actually occurred (Howard and King 2008, chapters 2, 6, 7).

The book also pointed to strengths of historical materialism compared to alternative forms of explanation. Those that prioritize the importance of 'ideas' in explaining the development of neoliberalism were shown to be exceedingly weak because the examination of the history of economic thought revealed that the intellectually dominant ideas into the 1970s held that there was a trend toward market elimination in the ACEs. Since 2008, there have been other attempts to explain neoliberalism by the influence of thinkers connected to the Mont Pèlerin Society.[8] But not only do they neglect the wider history of economic thought, they pay no attention to the very serious and damaging critiques levelled at Hayek and the Chicago School who play the chief role in the stories they tell. They also neglect to mention that many of the ideas of the Chicago School were abandoned by governments very early in the neoliberal era, including Friedman's monetarism and New Classical macroeconomics. Most serious of all, they fail to recognize that Chicago economists were, and remain, much closer to classical liberalism than they are to neoliberalism.[9]

Historical sociologists have proved more informative on matters related to neoliberalism (notably Mann 2012, 2013). But they have a problem with causation, in which the different 'powers' of social life (economic, ideological, military and political) are treated as having causal autonomy, with no power being primary. There is no specification of the general principles explaining why at any specific time one particular constellation of social powers was dominant rather than another. Instead, events are described and the complex of causal imputation that seems to fit best is utilized, in a way not altogether different from narrative historians dealing with 'one damn thing after another'. *RONACE* traced the sequence of factors that brought about neoliberalism in the 1970s, and retarded it prior to these years, but both were informed by historical materialism as to the hierarchy of causal forces.

Many other explanations of neoliberalism are circular, pointing to the effect that one aspect of neoliberalism has on others. These have sometimes been very useful (as will become clear in the next section), but they cannot be explanations of the change from one form of capitalism to another. The development of financialization, globalization, privatization, deregulation, flexible labour markets and so forth, form a loop of causation in which each component tends to reinforce the others. Consequently, the crucial question is what determines the loop itself. The answer of *RONACE* was in terms of historical materialism, where the productive forces are primary. And it is the development of computers, combined with statistics and big data, which is at the heart of the new general-purpose technology that in recent decades has engendered neoliberal capitalism.[10] They have revolutionized computation, data storage and analysis, communications, monitoring and surveillance, along with much else, and in so doing have significantly changed advanced capitalist economies by promoting marketization and globalization. In the forefront were changes in finance, and these changes have been powerful forces neoliberalizing other sectors of these economies.

The nature of neoliberal finance

RONACE treated finance as infrastructural in all types of capitalism because economic activity is not only commodified, it is also monetized. And, since most money is created by financial institutions in the form of credit, the financial system is, metaphorically speaking, the headquarters of the capitalist system (Schumpeter 1934, chapter III). It determines more than any other sector the allocation of capital and the distribution of risks and is therefore central to the activities of producers, consumers and governments (Crane 1995). Furthermore, in the neoliberal era, finance is infrastructural for the American Empire. The US rules most of the globe in a hub and spoke structure of nation states and capitalist relations, with Wall Street the largest financial centre, the American financial markets the most liquid and the US dollar the key currency, all of which contributes to American geopolitical dominance.[11]

Neoliberal finance involves what is frequently referred to as 'financialization'. Finance expands in size relative to other sectors, financial relations widen to include more transactions and they deepen in complexity. Many institutions grow to enormous size and supply the full array of financial products and services.[12] Others, including investment banks, become much larger and change into corporations with limited liability. Credit provision is significantly rationalized, frequently operating at arm's length on the basis of formalized risk calculations. New financial instruments proliferate along with an enlarged and more complicated structure of private debt. Regulations change to accommodate all this, but financial institutions and financial markets remain subject to huge array of rules concerning capital ratios, deposit-taking, risk exposure, reporting and disclosure, corporate governance, credit rating standards, fraud and due diligence. And all governments have an array of financial ministries and agencies to monitor compliance.

Financialization has been the proximate cause of extending neoliberalism to many other sectors of the economy.[13] A central role was played by the development of the science of 'quantitative finance' in the post-war years. Harry Markowitz provided a theory of optimal portfolio selection, William Sharpe derived the capital asset pricing model, Franco Modigliani and Merton Miller began the rigorous analysis of the determinants of equity-debt mix in corporate funding, Eugene Fama formulated the efficient market hypothesis and Michael Jensen applied the results to the incentive systems for corporate executives, while Fisher Black and Myron Scholes extended asset pricing theory to options.[14] The practicality of using all the results was transformed by improvements in computer technologies in the 1970s and 1980s, which also proved to be an important force behind changes to financial regulation so as to facilitate innovation in financial organization and financial instruments.

Prior to the 1980s, corporations were frequently vertically integrated con-glomerates of diverse activities, managed by executives whose incomes were heavily taxed, and whose remuneration was thus usually augmented through occupational perks which escaped income taxes, while they financed company investments primarily through retained earnings. Non-financial corporations were thus substantially 'free' from the control of the financial sector. All this began to change in the 1980s. Executive remuneration became much more closely related to changes in 'shareholder value' by being linked to the stock price of their firms, and was subject to far lower marginal rates of taxation, which often incentivized the substitution of debt for equity in order to lever-age profits. The same changes to incentives included financial institutions too, resulting in a large increase in indebtedness to finance their own activities. The focus on shareholder value often brought a specialization on core com-petence, resulting in a decline in vertical and horizontal integration. Coupled to much less restricted capital mobility and electronic monitoring technology, much of this went hand in hand with globalization. Complex supply chains resulted, requiring much denser structures of payments and receipts, as well as containing many new risks and taxation options, all of which brought more intimate relations with large, universal and globalized banks (Cortada 2011; Head 2013; Helpman 2011).[15]

Successive American and British governments played a particularly coopera-tive role in facilitating all of these changes. In both countries, strategic thinkers and ruling elites became increasingly of the mind during the 1970s that their countries were in 'relative decline', and they sought means of reversal. Neoliberalizing finance was a major component of this, together with other changes that reinforced it, such as ending capital controls, lowering marginal rates of taxation and ensuring labour markets were more 'flexible'. And since all this went with the grain of the new productive forces, the US and the UK were followed at varying speeds by the other ACEs.

The effects have not been confined to production, but have also had a dramatic impact on consumption. Consumer credit has mushroomed along with the means of accessing it and hedging the risks involved in doing so. No doubt, this was influenced by the changes in corporate organization and management just discussed because they resulted in a substitution out of defined benefit occupational pension plans and into defined contribution plans. The management of financial assets thereby became a significant problem for many middle class and working class individuals, and their demand for financial services increased. But there were other changes taking place with the same effects, including increases in the ownership of houses and consumer durables, all of which needed financing. And, most important of all, disposable incomes had risen dramatically in the 'golden age' growth of the early post-war years, making the mass of the population far more 'credit worthy',[16] and at the very time consumption was becoming more of a cultural experience conferring meaning on life (Baudrillard 1970; Hirsch 1976).

All credit provision was progressively subject to rationalization by assessing recipients in terms of computerized models of risk rather than in the more personalized ways of assessment prior to neoliberalization. And financial institutions moved from an 'originate and hold' model to one of 'originate and distribute' securitized loans, which again was made possible by the new computational technologies married to statistics and big data. This underpinned claims of a revolution in risk assessment and risk allocation, with some economists even claiming that the world of advanced capitalism was moving much closer to that of the perfectly efficient Arrow-Debreu model of complete markets in contingent commodities (Ross 1976; see also Athreya 2013).

The neoliberal financial crisis

The financial crisis revealed clear fault lines in all of this because it was very much a crisis of neoliberal finance. However, it is also true that the 'particular' lies within the 'general' (Eichengreen 1992, 2011, 2015; Kindleberger 1996; Krugman 2012; Wolf 2014; Reinhart and Rogoff 2009) and the most important feature of capitalist finance for understanding recurring instability is Hyman Minsky's depiction of the process of increasing financial fragility (Minsky 1986). This periodically makes an appearance unless there is significant financial repression in place. Stability itself generates instability because it involves low volatility, which generates a lower pricing of risk, and this encourages risk-taking. The process becomes self-reinforcing because finance is the principal sector of an economy whose own actions impact on itself in the form of signals which create positive feedback. In this way, credit expansion indicates that further credit expansion is profitable, bringing about a degrading in the quality of debt and, ultimately, a financial crisis. The process then works in reverse as a consequence of a credit crunch sending signals which encourage further credit contraction. That is why *RONACE* argued that a financial crisis would occur in neoliberal capitalism, even though we were not aware of where and when it would appear.[17]

As already noted, it took a very neoliberal form. The original disturbance arose in securitized American mortgages that had fuelled the preceding real estate boom beginning at the turn of the century. Several years later, rising interest rates made mortgages with adjustable rates more expensive and resulted in increased foreclosures between 2005 and 2007. House prices actually began to fall in early 2008, which made financial problems connected to housing even worse. Nonetheless, real GDP growth in 2006 and 2007 still stood at around 2 per cent, and the unemployment rate held fairly steady. There was some financial distress on Wall Street, but the Federal Reserve and the US Treasury managed the system, including the incorporation of the investment bank Bear Stearns, which was heavily invested in securitized mortgages and therefore weak, into the stronger JP Morgan Chase, and approving the takeover of Merrill Lynch by Bank of America. This involved some departures from previous practices, but in the implementation details including overt subsidization of the Bear Stearns merger with public money, not in the overall strategy of repairing problems of financial fragility as they materialized (Blinder 2013, chapter 5).

The discontinuity came in September 2008 when Lehman Brothers found itself in similar difficulties to Bear Stearns. This time the Federal Reserve and the US Treasury acted completely differently, and allowed the company to go bankrupt. This was a sharp change in policy for which no warning had been issued, and it brought about the crisis. 'The U.S. economy was crawling along that summer ... hardly in great shape but neither was it a disaster area. It wasn't even clear that we were headed for a recession, never mind the worst recession since the 1930s. Then came the failure of Lehman Brothers ... on September 15, 2008, and everything fell apart' (Blinder 2013, p. 3; see also Lybeck 2011, p. 369).

The act of allowing a moderately sized investment bank to fail brought on the neoliberal equivalent of an old-fashioned 'bank run'. The new version centred on the wholesale money markets which all financial institutions used to leverage their own activities. There was 'contagion'[18] and the markets ceased to function for the very good reason that no lender knew the true financial health of borrowers, and feared that Lehman might only be the first of a series of bankruptcies.[19] The seize-up was global because the leading financial institutions and markets were global. The markets were only coaxed back into operation, and further bankruptcies stopped, through radical action by central banks and finance ministries, including capital injections by public agencies and state guarantees of the debts of private financial institutions, as well as central banks extending swap facilities to each other on an unprecedented scale.[20] These actions stopped the financial meltdown, but did not curtail the reverse Minsky process of credit contraction or stop the onset of depression conditions. Financial institutions attempted to deleverage by selling assets, and cut back on renewing loans. In other words there was a classic credit crunch, forcing deleveraging on other debtors, so bringing about a sharp contraction in aggregate demand in most of the ACEs.

These events were very revealing as to the nature of the neoliberal financial system in at least five ways. First, they confirm that the US is the hub of the whole system. As such, the global crisis was a failure of the American Empire in the sense specified by hegemonic stability theory.[21] Second, they also confirm that finance is infrastructural in all ACEs, and in much the same way as the electricity grid or transportation system is infrastructural. If they are destroyed, so is the rest of the economy, and in short order. Third, it is evident that state failure played a major role in causing the financial crisis of 2008, and not just in the US. The governments and central banks of the ACEs had intervened repeatedly since at least the 1980s to protect 'their' financial institutions and markets. They had used their own power and that of international agencies like the International Monetary Fund (IMF) to ensure that international debtors to banks in the ACEs paid their creditors. Prior to the Lehman bankruptcy, whenever finance malfunctioned in the homelands of capitalism, they came to the rescue. Not surprisingly, financial firms and markets factored this into their (rational) expectations, and conducted their activities accordingly by raising their risk exposures because this increased their returns. In other words, state regulatory agencies created moral hazard on a grand scale, and when the US Treasury and Federal Reserve behaved inconsistently in September 2008, they triggered the crisis. Fourth, as it presently stands, neoliberal finance is a system where state and private institutions intimately intertwine, and the former cannot limit themselves to regulation and liquidity provision. They have to act as guarantors of all systemically significant financial institutions and all systemically significant contracts on financial markets. The capitalist rules of the game are very different from those for non-financial organizations and markets.[22]

Fifth, the previous two observations might suggest that neoclassical macroeconomics can claim a degree of validity because they allow the bankruptcy of Lehman Brothers to be classified as an exogenous shock. However, the conception of shocks in neoclassical macroeconomics does not obviously extend to this event.[23] And if the concept of 'shock' were expanded to incorporate events such as the Lehman bankruptcy, this would require jettisoning the efficient market hypothesis as operative in the preceding years since the moral hazard induced by the expected behaviour of the public authorities must have distorted market prices considerably. This would have hugely negative implications for the rest of neoclassical macroeconomic theory. Furthermore, the evidence of economic contraction after the financial crisis is not consistent with neoclassicism since most of the data has a Keynesian signature involving an effective demand failure, which neoclassical macroeconomics does not recognize as possible under any circumstances (see e.g. Lazear and Spletzer 2012). Moreover, predictions based upon neoclassical macroeconomics as to the consequences of states running large fiscal deficits and substantially expanding their monetary base have proved wholly at variance with actual consequences: interest rates have not risen, and inflation has not accelerated. In short, the experience of the financial crisis and its aftermath has comprehensively rubbished neoclassical macroeconomic theory.

Neoliberal financial reform

Does all this mean that neoliberal finance operates to impede the reproduction of neoliberal capitalism in a manner most conducive to the growth of productive power? In its present form, it certainly does. Without changes that significantly reduce financial fragility, there will be new crises, and they could well have much more destructive effects than those of 2008.[24] However, it is highly unlikely that financial fragility can ever be entirely eliminated in neoliberal finance, and the best that can be achieved is that the incidence and severity be reduced, thereby allowing the productive effects of finance to predominate.[25]

One might think that the most obvious way to do this would be to return to something similar to the kind of financial repression that prevailed from the

1930s to the 1970s. However, not only would such reforms kill off much of neoliberal capitalism generally, they would not foster development of the productive forces, and would not work to preserve financial stability. The 'sound' financial conditions of the 'Golden Age' had as much to do with rapid economic growth and the stability of economic conditions that prevailed, especially the stability of interest rates, inflation and exchange rates, as they did with financial repression. The Bretton Woods system which did a great deal to ensure this tranquillity collapsed because of its own contradictions, as *RONACE* made clear (Howard and King 2008, chapter 7; see also Eichengreen 2008), and from the early 1970s there was lower economic growth and much more volatility in interest rates, inflation and exchange rates. It was this that brought about the bulk of the deregulation that ended the financial repression, rather than the other way round.[26]

The central issue in the reform of neoliberal finance is to improve significantly the self-regulating properties of the financial system as a whole, not just that of the 'private sector'. So far as the public component is concerned, regulators must be given less discretion except in emergencies. This would make for clarity and stop problems festering as they do now. For example, if a bank falls below the mandated capital ratio, dividends to shareholders should be prohibited until capital is raised sufficiently to meet the capital requirements. And if the assets of banks fall in value, their pricing in the bank's accounts should immediately reflect this. In short, regulations need to be enforced in a clear and simple manner, which is not always done at present, and was certainly not done in the past (Financial Crisis Inquiry Commission 2011). Furthermore, regulation must have comprehensive coverage, including the shadow banking system.[27] So far as the private sector is concerned, the fragility of financial institutions and the fragility of the financial system must both be reduced. This translates into lowering bank leverage, and eliminating those inter-connections of the financial system which could underpin possible contagions. In more concrete terms, the following measures are needed.

First, in order to minimize disruption and contagion, a bankruptcy resolution procedure for financial institutions needs to be created that would maintain the operations of any insolvent institution until its positions are unwound in an orderly fashion, with the losses concentrated upon shareholders and bond-holders, and with contractual counterparties in short-term borrowing contracts substantially protected by insurance facilities. Second, to reduce the incidence of bankruptcies, financial institutions must be strengthened. The simplest way to do this is to increase their minimum capital-asset ratios significantly, which would also have the beneficial effect of increasing the incentive for equity holders to monitor the executives that manage the institutions they own.[28]

Third, since moral hazard would remain, speculation must be contained. The most straightforward manner in which to achieve this is to prohibit deposit-taking institutions from such activity, and place high margin requirements on other institutions. (Margin requirements are really transaction specific capital ratios.) Fourth, and in the same spirit, fraud and failures of 'due diligence' need to be prosecuted and carry severe penalties if prosecutions are successful. Ideally, this would include individual executives, as well as the corporations involved, and should not be limited to the 'small fry'.

Fifth, and finally, regulators need to focus much more on matters of systemic stability. The issue here is to improve the robustness of the interconnections of financial institutions and markets. Limiting regulation to individual institutions and markets is inadequate because they cannot properly assess risks without full information on systemic properties, which they do not generally have and lack the power to obtain. Nonetheless, one component of this endeavour to increase systemic stability should be to increase the transparency of transactions and positions held by individual institutions. The oxymoronic 'off-balance sheet' activities should be brought onto balance sheets, customized 'over the counter' derivatives reduced, secret trading strategies prohibited, and full disclosure of all positions held made mandatory. But the overall system also needs to be subjected to much more surveillance, including a close examination of new financial instruments, and with potential instabilities anticipated and stress tests (including contagion possibilities) done as a matter of routine.[29]

Implementing such measures would significantly strengthen financial institutions and the financial system of which they are parts. They would also reduce financialization. The size of the financial institutions and of the financial system would contract because private costs would rise closer to social costs, and the complexity and interconnectedness of the system would fall. And both of these effects could be expected to engender some roll back of neoliberalism more generally given the huge effect financialization has had on promoting neoliberalism.[30] However, this would not induce inefficiency precisely because the reforms would align private and social costs of financial activities. Neoliberal capitalism would become *more,* not less, efficient in promoting the development of productive power.

The operative question, however, is whether these types of reform are being implemented in the principal financial centres, and on the required scale. This is currently a somewhat opaque matter. Regulatory reform is very much still 'work in progress' and statements by government officials are often misleading. This is because agreements at the international level need to be embodied in national laws before they become effective. Such legislation, in turn, often treats only generalities and has to be translated into regulations by regulatory bodies in consultation with financial organizations (see e.g. Wolf 2014, pp. 232–37). Furthermore, many requirements that have been legislated will not come into force for many years, so facilitating the development of evasion strategies and lobbying for modification or reversal. The lobbying by financial interests can be intense and is greatly aided by the fact that the financial centres are in competition with each other. Nonetheless, even with all this indeterminacy recognized, the reforms actually being enacted appear to be overly modest.

True, both the US and the UK have legislated new bankruptcy resolution procedures that are very similar.

However, the challenge of effective resolution of large, complex financial institutions such as JP Morgan Chase ... is daunting. Such institutions have thousands of subsidiaries, or other related entities, many of them in different countries.... Resolution would require coordination between ... authorities and procedures, which may be incompatible with prevailing laws.... [And] as yet there is no internationally agreed mechanism that would preserve a failing bank and its subsidiaries as an operating unit to minimize the fallout for the financial system and economy. Moreover, given the inherent conflict over how losses should be shared and the intricacies of negotiations about international legal reform, reaching an agreement is unlikely to be achieved anytime soon.

(Admati and Hellwig 2013, pp. 76–77; see also
Blinder 2013, pp. 269–70)[31]

The news is hardly much better on capital ratios. 'One of the most remarkable features of the financial crisis of 2008 was the razor-thin capitalization of many of the world's largest banks.... When the crunch came ... the actual loss-absorbing capital available to many big banks was less than 2% of their total assets' (Anon 2014a).[32] The Basel Committee's new standards on minimum capital-asset ratios are hardly much higher, and there remain huge differences between risk-weighted capital ratios and capital ratios *per se* (Anon 2014b). In contrast, speculation is being reined in via implementation of the Volker Rule in the US and 'ring-fencing' in the UK. But, these apply only to deposit-taking institutions, not the many other institutions that make up the finance system. This, of course, included Lehman Brothers, the bankruptcy of which constituted the proximate cause of the 2008 crisis, and many other similar dangers remain (Admati and Hellwig 2013, p. 72 and see also Wolf 2014, pp. 225–27, 237–52).

Widespread fraud and failures of due diligence were manifest in the American and British financial systems in the years preceding the crisis, and have continued in the years following it (Blinder 2013; Ferguson 2012). The response has been totally inadequate. There has been new legislation in Britain on the matter (Treanor 2013), but the principal problem in both the US and the UK seems to have been, and remains, a failure to use existing laws, to the point in fact that senior judges have given public voice to their outrage (Rakoff 2014; see also Eichengreen 2015, p. 113; Garrett 2014).

Finally, while there has been much discussion of the need to monitor systemic stability, and stress tests are becoming routine and off-balance sheet activities have been eliminated, little progress has been made in determining all the properties of financial interconnections which are dangerous (Wolf 2014, pp. 252–56). Moreover, there has been no appropriate institutionalization of the authority required to act on dangers. This would require continuous collection of much more information on the positions held by individual institutions and the regulatory capacity to order and enforce changes. Furthermore, since the financial system is global and the regulators are predominantly national, the problems parallel those of constructing an effective bankruptcy resolution mechanism. This should not be surprising as the two issues are intimately connected, and both exhibit the central problem inherent in globalization: it is much more developed economically than it is politically.

Not everything is completely lost in the reform of neoliberal finance since, as already noted, implementation of the relevant legislation in the US and the UK is still 'work in progress', and both the EU and Japanese systems of finance are in the early stages of renovation. However, more than six years since the crisis broke, there are few signs that the 'clear and present dangers' will be adequately addressed. The financial systems of the ACEs remain organized and ruled very much as they were on the eve of the crisis. The reforms are weak and it looks as if they will stay that way. While they may produce some reversal of neoliberalism at the margins in particular areas, the judgment of *RONACE* that 'neoliberalism would be reversed on a wide front' (Howard and King 2008, p. 236) seems clearly incorrect.

However, the implications of this failure are not obvious. Perhaps the prediction will be saved by the experience of more financial crises engendering the requisite degree of radicalism. Alternatively, maybe the failure indicates that the materialist approach used to explain neoliberalism in *RONACE* is incorrect. Instead of the marked persistence of financial fragility constituting a contradiction of actually existing neoliberal capitalism, it is perhaps an indication that neoliberalism has a deeper contradiction which has already begun to bring about another type of transformation.

Another transformation?

An alternative theory of neoliberalism to that formulated in *RONACE* focuses on the decline of profitability that engulfed the ACEs in the late 1960s. This, it is claimed, activated capital and states to break the power of the organized working class, and restore the profitability through neoliberal reforms (Armstrong et al. 1991; Brenner 1998; Dumenil and Levy 2004; Glyn 2006; Kotz 2003; Overbeek 1993). We can accept the facts upon which the account is based, but the narrative fits the UK and New Zealand far better than Western Europe or the US. And it fails to explain why the working classes were defeated so easily, and remained defeated in the ensuing decades. Nor is it explained why defeat brought an extension of neoliberal policies rather than more authoritarian alternatives. In addition, the abandonment of social democratic principles in favour of neoliberalism by the political parties of the left hardly fits with this class struggle perspective. Moreover, this alternative account of neoliberalism pays no attention to the effect affluence has had on the atomization and privatization of the working classes, which has reduced their radicalism and militancy. Consequently, *RONACE* was rather dismissive of the relevance of class, other than its decline, in explaining neoliberalism.

This may have been wrong. But the problem is not that anything we explicitly wrote about class needs to be withdrawn. It is rather that something we relegated to the 'excesses' of neoliberalism may have been wrongly categorized (Howard and King 2008, pp. 224–28). The key point is that wealth can be produced and it can also be redistributed from others. Most economic systems involve both, and *RONACE* took the position that production was vastly more important than predation in neoliberal capitalism. However, the evidence suggests that both the market power of many corporations and rent-seeking behaviour on the part of the propertied classes has become very much more important than we believed. Moreover this may be no accident, but rather a trajectory structurally inscribed in neoliberalism.

The very nature of the system requires extensive and intimate relations between state agencies and private businesses. Historical materialism must claim that the institutions of the modern state prevail and promote the general interest in enhancing productivity. That, after all, is the 'function' of the superstructure and, insofar as historical materialism is correct, realized by the selection mechanisms underpinning historical causation. But even allowing for the inevitable uncertainty and messiness of social affairs, there has been a sufficient accumulation of evidence to put this in more doubt than prevailed before the crisis. Perhaps what *RONACE* called neoliberal capitalism may turn out to be, instead, a version of 'political capitalism' as understood by Max Weber, in which property owners capture the state for their own interests in redistribution as well as production, and make secondary the general interest in developing the productive forces (Swedberg 1998, pp. 46–53).[33]

Evidence in support of this hypothesis includes the lax regulatory regime in operation prior to the financial crisis, the subsequent 'bail out' of financial capital, the puny nature of the initial fiscal stimulus and the reliance almost wholly on monetary policy to engender recovery. This is coupled with the minimal financial reform evident since the crisis, along with the complete failure to prosecute leading bankers. The common thread behind all this, continually espoused by governments everywhere, is the need to preserve and foster business 'confidence'. Other supportive evidence comes from the weakening of professional civil services in virtually all the ACEs, and their replacement by business consultants, as well as the direct employment of business executives as state managers, and the 'revolving door' behaviour of senior civil servants who do remain and later find highly remunerative employment in the private sector (Crouch 2011).

One can also point to the corruption of university education and research as a result of the imposed commercialization, and the incorporation of the professoriate, including economists, into state and business institutions (Mirowski 2013; Stedman Jones 2012). The taxation of capital has been markedly reduced everywhere over the last thirty years, and the progressivity of tax codes has been almost eliminated. Political parties have virtually ceased to represent oppositional interests, and have transitioned toward becoming alternative camps of careerists who are apt to renege on whatever promises help elevate them to office (Mair 2013). Most dramatic of all is the very large increase in inequality that has occurred in all ACEs since the 1970s, and especially the spectacular income and wealth gains at the very top. Market processes and technological trends are no doubt partly responsible, but so too are the rent-seeking and other redistributional activities of the very rich. And whatever the precise mix of causes, wealth is a form of power, and concentrated wealth implies concentrated power (Bartels 2008; Galbraith 2008; Gilens and Page 2014; Johnson and Kwak 2010; Piketty 2014).

Quite possibly, all this is misleading and these phenomena really are diverse and do not constitute elements defining a 'political capitalism'. Perhaps the system remains neoliberal in the way understood by historical materialism but with the 'excesses' rather more prevalent than *RONACE* believed. In this case, the 'excesses' will only be curtailed after the experience of yet more financial crises, or other problems of capitalist reproduction arise, when the five 'selection mechanisms' that aim to promote efficiency are intensified. This is still my 'best guess' because the selection mechanisms are very powerful and can take a long time to work out. However, this said, the alternative scenario of the development of a 'political capitalism' certainly needs to be treated with much more seriousness than it was prior to the global financial crisis.

Notes

1 Howard and King (2008).
2 Blinder (2013) makes it clear that the bankruptcy of Lehman Brothers was the trigger of the financial crisis. See the section on 'The neoliberal financial crisis'.
3 States acted as 'market makers' in their own operations in an endeavour to improve the efficiency of public services, and they have maintained and extended regulation of markets generally to control market failures: externalities, information asymmetries, fraud and market power. See also Mazzucato (2014).
4 General government expenditures in the ACEs have risen from an average of around 10 per cent of GDP in 1870 to an average of about 45 per cent in 1996. From then to 2007, there was a decline of 3 per cent to 42 per cent of GDP (see Tanzi 2011, p. 9). One immediate effect of the financial crisis was that the upward trend of government expenditures as a percentage of GDP resumed as a result of numerators increasing in consequence of automatic stabilizers and denominators contracting due to depression. As for changes in regulation, see Tanzi (2011, pp. 4–5, 83–85, 213–16, 317–19) and Vogel (1996), whose title *Freer Markets, More Rules* summarizes the main thrust.
5 Historical materialism is a complex doctrine and the summary of the main ideas in this section is presented in stark terms, without nuance or qualification.
6 And, of course, they may sometimes reinforce the drive to overcome scarcity.
7 Historical materialism is thus not a monistic technological determinism or even an economic determinism. While the account of the theory in terms of functional causation would be most amenable to being described as technological determinism, it would be incorrect because it is the function of the productive relations to *develop* the productive forces. And the account of causation in terms of the selection mechanisms obviously does not allow the description of historical materialism as a form of technological determinism or of economic determinism. See Howard and King (2008, pp. 16–17).
8 See e.g. Burgan (2012) and Stedman Jones (2012). Dardot and Laval (2013), Mirowski (2013) and Rodgers (2011) are much superior accounts.

9   Nonetheless, some economists of the Chicago School are classical liberals for idiosyncratic reasons as well as classical reasons. For example, George Stigler believed that attempts to regulate business would tend to lead to regulatory capture and rent-seeking, so that preference for a minimalist state on the basis of this argument is not because the state acts to crush economic freedom but because business groups act to co-opt policy makers and administrators and use the power of the state to further their own interests. This, of course, further distances Stigler from neoliberalism as outlined in 'The nature of neoliberal capitalism' above. See Stigler (1975) and 'Another transformation?' below.

10 Of course, the technological changes underpinning neoliberal capitalism are more complex than this and extend further back into the twentieth century (see Howard and King 2008, chapters 6, 7).

11 'Empire' may be thought an inappropriate descriptor, but the substance of empire is not really a contentious issue except at the level of propaganda. Analysts holding varied ideologies broadly agree on what is involved. See Anderson (2013), Bacevitch (2002), Johnson (2000, 2004, 2006), Eichengreen (2011), Friedman (2009), Gowan (2010), Kagan (2012), Mann (2003), Mearsheimer (2014) and Rosenberg (1994).

12 Admati and Hellwig (2013, pp. 83–87) explain just how very large is 'enormous'.

13 Of course, different perspectives are possible because each aspect of neoliberalization tends to affect the others, as was noted in the section 'Explaining neoliberal capitalism' above. However, it seems clear that financialization was a particularly powerful force in contributing to neoliberalizing virtually everything else.

14 More generally, the implementation of neoliberal measures was greatly aided by other developments in neoclassical economics, such as auction theory, mechanism design and contract theory.

15 See also n. 29 below.

16 This was reflected in the development of neoclassical consumption theory in terms of 'permanent income' and 'life cycle' models, whose principal message was that consumers were far less constrained by current income and thus engaged in optimizing intertemporally.

17 Others were more perceptive (see Keen 2011, pp. 12–15). The problem of predicting the onset of financial crisis includes the fact that Minsky processes are not the only source of change. Capitalist systems are turbulent, and technologies and structures change, generating claims that 'this time is different', which are sometimes valid, but often fanciful, and never obviously true or false. See also n. 25 below.

18 Contagion is a 'normal' market process in finance and occurs when there is a widespread recognition of 'financial fragility'. It is not something analogous to a natural disaster such as a tsunami.

19 It is sometimes said that the new type of bank run reflected the rise of 'shadow banking', where banks in the economic sense of 'borrowing short and lending long' were not always banks in the legal sense, so they could not take deposits and were not covered by deposit insurance. This is analytically correct but it is confusing insofar as major players in the shadow banking system were the deposit-taking commercial banks and well established investment banks. 'Shadow banking' is not a separate system of finance from that involving regular banking. See Eichengreen (2015, pp. 64–66, 100–01), Krugman (2012, pp. 114–15), Lapavitsas (2013, pp. 277–78) and Wolf (2014, pp. 20–21, 359 n. 10).

20 The Chairman of the Federal Reserve, Ben Bernanke, told the Financial Crisis Inquiry Commission that 'out of maybe … 13 of the most important financial institutions in the United States, 12 were at risk of failure within a period of a week or two' after the Lehman Brothers bankruptcy (Financial Crisis Inquiry Commission 2011, p. 354). However, this did not stop Bernanke later claiming that the Federal Reserve could not save Lehman because it lacked suitable collateral!

(Bernanke 2013, pp. 94–96). This is nonsense, as Eichengreen makes clear (2015, pp. 145–50, 162–73, 177–202, 206–02, 290–92).

21 This is not to deny that there were serious financial problems in other ACEs. See Kindleberger (1987) for a statement of the hegemonic stability theory.

22 This remains true even when it is recognized that large corporations no longer go 'bankrupt', but enter 'bankruptcy protection'. However, the treatment of the automobile producers in the US and Canada suggests that financial corporations may prove to be the model for state actions in relation to large corporations more generally. See the section 'Another transformation?' below. It is disturbing that Bernanke (2013) shows little or no recognition of these problems. Of course, he is a very intelligent and informed man, and may well be fully apprised but chooses to keep his views private. But why then does he argue for 'transparency' (Bernanke 2013, pp. 62–63)?

23 Orthodox, or neoclassical, macroeconomics recognize the possibility of crises and output contractions, but they are treated as resulting only from shocks concerning the fundamental determinants of economic actions (preferences, technologies, endowments and institutions).

24 The crises may at some point cease to be containable. For example, in the case of the UK, the 'City' is very large relative to the size of the economy, and the resources of the British state could well fall short of what is required to preserve the solvency of leading financial institutions, which would have a catastrophic impact globally. While the British state is monetarily sovereign, it is so only in Sterling, and financial transactions in the 'City' take place in all significant currencies, and on a very large scale. London might well become 'Reykjavik on the Thames' if more crises occur. It is, perhaps, the recognition of this danger that underpins the coalition government's commitment to austerity because no other consideration seems very persuasive. In which case, the matters dealt with in 'Another transformation?' below become relevant.

25 This is a widespread view. For example, *The Economist*'s long-held position is that 'The frequency and severity of financial crises suggest that they are an inevitable part of capitalism. This does not mean policymakers should give up trying to limit the damage they cause' (Anon 2014c). Andrew Tyrie's position is very similar. 'Economic history also tells us that there is an economic and business cycle. That will bring another period of heady over-optimism, then hubris followed by crisis and, finally, overdone gloom.... All we can do is put in place rules and structures that reduce the likelihood and increase the chance of a less painful cycle' (cited in Treanor 2013). Blinder (2013, p. 265) says much the same. See also Bernanke (2013, p. 122; Bove 2013, pp. 187–88; Lybeck 2011, pp. 112–13). This, of course, is the position of Hyman Minsky, which was, in turn, heavily influenced by Joseph Schumpeter, whose own perspective on capitalism was greatly indebted to that of Marx. As summarized by Joan Robinson, 'The system is cruel, unjust, turbulent, but it does deliver the goods, and, damn it all, it's the goods that you want' (1964, p. 130). In short, since finance is both infrastructural and crisis prone, some degree of financial malfunctioning is a 'cost of doing business'.

26 Traditional banking, even when heavily regulated, can be a very risky business. And it was the riskier world from the 1970s on that drove much of financial innovation. However, it is also the case that, over time, this financial innovation acted to increase complexity and promote fragility (see Admati and Hellwig 2013, pp. 55–59, 68–72, 95–96; Bove 2013).

27 See n. 19 above.

28 Historically, banks have held far more capital than they do today. Capital ratios of 30 per cent or higher were common in the nineteenth century. And, at the same time, bankruptcy was treated much more severely. The extension of government 'safety nets' for banking operations and the softening of penalties for defaulting on

debts has gone hand in hand with the very substantial lowering of capital ratios in banking in the ACEs. Today, banks borrow far more relative to their assets than do non-financial corporations (but this does not stop banks demanding substantial equity from those who would borrow from them!). See Admati and Hellwig (2013, pp. 30–31, 36, 45, 146, 150–53, 178).

29 The so-called 'too big to fail' problem is deliberately not mentioned for two reasons. First, any bank is either too big or too interconnected, or both, to be allowed to fail in the way Lehman Brothers went bankrupt. Second, as Alan Blinder says 'forcing financial giants to shrink is certainly *feasible*. The question, then, is whether it is desirable, given the financial needs of large global corporations. Bernanke has plenty of company in thinking that it is not. Is it really realistic to expect megacompanies like GE, IBM and Apple to deal with modest-sized banks? Or would they take their business to the likes of Deutsche bank, UBS, and Banco Santander? The question answers itself. Furthermore, a country as large as the United States has gigantic firms in virtually every industry. Even a fragmented industry like retail has Walmart. Why should finance be different?' Blinder (2013, p. 269; see also Bove 2013). In other words, seeking to reduce the size of financial giants significantly would go wholly against the grain of neoliberalism, and from this perspective the financial fragility of neoliberal economies is best tackled in other ways. However, some measures to discourage large size which are consistent with neoliberalism would certainly be appropriate.

30 See also section 'The nature of neoliberal finance'.

31 The Dodd-Frank Act and similar legislation in the UK seek to put an end to state 'bailouts' altogether. But the measures introduced to achieve this are not up to the task and therefore not credible. Bankers as well as professors know this! (Admati and Hellwig 2013, pp. 138–39, 188–89).

32 Applying risk weights to assets in order to compute required capital ratios can in practice substantially dilute the ratio. 'For example, the roughly 55 billion euros in equity that Deutsche Bank held on its reported balance sheet at the end of 2011 represented more than 14 percent of the bank's risk weighted assets of 381 billion euros but only 2.5 percent of the bank's total assets of 2.2 trillion euros' (Admati and Hellwig 2013, p. 176).

33 As George Stigler might have remarked, once the state regulates all businesses, all of the state becomes subject to regulatory capture. See n. 9 above as well as Mazzucato (2014, pp. 165–91).

References

Admati, A. and Hellwig, M. (2013), *The Bankers' New Clothes*. Princeton: Princeton University Press.

Anderson, P. (2013), American Foreign Policy and its Thinkers, *New Left Review* second series 83, pp. 5–167.

Anon. (2014a), *The Economist*, 18 January, p. 72.

Anon. (2014b), *The Economist*, 25 January, p. 60.

Armstrong, P., Glyn, A. and Harrison, J. (1991), *Capitalism Since 1945*. Oxford: Oxford University Press.

Athreya, K.B. (2013), *Big Ideas in Macroeconomics*. Cambridge, MA, USA: MIT Press.

Bacevitch, A. (2002), *American Empire*. Cambridge, MA, USA: Harvard University Press.

Bartels, L.M. (2008), *Unequal Democracy*. Princeton: Princeton University Press.

Baudrillard, J. (1970), *The Consumer Society*. Thousand Oaks, CA, USA: Sage (1998).

Bernanke, B.S. (2013), *The Federal Reserve and the Financial Crisis*. Princeton: Princeton University Press.

Blinder, A.S. (2013), *After the Music Stops*. New York: Penguin.

Bove, R.X. (2013), *Guardians of Prosperity*. New York: Penguin.

Brenner, R. (1998), The Economics of Global Turbulence, *New Left Review* first series 229, pp. 1–265.

Burgin, A. (2012), *The Great Persuasion*. Cambridge, MA, USA: Harvard University Press.

Cohen, G.A. (1978), *Karl Marx's Theory of History*. Princeton: Princeton University Press.

Cortada, J.W. (2011), *Information and the Modern Corporation*. Cambridge, MA, USA: MIT Press.

Crane, D.B. (1995), *The Global Financial System*. Boston: Harvard Business School Press.

Crouch, C. (2011), *The Strange Non-Death of Neoliberalism*. Cambridge, UK: Polity Press.

Dardot, P. and Laval, C. (2013), *The New Way of the World*. London: Verso.

Dumenil, G. and Levy, D. (2004), *Capital Resurgent*. Cambridge, MA, USA: Harvard University Press.

Eichengreen, B. (1992), *Golden Fetters*. Oxford: Oxford University Press.

Eichengreen, B. (2008), *Globalizing Capital*. Princeton: Princeton University Press.

Eichengreen, B. (2011), *Exorbitant Privilege*. Oxford: Oxford University Press.

Eichengreen, B. (2015), *Hall of Mirrors*. Oxford: Oxford University Press.

Ferguson, C.H. (2012), *Predator Nation*. New York: Crowne Publishing Group.

Financial Crisis Inquiry Commission (2011), *Financial Crisis Inquiry Report: Final Report of the National Commission on the Causes of the Financial and Economic Crisis in the United States*. Washington DC: US Government Printing Office. At http://www.gpo.gov/fdsys/pkg/GPO-FCIC/pdf/GPO-FCIC.pdf, accessed 11 August 2015.

Friedman, G. (2009), *The Next 100 Years*. New York: Doubleday.

Galbraith, J. (2008), *The Predator State*. New York: The Free Press.

Garrett, B.L. (2014), *Too Big to Jail*. Cambridge, MA, USA: Harvard University Press.

Gellner, E. (1974), *Legitimation of Belief*. Cambridge, UK: Cambridge University Press.

Gerth, H.H. and Mills, C. Wright. (eds.) (1948), *From Max Weber*. London: Routledge and Kegan Paul.

Gilens, M. and Page, B.I. (2014), Testing Theories of American Politics: Elites, Interest Groups, and Average Citizens, *Perspective on Politics* 12(03), pp. 564–581.

Glyn, A. (2006), *Capitalism Unleashed*. Oxford: Oxford University Press.

Gowan, P. (2010), *A Calculus of Power*. London: Verso.

Head, S. (2013), *Mindless*. New York: Basic Books.

Helpman, E. (2011), *Understanding Global Trade*. Cambridge, MA, USA: Harvard University Press.

Hirsch, F. (1976), *Social Limits to Growth*. Cambridge, MA: Harvard University Press.

Howard, M.C. and King, J.E. (1985), *The Political Economy of Marx*. Harlow, UK: Longmans.

Howard, M.C. and King, J.E. (1989), *A History of Marxian Economics, 1883–1929*. Princeton: Princeton University Press.

Howard, M.C. and King, J.E. (1992), *A History of Marxian Economics, 1929–1990*. Princeton: Princeton University Press.

Howard, M.C. and King, J.E. (1994), Is Socialism Economically Feasible, *Review of Political Economy* 6(2), pp. 133–152.

Howard, M.C. and King, J.E. (2008), *The Rise of Neoliberalism in Advanced Capitalist Economies*. Basingstoke, UK: Palgrave Macmillan.

Johnson, C. (2000), *Blowback*. New York: Henry Holt and Co.

Johnson, C. (2004), *The Sorrows of Empire*. New York: Henry Holt and Co.

Johnson, C. (2006), *Nemesis*. New York: Henry Holt and Co.

Johnson, S. and Kwak, J. (2010), *13 Bankers*. New York: Pantheon Books.

Kagan, R. (2012), *The World America Made*. New York: Knopf.

Keen, S. (2011), *Debunking Economics*. London: Pluto Press.

Kindleberger, C.P. (1987), *The World in Depression 1929–1939*. Harmondsworth, UK: Penguin.

Kindleberger, C.P. (1996), *Manias, Panics and Crashes*. New York: Wiley.

Kotz, D.M. (2003), Neoliberalism and the Social Structure of Accumulation Theory, *Review of Radical Political Economics* 35(3), pp. 263–270.

Krugman, P. (2012), *End This Depression Now!* New York: Norton.

Lapavitsas, C. (2013), *Profiting Without Producing*. London: Verso.

Lazear, E.P. and Spletzer, J.R. (2012), *The United States Labor Market: Status Quo or A New Normal*. At http://www.kansascityfed.org/publicat/sympos/2012/el-js.pdf, accessed 11 August 2015.

Lybeck, J.A. (2011), *A Global History of the Financial Crash of 2007–2010*. Cambridge, UK: Cambridge University Press.

Mair, P. (2013), *Ruling the Void*. London: Verso.

Mann, M. (2003), *Incoherent Empire*. London: Verso.

Mann, M. (2012), *The Sources of Social Power: Global Empires and Revolution, 1890–1945*, volume 3. Cambridge, UK: Cambridge University Press.

Mann, M. (2013). *The Sources of Social Power: Globalization, 1945–2011*, volume 4. Cambridge: Cambridge University Press.

Mazzucato, M. (2014), *The Entrepreneurial State*. London: Anthem Press.

McCloskey, D.N. (1990), *If You're So Smart*. Chicago: Chicago University Press.

Mearsheimer, J.J. (2014), *The Tragedy of Great Power Politics*. New York: Norton.

Mills, C. Wright. (1959), *The Power Elite*. Oxford: Oxford University Press.

Minsky, H.P. (1986), *Stabilizing an Unstable Economy*. New Haven, USA: Yale University Press.

Mirowski, P. (2013), *Never Let a Serious Crisis Go to Waste*. London: Verso.

Overbeek, H. (ed.) (1993), *Restructuring Hegemony in the Global Political Economy*. London and New York: Routledge.

Piketty, T. (2014), *Capital in the Twenty-First Century*. Cambridge, MA, USA: Harvard University Press.

Popper, K.R. (1957), *The Poverty of Historicism*. London: Routledge and Kegan Paul.

Rakoff, J.S. (2014), The Financial Crisis: Why Have No High-Level Executives Been Prosecuted? *New York Review of Books* 61(1), pp. 4–8.

Reinhart, C.M. and Rogoff, K.S. (2009), *This Time is Different*. Princeton: Princeton University Press.

Robinson, J. (1964), *Economic Philosophy*. Harmondsworth, UK: Penguin.

Rodgers, D.T. (2011), *Age of Fracture*. Cambridge, MA, USA: Harvard University Press.

Rosenberg, J.P. (1994), *The Empire of Civil Society*. London: Verso.

Ross, S.A. (1976), Options and Efficiency, *Quarterly Journal of Economics* 90(1), pp.75–89.

Schumpeter, J.A. (1934), *The Theory of Economic Development*. Cambridge, MA, USA: Harvard University Press.

Stedman Jones, D. (2012), *Masters of the Universe*. Princeton: Princeton University Press.

Stigler, G. (1975), *The Citizen and the State*. Chicago: University of Chicago Press.

Swedberg, R. 1998. *Max Weber and the Idea of Economic Sociology*. Princeton: Princeton University Press.

Taleb, N.N. (2004), *Fooled By Randomness*. London: Penguin.

Taleb, N.N. (2007), *The Black Swan*. New York: Random House.

Tanzi, V. (2011), *Government versus Markets*. Cambridge, UK: Cambridge University Press.

Torrance, J. (1995), *Karl Marx's Theory of Ideas*. Cambridge, UK: Cambridge University Press.

Treanor, J. (2013), Andrew Tyrie on Banking Reform, *Guardian*, 29 December. At http://www.theguardian.com/business/2013/dec/29/andrew-tyrie-banking-reform-industry-stronger, accessed 11 August 2015.

Vogel, S.K. (1996), *Freer Markets, More Rules*. Ithaca: Cornell University Press.

Williamson, O.E. (1985), *The Economic Institutions of Capitalism*. New York: The Free Press.

Williamson, O.E. (1996), *The Mechanisms of Governance*. Oxford: Oxford University Press.

Wolf, M. (2014), *The Shifts and the Shocks*. London: Allen Lane.

Conclusion

The road to reclaiming pluralism
in economics

19 In from the cold

From heterodoxy to a new mainstream pluralism

Jerry Courvisanos[1]

This chapter synthesizes the work presented in the previous 18 chapters of this book, and, in this way, enables pathways for heterodox economics to emerge out of its niche on the periphery into the mainstream. The existing mainstream does not embrace heterodox economics in its identification of the discipline. Thus, pluralism is anathema to it, and it maintains instead a resolute, monistic approach in which methodological individualism and systemic stability through market forces in effect *define* economics. In this monistic intellectual environment, pluralism in economics cannot exist by definition. Out of the synthesis employed in this chapter a strategy with diversity emerges that is based on a framework of epistemic coherence. This set-up could provide a variety of pathways to a new pluralist mainstream of economics-learning, research and policy-making.

Included in this synthesis are the thoughts expressed in a panel discussion held at the end of the 2014 Festschrift Conference in honour of John King. The panel comprised Mike Howard, Therese Jefferson, Peter Kriesler, John King and John Lodewijks. It was asked to address this question of moving economics as a discipline from the bifurcated orthodox mainstream and heterodox periphery, as currently exists, to an all-embracing pluralist mainstream. Following the panel's observations, conference attendees were invited to provide feedback.

What emerged was an interesting dichotomy among the participants. The older established academic participants expressed hope, tinged with pessimism and wariness, in a possible movement away from the periphery of a diverse set of alternative economics schools of thought (or strands). In contrast, the younger participants expressed a stronger, perhaps defiant, perspective that economics might transform itself into a pluralist discipline. A variety of views did arise among participants in the discussion on whether this pluralism can, or should, emerge within or outside the existing university economics departments currently dominated by the mainstream.

The new mainstream

Given the entrenched position of the neoclassical strand in the economics discipline, the first theme of this book outlines the nature of the challenge to undermine neoclassical theory as the mainstream. First, the new pluralism needs to be distinctly different from the old one (King, Chapter 1). Second, it needs to have epistemic coherence in methodological terms (Stilwell, Chapter 2). Third, a consistent style in communicative terms is needed to enable any analysis to reach a resolution (Dow, Chapter 3). Having a diverse set of theories and analyses in the mainstream would require a conceptual framework that works across all strands to be specified clearly with consistent use of language and terms.

The new mainstream will not look anything like the 'old' pluralist economics that King (Chapter 1) encountered during his education in economics. The world has moved on, as has the political economy in which the nature of economic reality experiences day-to-day existence. 'The Age of Growth', so accurately identified at the time by Joan Robinson (1976) is no more. Pluralism at that time reflected a confident, if insular, western capitalism. Harry G. Johnson (1974) exemplified this in his appraisal of the state of economics at that time. Johnson discusses the various strands of 'scientific economics', cursorily dismissing both 'dead religious protest' (Marxism) and 'miracle-working necessity of government intervention' (development economics). Nevertheless, Johnson includes in the evolution of scientific economics 'three revolutions' (imperfect competition, welfare and Keynesian economics). He mentions within this scientific economics the works of John Kenneth Galbraith, Joan Robinson, Piero Sraffa, Michał Kalecki, Nicholas Kaldor, Milton Friedman, Ronald Coase and Anthony Downs. Finally, Johnson outlines 'certain factors which may make actual performance fall short of potential' (1974, p. 25), in the process making disparaging remarks of what could be considered Post Keynesian economists like Joan Robinson. Despite his condemnation of heterodox positions, Johnson's 1974 article amply demonstrated that 'old' pluralism did exist and that various strands across the whole spectrum could be debated in mainstream economics journals. This no longer occurs.

The new pluralist mainstream needs to reflect a more sober economic reality in which inequality and crises (ecological and financial) are endemic in a world in which neoliberal capitalism dominates in all major centres of economic activity, including China, India and Brazil (van Appeldoorn and Overbeek 2012, p. 11). Competing economic systems that existed and provided viable alternatives during 'The Age of Growth', notably, collective capitalism, communitarianism, democratic socialism and communism (Heilbroner and Ford 1971) are no longer. The 'new' pluralist economics needs a commitment to address this 'sober economic reality' with robust critical analyses of all theories and their application to flexible and effective economic policy.

Pluralism requires an obligation to 'epistemic progress', not alternative ontological systems. The view in this chapter therefore differs from the position taken by Tim Thornton (Chapter 15) that 'pluralist economics' can not include a closed system orthodox economics. The new pluralist mainstream envisaged in this chapter would necessarily include neoclassical economics along with other major economic strands. Axiomatically, given that 'pluralism' implies observing phenomena (in this case, economic) from multiple and diverse methodological approaches, the neoclassical strand offers a perspective that needs to be included in any study of economics. However, as Stilwell (Chapter 2) cautions us, 'the restructuring of the economic discipline along pluralist lines requires the mainstream practitioners to come on board'.

However, including neoclassical economics in pluralist economics does raise a conundrum. As Stilwell (Chapter 2) notes, neoclassical economics is an approach based on the monism of methodological individualism and systemic stability through market forces. Research is seen, therefore, only in the context of closed equilibrium systems with a positivist paradigm and quantitative econometric methods, in which optimization is the pinnacle. Such an approach eschews diversity of theoretical constructs, alternative methodological paradigms and variety of research methods, particularly critical realism (Jespersen 2011) and pragmatism (Walrave 1993). Can such a monistic perspective be brought into a pluralist economics agenda? If one were to approach this ontologically, the answer is 'no'. There could be no debate between economists imbued with either the ontological principles of neoclassical orthodoxy (Mirowski 2011, p. 501) or those of shared heterodoxy (King 2015, p. 126). The result is that their languages, terms and approaches would be divergent, virtually preventing any meaningful dialogue. For example, terms like uncertainty and sustainability have very different meanings in the two paradigms. Even the title 'new political economy' has a neoclassical interpretation and is not the intellectual property of heterodoxy (see Besley 2007).

Extrication from this conundrum requires that the new pluralist mainstream be based on what Stilwell (Chapter 2) calls 'epistemic progress'. This is an epistemological pluralism that allows economic phenomena to be examined by a diversity of theoretical strands and with multiple methods of empirical enquiry. Dow (Chapter 3) focuses upon the 'Babylonian' style to communicate within the new pluralism. Such a style builds up knowledge by means of a range of arguments that derive from diverse theories and analyses, which are not strictly commensurate with each other. Thus, the 'debate' on all economic phenomena under investigation then changes both its forum and its resolution. The forum occurs where discussion and analyses are conducted by economics research academics and students (not necessarily labelled as 'economists') who investigate issues that involve economic phenomena. In this forum, diverse investigatory theories and methods can be used by different individuals and groups of researchers. Then meta-analysis allows divergent studies to be scrutinized in a variety of academic fora. Resolution out of such scrutiny is a role for policy-makers who apply policies in the environmental context in which they were designed to be implemented. For this to emerge, Dow argues for a communicative coherence across strands.

Strategy

The question arises, what are the means to bring about a communicative and epistemic coherence? In keeping with the pluralist approach of this book, there cannot be a singular strategy towards reclaiming pluralism. Two of the book's themes (see table of contents) relate to this issue of strategy. Theme 2 illustrates how the history of economic thought (HET) has interacted within the economics discipline in the face of the neoclassical mainstream's dominant position and its indifference to HET (Kates, Chapter 4; Lodewijks, Chapter 5), as well as HET's positive influence on the enhancement of pluralist ideals (Millmow, Chapter 6). Theme 5 examines the role of mainstream economics in justifying the neoliberal political agenda from the perspectives of scientific method (Barone, Chapter 16), industrial relations (O'Leary, Chapter 17) and the global financial crisis (Howard, Chapter 18). Both themes note the strong resistance encountered from the established monistic mainstream and the massive effort needed to transform the discipline into a polycentric one in which there is inclusivity in theoretical perspectives. However, working through the contributions to these two themes does not need to be disheartening. Instead, it can identify strategies toward polycentrism.

In Theme 2, Kates's message is that HET is an integral part of the study of economics and not merely part of the domain of sociology of knowledge. In this chapter, mainstream economists are HET's 'enemies' because they see the need to protect the monopoly position of neoclassical theory as the only legitimate approach to how economies operate in the modern world. This political economy reality needs to be addressed, and Kates believes that HET can play its part in making economists better at their job. Lodewijks shows how the pluralist movement could draw valuable lessons from the successful vigorous campaigns waged by HET scholars in Australia. These campaigns create both scholarly and political pressure to ensure HET is recognized as a crucial tool in the teaching and education of economists. In essence, these political campaigns in Australia reflect the view of HET scholars everywhere that economics is the field of research to which they belong. But the mainstream needs to appreciate the diversity HET brings to the discipline. This can only be achieved by creating a field of enquiry out of HET that is communicative to all strands.

Millmow, writing about a polycentric economics department in post-war Cambridge, identifies the processes that create an environment for alternative visions of how economies should function to be debated. This then builds a long-term milieu of social learning and enlightened policy-making by the state (Hall 1993), in contrast to classical conditioning instruction and policy application emphasized by monistic neoclassicals (Courvisanos 1985). However, from this chapter it is also very apparent that debates emerging from a polycentric academy, unless bounded by strong cultural values of collegiality and tolerance, can result in acrimony and vindictive behaviour undermining mutual respect. There needs to be awareness of such potentiality when plotting out strategies and a framework for a pluralist future. While united against the orthodoxy in the current situation, economists from particular alternative strands may not be all that collegial to their neoclassical brethren or fellow travellers with different perspectives in a future polycentric academy. Lack of respect for alternatives occurs in a conscious effort to develop an alternative monist tradition, or in an unconscious ardent attempt to promote one specific vision of the future held very passionately. Such disrespect will definitely undermine a pluralist economics future.

Theme 5 also considers resistance by the mainstream to pluralism. Having by the early 1980s gained its monopoly position, the theoretical authority of neoclassical economics provided the basis for a set of broad state-based economic policies that focused exclusively on individualist market-driven processes. The term 'neoliberalism' encompasses this policy approach, and mainstream economics is committed to maintain its dominance in the economic policy field due to its theoretical and political legitimacy.

Barone, however, dismantles the scientific legitimacy that neoclassical economics has created as the basis for neoliberalism. He undermines the unequivocal implication that any 'so-called' economics conducted outside the neoclassical mainstream is 'bad' science. With mathematics providing the veneer for neoclassical 'science', Barone exposes both its teleology and its individual-based 'natural laws' as invalid epistemic foundations. Yet the mainstream, from a strategic perspective, will not abandon its existing conventional wisdom (Galbraith 1958) and its monistic epistemological position, despite the evolutionary forces that shape the community and its economic system (Veblen 1898). This explains why the enemies of HET are within mainstream economics departments. Stilwell (Chapter 2) and Thornton (Chapter 15) support institutional independence from economics departments and links with other departments, notably political science. Exposure to the broad community would come from heterodox economists supporting more investigative public/social media and joining forces through public fora with concerned scientists and activists on public issues of distress (e.g. environment, gender, indigenous and migration issues). This must be part of any strategy towards pluralism.

Arising from Barone's analysis is also the issue of 'science-recognition' for current heterodox economics and HET scholars. In most universities, the instigation of research assessment metrics leads to the question of how research in economics is defined for its research output to be measured. As King (Chapter 1) observes, these research metrics provide the mainstream with an opportunity to strengthen its monopoly position. This has enabled neoclassical theory to prevail both in respect to an absolutist view of HET (allowing only one trajectory in the development of economics as a science) and the dismissal of heterodox strands (allowing no alternative theoretical underpinnings). The 'zoo principle' does not apply. The approach expressed in the chapters of this book to these metrics and their regulatory managerialist problems is dichotomous. The different views in Theme 2 reflect, on the one hand, the need for HET to be 'inside the economics tent' in order for HET academics to be recognized as valid economics researchers, and also to secure their positions within economics departments. On the other hand, for pluralism to succeed, and for heterodox economics researchers to apply HET insights to address contemporary economic issues, might require that they be 'outside the economics tent', that is, in other departments.

The only resolution to this dichotomy is to accept that there needs to be diversity in strategies towards pluralism, just as there should be diversity in the strands of economic theory. 'Horses for courses' applies here, too. Economics academics who work outside the monopolist centre must choose their own appropriate strategy for furthering their careers, as they see them develop. However, a polycentric approach with a coherent epistemic framework to the science of economics must be part of that strategy. That is how the diverse group of authors has been able to contribute to this volume, in recognition of John King's continued effort for such a pluralist centre.

In Theme 5, O'Leary and Howard reflect from perspectives outside theoretical economics on the mainstream resistance to pluralism. O'Leary provides a case study on how the neoliberal political agenda, derived from a dominant free-market neoclassical economics, has strengthened employer discretion in industrial relations (IR) strategies. Such an IR approach in the meat industries of the US and Australia is shown to have damaged the ability of trade unions to negotiate with employers. As a strategy for moving away from neoliberal IR policies, there need to be pluralist economic voices demanding 'neo-pluralism' reform along the lines of 'associational' social relations and workplace partnerships for the community. For example, drawing upon Kalecki (1943), two Australian economists, Eric Russell and Wilfred Salter, argued for a full-employment policy with conciliation and centralized wage-fixing incomes policy (see Harcourt 1997). In this approach, strategy needs to focus on the community as well as the individual enterprise.

Howard's analysis first shows that neoclassical economics is highly resilient to non-neoliberal challenges, as evidenced by the short-lived stimulus in response to the crisis before austerity was imposed to address the accompanying moderate increase in public debt. Second, Howard notes the shift away from production to predation has increased both the market power of many corporations and rent-seeking behaviour by property owners. For legitimacy in a democratic system, financial regulation needs to control the worst excesses of financial predation (Offe 2013). However, neoclassical theory prescribes that the market still nominally rules: hence, the emotive term 'financial repression' adopted within conservative finance circles (Reinhart et al. 2011). Howard notes moreover how, while the state regulates business under the neoliberal 'camouflage', powerful (especially financial) business can better engage in regulatory capture. Strategically, for pluralism, this demands a critique of the neoliberal agenda, in order to unshackle economic policy from monist neoclassical theory.

Diversity

The new pluralism must reflect diversity, including neoclassical theory in that diversity. No analysis of modern day capitalism or any alternatives (potential and actual) can have relevance without contextualizing the dominant neo-classical strand in the analysis. For the neoclassical doctrine drives existing teaching, research, public discourse and policy-making while being under-pinned by the ideological power of the free market. Set against the neoclassical strand are classical economic ideas, including Marxism. These ideas are revisited in Theme 3 of this book by Kurz (Chapter 7), Doughney (Chapter 8), Schneider (Chapter 9) and Harcourt and Kriesler (Chapter 10), in order to establish a compass free of neoclassical hegemony. This compass allows re-evaluation of the nature of economics based on a diverse pluralist tradition that needs to emerge in the twenty-first century. It also is a compass to assist understanding of the development of neoclassical ideas.

By resuscitating a 'submerged and forgotten' classical theory of value and distribution, Kurz is able to argue cogently that it is the individual as well as the community as a whole which operates together to determine the social surplus of an economy. Two conceptual implications arise from this. One is that the individual utility of a commodity depends also on consumption by the 'community' as a whole. In this broader holistic situation, mechanical, individualist, marginalist thinking, so imbued in neoclassical doctrine, cannot be sustained. The other implication is that capital accumulation is part of a holistic transition process in which technical changes (or innovations) need to be specified. From such implications, diversity in economic theory beckons – whether with Schumpeter, and how innovative entrepreneurs respond through investment to waves of optimism and pessimism in the community, with Kalecki, and the adaptive non-optimal mechanism of social learning via conventions and rules, or with a synthesis of the two (Courvisanos 2012, pp. 25–28, 195–98).

Dominance of one theoretical perspective is the central issue in the remaining three chapters of Theme 3. By identifying errors in abstraction in Marx's work on the falling rate of profit, Doughney (Chapter 8) casts doubt on a fundamental Marxist doctrine. This provides a completely different picture of diversity, by asking heterodox economists – in this case Marxists – to not consider their own doctrine as fundamentalist and monist. Doughney's ana-lysis points to a broader pluralist agenda in which Marxist value/distribution theory is integrated with Kaleckian short-period investment (capital accumu-lation) decision-making to determine the rate of exploitation in a specific historical context.

Similarly, Schneider's investigation of multiple theoretical discoveries shows the Ricardian theory of rent as being of two types, both of which were 'dis-covered' from different strands of economic thought. Such discoveries lead to the conclusion that one monistic perspective denies simultaneity of discoveries and may also ignore the different ways in which a concept can be integrated and applied in a variety of theoretical frameworks. Finally, by examining eight economists who researched at Cambridge and who contributed to interpretations of Ricardo's 1817 book, *Principles of Political Economy and Taxation*, Harcourt and Kriesler discern two extremely divergent views of

Ricardo's place in the development of economic thought, namely the surplus approach and the marginal principle. This in itself clearly shows that pluralism, and not monism, needs to be recognized in the social science that is economics. Further, the authors' analyses uncover the lacunae between the short and long periods that were at the root of Ricardo's debate with Malthus.

All the chapters in Theme 3 underline the diversity that is required under a reclaiming-pluralism banner. They all show clearly that divergent views, puzzles and dilemmas cannot be resolved by one monistic approach, be that neo-classical, Marxist, Kaleckian or Austrian. Theme 3 provides, therefore, a restored compass for reclaiming pluralism in economics. This compass is a commitment to an epistemological stance that is pluralist and entails a pledge to allow diversity of economic strands and to encourage genuine attempts at synthesis or, at least, debate on specific issues/problems across these diverse strands.

Coherence

The major issue with a pluralist diversity is how to develop a framework of epistemic coherence that can then be researched, learned, communicated and acted upon. The issue is addressed by Dow (Chapter 3), who explains that coherence is not based on formal consistency of a theoretically perfect body of knowledge. Such formal consistency leads inexorably to a monistic episte-mological position. Instead, coherence for Dow is philosophical consistency based on an open-system ontology. This means epistemologically a pluralist frame of reference is needed that allows researchers to analyse the economic problem at hand using a methodologically consistent approach. The tools of analysis or theoretical perspectives adopted can be from across the complete gamut of economic theories and strands. This means determining what works best in an open-system ontology. There should be no restriction on what theoretical approach or synthesis is adopted. What is crucial is for the frame of reference to be clear so that it provides consistency in communication across the pluralist diversity.

With the diversity compass now in place, Theme 4 consists of five chapters that span a variety of theoretical approaches in HET in the twentieth century. Toporowski (Chapter 11) also looks at a multiple discovery, this time by Keynes and Kalecki in the context of the Great Depression. This discovery is the inability of free markets in capitalism to attain equilibrium, particularly that the labour market cannot be brought into equilibrium by changes in wages. Coming from different economic traditions (Marshallian and Marxist, respectively), this 'discovery' allows a synthesizing approach to non-market clearing processes across diverse HET strands. What unites this joint discovery is that up until full employment, changes in real wages are not the crucial variable in short-period fluctuations, even when there is marked unemploy-ment. From a Marxist perspective, Kalecki was able to add the observation that technical change (or innovation), as a trend over cycles, contributes to rising real wages. The dynamics of the economic system are inherent in this discovery, even if in Keynes the Marshallian perspective obscures this detail.

On the diversity of alternative views, Hart and Kriesler (Chapter 12) argue for a clear distinction between Sraffian and Post Keynesian strands. In terms of neoclassical theory, the former acts as a long-period critique while the latter is a short-period alternative model. Thus, coherence across the two is not ontological but epistemological. Together, Sraffian and Post Keynesian strands provide crucial different-time-period critiques of the teleological underpinnings of the neoclassical strand and, in so doing, help to identify when, where and whether the neoclassical strand has economic relevance.

Bloch (Chapter 13) also examines diversity of alternative views, these being Post Keynesian and Schumpeterian strands. The focus of his study is innovation, such that the short-period adjustment to aggregate demand shocks in the Post Keynesian strand is complemented with the long-period Schumpeterian supply and demand changes due to innovation. Together, Post Keynesian and Schumpeterian insights provide another crucial different-time-period analysis, in this case incorporating 'gales of creative destruction' with diffusion through changes to mark-up pricing.

The final two chapters in this theme reveal another form of coherence within diversity. In these two chapters, the work is more speculative and outside the customary economics literature (even for most heterodox economists). However, each adds significantly to 'epistemic progress'. Jefferson (Chapter 14) examines George Katona's contribution from psychology to behavioural macroeconomics. Katona's psychology-based behavioural research methods enable the framing of changing perceptions in the willingness of individuals or collections of individuals (in firms, clubs, unions, etc.) to spend, save or invest. This framing allows pluralism to be reclaimed in the 'sober economic reality' of inequality and crises. Thornton (Chapter 15) focuses on actual and potential contribution of complexity theory to economics. Coming out of ecological science fifty years ago, Buzz Holling views 'complexity inherent in ecology' (Holling 1966, p. 200) and then adapts this idea to establish complexity economics. Thornton notes that complexity ideas are actually long established within political economy. However, putting them all together in a holistic complex adaptive system allows for an integrated set of causal mechanisms to emerge that sustain diversity and enable flexible resilience in the face of crises (Levin 1998). Thus, complexity theory provides a tool of coherence. This can be achieved by creating syntheses between heterodox economics strands that are compatible in their theorizing of the causal mechanisms of a complex adaptive open system.

Two elements can be identified throughout this discussion of coherence, and they are both epistemological in character. One is that pluralism comes with a wide variety of research methods (notably critical realism and pragmatism), and not merely the single positivist econometric method applied to the monistic neoclassical model. The other is that framing economic decisions is critical to the determination of what economic strands, social science theories and research methods are applied to any specific issue under investigation. These two elements need to be set within a framework that has a coherence that empowers pluralist economists to determine appropriate strands, theories and methods. Table 19.1 sets out a proposed framework for a new pluralist economics based on the work developed throughout this book.

The framework encapsulates a philosophical dialectic with a series of outermost antinomies. The dialectic is based on the classical economics foundation identified by Kurz in which 'The Individual' and 'The Community' represent the two extremes, but which operate together to determine the surplus outcome that society requires over a specified period in order to reproduce itself. The Individual is based on static methodological individualism that eschews reality. Appropriately noting a strong King (2012) caution, the core character of 'The Individual' is that of microfoundations, which breaks down all economic activity to the microeconomic role of the individual (or collection of individuals like the firm). As King (2012) makes clear, this ignores emergent properties that arise from dynamic evolutionary forces in modern capitalism like innovation, income distribution, monopoly control and global warming which are elements from the core character of 'The Community'.

Surplus outcome allows the system to create, extract, distribute and use what is produced (Harcourt 2006, p. 85). The term 'surplus' (whether narrow firm-based or broad social-based) applies to all economic systems and is represented in different guises by all economic strands: whether 'profit', 'return on investment', 'interest', 'supra-surplus' or 'reward for innovation'. The appropriation and distribution of this 'outcome' emerges from interaction (or the political economy) of individuals and their communities. Between the top

Table 19.1 Proposed framework for a new pluralist economics

	The Individual	The Community
Methodology	positivist/normative	critical realist/pragmatic
Agency	entrepreneur/consumer	group/class/nation state
Structure	firm/enterprise	industry/sector/region
Principle	marginal analysis	surplus approach
Period	static	dynamic
Focus	economy	ecosystem
Core	microfoundations	emergent properties
Processes	markets (prices/utility)	institutions (rules/legislation)
Interaction	competition/cartelisation	conflict/contradiction
Analysis	equilibrium/model	complexity/reality
Instruction	classical conditioning	social learning
Outcome	surplus/profit/return/interest/reward	

and the bottom of the table are aspects that characterize the individual and community extremes. Since all economic strands are an amalgam of many diverse elements, there can be much interplay between the dichotomous characteristics. Thus, this is not a simplistic bifurcation of economics into orthodox and heterodox. For example, neoclassical theory is essentially based on 'The Individual' column, yet various versions of neoclassical theory include institutions, group behaviour and the role of government. There is also room in this table for synthesis across various strands by including characteristics between the two columns. For example, Courvisanos (2012) argues for a significant focus on 'The Community' column, but with crucial individual agency roles reserved for the entrepreneur and the institution of the enterprise that commercializes innovation.

Pathways

To conclude, there is the issue of how a new pluralism economics can be installed into research, teaching, public discourse and policy-making. This is the nub of reclaiming pluralism in economics. This new pluralism, once initiated with a diversity of economic thought (including neoclassical), must never become monocentric, for this would undermine the pluralism principle itself. As Mariyani-Squire and Moussa (2015, p. 202) perceptively point out, the proposition 'that long-run scientific "progress" is marked by the elimination of inferior rival paradigms from the cognitive and disciplinary landscape' cannot be sustained under the rubric of pluralism. As Cohen (2014, p. 6) notes, using the biological ecosystem as an analogy for the economic ecosystem: 'A research community without factions is like a monoculture in farming, dominated by a single biological species.' This results in a lack of adaptability and applicability to the economic matters at hand (i.e. no scientific progress).

The concept of 'epistemic progress' must be judged by how the new polycentric economics discipline can create research and learning spaces for various economic strands to contribute separately and, in tandem with other strands, provide new theoretical and empirical insights that address contemporary economic problems. Thus, to paraphrase a revolutionary leader, 'let a thousand economic ideas flower', be they concepts, theories, schools, paradigms or 'centres of excellence'. They are all needed, but some epistemic coherence is suggested. Table 19.1 offers a framework that can be used for both research and teaching to identify the polycentric space within which the new economics pluralism operates. The framework needs to be engaged not as a paradigmatic guide, but as a problem-based guide. Courvisanos (1985) outlines how such a problem-based guide can be used for the development of teaching curricula in economics. A similar approach can be developed for research. Once the research and teaching processes are adopted in this manner, the polycentric economics can more effectively extend its knowledge base into public discourse and policy-making.

This chapter ends where it began, with the panel discussion of how the new pluralist centre can come about. As students at the conference stated, 'it's all political'. This is nothing new. Kalecki (1943) recognizes that opposition to full employment is 'poor' economics despite the advancement of such poor economics by 'captains of industry' and their economics 'experts'. This is in fact 'a manifestation of underlying political motives.' The same can be said for the retreat to austerity economics after the global financial crisis. What is new are the political pathways suggested. There are students' movements that echo the dissatisfaction with mainstream economics, calling for pluralism in economics. Reference can be made here to the 1970s Political Economy Movement (at the University of Sydney), and much later the Post-Autistic Economics Movement (in France), the Post-Crash Economics Society (in Manchester, UK), and the International Student Initiative for Pluralism in Economics (ISIPE, across many countries). All are active at time of writing. Some panel participants recommended the establishment of an Australian College of Political Economy. There is also a need to build bridges outside economics to disciplines that have sympathy and concordance with the values and ideas of pluralist economics. An example is the Politics, Philosophy and Economics (PPE) degree, first established at Oxford University (UK) in the 1920s and offered in around 60 universities globally, which was followed by La Trobe University (Melbourne) in 2011. Further, pluralist economists have set up associations (with the umbrella organization being the International Confederation of Associations for Pluralism in Economics, ICAPE), journals (*World Economic Review, International Journal of Pluralism and Economics Education*) and networks (World Economics Association and its newsletter). Finally, there are modern information technology tools at hand to use as instruments of political warfare to expose polycentric economics to potential and actual economics students, the public interested in alternative economics, policy-makers and any mainstream economists willing to listen and be critical. These include open access publishing, blogs, massive open online courses (MOOCs) and tertiary education online newspapers.

In the end, what is required is a tolerant, accepting, diverse economics discipline with an epistemic framework of coherence and the pathways described above. The banner of pluralism needs to be raised by the young optimistic students who will drive this agenda in the future. Acknowledging that diversity will always exist in economics, whether the mainstream accepts it or not, leads to an incontestable proposition that is well expressed in a statement from a long way from economics. It is in a book on critical cinema studies and goes like this: 'ultimately only a pluralist vision could account for the diversity of forms. In taking an inventory of this diversity, I found it useful to try and define the thematic and ideological structure that so many of the films have in common, and that makes its range of viewpoints possible' (Kitses 2004, p. 13).

Note

1   Thank you to Harry Bloch and Alex Millmow for suggesting substantial improvements to an earlier draft.

References

Besley, T. (2007), The New Political Economy, *The Economic Journal* 117(524), pp. F570–587.

Cohen, B.J. (2014), *Advanced Introduction to International Political Economy.* Cheltenham, UK and Northampton, MA, USA: Edward Elgar.

Courvisanos, J. (1985), A Problems Approach to the Study of Economics, in D. Boud (ed.), *Problem-Based Learning in Education and the Profession.* Kensington, Australia: HERDSA, pp. 121–134.

Courvisanos, J. (2012), *Cycles, Crises and Innovation: Path to Sustainable Development – A Kaleckian-Schumpeterian Synthesis.* Cheltenham, UK and Northampton, MA, USA: Edward Elgar.

Galbraith, J.K. (1958), *The Affluent Society.* Boston: Houghton Mifflin.

Hall, P.A. (1993), Policy Paradigms, Social Learning, and the State: The Case of Economic Policymaking in Britain, *Comparative Politics* 25(3), pp. 275–296.

Harcourt, G.C. (1997), Pay Policy, Accumulation and Productivity, *The Economic and Labour Relations Review* 8(1), pp. 78–89.

Harcourt, G.C. (2006), *The Structure of Post-Keynesian Economics: The Core Contributions of the Pioneers.* Cambridge, UK: Cambridge University Press.

Heilbroner, R.L. and Ford, A.M. (eds.) (1971), *Is Economics Relevant? A Reader in Political Economics.* Pacific Palisades, California: Goodyear.

Holling, C.S. (1966), The Strategy of Building Models of Complex Ecological Systems, in K.E.F. Watt (ed.), *Systems Analysis in Ecology.* New York: Academic Press, pp. 195–214.

Jespersen, J. (2011), *Macroeconomic Methodology: A Post-Keynesian Perspective.* Cheltenham, UK and Northampton, MA, USA: Edward Elgar.

Johnson, H.G. (1974), The Current and Prospective State of Economics, *Australian Economic Papers* 13(22), pp. 1–27.

Kalecki, M. (1943), Political Aspects of Full Employment, *Political Quarterly* 14(4), pp. 322–331, in J. Osiatyński (ed.) (1990), *Collected Works of Michał Kalecki: Capitalism: Business Cycles and Full Employment*, volume I. Oxford: Clarendon Press, pp. 347–356.

King, J.E. (2012), *The Microfoundations Delusion.* Cheltenham, UK and Northampton, MA, USA: Edward Elgar.

King, J.E. (2015), *Advanced Introduction to Post Keynesian Economics.* Cheltenham, UK and Northampton, MA, USA: Edward Elgar.

Kitses, J. (2004), *Horizons West*, new edition. London: British Film Institute.

Levin, S.A. (1998), Ecosystems and the Biosphere as Complex Adaptive Systems, *Ecosystems* 1(5), pp. 431–436.

Mariyani-Squire, E. and Moussa, M. (2015), Fallibilism, Liberalism and Stilwell's Advocacy for Pluralism in Economics, *Journal of Australian Political Economy* 75, pp. 194–210.

Mirowski, P. (2011), The Spontaneous Methodology of Orthodoxy, and Other Economists' Afflictions in the Great Recession, in J.B. Davis and D.W. Hands, (eds.), *The Elgar Companion to Recent Economic Methodology.* Cheltenham, UK and Northampton, MA, USA: Edward Elgar, pp. 473–513.

Offe, C. (2013), Democratic Inequality in the Austerity State, *Juncture* 20(3), pp. 178–185.

Reinhart, C.M., Kirkegaard, J.F. and Sbrancia, M.B. (2011), Financial Repression Redux, *Finance and Development* 48(2), pp. 22–26.

Robinson, J. (1976), The Age of Growth, *Challenge* 19(2), pp. 4–9. Reprinted in J. Robinson (1980), *Further Contributions to Modern Economics*. Oxford: Basil Blackwell, pp. 33–42.

van Appeldoorn, B. and Overbeek, H. (2012), Introduction: The Life Course of the Neoliberal Project and the Global Crisis, in H. Overbeek and B. van Appeldoorn (eds.), *Neoliberalism in Crisis*. London: Palgrave Macmillan, pp. 1–22.

Veblen, T. (1898), Why Is Economics Not an Evolutionary Science? *Quarterly Journal of Economics* 12(4), pp. 373–397.

Walrave, M. (1993), The Development of High Speed Rail Innovation and Tradition: Prospects for the Future, *Rivista Internazionale di Scienze Sociali* 101(3), pp. 375–397.

Name index

Bold numbers refer to appearance in tables.

Subject index

Bold numbers refer to appearance in tables.

Abbott Government (Aust.) 26
academy: and monist economics 5, 9,
  14–15, 17; and pluralism 3, 9, 21, 22,
  25, 26, 27, 28; *see also* history of
  economic thought
Academy of Social Sciences in Australia
  (ASSA) 59, 60, 61, 62, 66
advanced capitalist economies: and
  long-run development 217; and
  neoliberal finance 279, 281, 283, 285,
  286, 287, 292, 293–4, 294n4, 297n28;
  see also Australia; United Kingdom;
  United States
age of growth, and its end 304
agents, and complexity economics 239,
  239, 247
anthropology 7; and economics 10–11,
  113, 241, 261; *see also homo
  economicus*
Association for Heterodox Economics
  (UK) 14
austerity, economics and politics of 27,
  296n24, 308, 314
*Australasian Journal of Economics
  Education* 22
Australia: consumer sentiment indexes in
  235; heterodox economics in 10–11,
  14, 16, 47, 50–1, 53, 55–6, 58–74, 306,
  308, 314; industrial relations in 26,
  251–2, 265–6, 267, 269–70, 272–6,
  308; neoclassical economic mainstream in 6, 19; neoliberal capitalism
  in 24, 26, 28, 251–2, 265–6, 267–8,
  269–70, 275–6; pluralism, old style in
  47–8, 76, 77, 80–92; *see also* especially
  history of economic thought;
  University of Sydney

Australia Meat Holdings (AMH) 265,
  272–3, 275
The Australian (newspaper) 64, 67
Australian Bureau of Statistics (ABS) 50,
  51, 56, 59, 60, 62, 63, 64, 65, 66, 67
Australian Business Deans Council
  (ABDC) 68, 69–71, 72, 73, 74;
  Business Associate Deans of Research
  sub-committee (BARDsNet) 70–1, 73
Australian College of Political Economy,
  recommendations to establish 314
Australian Economic History Review 71
Australian Economic Papers 88, 92
Australian Financial Review 64
Australian National University 77, 84,
  85, 87, 90
Australian Research Council (ARC) 60,
  65, 68, 72; Federation Fellows 66
Australian Standard Research
  Classification (ASRC) 60
Australian Workplace Agreements
  (AWAs) 269, 275, 276
Austrian political economy 10, 20, 52,
  146, 157, 176, 247, 262n2, 280, 310

Babylonian thought, and pluralism 37,
  305
banks: central 9, 176, 178, 191, 287, 288;
  commercial 178, 295n19; globalized
  285; investment 284, 286, 295n19;
  shadow 289, 295n19; 'too big to fail'
  297n29; *see also* credit policies;
  Federal Reserve (US); Lehman
  Brothers; Treasury (US)
behavioural economics, new: and
  neoclassicals 17, 36, 192–3, 247 (*see
  also* rational choice); old 240, 242,